SAINT
and
NATION

Erin Kathleen Rowe

SAINT

and

NATION

Santiago, Teresa of Avila, and Plural Identities in Early Modern Spain

The Pennsylvania State University Press
University Park, Pennsylvania

Library of Congress Cataloging-in-Publication Data

Rowe, Erin Kathleen, 1974– .
    Saint and nation : Santiago, Teresa of Avila, and
    plural identities in early modern Spain / Erin
    Kathleen Rowe.
        p.   cm.
Includes bibliographical references and index.
Summary: "Examines the controversy in early
seventeenth-century Spain over the elevation of Saint
Teresa of Avila to co-patron saint alongside the
traditional patron, Santiago. Assesses the crucial role
of sanctity in the symbolic representation of the nation
in early modern Europe"—Provided by publisher.
ISBN 978-0-271-03773-8 (cloth : alk. paper)
1. Christian patron saints—Spain—History—17th
century.
2. Spain—Church history—17th century.
3. James, the Greater, Saint.
4. Teresa, of Avila, Saint, 1515–1582.
I. Title.

BX4656.5.R69   2011
274.6'06—dc22
2010031390

CONTENTS

MAPS

ACKNOWLEDGMENTS

This project would not have been possible without the support and encouragement of many people. I owe my greatest debt to Richard L. Kagan, my mentor and advisor. While anyone who has had the privilege of working with Richard is familiar with his generous spirit and intellectual acumen, he played a particularly instrumental role in the development of this project. When I first met Richard as a graduate student, I was studying the medieval French Inquisition. I stumbled on the co-patronage controversy as a research paper topic in his seminar; in our meeting to discuss the paper, he told me that this would make an ideal dissertation topic. I reminded him that I was not an early modernist, that I didn't really know anything about Spain, and that I didn't speak a word of Spanish. He swept those concerns away with one hand gesture. And so I was off on the long adventure that has culminated in this book. I am grateful to many faculty members who provided invaluable advice and support throughout my graduate career at Johns Hopkins University, especially Gabrielle Spiegel, Judith Walkowitz, and David Nirenberg.

The research for this book was made possible by generous grants from the Fulbright Program and the Program for Cultural Cooperation between the Spanish Ministry of Education, Culture, and Sports and United States Universities. I received support for additional research from the University of Oregon, the UO Department of History's Spencer Brush Fund, and the American Philosophical Society's Franklin Grant. Portions of this book have appeared previously in the *Sixteenth Century Journal* and the *Catholic Historical Review*. I am indebted to the generosity and knowledge of archivists and librarians throughout Castile—in particular, those at the Biblioteca Nacional, Real Academia de Historia, Biblioteca Universitaria de Sevilla, Archivo Catedralicio de Sevilla, and the Archivo Catedralicio de Santiago de Compostela—as well as the Archivio Segreto Vaticano. I have especially fond memories of my weeks working in the Archivo Catedralicio de Santiago de Compostela, where *técnico* Arturo Iglesias provided invaluable help and advice. Ofelia Rey Castelao, professor at the University of Santiago de Compostela, shared her time, wisdom, and thorough knowledge of the ACSC with me. Like many American scholars, I was invited to participate in seminars and intellectual exchange at the Universidad Autónoma by James Amelang. Finally, my initial research year in Madrid would have been far less fruitful without the friendship and advice of my lunch companions at the BNM, Sasha Pack and Tanya J. Tiffany.

Most of this book was completed during the three years I spent at the University of Oregon. I thus owe several great debts to the UO and its Department of History for providing the perfect environment to nurture a young scholar. The two terms of leave I received were particularly valuable for the advancement of this project. I also received much advice and support from my colleagues, especially David Luebke, Ian McNeely, and Lisa Wolverton. My work was also greatly strengthened by the comments of an interdisciplinary group of early modernists at UO, of whom I would particularly like to thank Amanda Powell, Dianne DuGraw, James Harper, and Leah Middlebrook for their thoughtful responses to my chapter on gender. Nathalie Hester and Andrew Schulz brightened several gloomy Oregon winters with lively conversations about Spain and the Mediterranean, excellent meals, and warm friendship. I would also like to thank Nathalie for sharing with me her experience at the Archivio Segreto Vaticano. I am also grateful to Jesse, Laura, and Sophie Locker for showing me around Rome during my first research visit there in 2006.

In the broader intellectual world, I would like to thank Jodi Bilinkoff, Katie Harris, Lu Ann Homza, Allyson Poska, Molly Warsh, Guy Lazure, Kimberly Lynn, Xavier Gil, and Kate van Liere for their many probing questions, advice, and suggestions. Katrina Olds spent many hours discussing Dextro with me, and shared her knowledge of the cathedral archives in Jaén. Scholarship on Teresa of Avila can be dauntingly extensive and complex, but Teresian scholars are famously friendly and supportive to younger scholars. In addition to Jodi, I owe particular debts to Alison Weber and Christopher Wilson—their work and friendship have inspired and sustained me over the years. Trent Pomplun of Loyola College of Maryland provided invaluable aid in my journey through the labyrinth of canon law and the *perinde valere*. Finally, I am deeply grateful to two eminent scholars whose generosity and interest in my topic led them to seek me out with invaluable advice, recommendations, and support: Simon Ditchfield and Tony Thompson. Both Simon and Tony challenged me to examine the co-patronage debate in a broader context by looking beyond Spain to the larger devotional landscape of seventeenth-century Europe.

I also grateful to the editorial staff at PSU Press, especially Eleanor Goodman. I owe special thanks to my copyeditor, Suzanne Wolk, for her tireless work in clarifying and systematizing the complicated bibliography and to Kelly Johnston (UVa–The Scholar's Lab) for extending his time so generously to helping me make the maps. I would also like to thank the two anonymous readers of the manuscript whose thoughtful and thorough comments helped me refine my thinking during the final stages of revision.

A project of so many years would not have been possible without incurring a great number of personal as well as professional debts. My family always manifested patience and good humor with my saintly ramblings, particularly my parents, Richard and Cheryl Rowe, and my brother, Matthew. My father made a special trip with me to the quiet town of Alba de Tormes for the sole purpose of visiting Teresa's sepulcher (where we viewed her heart). I am also grateful for the love and support of my family of friends, including Matthew Miller, Aviva Cristy, and the Howe-Kubiaks. Daniel and James Rowe imbued the last couple of years with a great joy that has supplied me with the energy to finish this project. In the end, however, I must dedicate this book to Andrew A. G. Ross, the best reader, editor, and friend I could have hoped for.

ABBREVIATIONS

ACC	Archivo Catedralicio de Córdoba
ACSC	Archivo Catedralicio de Santiago de Compostela
ASV	Archivio Segreto Vaticano
BAE	Biblioteca de Autores Españoles
BCC	Biblioteca Capitular y Colombina de Sevilla
BNM	Biblioteca Nacional de España, Madrid
Col.	Collection
HSA	Hispanic Society of America
Leg.	Legajo (bundle)
MAE	Archivo del Ministerio de Asuntos Exteriores, Archivo de la Embajada, Madrid
MS	Manuscript
RAH	Real Academia de Historia, Madrid
VE	Varios especiales (special miscellaneous)

Map 1   Early modern Iberia, ca. 1617

Map 2 Cities mentioned in the co-patronage debate, 1617–1630

INTRODUCTION

In the autumn of 1627, the capital city of Madrid hosted eight days of lavish festivities, including religious processions, sumptuous decorations, sermons, games, and fireworks. The king, who was convalescing from a life-threatening illness, observed the main procession from a high window with full views of the streets. Crowds of people pushed into local churches to view the richly decorated images of the saint being honored, Teresa of Avila, and to listen to the royal musicians accompanying the mass. This festival marked the first official celebration of Teresa in her newly elected position as patron saint of Spain. Yet, in spite of the joyous events unfolding in Madrid, not everyone approved of this new spiritual representative. In fact, the cathedral chapters of Castile, headed by the powerful archbishop of Santiago de Compostela, had begun a campaign in the preceding weeks to prevent other cities of the kingdom from following Madrid's example, in defiance of royal orders. The cathedral chapter's efforts marked the beginning of a bitter three-year battle between those advocating Teresa's patron sainthood and those who felt that her elevation alongside Spain's existing patron, Santiago (Saint James the Greater), represented a grave insult both to the apostle and to Spain's spiritual traditions.

This book focuses on the period from 1617 to 1630, when the issue of who was or could be the patron saint of Spain burst onto the political and religious scene. Teresa and Santiago are two of the most iconic figures in Spanish cultural life; even today, they have maintained persistent and explicit associations with *españolidad* (which can best be translated as "Spanishness"). While both saints (Teresa especially) have received a great deal of scholarly attention, few studies have assessed their vital roles in historical-cultural imaginings of Spain.[1] The conflict

---

1. For a notable exception, see Carlos Eire's discussion of Teresa's *españolidad* in *From Madrid to Purgatory: The Art and Craft of Dying in Sixteenth-Century Spain* (Cambridge: Cambridge University Press, 1995), 379–82.

over their patron sainthood signified a seminal moment in Spanish history because Teresa's ascendancy marks the first substantial challenge to Santiago since the High Middle Ages, and suggests a shift in Spanish political, spiritual, and ideological culture. Teresa's elevation to co-patron saint proved alarming to many Castilians because it challenged not just Santiago's cult but traditional understandings of the Spanish nation. It interrupted the accepted historical narrative touted by Santiago's devotees to create what was, for the most part, a new historical-spiritual narrative, with new foundations. This new narrative was bound to recent events and current problems facing the nation—spiritual, political, and cultural. The largest of such events was a gradual geopolitical shift from perennial conflict with Muslims (reconquest) to a more multifaceted and spiritual conflict within Christianity (European religious wars). At the same time, the Spanish monarchy began to lose ground in its struggle to maintain hegemony in Europe. What on the surface may seem to be a simple devotional decision to name Teresa the national patron took on extraordinary importance to contemporary Castilians, who viewed the results of this decision as potentially cataclysmic. This book investigates the cultural, social, and spiritual stakes for participants.

At the heart of the controversy lay the idea of Spain itself, as national patron sainthood presented Castilians with an opportunity to imagine and contest their relationship to the larger national community, in much the same way that local saints had supplied a way to express local identities.[2] As Simon Ditchfield has recently argued, "when early modern Catholics wanted to express their collective identity or articulate their collective memory, more often than not they did so in terms of their devotion to their local churches whose holy custodians were the saints."[3] Early modern historians have been quick to assess such expressions of collective identity and sanctity in the context of civic identities, yet the national level has been largely overlooked.[4]

2. For a few examples of local studies, see Simon Ditchfield, *Liturgy, Sanctity, and History in Tridentine Italy* (Cambridge: Cambridge University Press, 1995); A. Katie Harris, *From Muslim to Christian Granada: Inventing a City's Past in Early Modern Spain* (Baltimore: Johns Hopkins University Press, 2007); and Diana Webb, *Patrons and Defenders: The Saints in the Italian City-States* (London: St. Martin's Press, 1996).

3. Simon Ditchfield, "Thinking with the Saints: Sanctity and Society in the Early Modern World," *Critical Theory* 35 (Spring 2009): 572.

4. As Ditchfield observes, "the role played by such works of *historia sacra* in the construction of national historiographies has been seriously underrated until very recently." Ditchfield, "'Tota regio nil nisi religio': Nations, Nationalisms, and *Historia sacra*; Some Preliminary Reflections," *Annali di Stori Moderna e Contemporanea* 10 (2004): 597. One exception is Jason A. Nice, *Sacred History and National Identity: Comparisons Between Early Modern Wales and Brittany* (London: Pickering and Chatto, 2009).

During the Middle Ages, saints tended to fall into one of two main categories: universal (saints venerated throughout Christendom, like the Virgin Mary and the apostles) and local (saints venerated only in specific regions or towns). Both types of saints played a variety of important roles in the spiritual and cultural lives of medieval people. They could act as intercessors between human beings and God on behalf of a petitioner, whether individual or corporate. They could serve as patrons entrusted with the protection of lands under their patronage: Patrons stopped floods, drove away locusts, and brought generous harvests.[5] Some were associated with particular problems—Saint Roch, for example, was often called upon in times of plague. Saints could also serve as examples, either as inspiration or as models for ideal Christian behavior. But not all hagiographers expected their readers to pattern their lives after the saints— for some it was enough to present the saint's life as a demonstration of God's power and the wonder of his miracles.[6] Finally, saints fulfilled a central theological role in the Catholic Church: The incorruption of their bodies offered tangible proof of the ultimate triumph over death promised to all Christians through the resurrection of the body as part of the Last Judgment.[7] Thus saints played multiple roles within Christian society, which fluctuated depending on the specific historical, political, religious, or cultural contexts.

National patron sainthood began to develop slowly during the Middle Ages, when we begin to see the emergence of such figures as Santiago in Castile, Saint George in England and Catalonia, and Saint Denis in France. I should say here that the word "nation," as it was understood throughout this period, derived its meaning from its Latin origins—*natio,* a vague term loosely connecting people from the same region who shared customs, history, and possibly language. Such national patrons acted much as local patrons did, though they reached out beyond a limited geographic range. Both national and civic patrons interceded on behalf of a specific *space* while simultaneously being tied deeply to a sense of *place,* embedded in shared histories and memories.[8] The saints'

5. For the best overview of local religious practice in early modern Spain, see William A. Christian, *Local Religion in Sixteenth-Century Spain* (Princeton: Princeton University Press, 1981).

6. Patrick Geary, *Living with the Dead in the Middle Ages* (Ithaca: Cornell University Press, 1994), 22.

7. Peter Brown, *The Cult of the Saints: Its Rise and Function in Latin Christianity* (Chicago: University of Chicago Press, 1981), 76–78.

8. For a discussion of the philosophy of place and space in historical context, see Richard L. Kagan, with Fernando Marías, *Urban Images of the Hispanic World, 1493–1793* (New Haven: Yale University Press, 2000). Kagan contends, "Place, moreover, is (quoting the German philosopher Heidegger) a 'gathering of meanings,' the locus where memory, history, and collective experience intertwine" (17). See also Clare A. Lees and Gillian R. Overing, eds., *A Place to Believe In: Locating Medieval Landscapes* (University Park: Pennsylvania State University Press, 2006).

relationship to place constituted a key factor in their mutability into symbols of civic and national identity. National patron saints took on new meaning in the early modern period, as monarchies drew more closely together through literacy and the printing press, mobility of people, centralized bureaucracy, and, increasingly, the fixing of territorial boundaries.[9] National patrons thus became embedded in the histories of the peoples they came to represent, often playing pivotal roles in the preservation or defense of the nation at moments of crisis. They also became associated with values and characteristics that those in the national community held as fundamental to their identities during a given period of time.

The use of saints for expressing collective identity or memory connected liturgical time with historical time. The liturgy brings the past into the present through an ongoing celebration of a cycle of events. Key to this process is the belief that the sacred is made present through such celebrations; for example, the liturgy for a saint's feast day commemorates the deeds and miracles of the holy person who lived in the past, while simultaneously appealing to the saint's power and presence for protection in the immediate present or future.[10] Thus the celebration of specific saints' feast days renders the distant past deeply relevant and immediately present, while providing hope for the future. Communities eagerly adopted such understandings of time and place in the celebration of their patron saints. As William Christian contends, shrines and relics, establishing sacred geography and "outlasting individuals as they do, come to stand not only for the *pueblo* of the moment, but also for the eternal *pueblo*."[11] Through its sacred geography, a community could obtain permanence and immortality, which mirrored the immortality promised to all Christians.

Saints thus became part of larger discussions about the future and direction of the nation, which included a diverse variety of economic and political policies from a range of both regional and national perspectives. The late sixteenth and early seventeenth centuries marked a period of profound shift in the Spanish zeitgeist—the fiscal burdens and moral complications of empire, along with the changing political situation in

9. As part of the general lack of attention paid to national patron saints, historians have spent little time exploring this subject in the context of medieval history, in spite of the presence of many significant "national" patrons. A comparison of national patron sainthood in the Middle Ages and the early modern period might prove extremely fruitful.

10. The "presentness" of sacred objects and texts (and their place in the liturgy) has been much commented on by historians, particularly medievalists. Peter Brown argues, "When the *passio* was read [as part of the liturgy], the saint was 'really' there." *Cult of the Saints*, 81–82.

11. Christian, *Local Religion in Sixteenth-Century Spain*, 158.

Europe, created a sense of unstable identity and general crisis among contemporary Castilians.[12] Such instability led in turn to a search for new ways of representing the national community and its future. Co-patronage participants engaged in a sophisticated negotiation of plural identities through the dynamic interplay between traditional binaries: local and extralocal, royal authority and nation, tradition and modernity, church and state, and masculine and feminine. The idea of plurality in early modern Spain has become an important new area for study. James Amelang has recently noted that while plurality characterized the monarchy, it existed *alongside* unity.[13] The two forces worked together, not in opposition. My work offers an in-depth case study that exposes the multilayered nature of early modern ideas, structures, and identities.

Co-patronage affords an ideal vantage point from which to examine plurality, because the conflict was not just about rhetoric or ideals but also about power, since a patron saint could act as a vehicle through which individuals or institutions could acquire or augment power. As Xavier Gil Pujol astutely observes, one of the main sources of power in early modern Iberia was jurisdiction.[14] Since privilege and jurisdiction provided the main channels through which people demarcated and defended their individual or communal power, they often became sites of fierce contestation. Thus what we see in the co-patronage debate is a struggle over ideals and values, but also over jurisdiction—specifically, over who had the right to name and to celebrate a patron—and therefore power. In addition, disputes over local privilege, royal authority, and ecclesiastical rights in the co-patronage debate reveal plural discussions about the nation, its meaning and values, in early modern Castile.[15] Nevertheless, while co-patronage touched off explosive disagreements

12. The problem particularly of identity, empire, and gender has begun to be explored with fascinating results by literary scholars; see especially Sidney Donnell, *Feminizing the Enemy: Imperial Spain, Transvestite Drama, and the Crisis of Masculinity* (Lewisburg: Bucknell University Press, 2003); and Barbara Fuchs, *Passing for Spain: Cervantes and the Fictions of Identity* (Urbana: University of Illinois Press, 2003).

13. James S. Amelang, "The Peculiarities of the Spaniards: Historical Approaches to the Early Modern State," in *Public Power in Europe: Studies in Historical Transformations*, ed. James S. Amelang and Siegfried Beer (Pisa: University of Pisa Press, 2006), 45–46. For another excellent discussion of this issue, see M. J. Rodríguez-Salgado, "Christians, Civilized and Spanish: Multiple Identities in Sixteenth-Century Spain," in *Transactions of the Royal Historical Society*, 6th ser., 8 (1998): 233–54.

14. Xavier Gil Pujol, "Spain and Portugal," in *European Political Thought, 1450–1700: Religion, Law, and Philosophy*, ed. Howell A. Lloyd, Glenn Burgess, and Simon Hodson (New Haven: Yale University Press, 2007), 420.

15. The evolution of the court system in Castile made litigiousness a key characteristic of jurisdictional battles; the co-patronage debate proved no exception, spawning numerous legal complaints (*pleitos*) as well as polemical tracts and sermons. Richard L. Kagan, *Lawsuits and Litigants in Castile, 1500–1700* (Chapel Hill: University of North Carolina Press, 1981).

about power, politics, spiritual values, and authority, supporters of both Santiago and Teresa constructed narratives of the Spanish nation that had the power to unify through the invention of a shared past and shared values. Hence, even when the nation was a contested category, it could still cohere.

Beginning in the last decades of the sixteenth century, Castile was beset by a series of misfortunes. While not without interludes of calm and prosperity, the Spanish monarchy faced an onslaught of crises and disasters for which its members scrambled to find solutions. These solutions could be, and often were, simultaneously pragmatic and ideological, ranging from resisting the devaluation of coinage to preventing Spanish men from becoming too "effeminate." Economic, political, social, and religious remedies to the problems facing Spain consumed the minds of the educated class. Many of these men—like Pedro de Ribadeneira, Juan de Mariana, and Sancho de Moncada, to name a few—produced printed treatises that were sent to the court as advice for the king and circulated among officials and courtiers. The proliferation of such treatises and their widespread dissemination demonstrate the variety of ways in which the country's elite attempted to strengthen the monarchy or to stave off what some referred to as its decline. This outpouring of political writing has not escaped the attention of historians, many of whom have studied in great detail both the individual men involved in the production of such works and the rhetoric they deployed to describe their country, its problems, and potential remedies.[16]

The movement to have Teresa elevated to co-patron must be understood in the context of this larger attempt to discover potential remedies for the ills of the monarchy and of Castile in particular. Since patron saints played critical roles in the protection of the places they represented, anxieties over the choice of national patron attended larger anxieties about the state of the monarchy. Seventeenth-century writers advocating both for and against co-patronage invoked the existing language of economic and political reform by framing the debate explicitly within the context of what would be best for the monarchy. They argued fiercely over how Teresa's elevation might add to or detract from the ultimate goal of keeping Spain strong. At first glance, the spiritual choice of an additional patron

16. For a sample of secondary work on *arbitristas* and reformers, see Francisco J. Aranda Pérez, ed., *Jerónimo de Ceballos: Un hombre grave para la república—vida y obra de un hidalgo del saber en la España del Siglo de Oro* (Córdoba: Universidad de Córdoba, 2001), 981; John H. Elliott, "Self-Perception and Decline in Early Seventeenth-Century Spain," in Elliott, *Spain and Its World: 1500–1700* (New Haven: Yale University Press, 1989), 241–61; and José I. Fortea Pérez, "Economía, arbitrismo y política en la monarquía hispánica a fines del siglo XVI," *Manuscrits* 16 (1998): 155–76.

might seem to have little in common with the more serious and practical economic advice being produced at the same time. A closer examination of such treatises reveals that they often discussed the problems of the monarchy in terms of divine punishment and debated supernatural as well as practical remedies. The significance of choosing a new patron saint would have been immediately recognizable to contemporaries as integral to the monarchy's future and well-being.

We see, therefore, that polemics on the choice of a new patron saint grabbed the attention of many leading political and spiritual figures of the day. Both Philip III and Philip IV took an active interest in promoting Teresa's co-patronage, as did Philip IV's powerful minister, the count-duke of Olivares. Some of the greatest literary figures of Golden Age Spain leapt into the fray, including Francisco de Quevedo y Villegas, the humanist and painter Francisco de Pacheco (Velázquez's father-in-law), Lope de Vega, and the royal chronicler Tomás Tamayo y Vargas, as well as a host of other prominent political and economic writers. Teresa's elevation was voted on twice by the representative assembly of Castile (the Cortes), and twice more by the kingdom's ecclesiastical representative assembly. In addition, the most powerful prelates in Castile weighed in on the issue, including the archbishops of Santiago, Toledo, and Seville—most notably among these the influential archbishop of Seville, Pedro de Castro. Participants both famous and obscure wrote prolifically on the controversy: Almost one hundred treatises and sermons printed and circulated by both sides of the issue survive, most produced between 1627 and 1629. These treatises were also disseminated widely, enabling participants to respond directly to their adversaries and creating a written debate. Such broad circulation was aided by the widespread practice of printing cheap pamphlets, which allowed materials to be circulated quickly across a wide geographic span.[17] For example, one co-patronage author, Francisco Morovelli de Puebla, claimed that he had fired off his pro-Teresa treatise in seven days after reading no fewer than nine pamphlets debating her elevation.[18] Writers maintained a direct dialogue with one another, at times quoting their opponents verbatim.

17. For more on print culture in early modern Europe, see Roger Chartier, *The Cultural Uses of Print in Early Modern France,* trans. Lydia G. Cochrane (Princeton: Princeton University Press, 1987); Henry Ettinhausen, "The News in Spain: 'Relaciones de sucesos' in the Reigns of Philip III and IV," *European History Quarterly* 14, no. 1 (1984): 1–20; and María Cruz García de Enterría, ed., *Las 'Relaciones de sucesos' en España (1500–1750)* (Alcalá: Universidad de Alcalá, 1996).

18. Francisco Morovelli de Puebla, *Defiende el patronato de Santa Teresa de Iesus, patrona illustrissima de España, y Responde a D. Francisco de Quevedo Villegas, Cauallero del habito de Santiago, a D. Francisco de Melgar, canonigo de la Doctoral de Seuilla, y a otros que an escrito contra el* (Málaga: Juan René, 1628), fol. 30v. Morovelli refers explicitly both to the authors and their key arguments throughout his treatise.

While a variety of printed material proliferated in this period, the co-patronage debate marked an important moment in early modern Spanish print culture—it provided the opportunity for writers from all corners of Castile to participate in a large-scale, kingdom-wide, print-based movement. The majority of participants came from the gentry, which was at the time (as in other European kingdoms) the rising class of university-trained "new men" who held prominent positions in local and royal bureaucracies. This group of educated and socially mobile Castilians wrote prolifically on the major issues confronting their monarchy. Scholars have often located the origins of nationalism and the nation-state in the works of such men; Liah Greenfeld, for example, finds English nationalism developing in the sixteenth century as the direct result of this specific group of socially mobile men redefining nobility in terms of service.[19] While I do not wish to make such a broad claim for these Castilians, it is noteworthy that nearly all the participants in the co-patronage debate came from families associated with lower branches of the nobility and local elites, rather than from the artisan class, the peasantry, or the highest aristocracy, who remained largely absent from the debate.

The failure of historians to understand the broad appeal and political significance of the co-patronage debate explains its virtual absence from modern historiography. One tends to find brief discussions of the debate in works on key figures—most prominently, Francisco de Quevedo, Teresa, and Santiago.[20] Such treatments of the debate hinder our comprehensive understanding of its wider significance. For example, Isaías Rodríguez's study of Teresian spirituality provides an excellent basic chronology of the debate as well as references to some of the primary material, but it does so almost solely from a *teresiano* perspective; the viewpoint of Santiago's supporters is consequently eclipsed.[21] The lack of attention to the co-patronage debate within the vibrant historiography on Saint Teresa is largely a by-product of scholars' emphasis on the life

19. Liah Greenfeld, *Nationalism: Five Roads to Modernity* (Cambridge: Harvard University Press, 1992), 51–87.

20. See, for instance, Pablo Jauralde Pou, *Francisco de Quevedo (1580–1645)* (Madrid: Castalia, 1998); Thomas Kendrick, *St. James in Spain* (London: Methuen, 1960); and Isaías Rodríguez, *Santa Teresa de Jesús y la espiritualidad española* (Madrid: CSIC, 1972).

21. Rodríguez, *Santa Teresa de Jesús*. Examples in Quevedian historiography include María José Alonso Veloso, "La estructura retórica del 'Memorial por el Patronato de Santiago' de Francisco de Quevedo," *Bulletin of Spanish Studies* 79, no. 4 (2002): 447–63; Luis Astrana Marín, *La vida turbulenta de Quevedo* (Madrid: Editorial Gran Capitan, 1945); and John H. Elliott, "Quevedo and the Count-Duke of Olivares," in *Spain and Its World*, 189–209. Américo Castro analyzed the co-patronage debate in a larger synthesis about the importance of Santiago in Spanish history. See his *España en su historia: Cristianos, moros y judíos* (Buenos Aires: Editorial Losada, 1948), 174–86.

and writings of the saint and her followers rather than on her cult or iconography.[22] Until now, the most fully contextualized treatment of the debate can be found in Ofelia Rey Castelao's study of the Santiago cathedral's *voto* tax and its effects on Santiago's cult, which places the co-patronage debate within the broader context of the cathedral's struggle to uphold Santiago's traditional prerogatives as a way of protecting its prestige and economic interests.[23]

Political and intellectual historians—most prominently John H. Elliott, I. A. A. Thompson, and M. J. Rodríguez-Salgado—have made important contributions to the co-patronage debate by assessing it as a sign of an identity crisis in Castile, although they have not explored the topic in detail.[24] Such discussions tend to be embedded in works on political culture in Castile, since, in spite of the rhetoric about "Spain" in the debate, co-patronage remained a staunchly Castilian problem, reflecting Castilian concerns in pamphlets written by Castilians. But even within Castile, the various regions and individual cities expressed multi-layered attitudes about their own rights and privileges and those of the Crown; neither unstintingly loyal to the monarchy and royal policies nor unable to see over their town walls, Castilian cities and their leaders played an important role in imagining and developing a national community.[25]

22. For other studies of Teresa that also discuss co-patronage in some form, see Francis Cerdán, "Santa Teresa en los sermones del Patronato (1627)," in *Santa Teresa y la literatura mística hispánica: Actas del 1 congreso internacionales sobre Santa Teresa y la mística hispánica*, ed. Manuel Criado de Val (Madrid: EDI-6, 1984), 601–8; Eire, *From Madrid to Purgatory*, 379–80; Francisco López Estrada, "Cohetes para Teresa: La relación de 1627 sobre las fiestas de Madrid por el patronato de España de Santa Teresa de Jesús y la polémica sobre el mismo," in *Actas del Congreso Internacional Teresiano, 4–7 Octubre 1982*, ed. Teófanes Egido Martínez, V. García de la Concha, and O. González de Cardedal, 2 vols. (Salamanca: Universidad de Salamanca, 1984), 1:637–81.

23. Ofelia Rey Castelao, *La historiografía del voto de Santiago: Recopilación crítica de una polémica histórica* (Santiago de Compostela: Universidad de Santiago de Compostela, 1985). See also I. A. A. Thompson's recent "La cuestión de la autoridad en la controversia sobre el patronato de santa Teresa de Jesús," in *De re publica hispaniae: Una vindicación de la cultura política en los reinos ibéricos en la primera modernidad*, ed. Francisco J. Aranda Pérez and José Damião Rodrigues (Madrid: Silex, 2008), 293–320. Carlos Santos Fernández and Fermín de los Reyes Gómez have produced a complete bibliographic survey of co-patronage documents: *Impresos en torno al patronato de Santiago, siglo XVII* (Santiago de Compostela: Xunta de Galicia, 2004).

24. Elliott, "Self-Perception and Decline," in *Spain and Its World*, 241–61; John H. Elliott, *The Count-Duke of Olivares: The Statesman in an Age of Decline* (New Haven: Yale University Press, 1986), 323–24; I. A. A. Thompson, "Castile, Spain, and the Monarchy: The Political Community from *Patria Natural* to *Patria Nacional*," in *Spain, Europe, and the Atlantic World: Essays in Honor of John H. Elliott*, ed. Richard L. Kagan and Geoffrey Parker (Cambridge: Cambridge University Press, 1995), 125–59. As Elliott remarks astutely in "Self-Perception and Decline," "A violent polemic over the identity of a nation's symbolic representative hints at a deep underlying disagreement over national identity itself" (261).

25. Some of the most important work on Castile and its relationship to the monarch is found in histories of the Cortes, the representative body of the major towns of Castile. See, for example,

The Castilian focus raises a vital question: Did the national community the writers discuss refer to Castile or to Spain? What did the title "patron saint of Spain" mean to them? The title is not a modern imposition on the past but reflects the language employed by participants in the debate. Seventeenth-century Castilians had a wide variety of terms with which to describe both Castile and the wider monarchy. Throughout treatises on both sides of the debate, for example, the terms "Spanish monarchy" (*monarquía española*), "Spains" (*las Españas*), "Spain" (*España*), "Hispania" (*Hispania*), "the Crown(s) of Castile" (*la[s] Corona[s] de Castilla*), and "the kingdom(s) of Castile" (*el reino/los reinos de Castilla*) are used in ways that at first glance seem almost interchangeable to modern eyes. But these terms are not interchangeable, and early modern authors often used them with great precision.[26] We can divide these terms roughly into two categories: The first category refers to concrete juridical-political or territorial units, while the second invokes what may be called an idealized or imagined community.[27]

In the first category one may place the terms "Spanish monarchy," "the Spains," and "the Crown and kingdoms of Castile," since all refer to existing divisions of Spanish territories. The Spanish monarchy, naturally, refers to the entirety of Spanish holdings, including the entire Iberian Peninsula, the Low Countries, the kingdoms of Naples and Sicily, and the American colonies. "The Spains," while an awkward term in English, was frequently used in early modern Spain to denote the Iberian kingdoms, which comprise modern-day Spain (Castile, Aragón, and Navarre); it also occasionally included Portugal (part of the Spanish monarchy from 1580 to 1640). At the time of the debate, these kingdoms were loosely connected by a common monarch but had separate governments, laws, and customs. The Crown(s) of Castile, whether singular or plural, included Old and New Castile, León, Andalusia, Asturias, and

---

José I. Fortea Pérez, "Las ciudades, las Cortes y el problema de la representación política en la Castilla moderna," in *Imágenes de la diversidad: El mundo urbano en la corona de Castilla*, ed. José I. Fortea Pérez (Cantabria: Universidad de Cantabria, 1997), 421–45; and I. A. A. Thompson, *Crown and Cortes: Government, Institutions, and Representation in Early Modern Castile* (Aldershot: Ashgate Variorum, 1993).

26. While these terms are generally used with precision in co-patronage treatises, Richard Kagan points out a degree of slippage in the work of other authors. See Kagan, "Nación y patria en la historiografía de la época austriaca," in *Le sentiment national dans l'Europe méridionale au XVIe et XVIIe siècles*, ed. Alain Tallon (Madrid: Casa de Velázquez, 2007), 205–6.

27. While the phrase "imagined community" comes from Benedict Anderson, I have been inspired here more by the work of Michael Walzer, who argued, "The state is invisible; it must be personified before it can be seen, symbolized before it can be loved, imagined before it can be conceived." Walzer, "On the Role of Symbolism in Political Thought," *Political Science Quarterly* 82, no. 2 (1967): 194.

Galicia. Each of these Castilian Crowns represented distinct regions with differing histories and customs, though they were unified by one law.

In the second category of community—the idealized or imagined—one finds both "Spain," and "Hispania," neither of which reflected a political entity but rather what is better understood as an imagined site full of cultural and historical resonance. *Hispania*, the Latin name for the Spanish province ("España" was the term rendered in the vernacular), hearkened back to the unified kingdom of Spain and an idealized time before the Moorish invasions of 711, which fragmented and destroyed the Visigothic Kingdom. For the next seven centuries, the political leaders of Christian Spain worked (in a piecemeal fashion) to take territory from their Islamic neighbors. As they did so, new political states began to emerge, eventually resulting in the disparate kingdoms of Portugal, Castile-León, and Aragón-Catalonia. The "Spain" of the ancient world no longer existed, though it endured in the memories of Christian leaders of these Iberian kingdoms, several of whom attempted to resurrect the imperial title assumed by the Visigoths—emperor of all Spain.[28] One can trace throughout Spanish history a tension between the political reality of distinct kingdoms and the historical memory of "Spain."

Another way to describe Spain during the early modern period was with the term *nación*. This term retained much of its medieval resonance in the early modern period; since the word referred to a community of people from a general region, it possessed a certain plasticity that did not necessarily connote alignment with a political state. For Castilians, *nación* referred to the Spanish nation (*nación española*); it is clear from their usage that the nation comprised more than just Castile. For example, one author referred to the veneration of Santiago "throughout our entire nation" in a sentence that referred explicitly to the pilgrimage site of the Virgin of the Pillar in Aragón.[29] Another *santiaguista* author denounced a sermon by an opponent who spoke in favor of displacing Santiago with Teresa; he declared that this opponent "deserved to lose his Spanish nationality [*la naturaleza de España*], not only for publishing this idea, but for thinking it, which is an insult to the whole nation!"[30] The union of the terms "nation" and "Spain" indicates that references to Spain connoted nationhood. In addition, authors using the term

28. Joseph F. O'Callaghan, *A History of Medieval Spain* (Ithaca: Cornell University Press, 1975), 216–24.

29. "Memorial de la Congregación contra el patronato de Teresa, de Assientos de 1628," HSA, fol. 67r.

30. *Memorial a su Magestad en nombre de la Iglesia de Sanctiago, i del Clero de las de España, por el unico Patronato del Apostol Santiago* (1627), BNM, VE 211/46, fol. 11v. All translations are my own unless otherwise indicated.

"nation" frequently modified it with the pronoun "our" (*nuestra*), emphasizing the nation's communicentric rather than its political function.[31]

In addition to the term *nación*, early modern intellectuals also described both particular towns and the Spanish nation as republics (*repúblicas*), a term that explicitly evoked Roman political ideals as well as contemporary concerns about governance and Christian reason of state.[32] Another humanist term in common use was *patria*. At the dawn of the seventeenth century, *patria* largely retained its sixteenth-century meaning of "hometown" or region of one's birth.[33] Yet Xavier Gil Pujol has demonstrated that by the close of the century writers employed the same term to refer to the nation—to Spain, a place that united people with a common history and to which people owed their primary loyalty.[34] Although early seventeenth-century Castilians did not conceive of Spain as a nation in the modern sense of a sovereign political entity, the common use of the terms *nación*, *patria*, and *república* reflected a growing sense of political and cultural loyalty to a specific territory. Thus the battle over the patron saint of Spain remains embedded in a larger process through which early modern Castilians began to conceptualize the nation in a way that permitted the development of national consciousness.

The complexities involved in discussing the "nation" in medieval and early modern Europe have given rise to vigorous debate among historians.[35] Some early modernists have taken exception to arguments by modern historians that posit the origins of nationalism (and the nation) in the late eighteenth century, asserting instead that early modern states did in fact demonstrate an incipient nationalism.[36] Others have

31. See, for example, Alonso Rodríguez de León, *Carta a su Magestad que suplica que cerca del unico y singular titulo de Patron destos Reinos de España* (ca. 1627), BNM, VE 211/52, 27.

32. See Robert Bireley, *The Counter-Reformation Prince: Anti-Machiavellism or Catholic Statecraft in Early Modern Europe* (Chapel Hill: University of North Carolina Press, 1990), 1–14.

33. On the difference between *patria* and *nación*, see Kagan's excellent essay "Nación y patria," 204–25.

34. Xavier Gil Pujol, "One King, One Faith, Many Nations: Patria and Nation in Spain, Six-teenth–Seventeenth Centuries," in *"Patria" und "Patrioten" vor dem Patriotismus: Pflichten, Rechte, Glauben und die Rekonfigurierung europäischer Gemeinwesen im 17. Jahrhundert*, ed. Robert von Friede-burg (Wiesbaden: Harrassowitz Verlag, 2005), 105–38. See also Thompson, "Castile, Spain, and the Monarchy," 156–58.

35. Eric Hobsbawm, Ernest Gellner, and Benedict Anderson are the major proponents of the "modernist" theory of nationalism (i.e., that nationalism is a product of the modern era), which many premodernists have contested since the 1990s. Opposing the "modernists" are "primordial-ists"; for two important examples, see Anthony D. Smith, *Chosen Peoples* (Oxford: Oxford University Press, 2003); and Adrian Hastings, *The Construction of Nationhood: Ethnicity, Religion, and Nationalism* (Cambridge: Cambridge University Press, 1997).

36. See Greenfeld, *Nationalism*, 87; and Philip Schwyzer, *Literature, Nationalism, and Memory in Early Modern England and Wales* (Cambridge: Cambridge University Press, 2004). Schwyzer argues

eschewed the nationalism debate by focusing on the broader, and more vague, category of "national identity" in premodern Europe.[37] Yet many such historians assume, rather than investigate, the conceptual and geographic parameters of the nation as it existed prior to the formation of the nation-state. The larger question of exactly how early modern peoples imagined and understood the nation remains understudied. The nation during the early modern period was a messy concept, straddling both the older, medieval understanding of a *natio* and a newer, more politicized meaning encompassing sovereignty. I argue that it is necessary to explore precisely what early modern writers intended when they used the word "nation."

Historians and political scientists, most famously Anthony Smith, have also noted the centrality of religious symbols and rhetoric in the development of national identities before the eighteenth century.[38] Eric Olsen presents a provocative reworking of nationalism and nationalist movements in early modern Europe, which he connects to strands of medieval millenarianism, including messianism. One of the most important aspects of messianism in the context of nationalism is its emphasis on the monarchy's unique role in God's plan. This type of particularism countered the universalism of Catholicism and permitted the Spanish monarchy to see itself as the only true defender of the faith in Europe; we can see from a transnational perspective that the Spanish, Portuguese, French, and English all represented themselves as chosen peoples in the early modern era. The application of the Old Testament depiction of the Hebrew people to early modern national discourses served the key purpose of permitting a transition between the loose medieval understanding of a nation into a more rigidly fixed and politicized geographical and cultural entity. Central to such a transition was the distinctive destiny of the chosen people, a specific group not only imbued with superior virtue and ability but also granted God's special grace and a promise of territorial domination over neighbors. It is not surprising that a messianic ideology that could be easily linked to territorial domination would prove popular during an era when monarchies were consolidating their authority and forming global empires. Thus the sacred played a

---

that even if broad-based participation in the nation was not possible before the eighteenth century, "nationalist" sentiments were expressed by the politically and economically dominant sector of society, which had the effect of creating a nation *in potentia* (8–9).

37. See Simon Forde, Lesley Johnson, and Alan V. Murray, eds., *Concepts of National Identity in the Middle Ages* (Leeds: University of Leeds Press, 1995).

38. See David A. Bell, *The Cult of the Nation in France: Inventing Nationalism, 1680–1800* (Cambridge: Harvard University Press, 2001); H. Eric R. Olsen, *The Calabrian Charlatan, 1598–1603: Messianic Nationalism in Early Modern Europe* (New York: Palgrave Macmillan, 2003); and Smith, *Chosen Peoples*.

key role in the development and augmentation of the concept of the nation during this period.

It is not my intention, however, to argue that discussions of the nation in the seventeenth century proceeded uniformly and progressively to the eighteenth-century development of nationalism. In fact, I reject the notion of the development of the nation-state as a linear process.[39] Identities and experiences remain fluid and plastic throughout history; in the early modern era, fluidity was encouraged by the easy movement of peoples, ideas, culture, and identities. In contrast, proponents of nationalist ideologies generally portray national identities as fixed and stable.[40] Historians must struggle to read behind and beyond discourses of national identities, both past and present, in order to view the more complicated reality. For example, in sixteenth- and seventeenth-century Castile, one ideological goal of many historians was to erase or "conquer" the Moorish past, which they viewed as a disruption or aberration in Spain's glorious Christian tradition; while such efforts were most obvious in Andalusia, they echoed throughout the kingdom.[41] Yet, in recent work, Andrew Schulz demonstrates that eighteenth-century Spain saw an upsurge in reclaiming and celebrating its Moorish heritage.[42] Rather than understand the Moorish presence as an interruption of Spain's grand national narrative, some eighteenth-century artists and writers saw it as *part* of Spanish history and identity. Thus Spain's national story could and did change over time.

Spain provides a particularly intriguing and complex perspective on issues of national community. The attempt to create a patron saint of "Spain" at a time when Spain did not exist politically fostered a sense of connection among Spaniards, performed through the celebration of patron sainthood. Every major city was ordered to celebrate Teresa as patron with public processions and festivals; no matter how the viewing public may have reacted to these processions, people were exposed through them to a variety of images and types of rhetoric about royal power, Spain, and what it meant to be Spanish. At the same time, the

39. See David A. Bell, "Review: Recent Works on Early Modern French National Identity," *Journal of Modern History* 68, no. 1 (1996): 101.

40. Experiences of twentieth-century Spain have had a profound effect in shaping the way historians understand and interpret Spain's past. Cemal Kafadar highlights the dangers of historians organizing works around the idea of a necessary progression from pluralism and fluidity to exclusion and homogenization in the development of unified (ethnic) nationalism; see Kafadar, *Between Two Worlds: The Construction of the Ottoman State* (Berkeley and Los Angeles: University of California Press, 1995), 21–23.

41. For a discussion of this process, see Harris, *From Muslim to Christian Granada*.

42. Andrew Schulz, "The Porcelain of the Moors: The Alhambra Vases in Enlightenment Spain," *Hispanic Research Journal* 9 (December 2008): 388–414.

very language of patron sainthood (especially when connected to Santiago) reaffirmed the sense of a historical Spain that preceded the Habsburg dynasty. Since nationhood in early modern Europe relied on the experience of a shared past, both sides of the debate eagerly promoted narratives of the Spanish past in which their saint played an integral role. But it is important to emphasize that even though the king had a large stake in such narratives, the nation did not necessarily support royal aims and was not inevitably controlled by the monarch. The Spanish nation was not synonymous with the Spanish monarchy, and it could even be used as a method of resisting royal policies.

The phrase "patron saint of Spain" raises many questions that are not easily answered. Of what exactly had Teresa been made patron saint? Castile? Spain? The Spanish monarchy? Participants disagreed bitterly over the geographic jurisdiction of Teresa's patron sainthood. These questions reflect even greater uncertainty over whom exactly Teresa represented in her spiritual advocacy. The Spanish people? The king? The interests of the monarchy? All of these? A close reading of the debate reveals a variety of attempts to answer these questions, directly or indirectly; we see a wealth of possible interpretations from Castilians about how they viewed themselves in relationship to town, nation, and monarchy. Teresa's patron sainthood could be tied to the person of Philip IV and the Habsburg dynasty exclusively, to the idea of a Spanish nation utterly distinct from the monarchy, to a new civic communal identity that militated against an older medieval understanding of universal *Christianitas,* or to an offense against local pride or the privilege of a specific class or group (specifically, the privilege of the clergy). The coexistence of such disparate understandings of the nation demonstrates the elasticity of nation and identity in early modern Europe.[43] At the same time, elasticity does not necessarily entail fragmentation or incoherence. This study examines the key elements of the Spanish nation and identity that were assumed and shared by both sides of the controversy over patron sainthood.

The book begins by tracing two developments in Castilian history that were fundamental to the shaping of the Castilian past: the origins and growth of devotion to the apostle Santiago in medieval Castile, and sixteenth-century Castilian accounts of national foundations. I investigate how Santiago's slow evolution as the patron saint of Spain created

---

43. For a seminal study on the role of the periphery in the development of national identity, see Peter Sahlins, *Boundaries: The Making of France and Spain in the Pyrenees* (Berkeley and Los Angeles: University of California Press, 1989).

a crucial place for the apostle in the burgeoning understanding of the Spanish nation as it developed throughout the sixteenth century. Through this process, ideological, spiritual, and political conceptions of the nation of "Spain" deepened into an increasingly salient national consciousness in early modern Iberia. I further assess the controversy that unfolded when, by the end of the sixteenth century, Santiago and his foundational place in Spanish history became open to question and doubt.

Chapter 2 addresses how international scandal and domestic doubts concerning Santiago's continued efficacy as patron saint created a space that permitted a growing movement centered around another seminal Castilian saint: Teresa of Avila. This chapter briefly traces Teresa's life, career, and monumental popularity after her death in 1582. It discusses the first Carmelite efforts to have Teresa made co-patron saint of Spain in 1617–18 and the heated controversy that followed. The intensity of devotion to Teresa during this period stemmed largely from the lived experience of her holiness by contemporary Castilian people who met, saw, spoke with, or were miraculously cured by her—she was, as they described it, "modern." In addition, Teresa's supporters expounded the belief that, as a native of Spain, she would intercede more powerfully for her nation than would a foreign saint. Her supporters quickly found new and inventive ways of fashioning Teresa, no less than Santiago, as a crucial part of Spain's mythic past and messianic destiny, while reshaping the older historical narrative in favor of a modern one.

In the third chapter I investigate the issue of political and royal involvement in the co-patronage controversy, which became important in the second phase of the debate (1627–30). The new king, Philip IV, and his powerful chief minister, the count-duke of Olivares, seized the opportunities provided by Teresa's election to promote royal propaganda. Yet their support for this controversial election allowed those hostile to royal policies generally, and to Olivares more specifically, to transform the co-patronage debate into a platform for political attack. I argue that early modern political writers could invoke the nation as a method of protecting traditional rights and providing a check to royal authority. Thus, while the king could (and did) use patron sainthood to consolidate authority with new symbolic propaganda, other groups could also mobilize their patron for the purposes of resistance and criticism. The inchoate nature of the nation during the early modern period allowed it to be employed simultaneously for multiple, and opposing, purposes.

Chapter 4 turns to the symbolic role that patron saints played in representing their kingdom on an international stage as embodiments of the monarch's foreign policy. Specifically, I analyze how foreign policy and gender collided in the co-patronage debate as Teresa's femininity provoked anxiety over her ability to fulfill her new role as guardian of Spain's international reputation. Reason-of-state theorists privileged international reputation as vital for the efficacy of foreign policy and the maintenance of Spain's hegemony in Europe; patron sainthood thus became central to representing and maintaining Spain's reputation, as well as embodying concrete policies. Opponents of Teresa's election insisted that representation by a woman would lead to international ridicule. In response, some of her supporters constructed a powerful argument that a new saint was necessary to combat contemporary problems facing the monarchy. They viewed the Moorslayer as an increasingly obsolete cultural symbol and instead advocated in favor of Teresa as a warrior against heresy and a promoter of internal reform.

In chapter 5 the discussion turns to the question of who exactly might have embraced such a vision of Teresa. The focus moves from external to internal here, as I "map" support for Teresa's co-patronage along regional lines within Castile. The vital symbolic function of patron saints in early modern civic and religious culture led to powerful connections to local patrons. Local elites in the early modern period were busily constructing local narratives and identities based on local cults. Attempts to introduce a national patron into a city or town could (and did) result in outrage and rejection. Yet it would be a misreading of seventeenth-century Castile to see such outrage as a triumph of localism over centralized authority. Cities and towns often integrated themselves into a larger national context, even as they fought to protect local interests. I present Andalusia as an extended case study in this chapter, as both regional identities and the clash over co-patronage were particularly fierce in this region.

In addition to increasing tensions between local and national cults, the co-patronage debate shed light on the growing uses of saints for civic rather than ecclesiastical purposes. Chapter 6 addresses the tension between beliefs that national patron sainthood remained solely the prerogative of the church and new understandings of it as primarily communicentric in nature. This chapter develops the clashes between Castilian churches and royal and secular authority, as many churches sought to advance their own unique interests, occasionally at the expense of royal authority. Yet churches did not necessarily invoke the ancient privileges of the ecclesiastical estate in order to promote papal power or a vision of the universal church. Rather, local churches more often than not advanced local (and sometimes national) issues. To complicate the ecclesiastical picture, prelates (in contrast to cathedral chapters) inhabited a middle ground, sometimes backing their chapter and sometimes throwing their support behind the king. This chapter argues that expanded state power in the early modern period led to increasingly national churches, whether they promoted local, royal, or national interests.

Bitter division over who should control patron sainthood—the nation or the church—proved controversial not only on the national but on the international level as well. In the final chapter the debate relocates to Rome, where a group of ambassadors representing the cathedral chapter of Santiago de Compostela began to campaign for the repeal of the 1627 papal brief, following a stalemate back in Spain. The resolution of a national dispute in an international context highlights the fundamental but understudied way in which the papacy used its ecclesiastical authority to bolster its position in international affairs. Chapter 7 also draws on multiple case studies of conflicts over patron saints and cultic devotion outside Spain in order to demonstrate that increasing nationalization of patron sainthood was occurring throughout early modern Europe, in spite of the papacy's efforts to maintain control.

The picture that emerges from the diverse and complex issues put forth in these chapters is of national consciousness surfacing during a time of turbulence and change. What is fascinating about the co-patronage debate is that it signals a process more complex than the substitution of one set of cultural values for another. The bitter wrangling over Teresa's elevation reveals the depth of the crisis that had developed in early seventeenth-century Castilian political and spiritual life over the future of the nation and its goals and values. Those supporting the new patron saint viewed the role of mythic origins as increasingly obsolete in the world of the Renaissance and Reformation, a world fraught with religious conflict and a changing political landscape. Teresa's supporters shifted the location of Spain's salvation from the distant past to the recent present; in doing so, they fashioned a new vision of the Spanish nation in which faith was preserved not by protection in battle but by internal piety and reform. The opponents of Teresa's elevation, by contrast, argued forcefully that any changes to the national narrative would lead to disastrous results—the apostle would turn his back on them, their policies would fail, and Spain would lose its place of primacy in the world. Yet failure and disaster came for the monarchy, with or without

Santiago's singular patron sainthood, and new national narratives were crafted in the eighteenth and nineteenth centuries. But the enduring presence of both Santiago and Teresa in the Spanish cultural and historical imagination demonstrates their centrality to expressions and understandings of the Spanish nation.

1

SANTIAGO AND THE
SHADOW OF DECLINE

Europeans have long told a variety of stories about themselves and their origins. Though medieval and early modern authors generally grounded stories of origins in Genesis, many peoples recounted additional stories based on ancient mythology or distant historical events. Such stories were various, layered, and evolved over time; Colette Beaune's recognition of a "plurality of founding heroes" in France can be seen throughout Europe.[1] Interest in origins intensified during the Renaissance as history writing as a genre developed and deepened.[2] In sixteenth-century Castile, a series of medieval legends about the apostle Saint James (Santiago) and his close relationship with the Spanish people became progressively fused to histories of Spain's spiritual foundation. Through this process, ideological, spiritual, and political conceptions of the nation of "Spain" strengthened into an increasingly salient national consciousness. This chapter examines this complex process by assessing how Santiago's slow evolution as the patron saint of Spain created a crucial place for the

---

1. Colette Beaune, *The Birth of an Ideology: Myths and Symbols of Nation in Late-Medieval France*, trans. Susan Ross Huston (Berkeley and Los Angeles: University of California Press, 1991), 315. See also Smith, *Chosen Peoples*. The Spanish discussed their origins in terms of a mythological King Tubal, Heracles, and Santiago.

2. Roberto Bizzocchi, *Genealogie incredibili: Scritti di storia nell'Europa moderna* (Bologna: Società Editrice il Mulino, 1995), 93–188; and Marie Tanner, *The Last Descendant of Aeneas: The Hapsburgs and the Mythic Image of the Emperor* (New Haven: Yale University Press, 1993), 67–118.

apostle in the burgeoning understanding of the Spanish nation as it developed throughout the sixteenth century. While Santiago's patron sainthood is often seen from a modern vantage point as a fixed feature of Iberian history, it was in fact slow, incomplete, and contested.

The story of Saint James and his connection to the Spanish nation began in the ninth century with a glow of radiant light—a cluster of shooting stars illuminating the blue-black sky. Shepherds grazing their sheep nearby looked up in awe and wonder; they were immediately aware that this mysterious celestial activity was a divine portent, like the comet that heralded the birth of Jesus. They discussed the events among themselves, and eventually their whispers reached the ears of the local bishop, Theodemir (d. 847), who decided to investigate the mysterious occurrence. Proceeding to the large, empty field over which the stars had fallen, the bishop and his men discovered the ruins of an ancient sepulcher. They knew at once what they had uncovered: the tomb of Saint James the Greater, one of the twelve apostles, first among them to be martyred in the years immediately following the Crucifixion and Resurrection of Christ.[3] Legends had circulated that James had been sent to the province of Hispania to evangelize before his martyrdom; it therefore did not surprise Theodemir that after his death he would return to the land he converted.[4] In honor of the newly discovered relics, the bishop built a simple chapel to house them and to mark the site for pilgrims; within a few centuries, the chapel evolved into a cathedral and the empty field into one of the greatest pilgrimage sites in the medieval Christian world—Santiago de Compostela.

The locals who housed and protected the apostle's relics began to develop a special relationship with the apostle. They eventually began to call him "Santiago," a vernacular contraction of his name in Latin, Sanctus Iacobus. The miraculous translation of Santiago's relics from the Holy Land, where he had been martyred, to an isolated field in the remote corner of the Iberian Peninsula was a sign to the local Christians that they had been offered a special relationship with the apostle. The protection of a powerful apostle could not have come at a better time for the besieged residents of the northern peninsula. The once great Visigothic kingdom of Hispania, built out of the former Roman province, had fallen to the Arab and Berber army of the Umayyad Caliphate in the early 700s, a century before the discovery of Saint James's relics.

3. William Melczer, ed., *The Pilgrim's Guide to Santiago de Compostela* (New York: Italica Press, 1993), 21.

4. Kendrick, *St. James in Spain*, 15–17. See also Ofelia Rey Castelao, *Los mitos del Apóstol Santiago* (Vigo: Nigratrea, 2006).

The invading army had driven many of the Christian Visigoths north, almost into the sea. Very quickly, however, Christian forces rallied under the nobility of Asturias-León and carved out a precarious kingdom on the northern edges of Islamic Spain. They began a series of periodic incursions southward to increase their landholdings; this long epoch of intermittent warfare—the so-called reconquest—spanned seven centuries, ca. 722–1492.

During this long period, Santiago became increasingly associated with aiding Christian forces against their Islamic enemies. His first dramatic act of protection for Christian forces occurred during the battle of Clavijo in the ninth century (834/844).[5] According to the legend, the night before a battle against the overwhelming numbers of the Islamic army, Ramiro I, the king of Asturias-León, knelt in prayer to ask God for a victory against his stronger and more numerous enemies. The following day, the king's prayers were answered: The sky opened, and Santiago descended from heaven on a brilliant white horse, holding aloft a sword. The miraculous apparition caused fear and chaos among the enemy, while Ramiro's army gained courage, slaying seventy thousand enemy soldiers. Ramiro and his emerging kingdom vowed never to forget what Santiago had done for them; Ramiro's armies took the words the apostle had taught them for their battle cry: "God and Santiago, help us!"[6]

These three stories—of Santiago's evangelization, translation, and apparition—encompass the central legends concerning the apostle and the Spanish kingdoms. While these legends fit together smoothly, each has its own distinct history dating from the Middle Ages. Historians have struggled to untangle when, why, and from which sources these stories appeared. The clearest picture we can form from the fragmented source material indicates that the belief that Santiago had been assigned the province of Spain for the purposes of evangelizing surfaced as early as the seventh century; a breviary of Greek origin translated into Latin, the *Breviarium apostolorum* (Apostolic breviary), stated unequivocally,

5. Historians disagree over the exact date of the battle, usually putting it somewhere between 834 and 844; 844 is the year that King Ramiro granted Santiago a privilege in thanksgiving for his aid in the battle, though the battle is traditionally dated to 834. The former date reinforces the historical improbability of the battle; almost all modern historians accept the fictional origins of both the battle and the privilege. For one example, see Roger Collins, *Early Medieval Spain: Unity in Diversity, 400–1000* (London: Macmillan, 1983), 237.

6. Detailed versions of the battle of Clavijo began to appear in the thirteenth century. For one influential example, see Rodrigo Jiménez de Rada, *Roderici Ximenii de Rada Historia de rebus Hispanie, sive, Historia Gothica*, ed. Juan Fernández Valverde, Corpus Christianorum: Continuatio Mediaevalis, vol. 72 (Turnhout: Brepols, 1987), 132–33.

"James, the son the Zebedee . . . preached in Spain and [other] Western places and was decapitated under Herod and buried in Achai Mararica."[7] An eighth-century hymn agreed that Santiago had preached in Spain.[8] References to the apostle's evangelizing efforts in Spain arose both within and outside Iberia but do not seem to have been universally accepted or reproduced. Isidore of Seville (d. 636), for example, remarked on Santiago's Spanish visit in one of his works but neglected it in others.[9]

Despite such references to Santiago's preaching in Spain, medieval Castilian texts instead chose to emphasize the presence of the apostolic relics and the pilgrimage site. Although this discovery dated to the ninth century, the location in a remote corner of the Iberian Peninsula created difficulties in attracting large numbers of pilgrims. Claiming the entire corpus of an apostle and martyr, as Compostela did, conferred enormous prestige on the shrine. An ambitious Galician prelate, Diego Gelmírez (d. 1140), worked tirelessly to improve the international reputation of his church and shrine; during his prelacy, the pilgrimage route to Compostela along the northern coast took on new life, thanks in large part to Gelmírez's close ties the Benedictine monks of Cluny, who sponsored a series of monasteries along the route to provide housing for pilgrims. Once the Cluniac monasteries provided the route with basic infrastructure, Compostela rapidly gained international popularity in the High Middle Ages, eventually becoming Europe's second major pilgrimage site, after Rome.[10] In one of his most lasting accomplishments, Gelmírez succeeded in having the see at Compostela elevated to an archbishopric. In order to solidify and preserve the cathedral's privileges for subsequent generations, the archbishop commissioned a four-volume work called the *Historia compostellana* (History of Compostela), which detailed the history of the discovery of the relics and growth of the shrine.[11]

7. "Jacobus qui interpretatur subplantator filius Zebedei frater Johannis. Hic Spaniae et occidentalia loca praedicatur et sub Herode gladio caesus occubuit sepultusque est in Achai Marmarica." Quoted in Melczer, *Pilgrim's Guide to Santiago de Compostela*, 10.

8. Ibid., 12.

9. There is some debate over the Isidorian origin of the reference to Santiago; it might have been a later textual addition. See Katherine Elliot van Liere, "The Moorslayer and the Missionary: James the Apostle in Spanish Historiography from Isidore of Seville to Ambrosio de Morales," *Viator: Medieval and Renaissance Studies* 37 (2006): 519–43. Van Liere discusses the debates over Isidorian authorship of *De ortu* (523–25).

10. On the phenomenon of medieval pilgrimage, see Diana Webb, *Medieval European Pilgrimage, c. 700–c. 1500* (New York: Palgrave, 2002).

11. For an exhaustive study of Gelmírez's life, accomplishments, and historical context, see Richard Fletcher, *St. James's Catapult* (Oxford: Oxford University Press, 1984). A modern edition of the *Historia compostellana* can be found in Emma Falque Rey, ed., *Historia compostellana*, Corpus Christianorum: Continuatio Mediaevalis, vol. 70 (Turnhout: Brepols, 1988).

While the purpose of the *Historia* was to glorify the apostle's shrine and provide a historical account of its presence, it underplayed, even ignored, the tradition of Santiago's evangelization of Spain.[12] In keeping with medieval devotional practice, the mere presence of Santiago's relics in Spain justified his special attachment to the Spanish people, manifested through his patron sainthood. Early medieval cults tended to spring up around relics rather than individuals, although devotions sometimes did arise from the sepulcher of a local holy person whose body remained attached to the place in which he or she had lived. Though such local connections were an important aspect of medieval piety, the number of relics far exceeded the number of local holy people. It is worth remembering that every church was under an obligation to house the relics of a saint under its altar. This necessity, along with the practice of dismembering holy bodies and the lively trade in false relics, meant that relics could travel from one end of Christendom to the other. The higher the saint in the heavenly hierarchy, the more coveted the relics would become on the market.[13] Thus many medieval churches housed cherished relics of saints with no specific tie to the region. The lack of such a tie was not viewed as an impediment to the efficacy of the relics' powers, since medieval clerics believed that all saints chose where their relics landed. That the apostle had chosen this specific site as the resting place of his miraculous body established a connection to his relics in Galicia; the account did not require the element of Santiago's evangelization in order to bolster the legitimacy of the relics' presence.

Even before the apostle's choice of Galicia for the burial of his relics was revealed, hymns had begun to honor Santiago as "our protector and patron helper."[14] Yet it is important to keep in mind that the early medieval church lacked a bureaucratic or centralized process for naming saints or patrons; the recognition of saints derived from popular acclaim, tradition, and episcopal support. As a result, no definite date for the beginning of Santiago's patron sainthood can be established, though we can trace the development of a bond of mutual obligation between Santiago and (future) Castilians. The mutual bond required that the apostle

---

12. It was Katherine van Liere who first observed the lack of interest in the apostle's evangelization throughout the Middle Ages. Van Liere and Emma Falque Rey agree that Fletcher's reading of the *Historia* as validating the legend of Santiago's evangelization is based on a codicological error. See Van Liere, "Moorslayer and the Missionary," 525–26.

13. For a thorough discussion of many of these issues, see Geary, *Living with the Dead*. See also Michael McCormick, *Origins of the European Economy: Communications and Commerce, AD 300–900* (Cambridge: Cambridge University Press, 2001), 283–318.

14. "Tutorque nobis et patronus vernulus." Quoted in Melczer, *Pilgrim's Guide to Santiago de Compostela*, 12.

protect and intercede for Castilians, while Castilians, in return, had to venerate the apostle and honor his relics.[15] Although Santiago's original role as patron consisted of general intercession on behalf of his people in the heavenly kingdom, as the Middle Ages progressed he began to be associated with a specific form of aid: military intervention.[16] Unlike the discovery of Santiago's relics and development of the pilgrimage route, which had international as well as regional importance, legends involving apparitions of Santiago in battle arose exclusively in an Iberian context. Although medieval historians claimed that Santiago's military intercession for the Spanish began with Clavijo in the ninth century, stories of Santiago's appearance at critical moments in battle against the "infidels" actually originated in the political and military realities of the High Middle Ages.

The evolution of Santiago as warrior might not have been possible without the influence of the First Crusade (1095–1101), when crusading ideology, developed and circulated by the Franks, began to appear in Spain. During the First Crusade, crusaders and theologians disseminated a new discourse of spiritual warfare throughout the Latin West that valorized certain military endeavors.[17] In addition, the crusaders' travels to Byzantium opened them to the influence of aspects of Byzantine cultic devotion, which included an emphasis on warrior saints that theologians in the Latin West tended to discourage.[18] The iconography of saints as warriors, and as intercessors for warriors, fit perfectly with the development of crusading ideology in the West. Early accounts of the Crusades, like the widely read history of Robert the Monk, often included stories of saints appearing in battles to defend Christian soldiers at crucial moments.[19]

15. Christian, *Local Religion in Sixteenth-Century Spain,* 33.

16. José Luis Barreiro Rivas, *La función política de los caminos de peregrinación en la Europa medieval* (Madrid: Editorial Tecnos, 1997), 173. Barreiro offers a critical distinction between Santiago as warrior (the Matamoros), dating from the twelfth century, and depictions of the apostle as a protector, which were much older.

17. Christopher Tyerman, *God's War: A New History of the Crusades* (Cambridge: Belknap Press of Harvard University Press, 2006), 27–166.

18. Marcia Colish discusses the early development of a cult of warrior saints in Byzantium in the centuries following Justinian. See her *Medieval Foundations of the Western Intellectual Tradition, 400–1400* (New Haven: Yale University Press, 1997), 123. One of the best-known medieval soldier saints (Saint George) appears to have had Byzantine origins; see Samantha J. E. Riches, *St. George: Hero, Martyr, and Myth* (Thrupp: Sutton, 2000), 11–12. Nevertheless, the English in particular had maintained a lively early medieval tradition of king-saints who tended to be martyred during battle; see John Edward Damon, *Soldier Saints and Holy Warriors: Warfare and Sanctity in the Literature of Early England* (Burlington, Vt.: Ashgate, 2003).

19. For one primary source example, see Robert the Monk, *Robert the Monk's History of the First Crusade: Historia iherosolimitana,* trans. Carol Sweetenham (Burlington, Vt.: Ashgate, 2005), 141–42.

Of the three soldier-saints named explicitly by Robert the Monk—Saint George, Saint Demetrius, and Saint Maurice—Saint George became the most popular in the Latin West. Both the English and Catalans eventually adopted him as their patron saint. He was depicted not only as a soldier and martyr but also as a serpent killer, an iconography that connected him visually with the archangel Michael, commander of the heavenly host, with whom he was often depicted.[20] The cults of Michael and George, among others, might have provided both inspiration and a blueprint for the cult of Santiago in Spain, beginning in the early twelfth century. All three bear iconographic similarities: George and Santiago, for example, were often portrayed on white horses, trampling enemies underfoot.

Most historians agree that images of Santiago as a warrior, the so-called Matamoros (Moorslayer), arose only in the twelfth century.[21] The first image of Santiago as a warrior appeared in the cathedral of Santiago de Compostela, in a sculpture in which the apostle appears on horseback wielding a sword.[22] Thus the ascendancy of Santiago as a military saint occurred only after the First Crusade and the spread of crusading rhetoric throughout western Europe. Iberia was particularly ripe for the adoption of crusading ideology, as its Christian leaders began renewing their assaults on their Islamic neighbors with increased vigor and success during the twelfth and thirteenth centuries.[23] Santiago Matamoros, therefore, became a polemical addition to the new language of crusade being introduced in a renewed surge of military activity by Spanish kings.

But Santiago was never the exclusive patron saint of the reconquest, no matter what the Compostelan cathedral preferred to claim, largely because of the regional diversity of the emergent Christian kingdoms. The new Christian territories created by the conquest of lands from al-Andalus were not unified; instead, the peninsula became a patchwork of kingdoms and principalities with evolving relationships to one another—Galicia, Asturias-León, Navarre, Aragón, Catalonia, and Portugal. From the eleventh to the thirteenth century, the Christian territories were

20. For depictions of George with Michael, particularly in the Byzantine tradition, see Riches, *St. George*, 12; Riches discusses George and the Catalans on pp. 14–15. On the rise of Saint George and crusader ideology, see also James Reston Jr., *Warriors of God: Richard the Lionheart and Saladin in the Third Crusade* (New York: Doubleday, 2001), 11.

21. Barreiro Rivas, *La función política de los caminos*, 173.

22. Joseph F. O'Callaghan, *Reconquest and Crusade in Medieval Spain* (Philadelphia: University of Pennsylvania Press, 2003), 195.

23. Many historians of medieval Spain and the Crusades have noted the Frankish influence on the Spanish kingdoms in the evolution of the concept of *reconquista* as a form of crusade. For one example, see Marcus Bull, *Knightly Piety and the Lay Response to the First Crusade: Limousin and Gascony, c. 970–c. 1130* (Oxford: Clarendon Press, 1993), 72–114.

consolidated into larger kingdoms; for example, the twelfth century saw the emergence of the separate kingdom of Portugal, while the ancient kingdom of Asturias-León joined together with the newer kingdom of Castile and, in the east, Catalonia with Aragón. As a result, there could be no one patron saint of reconquest. At least three major saints who were also regional patrons were regularly invoked during battle: Santiago (regional patron of Asturias-León), Millán (regional patron of Castile), and George (regional patron of Catalonia).[24] Eventually Santiago's cult came to dominate that of Saint Millán in Castile, though the two were sometimes invoked together.[25] In addition to these, a small number of more minor saints, such as Isidoro and Hermenegildo, were also occasionally invoked in battle. Moreover, one of the most popular *reconquista* saints throughout the Iberian kingdoms remained the Virgin Mary.[26] Santiago's position as the most popular patron of warfare was thus far from inevitable.

The eventual dominance of Santiago over other patrons in Castile arose from a variety of complex devotional and political factors, the most important of which was certainly the cathedral of Santiago's power and influence. The cathedral assiduously tried to associate the cult of Santiago with the royal family of Castile-León, and it occasionally nursed dreams of pushing its Castilian ecclesiastical rival, Toledo, out of its primatial seat.[27] In its bid for dominance over all other holy sites in Castile, the Compostelan cathedral came to view Santiago's relics and military apparitions as pieces of evidence for its spiritual superiority. Unlike the legend of Santiago's evangelization of Spain, the apostle's presence at key battles in Spanish history underscored his closeness to God and continued protection of the Spanish people in their struggle against the infidels. It is no surprise that the cathedral of Santiago boasts the oldest known image of the saint as warrior, or that the *Historia compostellana* devoted much attention to military apparitions.

Santiago became the primary symbol of the ideology of Castilian reconquest as crusade, and the battle cry "God and Santiago, help us!"

24. Ibid., 193–99.

25. Unfortunately, there is no definitive account of how the cult of Santiago assumed a place of preeminence over Millán and other popular warrior saints; all historians know is that this was eventually accomplished, despite Millán's continued popularity. O'Callaghan, *Reconquest and Crusade in Medieval Spain*, 199.

26. For a discussion of the Virgin Mary as *conquistadora* in the Spanish world, see Amy G. Remensnyder, "The Colonization of Sacred Architecture: The Virgin Mary, Mosques, and Temples in Medieval Spain and Early Sixteenth-Century Mexico," in *Monks and Nuns, Saints and Outcasts: Religion in Medieval Society*, ed. Sharon Farmer and Barbara Rosenwein (Ithaca: Cornell University Press, 2000), 189–219.

27. Kendrick, *St. James in Spain*, 53.

echoed throughout Castilian battlefields.[28] Stories that included pleas to Santiago on the eve of battle also began to proliferate. The twelfth-century chronicle dedicated to extolling the deeds of Alfonso VII (d. 1157) included numerous references to spiritual appeals to Santiago during times of crisis and warfare, almost exclusively in the format of invocations rather than accounts of apparitions. For example, the soldiers "cried out to the God of heaven and earth and to Saint Mary and to Saint James in prayer, that they might help and defend them."[29] An account of a later battle depicted Muslims calling out to Mohammed and Christians to God, Mary, and Santiago.[30] A more detailed prayer, which also invoked Christ and Mary, asked that Santiago, "apostle of Christ, defend us in danger, that we do not perish in dreadful Judgment at the hands of the Saracens."[31] One of the most striking features of these invocations is that they are defensive pleas for protection rather than requests for aggressive military intervention. The soldiers appealed to Santiago (along with Mary) for help and protection, but they asked their saints to save them, not to kill their enemies; no apparitions followed such prayers, and apparently none was anticipated. Although it seems likely that stories of Santiago's appearance in battle were already circulating around the time that this chronicle was written, it is clear that the twelfth century was a period of evolution for Santiago, from patron and protector to Matamoros.

The full formation of the Matamoros ideology occurred in the thirteenth century. By this time one finds complete references to the third and crucial element of *santiaguista* legends: the apostle's purported appearance at the battle of Clavijo, described as the first time Santiago intervened in battles against Muslims. Although the ninth-century battle may have been discussed in earlier centuries, especially in the twelfth, it was not until thirteenth-century histories that the battle attained a central role in stories about the reconquest.[32] The archbishop of Toledo, Rodrigo Jiménez de Rada (d. 1247), wrote a highly influential history of the Spanish people in which he included a description of the battle of

---

28. For one famous example, see *The Poem of the Cid*, ed. Ian Michael, trans. Rita Hamilton and Janet Perry (Manchester: Manchester University Press, 1975), 68:1134–40.

29. "Chronica Adefonsi Imperatoris," in *Chronica Hispana Saeculi XII*, ed. Antonio Maya Sánchez, Corpus Christianorum: Continuatio Mediaevalis, vol. 71 (Turnhout: Brepols, 1990), 2.22.205.

30. Ibid., 2.26.207.

31. "Sante Iacobe, apostole Christi, defende nos in prelio, ut non pereamus in tremendo iudicio Sarracenorum." Ibid., 2.69.227.

32. Unfortunately, a systematic study of the legend of Clavijo has yet to be written. Early twentieth-century Spanish historians, particularly Galician historians, attempted to find evidence for the historical battle, with mixed results and endless controversy over dating. But, to my knowledge, no one has yet traced the history of accounts of the battle in primary sources.

Clavijo containing all the elements of the legend as we still know it: On the night before the battle, King Ramiro had a dream in which he was comforted by Santiago and assured of victory against the Arabs. The next day, the apostle appeared in the thick of battle on a white horse, brandishing a sword.[33]

While all thirteenth-century versions of the battle contained the same elements (the dream, the apparition, the white horse, the seventy thousand enemies killed), they were not all consistent. For example, the Castilian *Primera Crónica General* (First general chronicle) presented a detailed account of the battle of Clavijo and Ramiro's dream the night before, in which the apostle told Ramiro, "You know that our lord Jesus Christ separated the world into provinces for my brothers, the other apostles and me, and that he gave Spain to me alone that I might guard and defend it from the enemies of the faith."[34] This brief account of how Santiago originally came to Spain served the function of explaining to the king (and the audience) why the apostle took a special interest in Spain. It also drew a line of continuity from his first-century preaching in Spain to crusading ideology, representing Santiago as the liberator of the Spanish from faithlessness and unbelievers. Elsewhere, the *Primera Crónica* ignored legends about Santiago's preaching and interment in Spain; the focus remained on thirteenth-century preoccupations—the apostle and the spiritual impetus behind Christian armies' movement southward into Islamic territory.[35]

By the thirteenth century, then, all three legends about Santiago in Spain had been fully formed and integrated into Castile's political and cultural ideology, and the saint's prestige as patron was growing. No doubt the kings of Castile-León identified Santiago's cult as a potential source for consolidating their own authority and providing a legitimizing and motivating force to their political and economic desire to expand territorially to the south. Yet one of the most fascinating aspects of Santiago's cult in this period is the contrast between his role as predominantly

33. Jiménez de Rada, *Roderici Ximenii de Rada Historia de rebus Hispanie*, 133.

34. " 'Sepas que Nuestro Senor Jhesu Christo partio a todos los otros apostoles mios hermanos et a mi todas las otras prouincias de la tierra, et a mi solo dio a Espanna que la guardasse et la amparasse de manos de los enemigos de la fe.' " Alfonso X, *Primera Crónica General de España*, 3d ed., ed. Ramón Menéndez Pidal, 2 vols. (Madrid: Editorial Gredos, 1977), 2:360.

35. The version of Clavijo from the *Primera Crónica* was actually taken from a slightly older history of Spain, Lucas de Túy's world chronicle, which also included a reference to Santiago telling the king that he had evangelized Spain, though Van Liere argues that elsewhere Lucas expressed no interest in the legend of Santiago's evangelization. See Van Liere, "Moorslayer and the Missionary," 527–28. For more on Lucas and Jímenez de Rada, see Lucy K. Pick, *Conflict and Coexistence: Archbishop Rodrigo and the Muslims and Jews of Medieval Spain* (Ann Arbor: University of Michigan Press, 2004), 173–77.

a Castilian saint and the insistence of sources that the apostle protected all Spain.[36] As we have seen, the disparate kingdoms of the peninsula maintained their own preferred patrons, as well as their own languages, laws, customs, and political identities.[37] While the movement of Santiago's cult from locally important to one that gradually eclipsed other major patrons in Castile is easy to establish, it is more difficult to grasp how, when, and exactly why Castilians identified the apostle's cult with Spain rather than with Castile alone.

The key to understanding the association of Santiago with Spain emerges when we take a closer look at the legends surrounding the apostle. While devotion to the apostle in Spain was medieval (and largely Castilian), the *legends* about Santiago—primarily his foundation of the Christian church on the Iberian Peninsula—predate the existence of the disparate kingdoms, which emerged only during the reconquest period. Thus Santiago's evangelization occurred when the entire region remained a Roman province. Since his presence in Iberia predated the legal-political divisions of the peninsula that occurred during the reconquest phase, his followers were able to claim a more universal jurisdiction for his patron sainthood. He was thus the patron saint of Hispania, or Spain. The "Spain" invoked by these Castilians drew from a rich diversity of linguistic-cultural groups; even if the Castilians assumed that they inhabited the most important region of Spain, they still used the term, knowingly and deliberately, to refer to all the Spanish kingdoms, and not merely to Castile.[38]

Through links between Santiago's evangelization and his apparitions in battles against Muslims, Santiago became tied to the peninsula's Roman and Visigothic past. Subsequent historians often described this period as a golden age that preceded the devastating invasion of Islamic forces at the beginning of the eighth century. Thus the term "Spain" immediately invoked this idealized period of unity and Christianity, before the darkness and chaos of 711. The rhetoric of reconquest relied on this vision of the past for its force and legitimacy—Christians had the duty to "reclaim" the territory that had been wrested from them

36. For one example, see Alfonso X, *Primera Crónica General*, 2:360.

37. At the same time, devotion to Santiago did persist in some regions in Aragón, particularly around the archbishopric of Zaragoza, which houses the shrine marking the Virgin Mary's miraculous appearance to Santiago. See Diego Murillo, *Fundacion milagrosa de la capilla angelica y apostolica de la Madre de Dios de Pilar, y excellencias de la imperial ciudad de Çaragoça* (Barcelona: Sebastian Mateuad, 1616).

38. The term *natio* could, of course, be used in a more limited way to denote what today we might call an ethnic group. For a discussion of premodern uses of the term (especially in relation to the Old Testament), see Hastings, *Construction of Nationhood*, 16–19.

through deception, trickery, and the brutal force of the invading "infidels" from the South, and to restore the glory of Hispania. Just as this creed had little relation to the concrete realities of the political and military relationship between the Christian and Islamic territories within Iberia, it represented an ideological rather than a practical goal. The process of reconquest did not, of course, unify the peninsula; on the contrary, it created distinct political entities that became more and more separate and that occasionally went to war against one another. Medieval kings sometimes made grandiose claims of Iberian sovereignty under the title of emperor (*imperator totius Hispaniae*), and not only in Castile—Alfonso I of Navarre and Aragón (d. 1134), for example, fashioned himself emperor after an attempt to link the Spanish kingdoms dynastically (with the exception of the Catalan territories) through marriage with Urraca, the queen of Castile-León. Urraca's son, Alfonso VII of Castile (d. 1157), became preeminent among the Spanish kings, which led him not only to adopt Alfonso I's title of emperor but to have himself crowned so in 1135.[39]

During the Middle Ages, therefore, the dream of returning to the lost Visigothic empire resurfaced as part of the ongoing power struggle between the medieval Christian rulers in Iberia, rather than as the ideological goal of reconquest. The idea of empire retained particular symbolic power in the ancient kingdom of León (later Castile-León), which considered itself the direct heir of the Visigoths, as the birthplace of King Pelayo, who began the first Christian excursions against the Umayyads. At the heart of the concept of the "emperor of all of Spain" was the idea, or perhaps the historical memory, of the Spanish nation. Thus centuries after the destruction of Hispania, members of the disparate kingdoms of the peninsula sometimes invoked the Spanish nation as a relevant and salient identity marker. In the emerging kingdom of Castile-León, the apostle Santiago took the role of patron and protector of the nation, an idea that was reflected in the common use of the phrase "patron saint of Spain."

The historical memory of the Spanish nation took on new life and meaning at the end of the fifteenth century, when the Union of Crowns (1479) created a dynastic alliance between Ferdinand's Aragón and Isabel's Castile. The unity forged by this event, later solidified by the ascension of Charles V and the Habsburg dynasty in 1516, gave rise to the glorification

39. O'Callaghan, *History of Medieval Spain*, 216–24. On the historiography of Leonese imperial claims, see 164–65.

of "Spain" throughout the sixteenth and seventeenth centuries. In addition, less than two decades after the Union of Crowns, the new Spanish kingdoms witnessed the end of the reconquest with the surrender of the last Moorish kingdom, Granada, in January 1492. The capitulation of Granada and the official end of the reconquest were celebrated as the final reparation to the catastrophic events of the eighth century and the complete restoration of Spain. One might assume that Spain's unification would have led to a gradual lessening of devotion to Santiago, since he had been seen predominantly as the patron saint of the reconquest. Yet the dawn of the Renaissance saw the apostle's cult assume a new place of prominence in Spanish spiritual and ideological life. While Santiago remained a saint associated primarily with war during the Middle Ages, in the early modern period he evolved into the ultimate representative of the Spanish nation, reflecting for many what it meant to be Spanish.

The sixteenth century was a period of passionate veneration of the apostle's patron sainthood. Understanding the transformation of Santiago's cult in the early modern period requires a brief examination of both ideological shifts and clear evidence of veneration.[40] The foundation for sixteenth-century veneration of Santiago was laid by the Catholic Kings, who visited the apostle's shrine in Santiago de Compostela in part to pray to the apostle for his support in their upcoming war against the Islamic kingdom of Granada. José Manuel García Morales argues that following their 1492 victory against the Moors, Ferdinand and Isabel began a campaign to revitalize the cult of Santiago. First, they implemented the *voto* of Granada, a rent paid to the cathedral of Santiago de Compostela by the churches in Granada, presumably in thanksgiving to the apostle for his aid in their liberation from Islamic domination. Second, they founded the Royal Hospital in Compostela in 1499, built adjacent to the cathedral for the housing of pilgrims. The city thereafter became the site of royal patronage, and medallions depicting various Spanish monarchs (the Catholic Kings, Juana, Charles V) appeared on several buildings.[41] Subsequent rulers of the Spanish kingdoms also made their way to Galicia to visit the apostle's tomb, among them Queen Juana and her husband, Prince Philip, as well as Charles V and Philip II,

---

40. While Santiago's cult in the early modern period remains surprisingly unexamined, given its importance, a recent collection of essays published by the Xunta of Santiago de Compostela addresses some noteworthy facets of the apostle's early modern cult. See *Santiago y la monarquía de España (1504–1788)* (Madrid: Sociedad Estatal de Conmemoraciones Culturales, 2004).

41. José Manuel García Morales, "El apóstol Santiago y la monarquía de España," in ibid., 24–25.

the latter as a prince on his way to England for his marriage to Queen Mary.[42]

Members of the royal family commissioned artistic works of Santiago as Matamoros and occasionally depicted themselves as "new Santiagos."[43] Images of Santiago, particularly presiding over the battle of Clavijo, sprang up throughout Spanish Renaissance churches in painting and sculpture.[44] The royal family also played a crucial role in the expansion and exultation of the Order of Santiago, a medieval military brotherhood.[45] In the sixteenth century the royal family gained increasing control over the Order, promoting its most loyal courtiers to its membership. The Order of Santiago became the most prestigious of such orders in early modern Spain, increasingly associated with courtly ideals as well as military ones.[46] In this way the apostle became more strongly tied to royal policies and royal patronage; devotion to Santiago demonstrated one's devotion to the king. The apostle's image also appeared on many military standards throughout the sixteenth century; carried into battle, such standards came to represent the Spanish kingdoms in the same way as the royal arms.[47] It is perhaps unsurprising that the only religious festivity celebrated by the Spanish army as it marched to war in the Netherlands in 1576 was the apostle's feast day, 25 July.[48] His participation in all wars fought by the monarchy reflected his close relationship with the royal family and the monarchy's foreign policy.

The opening of a new frontier in the colonial Americas also provided an opportunity to expand the apostle's intercession onto a new stage. Stories began to spread that Santiago had appeared in the Americas in numerous battles; as a result, he earned a new sobriquet, Mataindios

42. Victor Nieto Alcaide and María Victoria García Morales, "Santiago y la monarquía española: Orígenes de un mito de estado," in ibid., 34.

43. Nieto Alcaide and García Morales, Monterroso Montero, and Consuelo Gómez López all make this point—Nieto Alcaide and García Morales in reference to a painting of Philip II, Monterroso Montero in reference to depictions of Charles V (ibid., 43–44), and Gómez López in "El apóstol Santiago y la corte: Mentalidad, imagen y promoción artística" (ibid., 88).

44. Gómez López, "El apóstol Santiago y la corte," 87–89; and Francisco José Portela Sandoval, "Santiago, miles Christi y caballero de las Españas," in Santiago y la monarquía de España, 71–85.

45. The royal chronicler Hernando del Pulgar devotes much attention to the role of the Order of Santiago in his account of the war against Granada. Pulgar, Crónica de los Reyes Católicos: Guerra de Granada, ed. Juan de Mata Carriazo, 2 vols. (Granada: Editorial Universidad de Granada, 2008). See, for example, 1:255, 426–27.

46. Gómez López, "El apóstol Santiago y la corte," 90–94.

47. On military standards, see ibid., 88–89; and Nieto Alcaide and García Morales, "Santiago y la monarquía española," 43–45. The latter essay mentions that the Royal Armory houses many examples of such standards from 1544 to 1558.

48. I would like to thank Geoffrey Parker for calling this celebration to my attention. See Parker, The Dutch Revolt (Ithaca: Cornell University Press, 1977), 103.

(Indian slayer), and his name dotted newly drawn maps of Spanish colonial towns.[49] Hernan Ojea, a Galician friar who lived in Mexico for several years at the beginning of the seventeenth century, wrote a lengthy history of Santiago in which he included an extensive list of battles in the New World in which Santiago had appeared. Ojea cited battles the apostle fought alongside Hernando Cortés and pointed to the proliferation of Indian villages that chose Santiago as their patron.[50] One of Ojea's ideological goals was to demonstrate that New Spain had been conquered by Santiago, thereby affirming divine support for the Spanish empire. "For he has shown and still shows himself many times in battles on the side of Christians," Ojea wrote, "especially us Spaniards, surging among the enemies of our holy Catholic faith, armed and on horseback, like a sudden and terrifying clap of thunder."[51] Descriptions of holy apparitions did more than justify conquest; they also stressed that Santiago's role as protector was not relegated to the past alone but lived in the present and would continue in the future. The evolving relationship of Santiago to his chosen people prevented the apostle from losing symbolic salience after the end of the reconquest period.

The impulse to reach back into the past to construct a historical narrative of virtue became a hallmark of early modern political, cultural, and spiritual life. The relationship of past to present became a subject of increasing fascination, even urgency, largely as the result of the Renaissance, which intensified the significance that intellectuals placed on the glorious past (particularly as a reflection of present greatness). Central to the establishment of past greatness was the study of genealogies—personal, institutional, and national.[52] Early modern Castilians proved no exception, and they crafted elaborate genealogies for the Habsburgs and histories of the Spanish kingdoms. Spain's ancient history became a

49. For a dispute over an apparition of Santiago, see Bernal Díaz del Castillo, *Historia verdadera de la conquista de la Nueva España*, ed. Carmelo Sáenz de Santa María (Madrid: CSIC, 1982), 63; and Francisco López de Gómara, *Historia de la conquista de México* (1552), ed. Jorge Gurria Lacroix (Caracas: Biblioteca Ayacucho, 1979), 38. For more on devotion to Santiago in the Americas, see Emilio González López et al., eds., *Galicia, Santiago y América* (Santiago de Compostela: Xunta de Galicia, 1991).

50. Hernan Ojea, *Historia del glorioso apostol Santiago, patron de España: De su venida a ella y de las grandezas de su Yglesia y orden militar* (1615), ed. Ignacio Cabano Vázquez (Santiago de Compostela: Xunta de Galicia, 1993), fols. 234v–241v.

51. Ibid., fols. 16v–17r. "Son of thunder" was one of Santiago's sobriquets; see Thomas F. Coffey, Linda Kay Davidson, and Maryjane Dunn, eds., *The Miracles of St. James* (New York: Italica Press, 1996), xxiii.

52. See Tanner, *Last Descendant of Aeneas*. See also Kimberly Lynn Hossein, "Was Adam the First Heretic? Luis de Páramo, Diego de Simancas, and the Origins of Inquisitorial Practice," *Archive for Reformation History / Archiv für Reformationsgeschichte* 97 (2006): 184–210.

subject of great fascination, particularly the Visigoths and the cataclys-mic end of their empire, which was celebrated in histories, epic poems, and theater. The Visigothic era took on a central role in early modern understandings of the Spanish past because it marked the moment just preceding the Islamic conquest. Renaissance historians inevitably read Spain's past as a triumphalist narrative of continuity—while the Visi-gothic king Rodrigo was betrayed and destroyed by his enemies, Pelayo, a Visigothic prince, rose quickly thereafter to right these wrongs. Gene-alogists and historians created elaborate family trees tracing the ancestry of the Habsburg kings to Pelayo.[53]

In addition to the celebration of ancient and pious royalty, historians and hagiographers extolled the glory of ancient saints. Guy Lazure remarks, "The reinvention of the Spanish past began with a return to the glorious origins of the country's first evangelization, the Visigothic Hispania Christiana, and to the heroic actions of the saints that had preserved this faith across the centuries."[54] Preeminent among such saints was Santiago, and no general history of Spain was complete with-out reference to the Spanish evangelizer. As we have seen, the early medieval story of Santiago as Spain's original missionary had been largely ignored or overlooked by medieval historians in favor of the apostle's relics or his role in battles. By the end of the fifteenth century, however, the story had exploded with new life and grew steadily throughout the sixteenth and seventeenth centuries until it became an essential fixture in *santiaguista* legends.[55] The importance of origins in Renaissance scholarship quickly wed itself to the spiritual climate of the sixteenth century, and Spain's conversion to Christianity was trans-formed into a pivotal moment in national history.

References to Santiago's conversion of Spain proliferated in early modern histories, both national and local. Richard Kagan's study of local histories in the sixteenth century demonstrates that these works invari-ably included an account of the city's conversion to Christianity, which credited the event whenever possible to the evangelization of Santiago and his disciples.[56] Although municipal histories attempted to emphasize

53. For early modern fascination with the story of the last Visigoth king, Rodrigo, see Patricia E. Grieve, *The Eve of Spain: Myths of Origin in the History of Christian, Muslim, and Jewish Conflict* (Baltimore: Johns Hopkins University Press, 2009), 122–204.

54. Guy Lazure, "Possessing the Sacred: Monarchy and Identity in Philip II's Relic Collection at the Escorial," *Renaissance Quarterly* 60, no. 1 (2007): 69.

55. Katherine van Liere first pointed out that Santiago's missionary activity was an early mod-ern—not a medieval—addition to *santiaguista* legends, and she generated a persuasive genealogy for the story of his missionary activities in the fifteenth and sixteenth centuries. Van Liere, "Moor-slayer and the Missionary."

56. Richard L. Kagan, "Clio and the Crown: Writing History in Habsburg Spain," in Kagan and Parker, *Spain, Europe, and the Atlantic World*, 89–90.

the uniqueness of each town, historians were aware that creating a spiritual genealogy for their town necessitated a connection to the apostle or one of his disciples. Such consistent dependence on the legend of Santiago's evangelization throughout the countryside created a spiritual network that tied together the sacred geography of Castile under the patronage of one saint.[57]

Sacred and classical origins could be found not only in archives but in the soil. The mid- to late sixteenth century saw a series of archaeological discoveries that served to reinforce early modern beliefs about the past. One of the most famous of these was the discovery of the catacombs in Rome, which held the tombs of the earliest Roman Christians, including the relics of many early saints. Two similar findings rocked late sixteenth-century Castile: the discoveries of the *plomos* of Granada and of a long-lost history alleged to have been written by Flavius Lucius Dexter, a late antique Hispano-Roman.[58] In 1595 the relics of Saints Cecilio and Thesiphon were discovered in a hillside outside Granada called the Sacromonte. Alongside the relics lay lead tablets (called the *plomos*) that provided a brief history of the two saints, their conversion of the city, and their discipleship under Santiago. Flavius Dexter's work detailed the story of Santiago's arrival in Spain, his foundation of churches, and the early Christian bishops.[59] Physical remnants of the past, such as the bones of saints and lost histories, provided historical evidence of Santiago's evangelization of Spain at the same time that the long tradition of Santiago's cult in Spain substantiated the validity of the new findings. The reciprocal relationship between new archeological discoveries, forged histories, and Santiago's cult coalesced into a powerful constellation of reinforcing sources.

Unification at the national level became increasingly evident in Spain throughout the early modern period. The advent of the Habsburg dynasty with the ascension of Charles V solidified new bonds between the members of what would now be called the Spanish monarchy. Although Castile and Aragón were linked dynastically, each kingdom retained its legal and political independence. While legal unification of

---

57. Bill Christian observes, "The pride with which New Castilians described the association of royalty with their devotions indicates the political value of this kind of devotional style for a monarchy in the process of consolidating a nation-state." Christian, *Local Religion in Sixteenth-Century Spain,* 157.

58. One of the most important studies of the history and impact of the *plomos* on Granada is Harris, *From Muslim to Christian Granada.*

59. Flavius Lucius Dexter, *F. L. Dextri necnon Pauli Orosii Hispanorum Chronologorum Opera omnia, juxta memoratissimas Bivarii et Havercampi editiones accurate recognita,* Patrologia Latina, vol. 31 (Turnhout: Brepols, 1968).

the two kingdoms remained elusive, cultural unity became an increasing concern for a host of Spanish political and historical writers. Thus, in the early modern period, we see more frequent references to *la nación española,* the Spanish nation, a term that clearly had resonance with both Castilian and Aragonese authors, in spite of enduring differences and tensions between the kingdoms. The writing of historical narratives also reflected the new emphasis on the Spanish nation. Beginning during the Renaissance, Spanish historians increasingly produced national histories, which were often sponsored by the royal government.[60] Called "general" histories by sixteenth-century authors, such works traced the origins of the Spanish people and political and religious developments, and often discussed the character or values of Spaniards.[61] Perhaps the most famous early general history is Florián de Ocampo's 1543 *Los quatro libros primeros de la crónica general de España* (The first four books of the general chronicle of Spain), later expanded by Ambrosio de Morales in 1575. Alexander Samson has argued that Ocampo, who held the title of royal chronicler, deliberately fashioned a history of a unified "Spain" in line with current royal claims to universal sovereignty.[62] Histories, then, were often ideological, cohering more often than not with royal policies.

As part of a larger ideological attempt to demonstrate Spain's ancient glory and special relationship to God, sixteenth-century histories almost always included the story of Santiago's evangelization. One of Philip II's royal chroniclers, Esteban de Garibay y Zamalloa, included all of Spain's founders—Noah's nephew Tubal, the Greek god-hero Hercules, and Santiago—in his 1571 *Los quarenta libros del compendio historial de las chronicas y universal historia de todos los reynos de España* (The historical account of forty books of the chronicles and universal history of all the kingdoms of Spain). A few decades later the Jesuit historian Juan de Mariana produced the most important (and complete) general history of Spain, which addressed the issue of Santiago's evangelization in more detail than many of his predecessors had done. Mariana briefly described how the apostle came to Zaragoza to preach the Gospel, returned to the Holy Land, and was martyred. Mariana detailed how Santiago's followers put his body on a boat and sailed it to Galicia; at this point, Mariana launched into a discussion of Spanish devotion to Santiago. The apostle's

60. Richard L. Kagan, *Clio and the Crown: The Politics of History in Medieval and Early Modern Spain* (Baltimore: Johns Hopkins University Press, 2009).

61. Ricardo García Cárcel, ed., *La construcción de las historias de España* (Madrid: Marcial Pons, 2004).

62. Alexander Samson, "Florián de Ocampo, Castilian Chronicler and Habsburg Propagandist: Rhetoric, Myth, and Genealogy in the Historiography of Early Modern Spain," *Forum for Modern Language Studies* 4, no. 4 (2006): 339–54.

followers celebrated Santiago's feast day not on 25 March (the day of his martyrdom), but on 25 July and 30 December, because these latter dates mark his arrival on the coast of Galicia and subsequent migration to Compostela. Thus the most important feast days for the apostle in Spain celebrated the unique relationship between Santiago and the Spanish nation.[63]

The story of Santiago's evangelization created a powerful spiritual genealogy for the Spanish people. Although Tubal, Noah's nephew, provided an Old Testament progenitor for the Spanish people, and Hercules a divine and classical one, these figures remained largely in the background of social and spiritual life in early modern Spain.[64] Other heroes, particularly Pelayo and Santiago, played more prominent roles. Santiago's role had particular significance in culture and ideology because his tie to the Spanish people not only existed in the past but continued into the present and future. The idea that Santiago created a bridge between the past and the present resulted in part from the universalizing tendencies of hagiography. The events that surrounded holy lives were at once bound to a specific historical moment and eternal; the eternal derived from the saints' exhibition of unchanging spiritual virtues and prefigurement of salvation (exemplified in the saint's continued *praesentia* on earth through his relics). It is important to keep in mind that in the early modern period the genre of hagiography as *historia sacra* remained solidly within the realm of history; thus, just as hagiographies came to provide more stringent historical evidence for devotional practices, local and national histories of the period contained many spiritual and universal elements more commonly associated with hagiography.[65]

The stories circulating about Spain's ancient past were varied and fluid. Some gave Santiago the place of prominence, while others emphasized the secular and political aspects of history. As mentioned above, one of the key events in discussions of the Spanish past, whether in formal histories or in poetry, was the moment of Spain's "loss" to Islamic forces. One of the central components of this story was the belief that the Spanish had been conquered because of their sinfulness; this notion had medieval roots but was taken up by sixteenth-century historians with new zeal. More often than not, the blame for Spain's divine punishment was placed upon the Visigothic king Rodrigo. The twelfth-century *Primera Crónica General de España* recounted how the king

63. Juan de Mariana, *Historia general de España*, ed. Francisco Pi y Margall, BAE 30 (Madrid: Atlas, 1950), 89–90.

64. Both figures, especially Hercules, often appear in royal art as symbols of the Habsburg dynasty.

65. Ditchfield, " 'Tota regio nil nisi religio,' " 601.

became smitten with the beautiful daughter of Count Julian, one of his lords, who held Ceuta, the territory that acted as the southern gateway into the peninsula. The king seduced, or perhaps raped, Julian's daughter (unnamed in this version); when he failed to marry her, her father turned against him and conspired with the Moors to allow them entry into Spain.[66]

Although this story first appeared in medieval accounts, early modern historians repeated it with greater frequency and emphasis. The accounts of the fall of Spain remained integral pieces of Spanish history well into the second decade of the seventeenth century. The story of sin and salvation, loss and redemption, often included Santiago as the central figure. One cathedral canon wrote the following account of the reconquest:

> The African Moors forced the Spanish into servitude of the body; after entering Spain from the Mediterranean with powerful armies and occupying these Provinces, they took them [the Spanish] as vassals and tributaries. . . . They remained in this state for many years without remedy, nor hope of any, until brave Pelayo, of the glorious blood of the Goths, began the restoration, which continued with King Ramiro the First, who was being beaten by the Moors, and in danger of losing the conquest: but thanks to our glorious Apostle, who, seeing the Spanish threatened by the enemies of our Faith, which would lead to the extinguishment of the fruit of his preaching (and that of his disciples), returned for this, and for them . . . so that the Faith would always be firm in these kingdoms, and would continue to be firm until the end of the world. He took the sword in his hand, and ventured forth in their defense like their true, unique, and singular patron, to redeem and to liberate them from the slavery and servitude in which he found them, and from this time forward the Spaniards began to call him their Patron.[67]

66. Alfonso X, *Primera Crónica General*, 307–8. O'Callaghan observes that the story of Count Julian and Rodrigo does not appear in early Christian accounts of the reconquest but is given in early Arab ones. Later Christians, he points out, picked up the theme in order to blame the loss of Spain on the sins of the Visigothic kings. O'Callaghan, *History of Medieval Spain*, 52–53. An early Arab version can be found in translation: Ibn Abd al-Hakam, "Narrative of the Conquest of al-Andalus," in *Medieval Iberia: Readings from Christian, Muslim, and Jewish Sources*, ed. Olivia Remie Constable (Philadelphia: University of Pennsylvania Press, 1997), 32–35. The story of Rodrigo in Spanish culture is the main subject of Grieve's *Eve of Spain*.

67. Benito Méndez de Parga y Andrade, *Discursos del unico patronazgo de España, perteneciente al glorioso Apostol Santiago el mayor* (Santiago: Juan Guixard de León, 1628), 28.

There are several important elements in the crafting of this narrative. First, the author insists that Santiago's decision to aid the Spanish in battle stemmed from his desire to preserve their salvation, which he originally had brought in the first century. As a result of the apostle's actions, therefore, Spain was preserved and simultaneously given assurances that it would always be safeguarded in its religious purity. Second, Santiago acted as the essential bridge between the Visigothic era and the eventual restoration of Spain's Christianity. Finally, far from giving a straightforward account of events, the author imbued the text with an extended metaphor of slavery and redemption. The story here has a mythical dimension, alluding to the biblical story of the Hebrew people, their exile in Egypt, their enslavement, and their redemption.[68] It was both universal and specific, invoking at once sacred history and Spanish history, melding them into one metanarrative that proclaimed the Spanish to be the new chosen people. Implicit in this reading of the Spanish past was the promise of present and enduring power and success as a crucial facet of Spain's messianic destiny—a reading ardently encouraged by the Habsburg dynasty.

Yet all was not well by the end of the sixteenth century, either for Santiago's cult or for the Spanish monarchy itself. Despite continuities, the changing intellectual, spiritual, and political realities of the sixteenth century rendered the Matamoros a symbolic figure at once deeply relevant and increasingly ambivalent. A close evaluation of the escalating political, religious, and cultural difficulties of the sixteenth century reveals that some of the intensity of the rhetoric about Santiago and the Spanish past was a loud—and sometimes desperate—attempt to deny or obfuscate political and religious realities. Politically, the hegemony of Spanish power in Europe had begun to be threatened by political alliances and growing European global empires. The unity of the Catholic Church had been shattered by the rapid success of a variety of Protestant reform movements, which also fragmented political leadership and led to widespread warfare, particularly in central Europe.

The Renaissance had encouraged the growth and spread of humanism, with its new standards for historicity and evidence. Humanist scholars, along with Protestant theologians and polemicists, produced blistering critiques of popular devotion in the Catholic Church, reserving their harshest language for the cult of the saints. The church began to increase efforts to centralize and streamline aspects of cultic devotion in

---

68. The author explicitly compares the Hebrews and ninth-century Spaniards in a section that I have excised here for purposes of brevity.

order to eradicate superstitious practices and gross historical inaccuracies.[69] By the middle of the sixteenth century, devotional legitimacy had become increasingly connected to the need for proper historical analysis, including the importance of evidence. Such concerns led to an examination of traditions regarding saints with a stricter eye. This shift sparked a bitter debate both inside and outside the Spanish monarchy about the historicity of Santiago's evangelization of Spain and the battle of Clavijo; the undermining of either legend, if proved false, would deliver a dramatic blow to the apostle's cult in Spain, as well as to the ways Castilians understood their history and themselves.

Within Castile, the brewing controversy over Santiago's history grew out of a regional feud over the payment of an unpopular tax, called the *voto*. Literally, *voto* means "vow"; in this instance, it refers to a specific vow that purportedly resulted from Santiago's first appearance in battle at Clavijo, where he came to the aid of King Ramiro I. In thanksgiving for Santiago's help, the king made a vow to the saint, which took the form of a rent in bread and wine to be paid annually to the Compostelan cathedral. The cathedral had a copy of the charter issuing the *voto* tax dated from the ninth century but probably forged in the twelfth.[70] Ramiro's decree mandated that the *voto* be paid in perpetuity and condemned anyone who interrupted its payment to excommunication.[71] While the tax first applied only to the lands surrounding the cathedral, the archbishops of Santiago eventually began to extend its boundaries. By the early sixteenth century the cathedral was trying to extend the *voto* to central and southern Spain, including Old and New Castile, as well as Granada. Attempts to expand the tax, however, led to widespread anger and resistance within Old Castile.[72]

Five bishops of Old Castile sued the cathedral of Santiago in 1572 to protest the extension of the *voto* in a lawsuit that continued intermittently for fifty years. In the beginning, the plaintiffs attacked the ability of the cathedral to extend the tax to areas of Spain that did not exist as Spain in the ninth century, when they were still under Islamic rule. Then

69. For an excellent overview of the reforming efforts of the church, see Simon Ditchfield, "Tridentine Worship and the Cult of the Saints," in *The Cambridge History of Christianity*, vol. 6, *Reform and Expansion, 1500–1600*, ed. R. Po-Chia Hsia (Cambridge: Cambridge University Press, 2007), 201–43.

70. Rey Castelao, *Historiografía del voto de Santiago*, 7–22. Rey provides the most comprehensive study of the *voto* from its inception to its revocation in the nineteenth century.

71. See Mauro Castellá Ferrer, *Historia del apóstol de Iesus Christo Sanctiago Zebedeo Patron y capitan general de las Españas* (1610), ed. José Ma. Díaz Fernández (Santiago de Compostela: Xunta de Galicia, 2000), fols. 253v–254v. The *voto* was established "in perpetuum permansurum" (fol. 253v).

72. Kendrick, *St. James in Spain*, 40–46.

they shifted tactics upon the advice of a lawyer, Lázaro González de Acevedo, who began a daring attack on the legitimacy of the *voto* itself by claiming that the cathedral's decree from Ramiro was a forgery and the battle of Clavijo a fiction. The defendants succeeded (temporarily) in winning their làwsuit in 1592, and the spread of the *voto* was halted though by no means abandoned.[73] It was a bitter blow for the archdiocese of Santiago and meant the loss of a great deal of income.

The open doubts about *santiaguista* traditions provoked by the *voto* debates were strengthened by the publication in 1593 of edicts from the councils of the Spanish church compiled by García de Loaysa, a canon in the cathedral of Toledo and later archbishop-elect. Loaysa's work contained a document alleged to be from the Fourth Lateran Council (1215), at which the archbishops of Santiago and Toledo battled each other over the primacy of Spain. During this thirteenth-century quarrel, the cathedral of Toledo, in an attempt to humiliate its rival, had claimed that Santiago's evangelization of Spain never actually happened. Loaysa's documents brought this evidence into early modern view. For its part, the cathedral of Santiago de Compostela continued agitating for the legitimacy of the *voto* and sponsored a series of histories of the apostle in the early seventeenth century aimed at proving the truth of all *santiaguista* legends.[74]

Works written for the purpose of assuaging sixteenth-century doubts about Santiago's journey to Spain began to appear; they devoted much attention to Santiago's evangelization, including long descriptions of his disciples and where they in turn preached.[75] One of the main sources on which such apologies relied was Flavius Dexter's history. The broad dissemination of this work created a network of powerful alliances between the cathedral of Santiago and other cities heavily invested in the legend of the apostle's evangelization. But doubts were quickly raised by intellectuals, both inside and outside Spain, about the historicity of both

73. Ibid., 48–53. This history is too complex for a full telling here. In short, the cathedral managed to get the ruling in favor of the Castilian bishops overturned in 1612. Then, thanks to the efforts of Prudencio de Sandoval, the bishop of Pamplona, the *voto* came under attack once more. The cathedral's victory was short-lived. In 1628 the Council of Castile declared the kingdom of Castile exempt from the *voto*.

74. One of the most famous of these histories, written by Castellá Ferrer, dedicated more than one hundred folios to a detailed defense of the *voto*. Some of the most prestigious Spanish historians of the sixteenth century, including Ambrosio Morales, weighed in on the debate. Morales decided in favor of Santiago, although the cathedral of Santiago rewarded him financially for doing so. Rey Castelao, *Historiografía del voto de Santiago*, 50.

75. See Castellá Ferrer, *Historia del apóstol*, fols. 173r–174r, which discuss Saints Cecilio and Thesiphon.

Dexter and the *plomos* of Granada, calling Santiago's evangelization further into question. Intellectuals fiercely debated the authenticity of the two works throughout Castile, and both were eventually revealed to be forgeries in the seventeenth century.[76]

The controversies raging within Spain over *santiaguista* legends spilled over the borders of Spain to the rest of Catholic Europe. The papal curia took seriously its role in combating superstitious and ahistorical uses of the cults of the saints. It issued a revised Roman breviary (1568) and Roman missal (1570) to institute a series of liturgical reforms aimed at ridding the cult of the saints of anything with the potential to bring scandal upon the church.[77] The papacy's greatest ally in this Tridentine goal was the great Cardinal Caesar Baronius, who was charged by Pope Gregory XIII with overseeing a series of important changes to the official church calendar and liturgy. The cardinal compiled a new official martyrology that would reflect the calendar changes of 1582–83, in which ten days of the year were dropped from the calendar. He approached his task with a firm desire to remove from the martyrology any saints he considered fictional and any legends for which he could find no evidence. Baronius had apparently been made aware of García de Loaysa's thirteenth-century documents over the primatial debate in Spain that had cast doubt on Santiago's evangelization of Spain. Persuaded by Loaysa's evidence, he coolly refrained from mentioning Santiago's evangelization of Spain in his section on the apostle.[78] He had done the same previously in his magisterial *Annales ecclesiastici* (History of the Church). Finally, Baronius's revised breviary of 1602 included Santiago's conversion of Spain, but it suggested that this was a common belief held in Spain rather than irrefutable fact.[79] The omission of cherished Spanish traditions, combined with the broad dissemination of Baronius's work, humiliated and enraged many in Spain. The sting was compounded by

76. Katrina B. Olds, "The 'False Chronicles' in Early Modern Spain: Forgery, Tradition, and the Invention of Texts and Relics, 1595–c.1670" (PhD diss., Princeton University, 2009). See also José Godoy Alcántara, *Historia crítica de los falsos cronicones* (Madrid: Colección Alatar, 1981). On the rise of early modern forgers and the increasingly sophisticated skills of textual evaluation, see Anthony Grafton, *Forgers and Critics: Creativity and Duplicity in Western Scholarship* (Princeton: Princeton University Press, 1990).

77. For an account of the introduction of the Roman missal into Spain, see Henry Kamen, *The Phoenix and the Flame: Catalonia and the Counter-Reformation* (New Haven: Yale University Press, 1993), 93–103.

78. Stefano Zen, *Baronio storico: Controriforma e crisi del metodo umanistico* (Rome: Vivarium, 1997); on Baronius's correspondence with Loaysa, see pp. 38, 86, 109n69. See also the discussion of Loaysa, Baronius, and other Spanish writers in defense of *santiaguista* traditions (Ambrosio de Morales and Juan de Mariana in particular) in Rey Castelao, *Historiografía del voto de Santiago*, 40–61.

79. Kendrick, *St. James in Spain*, 53–54.

the embarrassment of international exposure. The embittered Spanish Habsburg monarchs quashed both Baronius's papal nomination and a postmortem movement to have him canonized.[80]

International rejection of one of the most fundamental traditions in Spanish history provoked powerful and complex reactions from the Spanish. Some, like the Toledan canon García de Loaysa and the bishop of Pamplona, Prudencio de Sandoval, openly supported criticism of the legend. The cathedral of Santiago went on the offensive by sponsoring a series of polemics and histories. Yet despite the Compostelan cathedral's spirited defense on behalf of its apostle and its own economic welfare, the cult of Santiago found itself besieged from all sides by the beginning of the seventeenth century. Attacked internationally by renowned historians who chipped away at deeply held Castilian traditions, and targeted at home over the *voto,* Santiago's cult was greatly weakened. And the apostle faced further challenges: The scandals facing Santiago's cult in Spain multiplied during the same period that saw the monarchy confronted with increasing difficulties. Some began to wonder if the apostle was failing in his duty as Spain's patron.

The last decade of Philip II's reign (1556–98) proved a difficult time for the Spanish kingdoms, as the economic crisis increased and military defeats on the international stage multiplied. Internally, the kingdom of Castile bore the brunt of the economic burden for the Spanish monarchy and found itself increasingly hard pressed to finance the imperial policies of Philip II.[81] An increase in silver supplies from the Indies, however, helped the Crown fund a series of offensives in Europe aimed at the defense of Catholicism, which concentrated on challenging Protestant governments, like that of England, and on crushing the rebellions in the Netherlands. Yet the catastrophic defeat of the Armada by the English navy in 1588 left many Spaniards reeling, unable to comprehend how God could allow such a devastating blow by a Protestant nation. As John Elliott explains, "If any one year marks the division between the triumphant Spain of the first two Habsburgs and the defeatist, disillusioned Spain of their successors, that year is 1588."[82] After 1588 the situation seemed only to worsen. Spain faced more difficulties in its conflicts

80. Eric Cochrane, *Historians and Historiography in the Italian Renaissance* (Chicago: University of Chicago Press, 1981), 459. Baronius's antagonistic relationship with the Spanish monarchy was more complicated than this suggests; the strongest area of tension between Baronius and Spain was the cardinal's outspoken criticism of Spanish authority in the kingdom of Naples and Sicily, of which Baronius was a native. Zen, *Baronio storico,* 280–86.

81. For an example of the difficulties the monarchy faced in financing the invasion of England, see Geoffrey Parker, *The Grand Strategy of Philip II* (New Haven: Yale University Press, 1998), 198–99.

82. John H. Elliott, *Imperial Spain, 1469–1716* (London: Edward Arnold, 1963), 283.

with the United Provinces of the Netherlands. These Protestant counties struggled at first against violations of local privilege by the Spanish monarchy but eventually desired to break free of their Catholic lords and establish an independent state.[83] In addition, the Spanish government faced another bankruptcy in 1597, followed by the death of Philip II in 1598 and a series of famines and plagues.[84]

The ascension of Philip III (1598–1621) offered no respite. The devastating plague of 1599–1600 was followed by new crises in foreign policy. The monarchy sent forces to Algiers and Ireland, but those campaigns ended in failure and aggravated the monarchy's continuing financial woes, culminating in another bankruptcy in 1607. Meanwhile, the United Provinces continued their resistance to the Spanish Habsburgs. Two years after the 1607 bankruptcy, it became clear that financial constraints made continued military intervention impossible. Philip III and his advisors began to institute a policy of peacemaking on the European front, as part of an effort to give the monarchy time to recover its resources before entering into more conflict.[85] The monarchy agreed to a twelve-year truce with the United Provinces, in which Spain made important concessions regarding open trade in Europe.[86] Many contemporary Castilians considered the terms of this truce a humiliating concession to the rebels.[87]

The losses and uncertainties during the reigns of Philip II and Philip III provoked varied responses among Castilians, who attempted to comprehend what had happened to the monarchy and to find the appropriate solution. Some channeled frustration and fear by framing their discussions in moral and religious terms, as divine punishment for Spanish sins.[88] In the opening decades of the new century, many learned men

83. For a full account of the conflict between the Netherlands and the Spanish Habsburgs, see Parker, *Dutch Revolt*.

84. Elliott, "Self-Perception and Decline," in *Spain and Its World*, 246. For more detailed studies of the state of the Castilian economy, see I. A. A. Thompson and Bartolomé Yun Casalilla, eds., *The Castilian Crisis of the Seventeenth Century* (Cambridge: Cambridge University Press, 1993).

85. For a thorough study of Philip III's peacemaking policies, see Paul C. Allen, *Philip III and the Pax Hispanica, 1598–1621: The Failure of the Grand Strategy* (New Haven: Yale University Press, 2000).

86. For a thorough account of the tortuous truce negotiations, see ibid., 203–33. For a nuanced account of the politics of the truce, see Antonio Feros, *Kingship and Favoritism in the Spain of Philip III (1598–1621)* (Cambridge: Cambridge University Press, 2000), 192–97.

87. Elliott, *Count-Duke of Olivares*, 48–51.

88. The Jesuit Pedro de Ribadeneira wrote in 1589 in response to the loss of the Armada, "Two things among others, Christian reader, have moved me to write of tribulations. The first is the multitude and abundance of them that we have in these difficult times, in which our Lord visits and punishes us by the public calamities that we suffer." "Tratado de la Tribulación" (1589), in *Obras escogidas del Padre Pedro de Rivadeneira*, ed. Vicente de la Fuente, BAE 60 (reprint, Madrid: Atlas, 1952), 360.

wishing to address the monarchy's problems began to write treatises
that laid out potential solutions to a wide variety of concerns. These
treatises, called *arbitrios,* began appearing in increasing numbers after the
loss of the Armada and proliferated during the reigns of Philip III and
Philip IV. *Arbitrios* tended to be largely economic in nature, addressing
such concerns as the lack of trade, the depopulation of Castile, and continued devaluation of the coinage.[89] An anonymous *arbitrista* explained
the necessity of reform in a treatise addressed to Philip III: "Consider
the contrary events which we have suffered in these last years, on the
sea and on land, in Flanders and England and France. . . . They oblige
us to investigate with careful consideration the causes that could precede
such harms in order that once understood, we may take a convenient
and effective remedy, which may appease the wrath of God."[90] The
author maintained that the proper diagnosis of the monarchy's ills was
of vital importance to its present and future. His calm and measured
tone stressed the possibility of turning back the wrath of God and the
disasters of his time by such diagnoses. Logical thought and orderly
response were the keys to Spain's salvation.[91]

Towns and villages had long responded to God's wrath with appeals
to the saints. Such communal devotions consisted largely of vows to
venerate certain saints in exchange for protection or aid in times of crisis.
Public devotion to a saint performed important work in unifying the
community and protecting it from disaster, which was perceived as a
manifestation of God's anger. But who would advocate for Spain in
heaven during this new time of moral, economic, and political crisis? On
the one hand, Santiago's appearance in battles in defense of the monarchy reinforced Castilians' conceptions of themselves as the divinely mandated new chosen people, whose task it was to rid the world of heresy
and idolatry. The apostle was tied to Spanish history and to the ever-
strengthening idea of the Spanish nation; that is to say, many Spaniards
understood Santiago as central to tradition and history, as representing
their community and its values. On the other hand, others perceived the

89. Fortea Pérez, "Economía, arbitrismo y política," 155–76. "Sea como fuere, lo que afloran
todas esas obras es una aguda, pero todavía inconcreta, percepción de que se estaba viviendo un
periodo de crisis" (163). For a full catalogue of the works of *arbitristas* and other reformers in
Spain, see Evaristo Correa Calderón, ed., *Registro de arbitristias, económistas y reformadores españoles
(1500–1936)* (Madrid: Fundación Universitaria Española, 1981).
90. "Al Felipe III sobre los medios de remediar los males de la Monarquía española" (ca. 1615),
BNM, MS 13239 (2), fol. 36r.
91. John Elliott has emphasized how the use of a medical discourse was tightly bound to the
concept of hope and belief in the possibility of cure, as this anonymous writer suggested. See Elliott,
"Self-Perception and Decline," in *Spain and Its World,* 248–50.

humiliation of Santiago's cult and the failures of the monarchy as signs that the apostle might be failing his community. More broadly, such failings might indicate that traditional ways of imagining the Spanish nation required revision or reform. For Castile, as for any village, the response to a perceived failure of one patron was simple: Elect a new, more powerful patron who might be able to gain God's ear more successfully. This is precisely what the Discalced Carmelites tried to achieve by asking the Castilian parliament, the Cortes, to elect the newly beatified Teresa of Avila as a new co-patron saint of Spain in 1617.

2

SAINT TERESA AND THE LIVED EXPERIENCE OF THE HOLY

Anyone with doubts about the efficacy of Santiago's protection might have viewed the beatification of Teresa of Avila in 1614 as a wish fulfilled. During the period between Teresa's death and her beatification (1582–1614), her popularity skyrocketed. When she was beatified the excitement reached a fever pitch, inspiring the Discalced Carmelites to nominate their saint as a new patron for the Spanish nation. This chapter discusses the events leading up to the movement to have Teresa named co-patron, including the salient points of her life, the details of her death, and her miracles. It is primarily concerned, however, with the bitter controversy that followed Teresa's elevation to co-patron and the central issues at play during the first phase of the controversy (1617–18), specifically the tension between modernity and tradition, liturgical innovation and history. Teresa's supporters declared that because their saint had lived in the recent past, she endured in the living memory of the Spanish people in a way that connected her to them more deeply than saints long dead could be. With this argument they refashioned the traditional priorities of early modern devotional life and held Santiago's cult up to potential ridicule and doubt. Santiago's supporters, for their part, insisted that their saint's power and efficacy derived in part from ancient traditions and his deeply held place in Spanish history. Both sides espoused differing visions of the nation, grounded in their conflicting understandings of the relationship between spiritual devotion, temporality, and history.

Teresa de Ahumada y Cepeda (1515–1582) was born in the walled Castilian town of Avila. Her father was descended from a wealthy New Christian family that had moved to Avila from Toledo.[1] One of twelve children, Teresa spent much of her childhood and young adulthood immersed in books, a member of a new generation of literate Castilians who read widely in the vernacular and had a particular passion for saints' lives and chivalric romances. Caught up in tales of saintly virtue and knightly adventure, she and her brother planned to run away from home to Islamic lands, where they hoped to achieve martyrdom. When they realized the impossibility of this plan, they played "hermits," building little hermitages out of stone in the family's orchard. Despite a period in late adolescence when Teresa claims to have been drawn into frivolity and flirtation, she eventually entered Avila's Carmelite convent, Our Lady of the Incarnation, in 1535, where she set aside her family names for her religious one, Teresa de Jesús.[2]

Yet Teresa's early years as a nun did not end her spiritual struggle and feelings of sinfulness. Three years after entering Incarnation, Teresa suffered a serious illness that marked a dramatic transition in her spiritual development. During this period she began to experience ecstatic visions, including a mystical union with God.[3] At the same time, she became increasingly dissatisfied with the worldly nature of life at Incarnation, a wealthy convent that housed the daughters and widows of Avila's most important families. Many of the noble residents maintained distinctions of rank, such as the title doña (lady) and the employment of servants. As her spiritual commitment deepened, Teresa began to see the laxness at Incarnation as evidence that the Carmelite rule had

1. For the most comprehensive treatment of the conversion of Teresa's family to Christianity, see Teófanes Egido López, "Introduction," in El linaje judeoconverso de Santa Teresa (Madrid: Editorial de Espiritualidad, 1986), 9–31; and, also by Egido López, "Tratamiento historiográfico de Santa Teresa," in Perfil histórico de Santa Teresa, ed. Teófanes Egido López (Madrid: Editorial de Espiritualidad, 1981), 13–32. While many of Teresa's contemporaries knew of her converso background, the issue was never raised in the co-patronage debate.

2. Teresa describes all of these events in her life story. Teresa de Jesús, "Libro de su vida," in Obras completas, 3d ed., ed. Enrique Llamas Martínez (Madrid: Editorial de Espiritualidad, 1984), 4–21.

3. References to her first illness can be found in ibid., 22–28; for some of her visionary experiences, see 270–82. See also Jodi Bilinkoff, The Avila of Saint Teresa (Ithaca: Cornell University Press, 1989), 112–24.

departed from its ascetic medieval origins. Instead of trying to change the existing rule, she developed a new constitution for a reformed Carmelite order, called the Discalced, or Barefoot, Carmelites. After much struggle, Teresa was able to establish a new Discalced house in 1562, which she dedicated in honor of her personal patron, San José. The priorities of the Discalced reform were simplicity, equality among sisters, and an austere way of life.[4] The new reform soon gained wealthy patrons, and Teresa began to work with them to establish Discalced houses for both men and women throughout Castile.[5] She spent the last twenty years of her life traveling from one end of the peninsula to the other, during which time she directly oversaw the foundation of seventeen houses.[6]

By the time of Teresa's death in 1582, she had acquired a reputation for sanctity and the support of many powerful and noble patrons, including the admiration of King Philip II. While her foundations were the original source of her fame, she quickly became renowned for the intensity of her spiritual gifts, which included mystical visions, levitation during Communion, and theological sophistication, revealed in her numerous writings. Although her written work remained unpublished at the time of her death, it circulated in manuscript and earned her the respect of many contemporary theologians. Yet Teresa's career generated scandal and controversy as well. The Castilian holy woman wrote, spoke, debated, and traveled widely—all unusual endeavors for early modern women.[7] Throughout her career, Teresa was acutely aware of the potential censure of her work by male theologians, largely due to her advocacy of mental prayer and contemplation. Inward and silent spiritual experiences were sources of controversy during Teresa's lifetime, as many clergy believed that such experiences flirted dangerously with Protestantism. Both the Holy Office of the Inquisition and Teresa's male confessors kept a close eye on her throughout her public career, with a particularly critical focus on her written work; one confessor ordered her to burn a commentary she had written on the Song of

4. Teresa de Jesús, "Las constituciones," in *Obras completas*, 1133–57. For another account, see Bilinkoff, *Avila of Saint Teresa*, 130–33.

5. On Teresa's often troubled relationship with her noble patrons, see Alison Weber, "Saint Teresa's Problematic Patrons," *Journal of Medieval and Early Modern Studies* 29, no. 2 (1999): 357–80.

6. Houses were established in Avila (1562), Medina (1567), Malagón (1568), Valladolid (1568), Pastrana (1569), Salamanca (1571), Alba (1571), Segovia (1574), Seville (1575), Beas (1575), Caravaca (1576), Toledo (1579), Palencia (1580), Villanueva de la Jara (1580), Soria (1581), Granada (1582), and Burgos (1582).

7. Alison Weber, *Teresa of Avila and the Rhetoric of Femininity* (Princeton: Princeton University Press, 1990), 164–65.

Songs, an order with which she dutifully complied.[8] Although Teresa managed to avoid serious involvement with the Inquisition, church authorities did not allow her writings to be printed until thirteen years after her death, and then only after lively debate, which included opposition from some theologians who considered Teresa's ideas either potentially dangerous or downright heretical.[9]

Some theologians argued that the potential heresy embedded in Teresa's core teachings was compounded by her gender, as women's greater susceptibility to demonic temptation rendered their visions less trustworthy than men's. Francisco de Ribera, a Jesuit priest and author of the first spiritual biography of Teresa (published in 1590), defended her visions vigorously in response to critics who claimed that women's visions should be ignored. "Those women who conquer their passions through strength and subject themselves to God," he asserted, "are to be called men, and men who are conquered by passions are called women. This is not a result of bodily differences, but of the strength of the soul. . . . So here we are talking about the visions of a woman more manly than many great men."[10] Ribera thus distinguished between two kinds of difference—bodily and spiritual. While bodies maintained the biological distinction of sex, souls could be gendered—that is, souls took on gendered features according to virtue rather than biological determination. In the early modern world, virtue, asceticism, and strength were gendered masculine; anyone demonstrating these traits could thus achieve a masculine soul.[11] Although Ribera's argument was firmly grounded in Christian tradition, the fact that he dedicated thirty pages

8. The volume of recent work on the spiritual lives of holy women, and the attempts of the Inquisition to control them, is immense. For a few examples of Teresa's response to this control, see ibid.; Gillian T. W. Ahlgren, *Teresa of Avila and the Politics of Sanctity* (Ithaca: Cornell University Press, 1996); and Elena Carrera, "Writing Rearguard Action, Fighting Ideological Selves: Teresa of Avila's Reinterpretation of Gender Stereotypes in 'Camino de perfección,'" *Bulletin of Hispanic Studies* 79, no. 3 (2002): 299–308. For broader works on holy women and the Inquisition, see Anne J. Cruz and Mary Elizabeth Perry, eds., *Culture and Control in Counter-Reformation Spain* (Minneapolis: University of Minnesota Press, 1992); and Mary E. Giles, ed., *Women in the Inquisition: Spain and the New World* (Baltimore: Johns Hopkins University Press, 1999).

9. The most comprehensive treatment of Teresa's involvement with the Inquisition, both before and after her death, can be found in Enrique Llamas Martínez, *Santa Teresa de Jesús y la Inquisición española* (Madrid: CSIC, 1972).

10. Francisco de Ribera, *Vida de Santa Teresa de Jesús* (1590), introduction by P. Jaime Pons (Barcelona: Gustavo Gili, 1908), 88. Ribera's general defense of visions in the postapostolic era is lengthy (63–90); for the more specifically gendered part of the argument, see 88–90.

11. The complexities of assigning a gender to virtue and other human qualities are not limited to the early modern period. For a Merovingian example, see John Kitchen, *Saints' Lives and the Rhetoric of Gender: Male and Female in Merovingian Hagiography* (Oxford: Oxford University Press, 1998). In discussing Gregory of Tours's ambivalence about femininity and sanctity, Kitchen observes, "the author . . . clearly identifies manliness as an essential attribute of sanctity" (105).

of his biography to this issue underscores the depth of early modern theological opposition to women's discernment of spirits.

Despite the hesitation of some ecclesiastical authorities concerning Teresa's sanctity, at the moment of her death her followers were confident that their mother rested in heaven with the saints. Teresa had taken ill and died rather suddenly, during a stopover in the town of Alba de Tormes on her way back to her home convent of San José in Avila. She had stopped in Alba at the request of one of her patrons, the powerful duchess of Alba, where she had quickly become too ill to leave; she died on 4 October, the feast day of Saint Francis of Assisi. The days immediately preceding and following Teresa's death was filled with signs of her sanctity.[12] Her postmortem flesh immediately assumed a transparent radiance and filled the room with a miraculous odor of such pungent sweetness that the nuns present at her bedside were compelled to open the window and door in order to relieve the intensity of the odor.[13] Francisco de Ribera described the sweetness of the odor as intensely floral, but changing—one day it smelled like jasmine, other days like violets or lilies. Her body also exuded fresh blood, which continued for many months after her death.[14] Despite the convent's quick burial of Teresa, the miraculous treasure of her relics could not be kept intact as the news of her holy death spread throughout Spain. Nine months after Teresa's burial, the Carmelite provincial, Father Gracián, visited Alba and was asked by the nuns to exhume Teresa's body and inspect it for miraculous signs. This was the beginning of the dismemberment of Teresa's body and the dispersal of her relics, as Father Gracián cut off the saint's left hand and had it sent to Avila. The three years following the saint's death were marked by an ugly quarrel between the nuns of Alba and Avila over where Teresa's relics should rest. The partisans of Teresa's interment in Avila went so far as to steal the saint's body from Alba and restore it to Avila, though they were forced by papal order to send it back in 1586.[15]

When Teresa's body was returned to Alba, her relics were displayed to the public for the first time as part of a great celebration of the saint. The laity's desire to be in the presence of the relics was overwhelming.

12. An excellent and lively overview of Teresa's last days and the subsequent struggles over her body are provided in Eire, *From Madrid to Purgatory*, 401–501.

13. "Deposition of Isabel de la Cruz," in Silverio de Santa Teresa, ed., *Procesos de beatificación y canonización de Santa Teresa de Jesús*, Biblioteca Mistica Carmelitana, vols. 18–20 (Burgos: Monte Carmelo, 1935), 1:111. Isabel also remarked that the intensely sweet smell remained on her hands, which had shrouded Teresa's body, no matter how many times she washed them.

14. Ribera, *Vida de Santa Teresa*, 527, 532.

15. Ibid., 530–35. See also Eire, *From Madrid to Purgatory*, 411–45.

Ribera described the scene in the church: "And it was necessary to place her body behind bars, since the large crowd of people were so devout and forceful that, if the body had been outside the bars, they would have torn her habit to shreds to possess the relics, and the body itself would have been in danger. All afternoon the church was so full of people wanting to see the marvel who could not be turned away, that we could neither enter further inside nor leave until very late, because they never got tired of looking at her."[16] By waiting until nightfall, Ribera was able to achieve his ultimate goal—he pushed his face through the bars and kissed the corpse's holy feet. The general fervor created by Teresa's body did not abate after the initial excitement of its return, and the nuns of Alba reported at length about the high volume of pilgrims of all social classes and from all parts of Spain eager to look at or touch her glorious relics, held in a chapel lavishly decorated by the duke of Alba.[17]

The demand for Teresa's relics became so great that the body was subject to an endless stream of mutilations, large and small, as people received pieces of flesh or holy oil, either from the nuns or by theft.[18] These pieces of flesh or handkerchiefs soaked in oil all retained, like the body itself, portions of the saint's miraculous *praesentia* and power.[19] Thus, as the saint's body was physically spread throughout the Iberian Peninsula and Europe, stories of cures and other miracles quickly followed, along with fervent devotion to the new cult. One witness told ecclesiastical investigators, "And one can see how the blessed mother Teresa's relics have spread throughout Spain, and beyond, where they are venerated as though she were a saint by princes, cardinals, bishops, religious, and men of learning. . . . And also, just after her death, many people had her image painted, and it was printed many times, and continues to be printed in many parts of Spain and Rome and Paris."[20] By this account, devotion to Teresa explicitly followed dismembered pieces of saintly flesh and oil as they traveled eastward through Spain and western Europe. The physical relics and the *praesentia* they contained sparked and sustained devotional interest in the saint, which soon expanded to include her holy image as well as relics.

Veneration of Teresa's relics and images went hand in hand with quickly spreading stories of miracles worked by the holy woman. Most

16. Ribera, *Vida de Santa Teresa*, 533.
17. Silverio de Santa Teresa, *Procesos de beatificación y canonización*, 3:189–191, 212–13.
18. Eire, *From Madrid to Purgatory*, 448–50.
19. Brown, *Cult of the Saints*, 86–105.
20. "Deposition of Fray Luis Ruiz Caballero," in Silverio de Santa Teresa, *Procesos de beatificación y canonización*, 3:283.

of the early miracles attributed to Teresa came from religious, particularly from Discalced Carmelite nuns, though they were not confined to
one geographic location or social status. Cures discussed in the saint's
beatification and canonization records were usually connected directly
to one of the saint's relics, although she was also credited with the miracle of bringing her nephew back from the dead during her lifetime. Most
of the miracles involved cures of various illnesses. For example, one nun
in Avila, Antonia de Guzmán, reported that a novena to Teresa had
cured another nun's young foster son, who had become mortally ill.[21]
But her miraculous deeds did not focus exclusively on the religious: one
of the duke of Alba's men claimed that one of Mother Teresa's relics, a
cloth soaked in blood, saved the life of his terminally ill child.[22]

The outpouring of devotion following Teresa's death resulted from
a surfeit of excitement and joy over the presence of a powerful new saint
and her relics, which promised great miracles to the Spanish people. The
marvelous events following Teresa's death combined with people's vivid
memories of her considerable personal charisma, to which many from
all over Castile had been exposed during her extensive travel. Memories
of Teresa and tales of her postmortem miracles gave contemporary Castilians access to a lived experience of the holy. The immediacy of that
experience played a significant role in the quick success of her beatification and canonization processes and the rapidly increasing devotion to
her cult throughout Spain.

The Carmelites began an immediate campaign for Teresa's canonization, inundating Rome with panegyrics in Latin on Teresa's virtues
and detailed accounts of miracles she performed in Spain.[23] Royal support constituted a key element in any successful operation, but the Carmelites did not have to worry about this. The Spanish Habsburg kings,
beginning with Philip II, had taken great interest in Teresa's career. Philip
actively supported efforts to canonize Teresa; on 31 March 1597 he wrote
a letter to the duke of Sessa, his ambassador in Rome, asking him to
request papal support for Teresa's canonization.[24] The letter from Philip
II was not the only one flowing from Spain to Rome on Teresa's behalf.

21. "Deposition of Antonia de Guzmán," in ibid., 2:396.

22. "Deposition of Beatriz de Jesús," in ibid., 1:119.

23. *Papeles tocantes a la canonizacion de Teresa de Jesus* (ca. 1622), BNM, MS 7326, fols. 8r–109r,
287r–290r.

24. *Apuntamientos sobre la vida, la canonización, y los milagros de Santa Teresa de Jesús*, BNM, MS
2232, fol. 59v. Earlier that year, in February, the "Reinos de Castilla" also wrote a letter of support
to Pope Clement VIII (fols. 59v–60r). *Liber secundus actorum pro canonizatione beatae virginis Teresiae
de Iesu Ordinis discalceatorum Reformatae Religionis Beatae Mariae de Montae Carmelo Fundatricis*, BNM,
MS 2261, also contains canonization information and copies of the letters written to the pope.

A systematic letter-writing campaign continued from 1596 to 1627, although the majority of letters were sent between 1601 and 1617—that is, during the time leading up to and following her beatification in 1614. The Discalced Carmelites carefully preserved copies of more than a hundred letters sent to Rome on behalf of their founder, including letters from the kings and queens of Spain and France, the duke of Lerma, and nearly every church, municipality, and bishop in Castile and Aragón.[25] In response to these efforts, the official investigation of Teresa's sanctity began in 1595 under the direction of the papal nuncio in Spain, Camilio Caetano.

When Teresa's beatification was announced in 1614, festivals in her honor took place throughout Spain. The feast celebrated in Madrid was attended by king, nobles, and ambassadors, while the pontifical mass was celebrated by the papal nuncio. Cities throughout the Spanish kingdoms, from Barcelona, to Pamplona, to Segovia, printed accounts (called *relaciones*) of the festivals they held. The Discalced Carmelite Diego de San José collected forty-nine *relaciones,* which he bound together into a giant volume and sent to Rome, dedicated to Paul V.[26] In a separate volume, another Discalced Carmelite, José de Jesús María, assembled the sermons that accompanied the festivals and forwarded this 449-page work to Rome as well.[27] For both of these volumes the friars collected *relaciones* originally printed in each city for local distribution. Thus celebrations in honor of Teresa spread both locally—through the festival and the printed account—and internationally.

The quick succession of Teresa's death and beatification, as well as the triumphant celebrations that occurred across Spain in 1614, spread awareness of the saint and her cult throughout the nation. Building on the emotional outpourings during this period, Fray Luis de San Jerónimo, the *procurador general* of the Discalced Carmelites, formally petitioned the Cortes on 24 October 1617 to elevate Teresa to co-patron saint of the Spanish kingdoms.[28] On 16 November the secretaries of the Cortes, don Juan de Hinestosa and Rafael Cornejo, read aloud a letter they

25. Spaniards were not the only people writing to Pope Paul V on Teresa's behalf. *Liber secundus* contains letters from King Louis XIII and his wife Marie in the original French (fols. 71r–72v).

26. Diego de San José, *Compendio a las solenes fiestas que en toda España hicieron en la Beatificacion de N. M. S. Teresa de Iesus fundadora de la Reformacion de Descalzos y Descalzas de N. S. del Carmen* (Madrid: Alonso Martín, 1615).

27. José de Jesús María, *Sermones predicados en la Beatificacion de la Beata Madre Teresa de Iesus Virgen, fundadora de la Reforma de los Descalços de Nuestra Señora del Carmen* (Madrid: Alonso Martín, 1615).

28. *Actas de las Cortes de Castilla* (Madrid: Congreso de los Diputados, 1907), 30:507–9. The *Actas* contains a copy of Fray Luis's letter.

had drafted after the 24 October vote, which expounded at length the reasons for Teresa's elevation, which included her great virtues and merits; her "many and continuous" miracles, particularly in Castile, her birthplace; her books and doctrine; her reform of the Carmelite order; the miracles performed at her sepulcher in Alba; and the favor shown her by Paul V when he granted permission for her cult to be venerated with masses throughout Spain by both secular and regular clergy. They claimed that her role as patron saint against heresy made her an ideal national patron, because "God our Lord desires these Catholic and most Christian kingdoms to retain their integrity and purity of faith which they have constantly professed." They added that Teresa would be particularly obligated to aid them in all endeavors, because she had been born and raised in the Spanish kingdoms.[29]

Apparently delighted by the vote of the Cortes, Philip III sent a letter on 4 August 1618 to all the cities of his kingdoms, ordering them to receive Teresa as their patron and advocate. The letter cited some of Teresa's accomplishments and stipulated that each city celebrate Teresa as *patrona* "with applause" and a double octave—eight days of celebrations, beginning on the saint's next feast day, 5 October 1618.[30] A later author recounted a (possibly apocryphal) story to the effect that, after sending this letter ordering the celebration of the festival, the king came in to dinner, saying, "I come very content, because I have just signed one hundred and twenty-five letters for Saint Teresa's patronage."[31] By all accounts, Philip followed closely his father's devotion to Teresa and his interest in augmenting her cult within his kingdoms.

Supporters of Santiago sprang into action immediately following the king's mandate to celebrate Teresa's feast day. The archbishops of Santiago and Seville began a campaign against Teresa's elevation without delay, and adamantly refused to celebrate the feast.[32] The archbishop of

---

29. Ibid., 31:52–56.

30. Philip III to the Municipal Council of Seville, 4 August 1618, Archivo Municipal de Sevilla, sección IV, tomo 35, no. 18: "lo que deseo que en todos mis subditos se asiente la misma os querido avisar desto y mandasose como lo hago publiqueis y hagais notoria en esa ciudad lo uno y lo otro y con demostraciones de gozo y regocijo que ordenareis se hagan cinco de Octubre que es el dia del glorioso transito desta bienaventurada Santa la admitais y recibais por Patrona y abogada y con el aplauso."

31. *Respuesta al memorial que escrivió el arçobispo de Santiago, contra el patronazgo de Santa Teresa* (ca. 1627), BNM, MS 9140, fol. 218v.

32. The seventeenth-century historian Antonio de León Pinelo, who chronicled Madrid from antiquity to the mid-seventeenth century in his *Anales de Madrid*, mentioned the royal decision in his list of major events for the year 1618, but provided only this terse detail: "This year the Congregation of the Churches of Castile dealt with whether Saint Teresa of Jesus had been elected patron, and confirmed it. But leaving [the Congregation], the church of Santiago and its clergy refused to execute it." León Pinelo, *Anales de Madrid (desde el año 447 al de 1658)*, ed. Pedro Fernández Martín (Madrid: Instituto de Estudios Madrileños, 1971), 221.

Seville, Pedro de Castro, also wrote a letter to the king opposing his order, which circulated widely in manuscript and printed form. Faced with the strength of the opposition, King Philip began to prevaricate and sought advice in resolving this divisive issue. *Santiaguista* author Francisco Tamariz later claimed that the king held a meeting with the archbishop of Toledo, the president of Castile, the papal nuncio, and other major prelates to discuss the co-patronage controversy. The result of this meeting was the king's decision to suspend the celebrations until the pope could consider the case.[33] On 24 September 1618 the royal secretary Jorge de Tobar issued another royal command, suspending the festivals for Teresa's patronage that year. Tobar wrote: "Today his Majesty, due to just considerations, has ordered me . . . to tell you to cease all the feasts and celebrations mentioned before until receiving further word from His Majesty, because this patronage cannot be received without the knowledge of his Holiness."[34]

According to Francisco de Santa María, Philip's change of mind resulted from the persuasive arguments against Teresa made by "three of the most important prelates in Spain," presumably Santiago, Toledo, and Seville.[35] While the prelates had many reasons for opposing Teresa's elevation, they targeted the greatest weakness in their opponents' case: In 1618 Teresa had been beatified but not canonized, which they claimed prevented her elevation to the level of patron saint. Another contributing factor to the king's change of heart might have been the complex political situation evolving at court in the autumn of 1618. That autumn saw the collapse of the duke of Lerma's position as Philip's chief minister and the dissolution of his faction at court. What followed was a time of uncertainty and change within the royal government. It is possible that the king saw this period of transition as an inopportune moment to be at odds with his prelates and wished to minimize opposition at court.[36]

33. Francisco Tamariz, *A mi padre Fr. Pedro de la Madre de Dios, Difinidor General de la Orden de los Descalcos de NS del Carmen—Acerca de un memorial que dio a su Majestad en defensa del patronato de Santa Teresa de Iesus*, HSA, fol. 9r–v.

34. Jorge de Tobar to the City of Seville, 24 September 1618, Archivo Municipal de Sevilla, sección XI, tomo 7, no. 58, fol. 75r. Another, slightly different version of this letter can be found in Pedro de la Madre de Dios, *Memorial que Dio a su Magestad el padre F. Pedro de la Madre de Dios, Difinidor General de la Orden de los Descalços de nuestra Señora del Carmen, en defensa del Patronato de la Santa Madre Teresa de Iesus* (ca. 1628), BNM, MS 9140, fols. 129v–130r.

35. Francisco de Santa María, *Defensa del Patronato de nuestra gloriosa madre Santa Teresa de Jesús* (1627), BNM, MS 9140, fol. 243r.

36. For a full discussion of Lerma's fall from power, see Feros, *Kingship and Favoritism*, 243–47. See also Bernardo José García García, "Honra, desengaño y condena de una privanza: La retirada de la corte del cardenal duque de Lerma," in *Monarquía, imperio y pueblos en la España moderna*, ed. Pablo Fernández Albaladejo (Alicante: Universidad de Alicante, 1997), 679–95.

The combination of the liturgical problems and political turmoil at court made 1618 an inauspicious moment for Teresa's elevation.

Jorge de Tobar's letter, however, was not the end of the controversy that fall. Apparently, several cities in Andalusia, most notably Granada, proceeded with plans to celebrate festivals in honor of Teresa's patronage, much to the outrage of the archbishop of Seville. The Discalced Carmelite monastery of Granada, for example, posted broadsheets proclaiming a poetry contest to accompany the impending celebrations.[37] In addition, the Cortes of Castile continued its defense of Teresa's co-patronage, responding a mere three days after the king's September letter to reaffirm their vote in favor of Teresa.[38] They commissioned four representatives, Alvaro de Quiñones (León), Lorenzo Ramírez (Jaén), Gabriel Cimbron (Avila), and Martín de Castrejon (Soria), to write a treatise justifying their position from the previous year. The treatise reiterated most of the original arguments made on Teresa's behalf, requesting that the king write a letter to the pope urging him to grant Teresa the status of *patrona*.[39]

The situation turned ugly when a printed letter by Pedro de Castro sparked a series of spirited responses that devolved into charges and countercharges of heresy. In one of the most controversial passages in Castro's letter the archbishop declared himself incredulous "that one could prefer a blessed woman [*beata*] to all the saints of Spain, of whom there are so many in Heaven!" He reiterated the sentiment a second time: "Today a beatified maiden [*doncella Beatificada*] is preferred over these and other canonized saints in the heavenly Court, made patron . . . by secular hands."[40] The scornful tone of the letter is underscored by Castro's designation of her election as patron by "secular hands"—and thus implicitly invalid. But it was apparently Castro's use of the terms *beata* and *doncella* to refer to Teresa that caused the outcry from her supporters. While *beata* could be interpreted as the proper title for a beatified holy woman, its more traditional meaning in Spanish referred to a holy woman living outside an order. On a more popular level, the

---

37. "Iusta Poetica en el Convento Real de los Santos Martires de la Ciudad de Granada—dia de la gloriosa Virgen Santa Teresa, fundadora del Carmelo Reformado" (1618), BNM, MS 4011, fol. 288r. The festivities for Teresa in Málaga certainly took place. See *Traslado y Relacion a la Letra a de las Solemnidades que precedieron a las fiestas que la Ciudad de Malaga hizo, quando juró por Patrona de la misma Ciudad a la Madre Santa Teresa de Jesus* (Málaga: Juan René, 1618).

38. *Actas de las Cortes de Castilla*, 32:376–81 (27 September 1618). They continued this discussion on 11 October 1618 (32:414–19).

39. Ibid., 32:378, 415–19.

40. Castro to Philip III, 4 September 1618, BNM, MS 1749, fol. 421v. He listed the most famous: Santiago and his seven disciples, along with Hermenegildo, Lawrence, Isidoro, Ildefonso, Leandro, and Dominic.

term bore an increasingly negative connotation throughout the early modern period, in response to scandals involving *beatas* who were later denounced as frauds by the Inquisition.[41] His use of the term *doncella* also had a nasty edge. While *doncella* referred to a young unmarried woman, it was a secular term not generally applied to a nun, who would be referred to as a *virgen* (virgin). Castro's double-edged digs at Teresa's status became a way of demonstrating her lack of worthiness to be patron, particularly in contrast to Santiago and other established Spanish saints.[42]

Teresa's supporters understood Castro's words as a veiled attack on their saint and did not hesitate to denounce him. The most eloquent attack on Castro's lack of respect in addressing Teresa came from an anonymous author who wrote to the king from Granada on 1 October 1618:

> This way of talking is dangerous and scandalous, because it is heretical to speak openly with equivocation and to use terms with two meanings and two significations, one catholic and the other erroneous. . . . And even though the Archbishop of Seville would never be suspected of heresy, by me or anybody else . . . his way of speaking in his letter is in the above-mentioned ways, because this word *Beata* signifies two things: a beatified saint and a state between religion and marriage. Those who are called *beatas* have lost their reputation in public opinion, because of their free ways.[43]

The multiple meanings of *beata* were obvious to this author, who argued that the archbishop's double entendres in this case smacked of heresy. He went on to complain that in Spanish one did not traditionally refer to a beatified saint as a *beata,* because it would be disrespectful to refer to a holy woman with the same name one would use for an immoral one. An anonymous glossator of Castro's letter voiced similar arguments against the archbishop's use of the terms *doncella* and *beata.*

---

41. The subject of *beatas*, gender, and Inquisitorial persecution has become the focus of much scholarly attention. For two brief examples of work on Inquisitorial trials, see Gillian T. W. Ahlgren, "Francisca de los Apóstoles: A Visionary Voice for Reform in Sixteenth-Century Toledo," in Giles, *Women in the Inquisition,* 119–33; and Mary Elizabeth Perry, "Beatas and the Inquisition in Early Modern Seville," in *Inquisition and Society in Early Modern Europe,* ed. Stephen Haliczer (London: Croom Helm, 1987), 147–68.

42. Castro's list includes no Spanish female saints. In addition, the glossator of his letter accuses the archbishop of general hostility to modern saints. "Copia de una carta que escribio el Arçobispo de Seuilla . . . con unas Notas de un su deuoto" (1618), BNM, MS 9140, fol. 107r.

43. Anon. to Philip III, 1 October 1618, BNM, MS 20711 (6), unpaginated.

He chastised the archbishop for causing a "scandal" and setting a "bad example" by speaking of a highly respected holy woman with such little courtesy.[44] The two authors understood the archbishop's use of these terms as a deliberate and underhanded attack on the holy woman herself.

These two anonymous treatises were joined by a third, by Francisco de Cueva y Silva; the archbishop's supporters denounced Cueva's attack on Castro as "scandalous."[45] Accusations of heresy leveled against one of the most powerful archbishops in Castile could not go unanswered. Eventually, Gabriel de Céspedes, a canon in the church in Jaén and a representative in the Cortes for Seville, and Andrés de Aresto, a canon in Toledo, were asked by the Congregation of the Clergy to request that the Holy Office of the Inquisition collect the offending documents for review and halt their circulation.[46] In November 1618, Bernardo de Sandoval y Rojas, the archbishop of Toledo, together with the Council of the Inquisition ordered that all the extant treatises on the debate be sent to the Holy Office, effectively silencing it.[47]

The acrimony inspired by the election of Teresa as national patron put the saint's supporters immediately on the defensive. They began to construct elaborate arguments explaining the necessity, significance, and legitimacy of the Cortes's vote. One of the most important elements of their argument built on the widespread popularity of Teresa's cult. Although she had been born in the Castilian city of Avila, they argued that devotion to the saint could not be contained by one geographic center or one specific group of people. Discalced Carmelite Francisco de Santa María, in his treatise in defense of Teresa's patronage, cited the "universal" acclamation for Teresa by people of both genders and all stations in life: "And if this acclamation was only from the common

---

44. "Copia de una carta que escribio el Arçobispo de Seuilla," fols. 106v–107r. Antonio Pérez jumped to the archbishop's defense, claiming that *beata* could hardly be an offensive term, as it was frequently used to describe Mary, the Blessed Mother. Pérez, *Un memorial al Rey contra el patronato de Teresa de Jesús* (1618), BNM, MS 9140, fol. 27r.

45. Tamariz, *A mi padre Fr. Pedro de la Madre de Dios*, fol. 9v.

46. Ibid., fol. 9r–v. Although Tamariz claimed Céspedes as an ally against co-patronage, Sancho de Ahumada y Tapia contested this point vehemently. See his *Carta apologetica, en la qual se descubre, arguye y refuta gran numero de falsedades, indignamente supuestas a los padres Carmelitas Descalzos, y a un memorial, que por orden de su Magestad saco a luz el RPF Pedro de la Madre de Dios, difinidor General del dicho orden, por el Patronato de la gloriosa Virgen, y Patriarca, Santa Teresa* (Zaragoza: Antonio Torcio, 1629), fols. 13v–14r. On 13 November 1618, the Cortes recorded that several *procuradores* requested that the Cortes comply with the edicts of the Inquisition in the matter of Teresa's patronage. *Actas de las Cortes de Castilla*, 32:612–13.

47. Bernardo Aldrete to Pedro de Castro, 13 November 1618, BNM, MS 4011, fol. 282r.

people, or from women, perhaps then it would lose something of its significance. But included among those devoted to Teresa are the most eminent theologians, the most important prelates, magistrates, princes, kings, and popes."[48] Not only did Francisco move devotion to Teresa out of the context of a specific audience (common, female) to a more general one, he was careful to highlight its learned and authoritative base of support (popes, kings). Moreover, Teresa appealed to people from all walks of life, as befitted a national patron.

In addition to broad social appeal, a national patron also required universal geographical support. After Teresa's beatification, many cities began to elect her as their civic patron saint. José de Jesús María described the phenomenon in his letter to Paul V: "Also proving extraordinary and impassioned devotion, great cities and illustrious towns have elected this holy virgin for their advocate and patron, and have voted, with the authority of the diocese, to keep her feast day."[49] Although José failed to provide a list of these cities, Francisco de Santa María included them in his treatise in defense of Teresa's co-patronage. Referring to the period directly following her beatification, he wrote: "These kingdoms received the news with such great happiness, unlike any seen before on any other occasion. Mexico . . . elected her for patron. Avila, Alba, Salamanca, Baeza, Ecija, Antequera, Málaga, Velez, Alcaudete, Arjona, and other towns did the same."[50] Francisco's and José's words create an image of Spain rising up in sudden and overwhelming joy to embrace Teresa and her cult.

Once they established that Teresa was beloved by all Spain, her supporters began to emphasize the unique bond of obligation between a saint and her nation. In fact, they increasingly depicted Teresa's nationality as fundamental to her patron sainthood. Discalced Carmelite Pedro de la Madre de Dios proclaimed: "She was born in Spain, raised in Spain, founded [convents] in Spain, wrote in Spain, God communicated with her in Spain, she lived always in Spain, never left Spain, died in Spain, and left her virginal body in Spain. Spain beatified her and canonized her. Spain contributed to the expense of these causes. Spain gave her so many houses and convents."[51] Pedro's choice of the term "Spain" (España), rather than Castile, reflects both conscious design on his part and consistent *teresiano* usage throughout the co-patronage debate. By

---

48. Francisco de Santa María, *Defensa del Patronato*, fol. 250r.

49. José de Jesús María, *Sermones predicados en la Beatificacion*, unpaginated.

50. Francisco de Santa María, *Defensa del Patronato*, fol. 244v.

51. Pedro de la Madre de Dios, *Memorial que Dio a su Magestad el padre F. Pedro de la Madre de Dios*, fol. 128v.

eschewing the local in favor of the national, Teresa's supporters extended their saint's jurisdiction beyond both the city (Avila) and the kingdom (New Castile) of her birth. Pedro's rhetorical device of repeating "Spain" in every phrase emphasized the reciprocal relationship between the two: Spain supplied Teresa with the fertile ground for her work and recognized her sanctity through canonization, while Teresa acknowledged her obligation to Spain by leaving her uncorrupted body there to work miracles continually for her native land.

Teresa's supporters understood the close bond between the saint and her nation as the most suitable relationship between a native and her home. Even saints, declared one anonymous *teresiano*, should demonstrate perfect love for their country, as was the obligation of every native.[52] In Teresa's case, love of her natal land manifested itself in constant intercessory prayers for its perpetual well-being. In connecting the importance of birthplace to saints, *teresianos* reflected common legal and social attitudes about the loyalty of natives and the inconstancy of foreigners to sainthood; native citizens of Castilian cities, for example, jealously guarded their local monopolies over office holding and bitterly resisted attempts by "foreigners" to gain civic posts.[53] In the same way, early modern cities and towns often gave privileged positions like patron sainthood to their native citizens, or, barring this, to saints who had lived, preached, or died there.[54] While close connections between cities and their local saints had been widespread throughout Europe from the earliest evolution of the cult of the saints, the early medieval cult of the saints tended to emphasize the glory brought to the town by the presence of a saint's relics, whether or not the saint had any living connection to the town. The civic dimensions of devotions to the saints expanded beginning in the late medieval period and intensified during the Renaissance.[55] Humanist exhortations to love one's *patria* had a profound effect

52. "Por la conservacion del patronato de la gloriosa virgen Santa Teresa de Iesus Fundadora de la sagrada familia Descalça de la Virgen del Monte Carmelo" (ca. 1628), RAH, MS 9/3681, fol. 41r. "Ser natural destos Reynos, por lo qual estar obligada a continuamente rogar por ellos a Dios nuestro Señor: que tambien el amor de los naturales, proprios, y deudos llega a ser de tal calidad, que aun en los Santos se halla, y mas perfecto en la Patria."

53. Tamar Herzog, *Defining Nations: Immigrants and Citizens in Early Modern Spain and Spanish America* (New Haven: Yale University Press, 2003), 71. Herzog points out that *ciudadano* (citizen) refers to the citizen of a town, not a nation. *Natural* was the term used to describe someone from a larger geographic region, like the kingdom of Castile, or Spain.

54. Simon Ditchfield emphasizes the native-saint connection in his work on liturgy and hagiography, citing seventeenth-century Italian writers who claimed that reading works on the deeds of holy ancestors "reflected directly on themselves as their direct heirs." *Liturgy, Sanctity, and History in Tridentine Italy*, 133–34.

55. For late medieval devotions to local holy people, see Augustine Thompson, *Cities of God: The Religion of the Italian Communes, 1125–1325* (University Park: Pennsylvania State University Press, 2005), 193–216.

on devotional patterns and on the uses of saints' cults for civic, political, and patriotic purposes.[56] Both impulses united powerfully in the creation of a national patron saint. The close connection between the national patron and her people (derived from sharing the same place of birth) strengthened the growing idea that the nation should be viewed as the primary site of loyalty.

One can see this expanded idea of national loyalty in several *teresianos* who emphasized their saint's close relationship to her *patria*. One anonymous author insisted that Teresa had rightfully been chosen as patron saint over other famous Spanish founders, like Saints Ignatius of Loyola and Dominic, because although these saints had been born in Spain, they had lived most of their lives elsewhere and had died outside it.[57] Thus, even though there were many other notable Spanish saints, Teresa held a unique position among them that derived from her particularly close relationship with her nation. In addition, Francisco de Santa María explained that this close bond between saint and nation served to glorify Spain; specifically, he pointed out that although other foreign nations had given birth to powerful male founders, only Spain had given birth to a female founder.[58] The distinctive honor of such an accomplishment (of having a prodigy among prodigies as a native) showed the world that Spain alone had been chosen to receive rare divine gifts. The ability of the native saint to reflect the glory of the nation underscored an increasingly national understanding of both patron sainthood and the community.

Another profound shift in early modern understandings of sanctity revealed itself in discussions of temporality. Teresa's supporters argued that she would protect them from the problems Spain was currently facing better than any other saint because she had lived as their contemporary. To underscore this point, her supporters occasionally described her as "modern" (*moderna*). For seventeenth-century Spaniards, the word "modern" carried with it none of the resonance (or baggage) that we today associate with it. Instead, according to a seventeenth-century

56. On this development in the late medieval Italian city-states, see Webb, *Patrons and Defenders*. Webb quotes a sixteenth-century humanist author on this point: "it is none the less piously to be believed that there are very many of them [saints] who exercise a special care and protection over those places in which they were born, or where they lived for a long time" (3).

57. *Acerca del Patronato de la gloriosa santa Teresa de Iesus, a quien eligieron los Reynos en sus Cortes por Patrona, se han de tratar tres puntos* (1618), BNM, MS 9140, fols. 209v–210v.

58. Francisco de Santa María, *Defensa del Patronato*, fol. 247v. "Vence tambien a los gloriosisimos fundadores Santo Domingo, y san Ignacio en tres cosas. La primera, en que ellos fueron hombre, y ella muger. Con lo qual hizo a su nacion mas admirable en mugeres, que lo es en hombre. Porque Italia, Francia, y Egipto podran dar varones fundadores tan admirables como Santo Domingo y San Ignacio: y ninguna nacion del mundo podra dar fundadora como Santa Teresa."

dictionary, the word meant "that which was done recently, in contrast to the ancient. A modern author is one who wrote a few years ago, and for this reason has less authority than the ancients."[59] The term thus had two general meanings: the first, basically temporal, meaning something occurring relatively recently; the second, that recent things were less significant or trustworthy than their ancient counterparts. In many parts of early modern Europe, humanists often championed "modernity" and the inherent value of the present over the ancients. Yet in early seventeenth-century Spain, references to new things, through use of the terms *moderno* and its more popular synonym, *novedad* (novelty), were often terms of disdain.[60] Why, then, did Teresa's supporters employ this term to describe their saint?

Rather than accept a derogative understanding of "modern," *teresianos* responded with a radical reconceptualization. In doing so, they interrupted the deeply held assumptions of many early modern Castilian intellectuals about the inherent superiority of the ancient over the modern. They insisted that it was in fact the saint's modernness that rendered her an especially strong choice for national patron. They remembered and loved her; in return, she would protect them from the contemporary problems they faced, which she could understand and sympathize with as the child of the same times. The end result would be the elevation of a far more effective intercessor for the Spanish people. Thus Teresa's cult and patron sainthood were placed in tension with—if not outright opposition to—antiquity and tradition, which had previously been the central features of both spiritual devotion and understandings of the Spanish nation.

Francisco de la Cueva y Silva, for example, argued that the long lapse between the present day and the death of most older Spanish saints meant that people knew of their miracles only from old stories. In contrast, Teresa had lived in the present age and had been known personally by many living people; thus the miraculous events of her life and death could be both remembered and verified.[61] He boldly refused to shy away from the idea of Teresa's "newness"; instead, he privileged living memory as well as what could be *proved*, in accordance with the concerns of

---

59. Sebastián de Covarrubias Orozco, *Tesoro de la Lengua Castellana o Española* (1611), ed. Felipe Maldonado (Madrid: Editorial Castalia, 1995), 757.

60. Marc Fumaroli, ed., *La querelle des anciens et des modernes* (Paris: Gallimard, 2001). On Spanish hostility to so-called *novedades* (novelties), see José Antonio Maravall, *La cultura del barroco: Análisis de una estructura histórica* (Barcelona: Editorial Ariel, 1975), 450.

61. Francisco de la Cueva y Silva, *Informacion en derecho sobre el titulo de Patrona destos Reynos, dado a la gloriosa santa Teresa de Iesus, fundando la eleccion que los Procuradores de Cortes hizieron. Y respondiendo a todas las oposiciones contrarias* (ca. 1618), BNM, MS 9140, fol. 181v.

the Tridentine church. Connecting memory and proof, Cueva challenged the cult of ancient saints and what he called the vague certainties lurking in the distant past. This sly attack on the cult of Santiago, and the lack of historical evidence for certain of its most prominent legends, was certainly not lost on the apostle's supporters. But more than taking a simple jab at his opponents, Cueva suggested that a saint who had lived among them, who had personal and professional relationships with people still alive to tell the stories to their neighbors and children, made the holy more vitally present. In addition, Teresa could be seen as more sympathetic to the problems and anxieties of her contemporaries than saints who had been dead for centuries. This kind of argument had the potential to shift the traditional emphasis of the cult of the saints, in which ancient saints tended to hold the place of greatest honor.

Along with their bold assertions of the importance of modern saints, most defenders of Teresa's elevation worked to insert their saint into the established narrative of Spanish history. They advocated strongly for the co-intercession of both saints and took pains to argue that none of Santiago's glorious traditions would be diminished by adding Teresa as his helper. Francisco de Santa María clarified this point in his treatise for co-patronage, first by admonishing the *santiaguistas* for having so little faith in the devotion of Spaniards and thinking them so fickle that they could easily forget their love for Santiago. Second, he asserted, "No one can look at the new patron without seeing the old one. And with this . . . I have proved that [devotion to Teresa] will only augment the cult of the apostle's sacred sepulcher."[62] Francisco expected his audience to understand that Teresa was a reflection of Santiago, because Teresa, as a Spaniard, owed her Christianity to Santiago's conversion; therefore, all of Teresa's successes and honors reflected glory on Santiago. Several writers referred to the Castilian saint as Santiago's daughter, while others explained that Teresa's career resulted from the apostle.[63] The "newness" of Teresa's sanctity and elevation could be read as a recent event in the ancient history of Santiago and Spain. In this way *teresiano* authors upheld and defended sacred Spanish traditions while simultaneously maneuvering for a place for their saint within those traditions.

Yet despite grounding their arguments within long-cherished Spanish traditions, advocates of Teresa's elevation still insisted on a reconceptualization of the role of modernity vis-à-vis antiquity. For example, one

---

62. Francisco de Santa María, *Defensa del Patronato*, fol. 255v.

63. Examples of Teresa as Santiago's daughter ("hija de Santiago") can be found in Antonio de Casuallo de Parada, "Discurso Apologetico de dichosa Patrona de la gloriosa Madre Sta Teresa" (1628), HSA, unpaginated; and Pedro de la Madre de Dios, *Memorial que Dio a su Magestad el padre F. Pedro de la Madre de Dios*, fol. 134v.

teresiano author argued that his saint surpassed all older Spanish saints because she possessed all their combined virtues and spiritual gifts in a way unprecedented among saints: She had been a virgin, a doctor of the church, a founder of an order, Spanish, a knight, an apostle of Spain, like Santiago's disciples, a teacher of doctrine, a martyr in desire, and an intercessor for every need.[64] Teresa thus encompassed every level of sanctity in the heavenly hierarchy. Another author described Teresa as the "last born" Spanish saint, beloved by Spain for this reason, a description that appealed to the Old Testament story of Jacob and his preference for his son Joseph over his older sons as a precedent for loving a younger child more than an older one.[65] The use of such a tactic by Teresa's supporters allowed them to present her as the spiritual heir to all the Spanish saints who had come before her, uniting their greatest qualities in one new super saint. Thus they portrayed her as a holy bridge between past and present, but in a way that privileged modern rather than ancient sanctity, since a modern saint was the fruit of generations of spiritual labor.

The Dominican preacher Domingo Cano supplied another genealogy for Teresa, which claimed that her patronage had been foreseen centuries earlier: "And even though these reasons (for her patronage) are sufficient, I cannot pass over in silence the fact that she is a native of Spain, who in her role as patron fulfills a prophecy and ancient desire of our Spanish nation, derived from the figure which Romans used to depict Spain—the figure of a woman wearing offensive and defensive arms, with two arrows in her right hand and a shield on her arm, and helmet on her head—which are the arms that Spain used in ancient times to defend herself against her enemies."[66] In Cano's explanation, Teresa's patronage was not only foreshadowed but prophesied—his choice of biblical language was certainly deliberate, part of an attempt to insert his saint into the glorious Spanish Golden Age before the Umayyad invasions. She had been chosen by God from those most ancient times to represent Spain; thus her elevation to patron saint merely fulfilled God's long-held desire for his people. Cano also emphasized the significance of Teresa's Spanishness (her *españolidad*); she

64. "Copia de una carta que escribio el Arçobispo de Seuilla," fol. 109r.

65. Melchor Alfonso Mogrovejo y Escovar, *Don Melchor Alfonso Mogrovejo y Escovar arcediano de Olmedo y Canonigo en la santa Iglesia de Auila, menor sieruo y deuoto de la Santa Madre Teresa de Iesus, en defensa de su Patronato* (ca. 1628), BNM, MS 9140, fol. 205v.

66. Domingo Cano, *Sermon que en la Fiesta de la gloriosa Santa Teresa de Iesus, en su convento de Religiosas Descalzas de Madrid predico el Maestro Fray Domingo Cano . . . en el Otavario de Fiestas que el Rey nuestro señor celebró en honor de la Santa, como nueua Patrona de España, y en hazimiento de gracias, por la salud que le alcançó de Dios* (Madrid: Juan González, 1627), fol. 12r–v.

became indistinguishable from the figure that allegorically represented Spain during the Roman period and was integrated seamlessly into Spain's most ancient history. More than being a part of Spain's history, Cano suggested, Teresa and Spain were one.

A similar appeal to Spanish history and the rhetoric of salvation came from the great royal preacher and Trinitarian Hortensio Félix Paravicino, who constructed another masterly narrative that incorporated Teresa into ancient history. He declared that God had "allowed Rodrigo and Florinda, a man and a woman, to lose Spain in universal ignominy, in order to show us that our weakness and sins were to blame. But now He permits a man and a woman, Santiago and Saint Teresa, to restore all its previous honor."[67] Paravicino thus evoked the myth of Rodrigo and Florinda, whose sinfulness had led to the loss of Spain to Arab invasion. Because the fall of Spain had occurred as a result of the sinfulness of a woman and man, Paravicino claimed that it was fitting for Spain to be restored by a woman and a man, which was clearly the role God intended for dual patronage.[68] Paravicino wove his narrative out of the same essential elements as Santiago's supporters (sin and redemption), but he relocated the key moment in Spain's history from Santiago's evangelization (or presence at Clavijo) to its dramatic fall in 711, framing his story within the narrative of Adam and Eve. In this metaphor, Paravicino identified the Visigothic era, rather than the earliest years of Spanish Christianity, as Edenic; at the same time, he created a narrative in which Spanish history mirrored the history of human salvation—Santiago and Teresa became the new Rodrigo and Florinda, just as Christ and Mary became the new Adam and Eve. Just as some *santiaguistas* claimed that Santiago's patronage stemmed from the moment when the apostle won Spanish freedom from Muslim tyranny at Clavijo, *teresianos* wished to make similar claims about their saint and the spiritual redemption of the Spanish peoples. Teresa, no less than Santiago, could be viewed as part of Spain's messianic heritage. Yet both Paravicino's and Cano's histories recast the moment of Spain's redemption, when Spain's "lost honor" was restored, in the period of Teresa's life, the sixteenth

67. Hortensio Félix Paravicino, *Oracion Evangelica del Maestro Fray Hortensio Felix Paravicino, predicador de su Magestad, al Patronato de España, de la Santa Madre Teresa de Iesus* (Madrid: Juan González, 1628), fol. 35r.

68. Ibid. For Paravicino's popularity, see Hilary Smith, *Preaching in the Spanish Golden Age: A Study of Some Preachers of the Reign of Philip III* (Oxford: Oxford University Press, 1978), 35. For more on Paravicino as a supporter of Olivares, see Fernando Negredo del Cerro, "La capilla real como escenario de la lucha política: Elogios y ataques al valido en tiempos de Felipe IV," in *La capilla real de los Austrios: Música y ritual de corte en la Europa moderna,* ed. Juan José Carreras and Bernardo J. García García (Madrid: Fundación Carlos de Amberes, 2001), 328.

century. As a result, they created a new temporal orientation for patron sainthood and the national narrative. In effect, these authors were saying: What is important to the Spanish nation is happening *now*, not in the ancient past; we need to adjust our ideas about ourselves based on the contemporary situation, not old stories.

While most *teresianos* integrated Teresa with Santiago and Spanish traditions, as Paravicino and Cano did, a few ridiculed and questioned Spain's apostolic pretensions. In his colorful and controversial work *Defiende el patronato de Santa Teresa de Iesus, teresiano* Francisco Morovelli de Puebla made several direct assaults on *santiaguista* legends; he directed particular venom at descriptions of Santiago's patron sainthood as "fifteen hundred years old." Morovelli pointed out that Pelayo, one of the oldest military heroes of the reconquest, had not invoked the name of Santiago in his battles; indeed, Santiago was not used this way until the ninth-century battle of Clavijo. Morovelli also expressed open doubt about Santiago's evangelization of the Spanish.[69] His treatise was one of the few that sought to secure Teresa's position as new patron by openly destabilizing Santiago's place in Spanish history. By tapping into debates over the apostle's cult that predated Teresa's election, he made the case that it was time to choose a new spiritual representative.

While few *teresiano* pamphlets attacked *santiaguista* traditions as aggressively as Morovelli did, there is evidence that lampooning Santiago was more common in poetry. Gaspar de Santa María, a Discalced Carmelite and a native of Granada, wrote several works in defense of Teresa's patronage, including one treatise and two poems, under a variety of pseudonyms.[70] The tone of the treatise is angry but measured, while in the poetry Gaspar assumed a viciously satirical voice, launching derisive attacks on Santiago and his followers. He constructed the two poems in the form of a dialogue, the first of which he attributed to Francisco de Quevedo y Villegas, a forgery that had the objective of both humiliating Quevedo and mocking *santiaguistas*. He ridiculed the

---

69. Morovelli de Puebla, *Defiende el patronato de Santa Teresa*, fols. 6r–11r.

70. His most formal treatise, for example, was printed under the name León de Tapia, as Gaspar León de Tapia had been the Carmelite's secular name. León de Tapia, *Examen y refutacion de los fundamentos, con que impugnaban el Licenciado Pedro de Losada, y otros, el Patronato de la gloriosa Virgen santa Teresa. Dado tres vezes por los Reynos de Castilla, y confirmado por la Santidad de Urbano 8 a instancia de la Catolica Magestad del Rey D. Felipe 4* (Barcelona, 1628). He also printed a long poem under the pseudonym Valerio Vicencio, *Al poema delyrico de don Francisco de Queuedo, contra el Patronato de la gloriosa virgen Santa Teresa, Patrona de los Reynos de Castilla, por nuestro muy Santo Padre Urbano, Papa Octauo* (1628), BNM, VE 155/59. Quevedo attributes this poem to Gaspar in *Obras de don Francisco de Quevedo Villegas*, ed. Aureliano Fernández-Guerra y Orbe, BAE 48 (reprint, Madrid: Rivadeneira, 1951), 450.

notion that Santiago could have ridden out to battle in defense of Spain, as his bones were safely tucked away in a crypt in Galicia.[71]

The challenge to the privilege of ancient saints was one of the most hotly contested issues of the co-patronage debate. The tension between modernity and antiquity partly reflected post-Tridentine concerns about establishing the legitimacy of Catholic doctrines in the face of Protestant criticisms of legends surrounding ancient cults like Santiago's. On a regional level, local cults and traditions found themselves facing stricter prohibitions from the church on proving the legitimacy of devotional traditions. Because *historia sacra* was deeply embedded in the history of a city, region, or nation, casting doubt on a civic patron was tantamount to unraveling local identity; defending one's saint equaled defending oneself, or at least one's communal identity. Such anxiety was particularly manifest in the cathedral of Santiago, which had already weathered a series of attacks on Spanish traditions regarding the apostle. Many opponents to co-patronage therefore interpreted *teresiano* emphasis on their saint's modernity as a direct assault on Santiago's cult, and on their traditional understanding of themselves as Spaniards.

Unsurprisingly, therefore, *santiaguistas* mounted their campaign against Teresa's election on the basis of two fundamental early modern spiritual and cultural values: tradition and history. They rejected the *teresiano* reconceptualization of "modernity" and instead focused on the concept of innovation—*novedad*, in Spanish—a term with rich and ambivalent meanings in early modern Spain. In his early seventeenth-century Castilian dictionary, Sebastián de Covarrubias Orozco defined *novedad* as "something new and unaccustomed. It is dangerous to change something from its ancient use."[72] Covarrubias's definition is telling, as it moved quickly from the more general (and largely benign) category of innovation to the more fearful one of altering custom from past use.[73] The danger implicit in overturning tradition resonated throughout *santiaguista* treatises, which viewed Teresa's displacement of Santiago as a quintessential example of dangerous innovation. They commonly referred to Teresa's

---

71. Vicencio, *Al poema delyrico,* unpaginated. "El cuerpo de Santiago está en Galicia / que el orbe nos codicia / de donde cierto infiero / que no anduvo en las lides caballero." For a brief discussion of this poem and Quevedo, see Castro, *España en su historia,* 176–78. For his part, Quevedo referred to the poem as a "shameful sacrilege" in "Su espada por Santiago," in *Obras de don Francisco de Quevedo Villegas,* BAE 48, 425–26.

72. Covarrubias Orozco, *Tesoro de la Lengua Castellana,* 780.

73. Maravall argues that the series of crises and disasters plaguing the Spanish monarchies imbued contemporaries with a sense of doom and an inability to believe that the future held anything better, which resulted in a fear of new ideas.

elevation as "esta novedad." In an appeal to the University of Valladolid, the Compostelan cathedral claimed that the university had an obligation to defend Santiago's prerogatives because the university itself had been "founded in order to repress *novedades* with authority and learning, as *novedades* in general bring grave harm to a Republic."[74] The harm brought to the republic by *novedades* was described by *santiaguista* Benito Méndez de Parga y Andrade, who stated baldly, "One of the things that most disturbs the peace of a Republic, the quietness of the kingdoms, and the tranquility of the provinces is the invention of *novedades* in matters that have already been agreed upon." He claimed that ancient authorities uniformly rejected any innovation that overturned ancient customs without reason, especially when it achieved nothing for the public good.[75] The key to Méndez's argument rested on the idea that customs were "agreed upon"; disharmony was the inevitable result when one group overturned a custom that had been universally recognized. Thus Teresa's elevation marked a deviation from Spanish custom as well as from history and tradition.

The danger that Teresa's co-patronage posed to important Spanish traditions was immediately manifest to her opponents when the celebration of her feast day on 5 October 1618 threatened to suppress the feast day belonging to an ancient martyr, Saint Placid. *Santiaguistas* rose up in outrage at this suppression, declaring that such a violation of liturgical traditions not only defied the breviary but undermined the foundations of the church itself. The displacement of Placid, a martyr and early Christian saint, in favor of a newly beatified contemporary holy woman epitomized to *santiaguistas* the great harm that would be done to the spiritual and social order if innovation usurped tradition. It further represented a first step in what some viewed as a vast conspiracy to destroy the apostle and his prerogatives.

The feast day of Saint Placid had its own peculiar history, which exemplifies several key features of sixteenth-century cultic devotion. Placid was a sixth-century monk, a companion and friend to Saint Benedict (d. 543). A twelfth-century document claimed that Placid had gone to Sicily and been martyred along with his companions by Saracen invaders. When bones were discovered at a monastery in Messina in the mid-sixteenth century, they were widely believed to be those of Placid and his companions. The cult was approved by Sixtus V and became

---

74. Bishop of Bugia to the University of Valladolid, 24 October 1627, BNM, MS 7326, fol. 297r. The term *inconveniente* in seventeenth-century Spanish had a much stronger negative connotation than the modern English "inconvenient."

75. Méndez de Parga y Andrade, *Discursos del unico patronazgo de España*, 3–4.

enormously popular.[76] Placid, therefore, was both an ancient saint and a contemporary one, connected to early Christianity but also to the massive relic findings during the sixteenth century in both Italy and Spain. Placid fit perfectly into Spanish devotional traditions, because his martyrdom occurred at the hands of Spain's traditional enemies (Muslims). In addition, when Placid's relics were discovered, the kingdom of Sicily was a member of the Spanish monarchy, which may help to explain the strength of his cult in Spain.

But before examining the skirmish over Saint Placid's feast day, I would like to make a few preliminary observations about liturgical practice and Teresa's celebrations. Part of centralizing and tightening cultic devotion of the sixteenth and early seventeenth centuries included stricter regulations about the celebrations of saints' cults. Before a holy person could be venerated, a bishop or higher ecclesiastical authority had to grant permission. These types of honors were restricted carefully until beatification was complete, when the brief issued in honor of the beatification would stipulate the exact terms of worship for the newly beatified person.[77] As such, the breviary outlined liturgical procedures for Teresa's prayer and veneration that were tightly restricted; her beatification brief allowed only Discalced Carmelites (but of both sexes) to celebrate Teresa's holy day with the divine office and a mass in their own churches; these offices and masses would follow the general prescribed order for "virgins," which was Teresa's official category as a holy person.[78] In 1616 Paul V issued another brief extending the celebration of the divine office on Teresa's feast day to ecclesiastics of both sexes throughout Castile, which was extended to all the Spanish kingdoms and Portugal the following year.[79] The divine office, also known as the canonical hours, consisted mainly of sung psalms but included no celebration of the Eucharist. It was therefore less formal and a smaller honor than a mass.[80] Thus, at the time of the Cortes's election of Teresa in

76. *Bibliotheca sanctorum*, ed. Iosepho Vizzini et al., 13 vols. (Rome: Istituto Giovanni XXIII nella Pontificia Università Lateranense, 1961–68), 10:942–47.

77. Some of the confusion over Teresa's status may have reflected the uncertainty in Rome, following the establishment of the Congregation of Sacred Rights (1588), over how to handle the veneration of holy people who were uncanonized but had significant lay followings.

78. See the preface by Silverio de Santa Teresa in Teresa de Jesús, *Obras de Santa Teresa de Jesús*, ed. Silverio de Santa Teresa, Biblioteca Mística Carmelitana, vol. 2 (Burgos: Monte Carmelo, 1915), 413–14.

79. Rodríguez, *Santa Teresa de Jesús*, 125. As a special honor, in 1629 Urban VIII extended to Teresa her own office, which meant that while the frame of the divine office followed the general order for virgins, worship included hymns written especially for Teresa during vespers and matins.

80. For a detailed study of the history and organization of the divine office, see John Harper, *The Forms and Orders of Western Liturgy from the Tenth to the Eighteenth Century: A Historical Introduction and Guide for Students and Musicians* (Oxford: Oxford University Press, 1991), 73–103.

1617, the celebration of her feast day had extended to all of the Iberian Peninsula; nevertheless, there was quite a disparity between these permitted services and those mandated by the breviary for patrons, which consisted of the celebration of a double octave—divine office beginning from the vespers of the evening before the feast day and continuing until the vespers eight days later.

The necessary extension of Teresa's feast day into a nationally celebrated double octave angered opponents of co-patronage, who pointed out the preexistence of celebrations for Saint Placid's feast day on 5 October.[81] Normally, a church would celebrate its ferial (daily) offices unless the day fell on the feast day of an important saint or holy day, in which case the ferial office would be superseded by the festal; when there was any overlap in feast days (as in the case of Placid and Teresa), the more solemn feast took precedence.[82] The new royal decree mandating the celebration of Teresa as patron saint would thus have resulted in the suppression of Placid's feast by Teresa's, since hers represented a higher degree of liturgical solemnity. *Santiaguista* opponents argued that celebrating Teresa as patron would create something of a liturgical paradox, since the solemn feast required for a patron contradicted her relatively low status on the liturgical hierarchy as beatified.[83] *Santiaguistas* clearly read Teresa's displacement of Placid, martyr and enemy of the Moors, as a portent of her displacement of Santiago.

The core of opposition to co-patronage rested less on the relatively small liturgical issue than on what this trend could mean for the apostle's cult. Opponents viewed the antiquity of Santiago's cult as a key feature in its importance to the Spanish people and their history. Francisco de

81. In February 1629 Urban VIII issued a jubilee for Teresa's feast, with plenary indulgences for those who visited a Discalced Carmelite monastery from the vespers of the day before her feast day to the sunset of the day after. One of the reasons for this jubilee was to advertise the change in Teresa's feast day. Teresa died on the night of 4 October; accordingly, her feast was established for the following day, the fifth. The year the saint died (1582), however, was the same one in which the Gregorian calendar reforms took effect and ten days were dropped from the calendar. Her feast day was accordingly adjusted to 15 October, where it stands today. "Iubileo plenísmo en la fiesta de la gloriosa Virgen y Madre Sancta Teresa de Iesus Patrona de los Reynos de la Corona de Castilla" (1629), BNM, VE 197/2.

82. The liturgical problems springing from the ferial and festal calendar are discussed at length in Ditchfield, *Liturgy, Sanctity, and History in Tridentine Italy*, 28–33.

83. Pedro de Castro to Philip III, 4 September 1618, BNM, MS 1749, fol. 421r–v. For their part, *teresianos* rejected the notion that Teresa's beatified status hampered her ability to become patron saint. Pedro de la Madre de Dios scathingly remarked that the church did not follow the ecclesiastical hierarchy when making decisions to celebrate certain saints over others. While the breviary delineated the style of worship, he insisted, local tradition, customs, and devotional preferences also affected the veneration of saints. *Memorial que Dio a su Magestad el padre F. Pedro de la Madre de Dios*, fols. 131v–132r.

Melgar, a canon in the cathedral of Seville and an ardent opponent of co-patronage, argued that Santiago's singular and unique patron sainthood resulted from his evangelization of Spain and the presence of his body, which had brought honor and fame to the nation as a site visited by many kings and important people throughout history.[84] In addition to these justifications for Santiago's patronage, his supporters emphasized that his traditional patronage had always been singular and that this uniqueness was a significant part of the apostle's traditional prerogatives. Other writers also underscored Santiago's role as a military captain and his corporeal presence in battles fought for Spain. His presence in battle was seen not as past but as eternal, and it thus served as evidence for Santiago's historical and *continued* presence in Spain and his enduring relevance to the Spanish nation.

Santiaguistas were extremely sensitive about the representation of their apostle. After decades of attacks regarding Santiago's conversion of Spain, the Compostelan cathedral and its allies viewed the new challenge to his patronage as the most recent in a long line of threats. They felt, therefore, that they must defend not just his patronage but all aspects of their saint's cult simultaneously, which is reflected in the structure of their treatises. For example, many of their treatises against co-patronage included lengthy defenses of Santiago's evangelization of Spain and the establishment of the *voto*. This defensive posture contained a kind of circular logic: Attacks on Santiago had left open a space for the Carmel-ites to take away his privilege as singular patron, while the loss of his unique privilege could lead to greater resistance to the *voto* and increased ridicule of Santiago's traditions. The defense of one constituted a defense of all, and the best strategy for defeating Teresa's patronage was to assert that all of Santiago's traditions were indisputable. Equally, the successful defense of Santiago's patronage would deliver a blow to those seeking to dismantle other *santiaguista* traditions. In a pamphlet addressed to the king, a Sevillian canon bewailed the assaults on Santiago's reputation: "They strengthen themselves at the expense of a just and agreed-upon right and utter most false and unjust slanders, with which they try to weaken the reasons for the apostle's unique patronage."[85] These "slanders"—like Morovelli's and Gaspar's—included the rejection of Santiago's role in battles and open doubts about whether he ever visited Spain.

84. Francisco de Melgar, *Proposicion, y discurso, sobre si debe ser admitida por Patrona General de España, juntamente con su antiguo, i unico Patron Santiago, la Bienaventurada Sancta Theresa de Iesus, conforme a lo determinado por los Procuradores de Cortes, i Breve de la Santidad de Urbano octavo* (Seville: Francisco de Lyra, 1628), fols. 17v–18r.

85. Alonso de Serna, "Carta al Rey sobre el patronato" (ca. 1617), BNM, MS 9140, fol. 73r.

The *santiaguistas* mounted a powerful campaign against such slanders on their apostle's traditions. The Portuguese abbot Joan Salgado de Aráujo dedicated a section of his treatise in favor of Santiago's patronage to a defense of his evangelization of Spain, in which he attacked García de Loaysa's publication of the conciliar records for the Fourth Lateran, which purported to deny that evangelization. Salgado cited a series of authorities in support of his position and penned a lengthy refutation of Loaysa's arguments.[86] Pedro González Guijelmo, a canon in the cathedral of Osma, supplied an extensive list of authoritative authors proving Santiago's foundation of numerous churches in Spain, ranging from Flavius Dextrus, Castellá Ferrer, the Council of Trent, Aragonese historian Diego Murillo, and ecclesiastical historian Francisco de Padilla. González also provided an eloquent defense of the traditionalist position: "There is no more effective proof than ancient traditions, not only in the churches and kingdoms of Spain, but in all the Church and nations, which have in the past and to this day venerate and proclaim Santiago as Spain's unique and only patron."[87] Others writing in defense of Santiago's singular patronage grounded his right to this honor in tradition and history, stressing the extent of its duration.[88] The chronological and geographical accumulation of celebrations for Santiago as patron served as a kind of living history in which the unbroken chain of customary beliefs bound together the past and present.

It is important to understand the immediacy of the history the *santiaguiastas* relied on, specifically its *living* nature. Historians have often described opponents of co-patronage as conservatives bent on preserving the status quo in Spain, no matter what the ultimate cost. But one must recognize that, for them, Santiago's sanctity was no less a lived experience than Teresa's, despite the fact that the apostle had died sixteen hundred years earlier. Their desire for the lived experience of the holy was no less intense than that of the *teresianos,* though it took a different form; for them, the many centuries that had elapsed since the apostle's death provided definitive proof of the saint's efficacy and power, and of the fact that he would continue to protect Spain in the future. Each side espoused differing visions of the source of holiness and power. While

86. Joan Salgado de Aráujo, *Memorial, informacion, y defension apologetica del patronato de España por el apostol Santiago* (1628), HSA, 7–12. Salgado's treatise contains the epigraph "Pro religione, pro patria, pro rege defensionem suscipere legitimum, ac naturale ius est."

87. Pedro González Guijelmo, *Discurso en derecho, a favor del unico patronazgo del Apostol Santiago* (ca. 1628), BNM, VE 211/51, 5–9, 10–11.

88. Benito Méndez de Parga y Andrade railed against those who presumed to deny Santiago's possession of this honor from time immemorial, to which he did not ascribe a specific time frame but referred to as being "centuries long" (*de muchos cientos*).

promoters of Teresa's modernity insisted that the youth of her cult would provide greater motivation and energy in her intercession, those arguing for Santiago claimed as passionately that the long history of their apostle's patronage enriched and deepened his protection of Spain.

The apostle's antiquity thus played a privileged role in *santiaguista* defenses of his prerogatives. One of their primary tasks was to provide historical evidence for the unbroken chain of Santiago's singular patron sainthood from his redemption of the Spanish people to the present. Evidence of such patronage came mainly from privileges granted by these royal figures to the cathedral, which it guarded carefully.[89] Yet some authors extended Santiago's patronage of Spain beyond the eight hundred years claimed by the cathedral (which dated from the battle of Clavijo) to Santiago's arrival in Spain nearly sixteen hundred years earlier. Alonso Rodríguez de León, a canon in the cathedral of Compostela, used these sixteen hundred years as proof of the absurdity of the Carmelite pretension. How, he wondered, could anyone doubt the annoyance Santiago must be feeling at the interruption of sixteen hundred continuous years of singular patronage?[90] Santiago's patron sainthood was woven into the very fabric of Spanish history—the apostle's story was also Spain's story, and one could not be disrupted without potentially unraveling the other.

Sacred and secular history assumed a central role in the co-patronage controversy from its inception, providing a stage for depicting and enacting both patron sainthood and nationhood. Proponents on both sides of the debate maintained clear and specific understandings of their shared past as Spaniards. The concept of "Spain" retained the salience it had developed in the sixteenth century. Both Teresa and Santiago were repeatedly described as national patron saints; because nationhood in early modern Europe relied on the experience of a shared past, both sides eagerly set forward narratives of the Spanish past in which their saint played an integral role. Teresa's supporters shared their opponents' privileging of the cultural, imaginary nation of Spain over the actual juridical and linguistic realities of Iberian diversity. While they produced an alternate reading of Spain's past, they did so without changing the essential elements: the glorification of the Visigothic-Roman past, which was in turn demolished by the invasions of 711, all interpreted in biblical and eschatological terms. Yet the innovation of Teresa's election and her relative modernity allowed the radical recasting of modernity and

89. *Memorial a su Magestad en nombre de la Iglesia de Sanctiago*, BNM, VE 211/46, fol. 3r–v.
90. Rodríguez de León, *Carta a su Magestad*, BNM, VE 211/52, 5.

antiquity. In addition, that Teresa had lived and died in Spain became a foundational argument for her supporters. Their conceptualization of nationality as a crucial factor in proper intercessory effectiveness highlights an important shift that was occurring in early modern devotions, which (not surprisingly) followed the path of centralizing political authority. The Catholic Church, though it remained a vital force in shaping devotional cults and their iconography, was no longer the dominating factor in giving meaning to holiness, as cities and nations elevated patron saints as their primary symbolic representations. Thus Teresa's primary purpose as her people's newest patron was to represent Spain; by taking on the attributes of the Roman allegorical statue of *Hispania,* Teresa embodied the Spanish nation and became its ultimate symbolic representation.

While the push for Teresa's election to co-patron in 1617–18 ended almost as quickly as it had begun, the stage was set for a second phase of the controversy, largely because the first attempt failed—primarily as a result of a liturgical technicality over Teresa's status as beatified. As Teresa's supporters anticipated, Pope Gregory XV quickly recognized the importance and authenticity of Teresa's cult with her canonization in 1622. At the same time, Gregory canonized three additional Spanish saints—Ignatius of Loyola, Francis Xavier, and Isidro Labrador, the patron saint of Madrid.[91] The Spanish kingdoms exploded with celebrations of thanksgiving for this momentous and unprecedented honor. Because the festivals generally celebrated all four saints at once, one of the greatest side effects of Gregory's proclamation was temporarily obscured: the removal of the only serious obstacle to Teresa's being named co-patron saint of Spain. Her supporters had waited, without forgetting; in 1626 they seized their opportunity.

91. The Italian saint Philip Neri was also canonized at this time.

3

THE POLITICS OF
PATRON SAINTHOOD

In the spring of 1626, King Philip IV (1621–60) and his chief minister, the
count-duke of Olivares, were in Aragón, carrying out their first royal
visit.[1] While on this journey, the king wrote a letter to the president of
Castile requesting a vote in the Cortes to reopen the issue of elevating
Teresa to patron saint. The Cortes voted and elected her "without lack-
ing one vote." When the king returned to Madrid, he was overjoyed at
the Cortes's decision; both Philip and Olivares immediately fired off a
series of letters seeking papal confirmation for the Cortes vote to the
necessary officials in Rome, including Pope Urban VIII and the count of
Oñate, the royal ambassador to the papal curia.[2] On 21 July 1627 Urban
issued a brief confirming the king's and Cortes's election of Teresa as co-
patron. "Therefore, for these reasons," he wrote, "and for the great
devotion which they have for Teresa, they elected her for patron and
advocate of these kingdoms in the last Cortes of the aforementioned

---

1. For more information on Philip IV's royal visit to Aragón, see Elliott, *Count-Duke of Olivares*, 255–66.

2. Olivares to the papal legate, 26 May 1626, Biblioteca Apostolica Vaticana, Fondo Barberini
(Latini), MS 8599, fol. 8or–v. See also "Relacion de los negocios que D Diego Saavedra hizo al Sor
Conde de Oñate" (14 December 1626), MAE, leg. 58: "Hable al sec^{rio} de la Congreg^{on} de Ritos sobre
la confirmacion del Patronato de la Santa Theresa de Jesus en los Reynos de Castilla y me dijo, que
para hazerla es menester, se remita authentico el Decreto de las Cortes, sirvase Vexca de escriuierle
embie luego, y tambien el que se hizo en las Cortes penultimas" (fol. 418r).

kingdoms. . . . And because . . . the representatives in the Cortes desired it so greatly that their vote be firm and perpetual, we grant it our patronage and the approval of the Holy Apostolic See." The papal brief also provided for the protection and safeguarding of Santiago's cult and his traditional prerogatives as patron. It stipulated that the patronage of Teresa be "without prejudice, or any innovation to the patronage of the Apostle Santiago in all the kingdoms of Spain."[3] With this brief, Teresa's place as *patrona* was confirmed in perpetuity by the highest authority in the church.

The news of the papal brief arrived in Madrid at a critical moment. In early August 1627 the twenty-two-year-old king had been struck down with a serious illness and was huddled in bed with fevers and chills. Despite careful medical oversight and treatment (including bleeding), the king collapsed again a few weeks later with fever and vomiting. By 1 September he hovered between life and death, and the churches in Madrid were ordered to uncover the host as an act of devotion and an entreaty to God for his health.[4] His subjects feared for his life—hanging in the balance was not only Philip's life but the future of the succession. Philip had no son, although his queen was once again pregnant.[5] According to Carmelite accounts, as Philip lay burning with fever and possibly dying, he received the news of Urban's brief elevating Saint Teresa to co-patron saint. He was healed instantly.[6]

Teresianos considered the king's sudden return to health a sign of divine support for their cause.[7] Discalced Carmelite and royal preacher Francisco de Jesús proclaimed it a miracle in a sermon in honor of Teresa's patronage. After describing the miracle to his listeners, he reminded them of the crucial importance of the king's health to Spain's strength

---

3. "Breve del papa Urbano VIII declarando el patronato de Santa Teresa en España, 21 julio 1627," in *Escritos de Santa Teresa*, ed. Vicente de la Fuente, 2 vols., BAE 53 and 55 (Madrid: Atlas, 1952), 425–26. A printed copy of the papal brief, in Latin, is located in RAH, Col. Salazar y Castro, MS 9/1042, fols. 233r–234v.

4. An account of the king's illness is provided in Gerónimo Gascón de Torquemada, *Gaçeta y nuevas de la Corte de España desde el año 1600 en adelante* (Madrid: Real Academia Matritense de Heráldica y Genealogía, 1991), 270–77.

5. The king and queen had lost their infant daughter earlier in the summer; the queen's pregnancy resulted in another daughter, who lived less than twenty-four hours. Ibid. By the second week of October, the king had apparently recovered but was still weak. Nuncio Pamphilio to the secretary of state, 11 October 1627, Biblioteca Apostolica Vaticana, Fondo Barberini (Latini), MS 8331, fol. 15r.

6. Court chronicler Matías de Novoa remarks at length on the king's illness, though he makes no mention of the miraculous cure. Matías de Novoa, *Historia de Felipe IV, Rey de España*, Colección de Documentos Inéditos para la Historia de España, vol. 69 (Vaduz: Kraus Reprint, 1966), 57–58.

7. Ahumada y Tapia, *Carta apologetica*, fols. 24v–25r. The account of the king's miraculous healing centered on the testimony of witness Alonso Pérez de Guzmán, the king's almoner and chaplain.

and prosperity, since ill leaders led to decaying nations.[8] To Francisco and many other *teresianos,* Teresa's ability to raise Philip IV from his deathbed to new life and vigor demonstrated the vitality she would bring to the ailing monarchy. According to the bishop of Córdoba, Cristóbal de Lobera, Teresa would rid Spain of heresy, pestilence, famine, storms, and floods, while providing victories, prosperity, royal good health, and a secure succession.[9] Because Teresa advocated the good of the republic, *teresianos* viewed her role as national patron saint as a public office. Furthermore, they saw her as complementing the reform program being implemented by Olivares, which also promised to strengthen and revitalize the monarchy.

Supporters of Santiago agreed that an effective patron saint was critical to Spain's future, though naturally they viewed Santiago as the guarantor of such protection. They argued that the loss or diminishment of the apostle's patron sainthood would bring down the wrath of both God and saint, and would erode the very foundations of the nation. They insisted that the king had no right to disrupt Spanish traditions in favor of his own preference, especially as such disruption would lead to national disaster. *Santiaguistas* often derided royal support for Teresa as an act of bad kingship, although most shifted the blame to Olivares. Opposing Teresa's elevation, therefore, provided an opportunity for a blistering critique of Olivares's policies and his role as the king's chief minister. The co-patronage controversy was not separate from the politics of early modern Castile; on the contrary, it was deeply embedded in it, as both sides adapted the language of national sainthood to contemporary political discourse, including the revitalization of the monarchy and the critique of plural authority represented by Olivares's power. In addition, the political wrangling revealed the contested relationship between king and nation. On one hand, a national patron saint could be used to consolidate royal authority and muster support for reform policies. On the other, the saint could help create a vision of the nation as distinct from the king in order to resist or even rebuke the monarch.

The tensions that surfaced in Madrid in the late summer of 1627 stemmed from more than the sudden onset of a royal illness and the

8. Francisco de Jesús, *Sermon que predico el dia primero de la octava, con que el Rey nuestro Señor quiso celebrar la Fiesta de la nueva Patrona de sus Reynos de España, NSM Teresa de Iesus* (Madrid, 1627), 56–58.

9. Cristóbal de Lobera, *Iusta Cosa a sido eligir por Patrona de España, y admitir por tal, a Santa Teresa de Iesus, y en ello no se hizo perjuyzio alguno al patronato de Señor Santiago Apostol y Patron de España,* BNM, VE 216/58, fols. 2v–3r.

elevation of a controversial patron saint. The period since Philip's ascension in 1621 had been a critical and uneasy time for the Spanish monarchy. The court was quickly divided between those who wished to see the continuation of Philip III's foreign policies and those who had viewed his truce with the Dutch as an unnecessary, even dangerous, concession to rebels. The new king, only a teenager, began to lean heavily on the advice of Baltasar de Zúñiga, former ambassador to the imperial court, and Zúñiga's nephew, Gaspar de Guzmán, the count of Olivares.[10] Though Philip III's reliance on the counsel of his favorite, the duke of Lerma, had been a source of bitter controversy in the first decades of the century, Philip IV followed in his father's footsteps and ultimately delegated much of his authority to Olivares.[11] Olivares in turn used his close relationship with the young monarch to fashion a powerful new faction at court, whose primary goal was the implementation of a series of bold (and controversial) new policies: increased military intervention on the Continent and reform programs at home to stabilize and improve the Spanish economy.

Olivares believed that the situation of the monarchy required decisive action. He considered it imperative to restore Spain's reputation abroad as a power to be feared and obeyed. But a strong presence in the international arena could not be maintained without improving the domestic economic situation. In 1623 the new government promulgated the Articles of Reformation, which attempted to reform several areas of Castilian economy: the banking system, sumptuary laws, tax relief for immigrants, and a reduction in local offices.[12] Although his reform scheme had mixed results, the mid-1620s saw a cluster of military victories that appeared to justify Olivares's new foreign policies. The so-called *annus mirabilis* of 1625 brought news of a major victory by Spanish forces against the Dutch at Breda; the retaking of the important port of Bahía, Brazil, from the Dutch; and the defeat of English forces at the port city of Cádiz. These early successes gave Olivares the space to draft bigger plans, many of which focused on attempts to augment royal power, both in Castile and in other kingdoms of the monarchy.[13] By 1626 Olivares had begun to reinforce the power of the monarch with effective royal

10. Elliott, *Count-Duke of Olivares*, 40–45.

11. For a discussion of royal favorites in early modern Europe, see John H. Elliott and L. W. B. Brockliss, eds., *The World of the Favourite* (New Haven: Yale University Press, 1999). On Lerma's *privanza* specifically, see Feros, *Kingship and Favoritism*.

12. Elliott, *Count-Duke of Olivares*, 146–50.

13. Ibid., 226–43.

propaganda.[14] He seized on the movement to name Saint Teresa as Spain's new co-patron as a key component of this effort.

The decision to restart the campaign for Teresa's co-patronage can be tied to the political concerns of Philip and Olivares in the middle years of the 1620s. Making Philip IV "king of Spain," rather than the king or titular lord of a diverse scattering of kingdoms, was one of Olivares's most ardent desires for the new king. The count-duke laid out his argument for increasing royal power in his "Great Memorial" of 1624, a private treatise for the young monarch that described how the royal government functioned and advised Philip on how to navigate it.[15] While Olivares expressed a desire to have the other kingdoms conform to the laws of Castile, his primary motive was to augment the powers of the monarch, rather than to create a unified nation-state.[16] In the spring of 1626, for example, the king and count-duke traveled to Aragón, in part because they had hoped a personal visit might help win Aragonese support for one of Olivares's newest reforms: the Union of Arms, the creation of a reserve army supported by all kingdoms in the monarchy. In Olivares's plan, the reserve army would provide multiple solutions, including greater defense of the monarchy, redistributing the burden of arms more effectively (particularly away from Castile), and drawing the disparate pieces of the monarchy closer together.[17]

John Elliott has argued that Olivares viewed the Union of Arms "as a necessary prelude to the still greater task of uniting their hearts."[18] The election of a new national patron saint provided the perfect opportunity for unifying hearts, a connection made even clearer given the close timing of the two events.[19] Olivares and Philip were hardly the first to use a patron saint to further a political agenda. Since the Middle

---

14. On Olivares's sharp eye for propaganda and staging, see Jonathan Brown and John H. Elliott, *A Palace for a King: The Buen Retiro and the Court of Philip IV*, 2d ed. (New Haven: Yale University Press, 2003).

15. Gaspar de Guzmán, "Gran Memorial," in *Memoriales y cartas del Conde-Duque de Olivares*, ed. John H. Elliott and José F. de la Peña (Madrid: Alfaguara, 1978), 95.

16. This view of Olivares's motivation is provided in Elliott, *Count-Duke of Olivares*, 198–99.

17. For a thorough discussion of the genesis of Olivares's Union of Arms, see ibid., 244–52. The visit to Aragón met with little success, as the fiercely independent Aragonese were wary of any attempt to draw them more securely into the monarchy.

18. Ibid., 243.

19. The location of the king and Olivares at the time of the petition to Contreras is described explicitly in *Relacion sencilla y fiel de las fiestas que el rey D. Felipe IIII nuestro Señor hizo al Patronato de sus Reinos de España Corona de Castilla que dio a la Gloriosa Virgen Santa Teresa de Iesus, año 1627* (Madrid: Juan González, 1627), fol. 1r–v. Olivares sent the Cortes a letter of gratitude for its election of Teresa dated 14 May, which is the same date Elliott provides for Olivares's return from Aragón. *Actas de las Cortes de Castilla*, 45:51–52; and Elliott, *Count-Duke of Olivares*, 255.

Ages, kings had understood the polemical and centralizing power of associating the Crown with specific saints. As Diana Webb explains, "The patron saint symbolized the public power, and rulers could with propriety demand, in the saint's name, demonstrations of obedience that . . . they might perhaps not feel fully entitled to demand in their own right."[20] In the case of Teresa, celebration of her feast as patron would mean that eight days of lavish rituals would occur simultaneously in every major Castilian city and town, transforming them into a stage for the performance of royal power and policies usually reserved for Madrid alone.[21] Such "political" saints were often drawn from local cults, which could be appropriated more easily than universal saints for national purposes.[22] While Santiago's cult had been associated with the Habsburgs during previous reigns, the apostle's deep historical significance to the Spanish past may actually have militated against his effectiveness in furthering contemporary royal policy. In looking for support for new policies, Olivares and Philip found fresh inspiration in a new saint.[23]

It made sense that Philip would choose a new saint with a preexisting relationship to his family. In addition to Teresa's cure of the young king in 1627, several other miracles on behalf of the Habsburgs were credited to her. Discalced Carmelite Pedro de la Madre de Dios explained how the prayers of Teresa's monks on behalf of Philip's grandfather, Philip II, had successfully released him from purgatory after a mere eight days. Pedro linked the two miracles—the grandfather's liberation from purgatory and the grandson's release from an untimely death—to demonstrate what, he argued, "Spain owes to Teresa." He further strengthened Teresa's tie with the royal family by attributing the birth of male heirs to Philip III to the saint's intercession.[24] *Teresianos*

20. Webb, *Patrons and Defenders*, 6.

21. Philip IV often used religious festivals as a way of transmitting a vision of royal power. See especially the section on the Corpus Christi festivals in Madrid in the mid-seventeenth century in María José del Río Barredo, *Madrid, urbs regia: La capital ceremonial de la monarquía católica* (Madrid: Marcial Pons, 2000), 205–33.

22. Gabrielle M. Spiegel, "The Cult of St. Denis and Capetian Kingship," in *Saints and Their Cults: Studies in Religious Sociology, Folklore, and History*, ed. Stephen Wilson (Cambridge: Cambridge University Press, 1983), 141–68. Spiegel contends that "the inherent universalism of Christian religious thought potentially militated against the growth of national feeling. To find unfailing support for national causes, the peoples of Europe turned instead to local saints" (141).

23. Both men also demonstrated great personal devotion to Teresa. Olivares declared in a letter, "Almost since I was born, I have taken her as my personal advocate." Olivares to Cardinal Torres, in *Escritos de Santa Teresa*, 425. Philip invoked Teresa in his will and testament, referring to her as a saint "to whom I have shown devotion with very particular demonstrations." Antonio Domínguez Ortiz, ed., *Testamento de Felipe IV* (Madrid: Editora Nacional, 1982), 3–4.

24. Pedro de la Madre de Dios, *Memorial que Dio a su Magestad el padre F. Pedro de la Madre de Dios*, fol. 127r–v.

thus emphasized that their saint was responsible for Philip IV's life on not one but two occasions, his birth and his miraculous recovery, creating a bond of personal obligation between saint and king.

Saints venerated by a monarch or royal family frequently became the symbolic as well as the sacred locus for kingdoms in the premodern world. The Capetians' preference for Saint Denis and the fourteenth-century Plantagenet choice of Saint George, for example, created a broader devotional base for the chosen saints than local or regional cults could do. Proximity to the royal person allowed the saints to draw on the sacred aura of kingship. Since the bodies of kings were unlike the bodies of ordinary men, the act of safeguarding a royal body created a unique and elevated status for the protector. The association of a saint with a particular king or royal dynasty resulted in the creation of royal or dynastic saints, which could have significant political uses for the royal family.[25] Yet Philip did not unilaterally declare Teresa the new patron. On the contrary, her elevation to this status originated in the representative assembly. She represented, therefore, the entire nation, rather than acting merely as the private patron of the royal person. It is here that we can begin to trace the movement from *dynastic* saint (a saint associated with a particular monarch or royal family) to *national* saint (Spain's patron, not just Philip's). The doubleness of her role—dynastic and national—served the ultimate goal of uniting people in a more effective way than a dynastic saint alone could do, since she protected more than royal interests.

The celebration of saint and nation began with Teresa's feast day, a double octave—eight days of liturgical observance at the highest level of formality—beginning on 5 October 1627. While the king appears to have been involved in the planning for the celebrations in Madrid, the real planner was Olivares. The count-duke carefully oversaw every detail of the lavish spectacle, ensuring that the festival would assert the continuing power and vitality of the king—and of himself by extension. Nevertheless, the official account of the event described the king as the "absolute master," in charge of every aspect of the celebration, right down to the decorations of the chapels and the use of royal musicians during mass. Philip sent decorations and silver from the royal chapel to the Discalced Carmelite church, provided his royal musicians, who

---

25. For discussion of this phenomenon, see Jean-Marie Le Gall, *Le mythe de Saint Denis entre Renaissance et Révolution* (Paris: Champs Vellon, 2007); and Gábor Klaniczay, *Holy Rulers and Blessed Princesses: Dynastic Cults in Medieval Central Europe*, trans. Éva Pálmai (Cambridge: Cambridge University Press, 2000).

would play at mass, and commanded the involvement of his main chaplain and almoner, Alonso Pérez de Guzmán. While the king's illness prevented his attendance at any of the masses, the account explained that as the solemn procession passed by the palace on its way to the Convent of San Hermenegildo (the Discalced Carmelite convent), the king and queen observed the activity from special windows, from which they could see but that protected them from being seen.[26]

Other nobles and princes observed the procession from high above the noisy and crowded streets, although many important people took part in the procession themselves, including representatives of the Cortes and members of the royal councils. The faithful flooded into the church to venerate the image of their new patron and to pay her homage.[27] While the official account of the events does not include much detail about the decorations, the processions were certainly accompanied by floats, pyramids, fireworks, and images of the saints in allegory. In addition, onlookers would have seen a series of processions in thanksgiving for the recovery of the king, which were separate from these festivities but occurred throughout October.[28]

In addition to the visual sumptuousness of the event, the octave was accompanied by sixteen sermons, two preached on each day. Philip ordered all sixteen sermons to be printed, in order that he might read them at his leisure, since his illness had prevented his attendance.[29] Aware of the king's careful monitoring of the event, royal preachers chose language for their sermons that harmonized with royal ideology, forcefully promoting the connection between Teresa's intercession, Spain's well-being, and Spanish piety. Discalced Carmelite Juan de la Asunción, for example, touted Philip IV as "more pious than powerful . . . more religious than rich." He further claimed that the king remained the church's only defense and support, the sole aid to the faith and the greatest protector of the saints: "This is a clear sign that his kingdoms will last as long as the kingdom of Heaven, which is the Church, because the infallible foundation of power is the defense of the Church and the protection of the faithful and the Faith."[30] In Juan's construction of royal

26. *Relacion sencilla y fiel de las fiestas*, fols. 8v–9r.

27. Ibid., fols. 5v–8v. With respect to the king's involvement, the anonymous author calls Philip the "dueño absoluto" of events.

28. Gascón de Torquemada, *Gaçeta y nuevas de la Corte de España*, 270–77. He reported that some festivities took place on 7 and 8 October, which directly coincided with co-patronage festivities.

29. *Relacion sencilla y fiel de las fiestas*, fol. 7v.

30. Juan de la Asunción, *Sermon que predico el P.F. Iuan de la Assuncion Religioso Descalço de la Orden de nuestra Señora del Carmen. En su Conuento de S. Hermenegildo de Madrid, el dia septimo de las Octauas, que el Rey D. Felipe IIII N. Señor celebró a una en los dos Conuentos de Carmelitas Descalços y*

power, defense of the faith was not merely a source of protection or a moral necessity but a way of transforming the terrestrial kingdom of Spain into the celestial kingdom of God. Such a transformation in turn imbued the monarchy with eternal and immutable qualities.

In the process of transforming the earthly monarchy into a mirror of the celestial kingdom, Teresa became fully integrated into court life as one of the king's most efficacious agents. Friar Juan continued, "It is the same thing for a Prince to take care of the divine cult and Catholic religion and to look after the common good of his kingdoms. . . . Just as the king appoints valiant captains to lead his soldiers to help them fight against the enemies of the Faith, he appoints patrons to his kingdoms, who fight in heaven with their intercession and help and defend [the kingdoms] with their prayers."[31] By comparing national patron saints to captains in the royal army, Juan depicted patron sainthood as a type of royal appointment. Further, if Teresa's main job as patron was to protect the monarchy from its foreign enemies, then she could be seen as part of royal policy for safeguarding Spain. As a result, co-patronage could be viewed as the king's *obligation*, part of his duty as a good king and necessary for the well-being of the Spanish monarchy, rather than as a personal or even a spiritual choice. Such an understanding of patron sainthood was echoed in other sermons from the octave. Francisco Pimentel, for example, proclaimed that Spain had been protected from divine vengeance—as specifically manifested in war, dissension, famine, loss of territory, and, worst of all, heresy—only as a result of Teresa's strenuous interventions on its behalf.[32] *Teresianos*, therefore, integrated patron sainthood into a larger discourse of how a good king defended and preserved his realms.

The duties of a good king, as outlined by Juan de la Asunción and Pimentel, drew from a body of political theory that would have been immediately recognizable to their learned listeners. These ideas, known as Christian reason of state, were widely discussed throughout early modern Europe. Exponents of Christian reason of state protested vigorously against the Machiavellian dismissal of service to God as the highest duty of political leaders; they produced numerous treatises in defense of the Christian prince that were highly influential throughout Europe, the

---

Descalças desta Corte. A la fiesta del Patronato de la gloriosa Virgen S. Teresa Fundadora desta Reformacion, Patrona de los Reynos de España, Corona de Castilla (Madrid: Juan González, 1627), 48–49.

31. Ibid., 49.

32. Francisco Pimentel, *Sermon que predico en la Octava, con que el Rey nuestro Señor quiso celebrar la fiesta de la nueua Patrona de sus Reynos de España, Santa Teresa de Iesus* (Madrid: Juan González, 1627), fol. 19v.

most important of which was by Giovanni Botero.[33] The Christian concept of kingship was particularly important in the Spanish monarchy, where the Habsburg monarchs had spent a century creating an image of themselves as God's new chosen instruments. One early seventeenth-century political writer, Juan Pablo Mártir Rizo, compiled a Christian reason-of-state treatise in which he explained that a king would achieve all earthly success if "he fears God above everything, and if he is observant of the Catholic religion."[34] Within the framework of this political theory, the monarch's primary responsibility was to provide for and sustain "the common good," an older, Thomist concept founded on peace, justice, and security.[35]

Castilian political thinkers were passionate about the monarch's duty to ensure justice and provide for the common good. They were not shy about counseling the king or complaining about policies they viewed as dangerous or injurious, and they wrote prolifically to the king on these subjects. In fact, the late sixteenth and early seventeenth centuries saw an explosion of cheaply printed pamphlets and memorials offering recommendations and complaining about every aspect of Spanish political and economic life.[36] One such author, Jerónimo de Ceballos, imagined the metaphor of the body politic in an updated version that focused on internal organs.[37] For example, he compared the brain to the ecclesiastical state as the most important part of the body. It was the liver that Ceballos equated with royal power, since it was the monarch's job to spread peace and justice to his vassals in the same way that the liver carried blood to all parts of the body.[38] In this formulation, the king's

33. On the theory of Christian reason of state in early modern Europe, see Bireley, *Counter-Reformation Prince*, 111–35; and Giovanni Botero, *The Reason of State* (1589), trans. P. J. Waley and D. P. Waley (London: Routledge and Kegan Paul, 1956).

34. Juan Pablo Mártir Rizo, *Norte de Príncipes y Vida de Romulo*, ed. José Antonio Maravall (Madrid: Centro de Estudios Políticos y Constitucionales, 1988), 21. See also Maravall's excellent introduction to this work.

35. Bireley, *Counter-Reformation Prince*, 35. Bireley cites the influential example of the sixteenth-century Spanish canonist Francisco Súarez. Such ideas are repeated in Philip II's law code, *Nueva Recopilación de las leyes destos Reynos*, 1640 facsimile ed., vol. 1 (Valladolid: Lex Nova, 1982): "La Ley ama, y enseña las cosas que son de Dios, y es fuente de enseñamiento, y Maestra de derecho, y de justicia, y ordenamiento de buenas costumbres, y guiamiento del pueblo" (58).

36. Manuel Colmeiro, *Biblioteca de los economistas españoles de los siglos XVI, XVII y XVIII*, 5th ed. (Madrid: Real Academia de Ciencias Morales y Políticas, 1979). Colmeiro lists almost two hundred *arbitristas* during the reigns of Philip III and Philip IV.

37. One of the most influential medieval thinkers to see the body politic in this way was John of Salisbury, *Policraticus: Of the Frivolities of Courtiers and the Footprints of Philosophers*, ed. Cary J. Nederman (Cambridge: Cambridge University Press, 1990), 67.

38. Jerónimo de Ceballos, *Arte real para el buen gobierno de los Reyes, Principes, y sus vasallos* (Toledo: Diego Rodríguez, 1623), fol. 4r–v. For similar metaphors of the body politic, see the dedication in Juan de Santa María, *Republica y policia christiana para Reyes y Principes; y para los que en el*

importance gravitated from the key position (head) to a functional one (spreading peace). The significance of Ceballos's metaphor lies in his understanding of the king as being in service to the body politic, to the church, and to natural law, rather than in a more exalted position of absolute authority.

To *teresianos,* therefore, electing Teresa as patron constituted an act of service for the benefit of all the Spanish people, part of the king's obligation. While *santiaguistas* offered similar ideas about the central tenets of good kingship and viewed the choice of a patron saint as integral to the nation's common good, they vehemently denied that Teresa's elevation would accomplish such good. When *santiaguista* churches refused to celebrate Teresa's feast day, they began to produce treatises that justified and defended their defiance of the royal decree using terms and arguments similar to those of their opponents, but to very different effect. Juan González Centeno, a canon in the cathedral of Seville, wrote, "A well-governed Christian Republic is one that supports these two poles consistently—belief and faith, the doctrine of the Gospels and of the saints, and government, reason, law, justice, and reward. If this new patronage does not lead to faith, does not conform to reason, is not founded on justice, it will erode the integrity of the law. . . . What reason can there be that this matter would go forward amidst such uproar?"[39]

González's language here echoes Juan de la Asunción's, since both agreed that a Christian republic owed its prosperity and stability to upholding faith and justice. Yet, for González, Teresa's elevation failed to support to either pillar; its only result, therefore, could be the erosion of the foundations of the republic. The "uproar" he mentions provided the strongest evidence of the deleterious effects of co-patronage, since an act of bad government resulted in acrimony and dissent in the republic.

But denouncing co-patronage as corrosive supplied *santiaguistas* with only part of their defense for refusing to celebrate Teresa's feast day; they also needed to explain how their refusal to act on an order of the king in no way constituted disloyalty. They approached this issue chiefly by appealing to the ancient right of the loyal vassal to offer counsel to the king. While the medieval language might seem archaic, the right was deeply held and frequently invoked in early modern Spain, largely because it provided a language of loyal resistance. Those who disagreed

---

gouierno tienen sus vezes (Barcelona: Lorenzo Deu, 1619). See also Pedro Fernández Navarrete, *Conservación de monarquías y discursos políticos* (1626), ed. Michael Gordon (Madrid: Instituto de Estudios Fiscales, 1982), 181.

39. Juan González Centeno, *Tres Puntos en que se resuelve lo que a Santiago Apostol compete por Patrono de España* (ca. 1628), BNM, MS 9140, fol. 121v.

with the king could thus portray themselves as obedient while simultaneously refusing to carry out a royal command. Such a refusal in Castile
most often entailed what was called "obeying, but not complying" (obe-
dezco, sino no cumplo); the individual or group would assert loyalty and
obedience to the Crown while simultaneously refusing to fulfill a particular royal order, usually stipulating that the group's right to counsel had
been violated and that compliance could occur only after counsel.[40] Key
to this formula was that it permitted those who invoked it simultaneously to insist on their obedience to the royal will. This tradition acted
as a check to royal authority and helped to foster a lively tradition of
debate about policies, reforms, controversies, and problems plaguing the
monarchy, including co-patronage.

Santiaguista treatises directed at the king's support of co-patronage
thus contained two main parts: a denunciation of co-patronage as an act
of bad kingship, and something a loyal vassal had the duty to refute as
such. The brilliant satirist and Golden Age luminary Francisco de Quevedo y Villegas, for example, explained to the king why it was necessary
for him to speak out against the king's desire for Teresa's elevation. In his
treatise—part apology, part declaration—Quevedo argued that while a
vassal was obliged to obey the will of the king, it was also "the obligation
of the vassal to inform your Majesty of the reasons why this co-patronage is not and cannot be a licit gift."[41] He then referred to a printed
letter to Philip from the cathedral chapter in Badajoz; the letter explained
that while the chapter had celebrated Teresa's feast day, it would not do
so again. The cathedral chapter insisted that it was "in obedience to your
Majesty" but added that its obedience remained "against our consent."[42]
The archbishop of Seville, Pedro de Castro, made a similar point, insisting that he always obeyed the king's orders but could "better complete"
these orders if he first gave the king his opinion on the matter.[43] The
duties of the vassal in these instances were twofold: first, to obey the
king, regardless of the individual's feelings about the decree, and second,
to inform the king in all honesty that he disagreed with the royal command and to explain why, in the hope that this information might produce a revocation. Obedience, it is important to note, did not necessarily

40. Ruth Mackay, The Limits of Royal Authority: Resistance and Obedience in Seventeenth-Century
Castile, Cambridge Studies in Early Modern History (Cambridge: Cambridge University Press, 1999),
1–3. See also Elliott, "Self-Perception and Decline," in Spain and Its World, 243.

41. Quevedo, "Su espada por Santiago," 427–28.

42. Ibid., 428 (emphasis added). Quevedo provided an exact quotation. This letter was printed
in "Copia de la carta que la santa Iglesia de Badajoz escribió a la Majestad del Rey D. Felipe IIII
nuestro Señor, tocante al pretenso Patronazgo de santa Theresa de Iesus" (1628). Two copies have
been preserved, one at RAH, Col. Salazar y Castro, MS 9/1032, fol. 70r–v, and the other at ACSC,
IG 301 (57).

43. Castro to Philip III, 4 September 1618, BNM, MS 1749, fol. 421r.

entail compliance. Pedro de Losada y Quiroga, canon of the cathedral chapter of Jaén, further refined such arguments, claiming, "Those who implement the laws first are not the most obedient; rather, [the most obedient] are those who try to put them right; the first group wish to seem obedient, but they are superficially obedient."[44] From his perspective, obedience transcended the mere act of compliance with the laws. The true nature of obedience required that a subject examine the good of the law and report any concerns or disagreement to the prince; compliance or noncompliance was secondary.[45] Such an understanding of relations between monarch and subject (or king and vassal) provided for the possibility of dynamic exchange between the two parties and gave subjects, whether through the Cortes or individually, a powerful tool for political involvement and activity beyond the boundaries of the royal councils.

In addition to invoking the traditional right of counsel, *santiaguistas* drew from political theory models that stressed the importance of continuity and tradition in kingship. The jurist Fernando de Mera Carvajal cited the example of Philip III's cessation of the 1618 co-patronage festivals in order to draw attention to the central role of tradition in the exercise of royal authority:

> In the time of the holy king Philip III our lord, this novelty began, but it was opposed by the ecclesiastical estate, which . . . asked his Majesty not to support it. . . . His Majesty ordered a council of the prelates and learned people to discuss this matter . . . and so the king [Philip IV] ought to impose perpetual silence on this matter, to execute a new decree, and to fulfill the royal word of his glorious father; for even though his [Philip III's] natural body had expired with his death, his intellect and the name of king, which is where his power lies . . . , lives, remains, and shines forth in his Catholic Majesty, as his son and successor. And in this way his word . . . produces a perpetual obligation.[46]

Mera's words offered a lesson on the essence of royal power: The office of the king was understood, at least in part, as something separate

44. Pedro de Losada y Quiroga, *Al illustrissimo y reverendissimo Señor Arzobispo y al Dean y Cabildo de la Santa Iglesia Metropolitana del Apostol Santiago* (1628), BNM, MS 9140, fol. 70v.

45. This idea is echoed in *Las Siete Partidas,* which states, "For not withstanding the law is a good and noble thing, the more it is deliberated upon and carefully examined, the better and more stable it is." *Las Siete Partidas,* ed. Robert I. Burns, trans. Samuel Parsons Scott, vol. 1 (Philadelphia: University of Pennsylvania Press, 2001), 6.

46. Fernando de Mera Carvajal, *Informacion en derecho por el unico y singular Patronato del glorioso Apostol Santiago Zebedeo, Patron, y Capitan general de las Españas con la sagrada Religion de Carmelitas descalços sobre el nuevo compatronato destos Reynos, que pretende para la gloriosa Virgen santa Teresa de Iesus* (Cuenca: Salvador de Viader, 1628), fol. 25r.

from the physical being of each individual monarch. While each king might die, the power and dignity of the office continued to the next king.[47] Another *santiaguista*, Andrés de Torres, declared, "Princes must fulfill the obligations of their vows and the promises made to God in their name by their ancestors."[48] According to both authors, therefore, laws and vows made by one king were passed to his successor along with the royal office. Each king had the right to issue new decrees, but he also had to be mindful of the existing laws and traditions of the kingdom, which he had no right to circumvent or ignore. Tradition and custom thus acted as important restraints on absolute royal authority in early modern Spain.

When tradition and custom were circumvented, or even flouted outright, chaos and divine punishment followed. Pedro González Guijelmo described the consequences starkly: "And now I prove well what harm results in the division of power—what dissension and disruption of the peace go with it!" He followed this admonition with yet another stern warning: "And what wars have been caused by such division between fathers and sons, brothers and neighbors!"[49] In both of these dark forecasts, González predicted that the clash over which saint should be patron would lead to disturbance in the republic, with chaos and civil war the inevitable result.[50] *Santiaguista* logic followed a pattern of inevitable consequence: Co-patronage constituted a violation of a most honored tradition; breaking tradition proceeded from bad kingship; bad kingship led to disorder and disruption; the end result must be chaos and civil war, the ultimate evils for a Christian republic.

The dark vision of Spain's future presented by *santiaguistas* like González reflected a mood of pessimism and disenchantment that some Castilians felt beginning in the early seventeenth century. As I mentioned in chapter 1, men like the *arbitristas* responded to crisis with theories that ranged from spiritual and moral (including the election of a new patron

47. The most important work on the nature of kingship remains Ernst H. Kantorowicz, *The King's Two Bodies: A Study in Mediaeval Political Theology* (Princeton: Princeton University Press, 1957). For an example of Spanish kingship specifically, see the fascinating discussion of Philip II's death in Eire, *From Madrid to Purgatory*, 255–367.

48. Andrés de Torres, *Por el dotor Don Andrés de Torres Abad de Santiago de Peñalba, dignidad y Canonigo de Letura en la santa Iglesia de Astorga: En defensa del unico Patronato del Apostol Santiago, hijo del Trueno, rayo de los enemigos de la Fe. Luz de la Christiandad de España* (Santiago de Compostela: Juan Guixard de León, 1629), 32.

49. González Guijelmo, *Discurso en derecho*, 36–37.

50. González's position fit squarely with contemporary reason-of-state theories. Martín González de Cellorigo warned his readers of the destructive results of social division by citing the example of warfare between Athens and Sparta, which ought to have been at peace. See his *Memorial de la política necesaria y útil restauración a la República de España y estados de ella y del desempeño universal de estos Reinos* (1600), ed. José Pérez de Ayala (Madrid: Instituto de Estudios Fiscales, 1991), 125–27.

saint, or resistance to such an election) to economic and political.[51] Some of the most vocal and well-known *arbitristas* writing in the 1620s became deeply involved in the co-patronage debate, among them Pedro Fernández de Navarrete, Jerónimo de Ceballos, and the political author Juan Pablo Mártir Rizo. The participation of such men in the co-patronage controversy illustrates the extent to which it was absorbed into larger political and economic concerns of the day, not only by those who were natural partisans (for example, a Discalced Carmelite, or a member of the cathedral chapter of Santiago de Compostela) but for a broader world of intellectuals and political thinkers. And while many prominent *arbitristas* developed innovative ideas for safeguarding Spain's future, in the co-patronage controversy they fell staunchly into the *santiaguista* camp.

Pedro Fernández de Navarrete is best known for his 1626 *arbitrio, Conservación de monarquías y discursos políticos* (The Conservation of the Monarchy and Political Discourses), in which he outlined the greatest economic problems facing the Spanish monarchies and offered potential remedies for them.[52] His involvement in the co-patronage debate stemmed largely from his position during the late 1620s as a canon in the cathedral of Santiago, as well as its representative in the royal court. In Madrid he advocated for the revocation of Teresa's patronage, among other issues.[53] In October 1627 the cathedral chapter acknowledged its gratitude for the support of the well-respected author, telling him, "We console ourselves that we have you in this Court in order to repress these *novedades* [novelties] . . . not only as our brother, but also because of your talent, capacity, education, and moreover because you share the same desire."[54]

The Toledan jurist Jerónimo de Ceballos, like Navarrete, was a prolific author of treatises addressing the political, social, and economic problems facing his town and Castile.[55] Ceballos advised on everything from the dangers of leisure, to the evils of selling Spanish raw materials to foreign merchants, to upsetting traditions in favor of novelty. Like Navarrete, he argued against Teresa's patronage. He wrote a letter to the town council of Toledo in 1618, urging it to reject Teresa's election

51. Fortea Pérez, "Economía, arbitrismo y política," 166–75.

52. Fernández Navarrete, *Conservación de monarquías.*

53. For more detailed information regarding Navarrete's relationship with the cathedral of Santiago, see Arturo Iglesias Ortega, "Pedro Fernández de Navarrete, un riojano en la catedral de Santiago," *Berceo* 138 (2000): 91–137. I am deeply indebted to señor Iglesias, who is one of the *técnicos* at the ACSC, for referring me to his article and to Navarrete's connection to the debate.

54. For the full text, see the appendix in ibid., 131.

55. Aranda, *Jerónimo de Ceballos,* 184–87.

for the sake of "the tranquil estate of the Christian Republic."[56] The main thrust of the treatise aimed at eliminating *novedades* in favor of antiquity, which conformed neatly to the content of his political treatises, in which he combined his dislike of novelty with hostility to the church's overabundance of wealth.

The links between reformers and co-patronage are significant to our understanding of both *arbitrismo* and the controversy largely because they demonstrate the overlapping layers of intellectual and political life in the early seventeenth century. Both Navarrete and Ceballos expressed antagonism toward the proliferation of religious festivals and clerical wealth, prominent concerns of the day that affected the way Castilians reacted to Teresa's elevation.[57] The *arbitristas,* like most participants in the co-patronage debate, tended not to be court figures in the service of the king. Rather, they often stood outside royal circles, as prominent men in their native cities who kept keen watch over royal policies that affected their cities and the nation as a whole. From Toledo, Seville, Valladolid, and Burgos, they viewed the choice of national patron saint as critical to Spain's future.

Santiaguistas, whether *arbitristas* or not, understood themselves as playing an important role in safeguarding the Spanish nation from ill-considered ideas, innovations, and policies. Alonso de Serna insisted that "the disquiet and rumors in a large part of this kingdom have resurged with the new patronage. . . . They are not the effects of the disobedience of Spain, which out of all the parts of the monarchy is the most loyal and devoted to your Majesty. They are the effects instead of this novelty."[58] One of Serna's main purposes here was to defend the *santiaguista* refusal to celebrate Teresa's feast day, on the grounds that the "disquiet and rumors" stemmed not from disobedience but from Teresa's elevation. "Spain," Serna claimed, could not be disobedient; it was in fact the most loyal of all the monarch's kingdoms. By creating distinct groups—Spain and the adherents of novelty—Serna excluded supporters of co-patronage from "Spain" as well as from loyalty and obedience. Thus he claimed uniform opposition to co-patronage among all "true" Spaniards. He also depicted the apostle's supporters not as a loosely affiliated group of individuals but as a unified group—Spain—distinct from the king, who oversaw a monarchy that encompassed additional territories.

56. Ceballos, "Parecer contra el patronazgo de España de la Madre Teresa de Jesús," in ibid., 378.

57. This issue is discussed in greater detail in chapter 6.

58. Serna, "Carta al Rey sobre el patronato," BNM, MS 9140, fol. 72r.

The separation of Spain from the monarch and monarchy emphasized the distinction between royal authority and tradition that was crucial to the *santiaguista* position. While royal authority and tradition were
not inherently or necessarily in opposition to each other (indeed, the
interests of the common good dictated that they be in harmony), the
frequency with which *santiaguistas* invoked the superiority of tradition
in the matter of patron sainthood transformed it into a powerful tool for
defending the Spanish nation against the misuse of royal authority. Many
santiaguistas went so far as to declare that the question of co-patronage
lay outside royal jurisdiction altogether. Losada stated quite clearly that
choosing a patron saint was "not in the power of any earthly prince."[59]
History and tradition revealed God's choice to intercede for the Spanish;
it was not a decision or a decree made by a terrestrial king or a representative body like the Cortes.

Responding to a *teresiano* argument that Santiago's patron sainthood
had in fact resulted from the decision of an earthly prince (in this case,
Ramiro's vow to the apostle following the battle of Clavijo), Quevedo
argued that the apostle's appearance at Clavijo served only as *proof* of
his patronage but did not mark its inception. Ramiro's ninth-century
vow had only confirmed what God had previously mandated.[60] Quevedo contended that Santiago's patronage was a position the apostle
held by divine right, stemming from his evangelization of Spain, and
therefore one he had held for sixteen hundred years. By connecting Santiago's patronage with his conversion of Spain rather than with the battle
of Clavijo, Quevedo drew on the wealth of sixteenth-century histories
that saw Santiago's evangelization as Spain's most important moment
and the apostle as the spiritual originator of the Spanish nation. The role
that the apostle played in Spanish history and tradition meant that, for
Quevedo, the current monarch had no right to alter his status; "Spain,"
as a historical and cultural entity that had existed for a millennium and a
half, maintained traditions that predated the Habsburg dynasty by fifteen
centuries (even if official genealogies traced their lineage to the Visigothic kings). The nation, according to Quevedo, had the right to maintain its own patron saint, no matter what the king thought. He, like
Serna, believed adamantly that to support Santiago and to be Spanish
were one and the same thing; in one letter to the Compostelan cathedral,

59. Losada proclaimed that appointing patrons "no estan en potestad de los Principes de la
tierra." Losada y Quiroga, *Defensa del unico y singular Patronazgo de las Españas, perteneciente al
glorioso Apostol Santiago Zebedeo* (Santiago de Compostela: Juan de León, 1628), 27.

60. Quevedo, "Su espada por Santiago," 433.

Quevedo proclaimed himself in "vassalage" to the apostle and claimed that to support Santiago's cause was "to be Spanish."[61]

Supporters of Santiago, therefore, attempted to divide dynastic from national cults, in spite of Philip's efforts to harmonize them. While dynastic and national cults often began as the same—that is, as cults associated with a king and disseminated through royal devotion—the permeation of royal cults beyond the family itself could in fact undermine, rather than enhance, royal authority. Cults associated with specific dynasties could be employed for the purposes of royal propaganda, but national saints represented all the people of the nation, not just the king and his family. As Gabór Klaniczay observes, such "saints ceased to be the agents of dynastic prestige, and were transformed into genuine national symbols, symbols which could, if need be, be turned against the dynasty itself."[62] A national patron saint, therefore, need not uphold royal prerogatives or dynastic claims. In fact, the saint could be mobilized in favor of competing visions of the nation from the one presented by the king or monarchy.

Tensions over the national patron could very quickly spill over into other realms of royal policy, particularly during a period of crisis and uncertainty. During the key years of the co-patronage debate, anger over the economic state of Castile and the monarchy's faltering foreign policies pervaded the court. In fact, the gloom that descended on Madrid during the king's near-mortal illness of August–September 1627 did not necessarily result from fear that he might die, despite *teresianos'* triumphant depictions of the event. Foreign observers at court reported that the masses ordered for the king's return to health were very poorly attended.[63] Few were sure they wanted him to recover.[64] Court chronicler Matías de Novoa claimed with some malice that many hoped for the king's death "in order to be liberated from the hands of the count of Olivares."[65] John Elliott has pointed out that the years 1627–30 were the

---

61. Quevedo to cathedral chapter, 1 February 1628, in Quevedo y Villegas, *La epistolario completo de Francisco de Quevedo,* ed. Luis Astrana Marín (Madrid: Instituto Editorial Reus, 1946), 177–79. "Por esta causa el ser español. Me pone en el vasallaje de nuestro unico i solo patron Santiago."

62. Klaniczay, *Holy Rulers and Blessed Princesses,* 367.

63. Elliott, *Count-Duke of Olivares,* 312. Elliott cites a dispatch from an Italian ambassador in this connection.

64. The papal legate reported back to Rome on the "little love" the Spanish people felt for Philip. Nuncio Pamphilio to papal secretary, 28 August 1627, ASV, Segreterio di Stato, Nunz. Diversi, vol. 120, fol. 25v.

65. Novoa, *Historia de Felipe IV,* 57–62. "Todos los deseos de los vasallos están contra la salud y vida de VM, deseándole la muerte por librarse de la manos del conde de Olivares" (62). The papal legate also reported on the "great hatred" felt at court for Olivares. Nuncio Pamphilio to the secretary of state, 1 September 1627, ASV, Segreterio di Stato, Nunz. Diversi, vol. 120, fol. 29r.

most critical and dangerous for Olivares and his position. The king's illness revealed to Olivares the true extent of nobles' hostility toward him, which was exacerbated by a bankruptcy of the royal government in 1627 and the Spanish monarchy's instigation of an ultimately humiliating struggle with France over the succession to Mantua in Italy.[66] A vicious anti-Olivares treatise addressed to the king circulated through the court in manuscript during the same period. Its anonymous author proclaimed that Olivares's ambition and the tyranny of his rule would bring ruin on the king and his country. He advised that the king follow the example of his grandfather and great-grandfather and rule absolutely and alone. Furthermore, he blasted Philip's ineffective rule, declaring, "You are not a king" and exhorting Philip to look to the crisis in his kingdoms and to take control of the situation before it was too late.[67]

The increasing hostility directed at the count-duke created a highly charged atmosphere for in the introduction of Teresa's patron sainthood. While Olivares did not waver in his support for Teresa's elevation, his advocacy transformed the election into a lightning rod for his detractors. Quevedo's controversial treatises against co-patronage afford the best illustration of the political forces at work in the controversy. For much of the 1620s Quevedo enjoyed a somewhat unlikely alliance with the count-duke. While scholars have put much emphasis on the disintegration of their relationship in subsequent decades, it is important to keep in mind that, at the outset of the co-patronage debate and for several years afterward, the two men worked together.[68] Matías de Novoa described their alliance with typical cynicism, claiming that the "great friendship" that seemed to exist between the two stemmed solely from Olivares's fear of Quevedo's satirical powers.

Quevedo's opposition to the elevation of Teresa caused considerable stress in their relationship. The first treatise published by Quevedo, "Memorial en defensa del unico patronato de Santiago" (Memorial in Defense of the Unique Patronage of Santiago), probably in February

66. John H. Elliott, *Richelieu and Olivares* (Cambridge: Cambridge University Press, 1984), 90–95; and Elliott, "Foreign Policy and Domestic Crisis: Spain, 1598–1659," in Elliott, *Spain and Its World*, 125–27. Thompson agrees with Elliott's assessment, observing that the crisis of 1627 provoked Olivares into taking "an increasingly authoritarian approach" and mounting an aggressive campaign of propaganda. Thompson, "The Government of Spain in the Reign of Philip IV," in *Crown and Cortes*, 31–32.

67. Novoa, *Historia de Felipe IV*, 74–76. This was not the only manifestation of antigovernment feeling at the time; the papal nuncio noted that "infinite speeches [were] given freely against the government." Nuncio Pamphilio to the secretary of state, 4 September 1627, Biblioteca Apostolica Vaticana, Fondo Barberini (Latini), MS 8331, fol. 7r.

68. For an important study of Quevedo's relationship with Olivares, see Elliott, "Quevedo and the Count-Duke of Olivares," in *Spain and Its World*, 189–209.

1628, was followed shortly by the more elaborate and argumentative "Su espada por Santiago" (His Sword for Santiago), sometime in early May. Quevedo had multiple motivations for producing these two treatises: he was a knight of Santiago, Spain's noblest and most prestigious knighthood; he continually expressed deep loyalty to Spain's long-held traditions; and he maintained a close relationship with the cathedral chapter in Santiago, which has led some historians to speculate that he was paid a commission by the chapter for his works.[69] In one of several surviving letters from the cathedral chapter of Santiago to Quevedo from January 1628, the chapter thanked Quevedo for his ardent support of Santiago, declaring that his talent would enable him to restore with his pen what the Carmelites had tried to destroy with their artifice.[70] With this lovely juxtaposition of Quevedo's inherent talent (true art) and the Carmelites' artificial machinations (false art), the cathedral chapter appealed to Quevedo's pride in his knighthood and skill as a writer.

On 27 February 1628, the new archbishop of Santiago, José González, sent Quevedo a letter acknowledging receipt of a copy of his "Memorial" and thanking him for his excellent defense of Santiago's patronage.[71] This is the first letter to Quevedo on the topic of co-patronage that addressed his work specifically by title; therefore, one can tentatively date the publication of the treatise to February 1628. The combination of Quevedo's literary fame, the excellence of the work, and the heated nature of the controversy made this treatise the most important produced by the debate, followed by his next treatise. Copies of the treatise spread rapidly throughout Castile. Quevedo received a series of letters from readers throughout the kingdom, either thanking or deriding him for his memorial. In addition to preserving a list of those who read and appreciated (or were angered by) Quevedo's work, this series of letters gives us a picture of its geographical dissemination. For example, the archbishop in Santiago, unsurprisingly, had a copy at the end of February. Sister Beatriz de Jesús, the prioress of the Discalced Carmelite monastery in Madrid and a niece of Teresa's, had read one by 5 March;

69. José Ma. Díaz Fernández, "Quevedo y el cabildo de la catedral de Santiago," in *Estudios sobre Quevedo: Quevedo desde Santiago entre dos aniversarios,* ed. Santiago Fernández Mosquera (Santiago de Compostela: Universidad de Santiago de Compostela, 1995), 105–18.

70. Cathedral chapter to Quevedo, 16 January 1628, in Quevedo, "Epistolario," in *Obras de don Francisco de Quevedo Villegas,* BAE 48, 539. RAH, Col. Salazar y Castro, MS 9/1032, houses many manuscript copies of Quevedo's letters.

71. Quevedo, "Epistolario," 539–40. González specifically names the archdeacon Santiago Sanz del Castillo as the one who gave him the treatise.

two days later, canons from the cathedral in Toledo were writing Quevedo both to congratulate him on his work and to support his position.[72] Shortly thereafter, a rector from the University of Alcalá, Rodrigo Gutiérrez, penned words of support and encouragement.[73] Juan de Salinas, a monk from Seville, wrote Quevedo a similar letter also at the beginning of March; by the end of the month, two additional letters were sent from Andalusia, this time Granada, one of them from the prioress of the *comendadoras* of Santiago.[74] One can see by following this pattern of epistles that Quevedo's treatise had spread within a month to all regions of Castile.

The popularity of Quevedo's work no doubt exacerbated the irritation felt by Olivares at his ally's defection. It is not clear whether words passed between them after the February publication of his "Memorial," but Quevedo did include a letter to Olivares in his preface to the follow-up treatise, "Su espada por Santiago," in which he attempted to explain his reasons and to appease the count-duke. He insisted that his motivation for writing the second treatise lay in the need to clear his name of false accusations and correct false claims put forward in *teresiano* works.[75] Getting his new treatise into Olivares's hands was another matter entirely. One of the influential men who served as an intermediary between Olivares and Quevedo was the powerful governor of the archbishopric of Toledo, Álvaro de Villegas.[76] Quevedo sent a copy of his treatise to Álvaro with a letter that asked the governor to pass it along to Olivares. In mid-May Álvaro sent the treatise back to Quevedo, unopened, with a letter letting the author know in no uncertain terms that he had aroused Olivares's wrath. He also gave the author a brief lecture on the election of patron saints, which testified to his own support of co-patronage.[77]

72. Sor Beatriz to Quevedo, 5 March 1628, RAH, Col. Salazar y Castro, MS 9/1032, fol. 52 r.–v. Quevedo received two letters from Toledo dated 7 March, one from Alvaro de Monsalve alone and one from Monsalve and Pedro de Rosales, on behalf of the cathedral chapter. Both can be found in ibid., fols. 24r and 19r, respectively.

73. Rodrigo Gutiérrez to Quevedo, 13 March 1628, ibid., fol. 21r.

74. Juan de Salinas to Quevedo, 7 March 1628, ibid., fol. 28r; Mendo de Benavides to Quevedo, 21 March 1628, ibid., fol. 29r; and doña Jerónima de Gaona to Quevedo, 27 March 1628, ibid., fol. 26r.

75. Quevedo, "Su espada por Santiago," 421–23.

76. Elliott, "Quevedo and the Count-Duke of Olivares," in *Spain and Its World,* 194. Elliott calls Álvaro de Villegas one of Olivares's "closest confidents" and presumes that he was a relative of Quevedo's.

77. Álvaro de Villegas to Quevedo, 18 May 1628, RAH, Col. Salazar y Castro, MS 9/1032, fol. 22r.–v.

At some point in the spring of 1628, Quevedo had been sent away from court, confined to the village of Torre de Abad Juan, where he apparently remained while writing "Su espada por Santiago." His seventeenth-century biographer, Pablo Antonio de Tarsia, passed over the incident briefly, commenting only that Quevedo suffered a period of difficulty in 1628 after the king banished him from court.[78] Several Quevedian scholars have connected his stay in Torre that spring with the wrath he incurred for his co-patronage treatise. One such biographer, Luis Astrana Marín, uncovered and printed excerpts of three letters regarding Quevedo and his calamities at court, as transmitted by Juan Jacobo Chifflet in Brussels to the papal nuncio in France, Juan Francisco Bagni. Chifflet explained to Bagni that his friend Quevedo had been ordered to leave the court by an enraged Olivares. Quevedo had complied, then returned to Madrid, presenting himself to the king and begging for mercy; the king sided with Olivares, who sent the troublesome author away again, this time interning him in a "tiny village" as a prison. Chifflet also mentioned that he had read Quevedo's work on Santiago's patronage and that he had received word from Spain that twenty-two pamphlets had already come to light on the topic but that he had seen only one, which he dutifully sent on to a Jesuit brother of his in Bologna.[79]

As Chifflet's foreign sources attest, Quevedo's work was as widely read as it was controversial. The combination of his works, political exile, and literary fame led to an explosion of printed responses, both critical and supportive, throughout Castile.[80] In spite of this spectacular scandal, little concrete information about how the co-patronage debate unfolded in the complex political atmosphere at court has survived. The sparse information we have comes largely from the Compostelan cathedral, which had organized a campaign to win the king's loyalty back to

---

78. Pablo Antonio de Tarsia, *Vida de don Francisco de Quevedo y Villegas* (1663), ed. Felipe B. Pedraza Jiménez (Aranjuez: Editorial Ara Iovis, 1988), 93–94. Tarsia says that Quevedo was invited to return to court with an official letter from the president of the Council of Castile at the end of December 1628.

79. Astrana Marín, *Vida turbulenta de Quevedo*, 393. Astrana obviously hispanized their names; in addition, he provided no proof of the provenance of the letters. John Elliott disputes Astrana's explanation of Quevedo's confinement in the context of the co-patronage debate, arguing instead that the banishment was the result of rumors circulating at court that *Política de Dios* contained anti-Olivares messages. Elliott, "Quevedo and the Count-Duke of Olivares," in *Spain and Its World*, 193–94.

80. Morovelli de Puebla launched the most bitter attack on Quevedo, which in turn provoked a series of responses, among them Reginaldus Vicencius, *Respuesta al papel de Don Francisco Morovelli, sobre el patronato de Santa Teresa* (Málaga: Juan René, 1628), fol. 3v; and *Memorial de Advertencias al papel que Don Francisco Morovelli imprimio derechamente contra don Francisco de Quevedo, y su Memorial en defensa de Santiago, y de recudida contra don Francisco Melgar, doctoral de Sevilla: y los demas* (Málaga: Juan René, 1628), fols. 1v–2r.

the apostle in the autumn of 1627. While the cathedral also had people at the papal curia working to undo the 1627 brief, from the autumn of 1627 to the spring of 1628, *santiaguista* hopes remained pinned on the royal court and the possibility of persuading the king and Olivares to change their minds.[81] The cathedral confessed to its ally, the chapter in Seville, that it had sent dignitaries to the court whose job it was to work for the revocation of the brief at any expense.[82] Writing to its secretary, Pedro Fernández Navarrete, the cathedral identified these dignitaries: the archdeacon of Santiago, Santiago Sanz del Castillo, Cardinal Alonso Rodríguez de León, and prior Gaspar Garnica. Rodríguez's job was to collect all the writings for Santiago "with those that can be found in this Court," in order to mount a more persuasive defense.[83]

With its delegates and those of its allies assembled at court, the cathedral of Santiago began its efforts to rally as much support in Madrid as it could, writing letters to royal councils, the king, Olivares, and Navarrete.[84] Subsequent letters of persuasion were sent to the king's confessor, Antonio de Sotomayer, the president of the Council of Castile Cardinal Trejo, the royal chronicler Tomás Tamayo y Vargas, the count of Lemos, and Álvaro de Villegas. These strategic choices reflect the cathedral's calculated attempts to reach people in close proximity to the king in order to obtain a royal audience.[85] They did not always win the support of the men to whom they wrote. While Tamayo was hired to write a treatise for the cathedral (printed anonymously) and the count of Lemos seems to have sympathized with the *santiaguista* cause, Álvaro remained staunchly allied with Olivares. The cathedral chapter remarked rather snidely to their representatives at court that Álvaro maintained a "particular interest" in the Discalced Carmelites.[86]

81. Compostelan chapter to don Gaspar Ortega de Villar, 22 October 1627, ACSC, IG 940, fols. 242v–243r.

82. Compostelan chapter to chapter of Seville, 19 December 1627, BCC, 9.147.6 (2).

83. Compostelan chapter to Navarrete, 26 October 1627, quoted in Iglesias Ortega, "Pedro Fernández de Navarrete," 131. The chapter made note of Rodríguez's importance to its cause in the court in a letter to the cathedral in Seville, 17 December 1628, BCC, 9.147.6 (2). Rodríguez also wrote a treatise in defense of the apostle called *Carta a su Magestad que suplica que cerca del unico y singular titulo de Patron destos Reinos de España*.

84. Compostelan chapter to Philip IV, 16 October 1627, ACSC, IG 940, fols. 239v–240r; Compostelan chapter to Council of Orders and Inquisition, 16 October 1627, ibid., fol. 241r–v; chapter to Navarrete, 26 October 1627, ibid., fols. 246v–247r; and chapter to Olivares, 26 October 1627, ibid., fol. 249v.

85. Letters to Sotomayer, Trejo, Tamayo, and Lemos, ibid., fol. 252v, fols. 253v–254r, 270v, 271v–272r, respectively. The letter to Álvaro of 13 December 1628 can be found in ACSC, IG 941, fols. 9v–10r.

86. Compostelan chapter to legates at court, 2 January 1628, ACSC, IG 941, fol. 10r–v. For a reference to Lemos's support, see chapter to Gaspar Ortega, 19 December, 1627, ibid., fol. 12r–v; this letter reads, "entre los valedores que VM tiene es el major Sor Conde de Lemos."

In spite of this letter-writing campaign to the king's close advisors and the work of the legates at the court throughout the fall and early winter of 1627, it was not until the middle of January 1628 that they achieved their long-sought audience with Olivares. When the meeting occurred, the cathedral believed it gained ground with Olivares, who purportedly confessed that he would not have pushed Teresa's elevation had he known what opposition it would arouse. The two sides began a negotiation in an attempt to find a compromise position between patron saint of Spain and nothing; the *santiaguista* delegates put forth an offer that Teresa be declared *abogada* (advocate) rather than *patrona*, which could allow both sides to claim victory. The delegates appear to have made this offer without receiving prior approval from the cathedral of Santiago. The cathedral expressed its relief that the offer was refused and admitted that it had no desire to concede to Teresa the title of *abogada universal* any more than it wanted her to be patron.[87] It would not make any concession to Teresa's cult other than the liturgy of the virgins assigned to her by the pope at her canonization.[88]

Despite Olivares's refusal to back down, the cathedral's legates found many sympathetic ears at court. Possibly inspired by Quevedo's memorial, some of the members of the Council of Castile initially refused to attend festivals held for Teresa in Madrid.[89] Perhaps delighted to find another method of antagonizing Olivares, the council later issued Quevedo a royal license to have his works opposing co-patronage printed in Castile.[90] Both of these decisions no doubt earned the council the count-duke's ire, which was almost certainly their intention, though it appears that recalcitrant members were nevertheless eventually compelled to attend the 1627 festivities. While genuine feeling over the issue of co-patronage may have played a role in motivating the council's actions, it was also involved in highly contentious negotiations with Olivares over royal finances throughout the fall of 1627.[91] The council's president, Cardinal Trejo, had been appointed by Olivares himself, but the two wrangled continually until Olivares concocted a scheme to have

87. Compostelan chapter to legates in Madrid, 16 January 1628, ibid., fols. 18v–19v.

88. Compostelan chapter to legates, 23 January 1628, ibid., fols. 21v–22v: "sin estenerse a cosa alguna, ni concession de otra veneracion a la sancta, sino quella que en el choro de las virgines de dar Romana Iglesia."

89. Archivo Histórico Nacional, Madrid, consejos, leg. 7145, expediente 34, consulta, 9 October.

90. *Memorial de Advertencias al papel que Don Francisco Morovelli*, fol. 7v. "Quando en la Corte se celebró el patronato de S. Teresa, los Consejos no quisieron hallarse en la procession y fiesta; y aviendose visto en la Real Consejo pleno el memorial de don Francisco de Quevedo, y leydole todo de comun acuerdo le aprobaron y dieron licencia para imprimirle."

91. Elliott places the council's refusal to attend in the larger context of arguments with the king over finances. *Count-Duke of Olivares*, 323.

Trejo removed. In 1629 Olivares invoked the absentee-bishop rule against Trejo to force him back to his bishopric in Andalusia.[92] Thus the council's sometimes acrimonious relationship with Olivares reflected the general dissatisfaction, even hostility, that his ministry faced. His enemies used any weapon against him they could find, even Teresa's elevation. Resistance to co-patronage on some level necessarily entailed resistance to Olivares, and vice versa.

Hostility to Olivares's ministry stemmed from more than dislike for his specific policies; it also drew on a long history of hatred for favorites in Spanish political culture. Opponents believed that it reduced royal majesty for the king to share his power; moreover, they feared such power sharing would result in increased factionalization and political corruption. As we have seen, Philip III's favorite, the duke of Lerma, drew bitter criticism and was eventually driven from power. Political theorists who distrusted the power of the favorite and his control over affairs of state conceived of the position as something unnatural and unhealthy, bad for both king and kingdom. In addition, favorites could act as lightning rods, absorbing dislike of royal policies for the monarch. One of the best-known *arbitristas* of the early seventeenth century, Juan de Santa María, blasted Lerma's rule in his book of advice to kings: "And would it not be a great monstrosity to have a body with two heads? So it would be a much greater one to have two people govern a kingdom. . . . Unity is the beginning of much good and plurality causes many evils."[93] Here Juan stresses the terrible consequences of favorites by invoking a distorted and monstrous body politic—an unnatural and potentially life-threatening deformation of nature and a danger to prosperity.

The image of the two-headed monster made numerous appearances in treatises that opposed co-patronage, as *santiaguista* authors employed political language to emphasize the disorder that would result from having two patron saints. For example, Mera lamented that in order for a body to be well governed, a head needed to be a head, an arm an arm, and that if all the body parts were to be the head, the result would be a monstrosity.[94] Authors like Mera asserted that the apostle's loss of status

---

92. On Olivares's contentious relationship with Trejo, see ibid., 393–94.

93. Juan de Santa María, *Republica y policia christiana*, fol. 4r–v. Antonio Feros calls Juan de Santa María's *República y policía cristiana* "the finest and most influential attempt by Lerma's opponents to challenge the political discourse he had promoted." *Kingship and Favoritism*, 236.

94. Fernando de Mera Carvajal, *Informacion en derecho, por el estado eclesiastico de las coronas de Castilla y León, con la sagrada Religion del Carmen descalço, . . . sobre quitar el reço de Patrona de España a gloriosa Virgen santa Theresa de Iesus, y borrar las insignias y blasones deste Patronato* (Cuenca: Salvador de Viader, 1631), fol. 15v. For another example, see González Guijelmo, *Discurso en derecho*, 36;

as the singular patron saint of Spain constituted a grave insult to his cult, because singularity represented the highest and most effective form of leadership. One anonymous author, who wrote under the pseudonym Reginaldus Vicencius, argued that the metaphor of the body politic applied as well to the mystical body as it did to the natural one; both drew strength and prestige from singularity.[95] Yet despite the spiritual context of *santiaguista* metaphors of singularity, they cannot be separated from the political (anti-favorite) discourse of singularity. Any reference to a two-headed monster, whether in Juan de Santa María or in a *santiaguista* treatise, alluded to the king's controversial choice of investing power in the hands of a favorite.

Keeping in mind the protests against Olivares at the time of the king's 1627 illness, the use of images of monstrosity and singularity in *santiaguista* treatises strongly suggests that these authors employed them deliberately as a critique of royal favorites. Alonso Rodríguez de León, for example, contended that singularity in government—one prince or leader whom everyone recognized and obeyed—constituted the highest form of government: "In this way, the sovereignty and majesty of unity consist in being one alone and in not having any equal. . . . And if there is not one alone, then the greatest monarchy falls down one level . . . to plural government and division, which God abhors."[96] While Rodríguez harnessed political language for a spiritual purpose, the passage clearly could be read as a denunciation of plural political authority as well as spiritual, since early modern readers understood that, ideally, the terrestrial should be an image of the celestial. Another *santiaguista* declared baldly that two-headed government would be a "monstrosity," and he directed the reader to a passage in Alfonso X's revered medieval law code, the *Siete Partidas,* which declared that the purpose of an emperor was to unite people under one ruler.[97] Emphasis on the "unique and singular" patronage of Santiago echoed throughout *santiaguista* treatises; such language provided an alternate vision of the terrestrial monarchy, which had strayed into dualism and monstrosity.

Santiaguistas appropriated additional anti-favorite language to apply to co-patronage. Perhaps the best example of such rhetoric comes from

and Rodríguez de León, *Carta a su Magestad,* 17: "y asi como no puede servir una cabeza a dos cuerpos, tampoco puede auer dos cabezas en un cuerpo, que lo uno y el otro seria monstruosidad."

95. Vicencius, *Respuesta al papel de Morovelli,* fol. 8v.

96. Rodríguez de León, *Carta a su Magestad,* 5–6.

97. González Guijelmo, *Discurso en derecho,* 36. He provided a reference to "1 tit. 1 p 2," by which he meant partida 2, title 1, law 1, which discusses the purpose of emperors: "First, to remove discord from among the people and unite them; which could not be done if there were many emperors, because, according to nature, sovereignty does not require a companion, nor does it have need of one." Quoted in Burns, *Siete Partidas,* 1:269.

Pedro de Losada y Quiroga. In his treatise against co-patronage, he provided a stern warning to kings who gave in to bad counsel and refused to change their minds. To illustrate this point he retold a well-known story from the book of Esther in which King Assuero sent out orders to have all the Jews in his kingdom put to death. Shortly thereafter, he recognized the injustice of his action and nullified the order, blaming his decision on bad counsel received from his favorite minister, Aman.[98] At the beginning of the seventeenth century, biblical commentators and political thinkers frequently used this story as the preeminent example of the dangers of bad counsel.[99] When describing Aman's position in the royal government, Losada employed the word *privado,* a Spanish term denoting a minister of special intimacy and power, which was also how Olivares's contemporaries usually described him. Losada said bluntly, "It is a very dangerous doctrine, to council princes."[100] Thus his application of this biblical story worked on two levels simultaneously: First, it acted as a nasty commentary on the deleterious effects of bad favorites; and second, it provided a way to blame Olivares for the co-patronage debacle, thereby absolving Philip of direct responsibility.

Teresianos were quick to address their opponents' critiques of plurality and political favorites. Olivares's support for Teresa created an environment in which it became politically advantageous to support co-patronage, as revealed by the many co-patronage treatises that were dedicated to him. Such dedications most probably represent a traditional blend of sycophancy and the hope for a promotion or some type of royal patronage.[101] In addition, *teresiano* treatises provide some of the richest examples of the defense of Olivares's role as royal favorite by justifying and glorifying co-patronage.[102] Those writing on behalf of co-patronage

98. Losada y Quiroga, *Al illustrissimo y reverendissimo Señor Arzobispo,* fol. 70r–v.

99. Commentaries on the book of Esther always emphasized this lesson as the most important part of the story. For an example of a contemporary commentary, see Gaspar Sánchez, *Gasparis sanctii centumputeolani, e societate Iesu theologi, in collegio complutensi sacrarum literarum interpretis, in libros Ruth, Esdrae, Nehemiae, Tobiae, Iudith, Esther, Machabaeorum Commentarij* (Madrid, 1627). Significantly, the Jesuit scholar dedicated this commentary to Olivares. Elizabeth R. Wright has also noted the use of the Esther story as part of prominent political rhetoric against favorites. See her *Pilgrimage to Patronage: Lope de Vega and the Court of Philip III, 1598–1621* (Lewisburg: Bucknell University Press, 2001), 112–15.

100. Losada y Quiroga, *Al illustrissimo y reverendissimo Señor Arzobispo,* fol. 70r–v.

101. Antonio de Casuallo and Francisco de Morovelli de Puebla dedicated their work to Olivares, as did Francisco de Santa María, because of the "great demonstration and fervent devotion you [Olivares] have for our saint." Francisco de Santa María, *Defensa del Patronato,* fol. 242r.

102. Antonio Feros points out how many historians have neglected to analyze the positive images of plurality, focusing instead on the negative. See his "Images of Evil, Images of Kings: The Contrasting Faces of the Royal Favourite and the Prime Minister in Early Modern European Political Literature, c. 1580–c. 1650," in Elliott and Brockliss, *World of the Favourite,* 205–22.

also used the metaphor of the heavenly kingdom, but in the opposite way from their opponents. Whereas *santiaguista* authors used the political language of singularity to insist that the post of heavenly intercessor ought to follow the same model (presumably because God had ordained singularity of kings), *teresianos* began with images of the heavenly kingdom, and argued that the earthly should follow the celestial example by having plural intercessors. One anonymous *teresiano* compared the saints in heaven to courtiers who were God's friends and admitted into God's presence; access to God's presence enabled the saints to gain God's ear and to ask favors of him.[103] This description of the heavenly court matched court life and etiquette in early seventeenth-century Madrid. The Habsburg kings tended to be invisible for the most part to their subjects, believing that absence was a symbol of majesty. Access to the royal presence, therefore, was severely restricted.[104] As a result, courtiers who had physical access to the king attained enormous power, as they could use this access to ask favors or gifts of the monarch.[105] As laid out by *teresianos*, in the celestial court God took the place of the king, while the courtier-saints were those few worthy beings who had direct access to his divine majesty. In this metaphor, Teresa appears as the courtier with the closest proximity to God; she was, therefore, the Olivares of the allegory.

To *teresianos*, both celestial and terrestrial images of plurality were natural, beneficial, and divinely sanctioned. The king, like God, was too distant to be approached directly; intermediaries and counselors were therefore a necessary part of royal and divine governing. Discalced Carmelite Francisco de Santa María emphasized the connection between heavenly and earthly counselors when he wrote, "Just as God placed [John] the Baptist, the greatest of the prophets, alongside Christ, and placed a Count on the side of the king, making him the greatest of all the nobles, so Spain placed Saint Teresa alongside Santiago."[106] By aligning Teresa and Olivares with John the Baptist, Francisco validated both

---

103. "Copia de una carta que escribio el Arçobispo de Seuilla," fol. 108v. "Porque qualquiera de los santos Bienauenturados es amigo de Dios, Cortesano de su Corte, y que puede mucho con el, y a qualquiera le reuela las oraciones que los fieles les hazemos, y ellos las ofrecen a Dios intercediendo por nosotros."

104. On the Habsburg court, see M. J. Rodríguez-Salgado, "The Court of Philip II," in *Prince, Patronage, and the Nobility: The Court at the Beginning of the Modern Age, c. 1450–1650,* ed. Ronald G. Asch and Adolf M. Birke (Oxford: Oxford University Press, 1991), 205–44.

105. Both Lerma and Olivares gained and held their positions as favorites partly through their careful control over the men and women who held positions in the royal household.

106. Francisco de Santa María, *Defensa del Patronato,* fols. 254v–255r. Antonio Feros points out the prevalence of comparisons between royal favorites and John the Baptist in pro-favorite works. "Images of Evil, Images of Kings," 205.

co-patronage and royal favorites, insisting that God had done the same himself. In addition, Francisco argued forcibly that placing John the Baptist alongside Christ in no way diminished Christ's majesty; plural authority brought honor to both parties. Francisco wrote at length on this point, responding explicitly to *santiaguista* authors who had claimed that the attempt to envision John as a partner to Christ constituted a form of blasphemy (because it assigned Christ's divinity to John). Rather, Francisco based this comparison on the idea that pluralism did not mean equality—the superior honor, dignity, and supremacy of Christ, the king, and Santiago was consistently maintained.

These glimpses of political maneuvering demonstrate how the close association of the king, Olivares, and royal policies with Teresa's elevation infused the liturgical and theological world of patron sainthood with political interests and contests. Resistance to the king's will compelled the *santiaguistas* to tap into an extant discourse on disobedience, disorder, and the limits of royal authority. The *teresianos,* for their part, exploited the fusion of divine and secular to mold co-patronage into part of politically astute reform policy, which would help Spain maintain its strength and status in the world. While each side implemented these ideas to bolster its own position, the use of certain kinds of rhetoric could also be deployed for political purposes, such as the critique of favorites. On a larger scale, the simultaneous proliferation of advice to the king and co-patronage treatises can best be understood in relationship to each other. Each represented a different facet of the same set of political, economic, and social questions that were being tackled in response to a crisis that was both material and ideological.

Disagreements over which patron would most benefit the monarchy revealed layers of bitter conflict over which policies would return the monarchy to its former strength. Both sides of the co-patronage debate agreed that the celestial world ran parallel to the terrestrial. *Santiaguistas* rejected plurality in heaven and on earth. They insisted on the return to earlier models of kingship in which the king accepted advice from a wide array of counselors but did not abdicate royal authority to a favorite. While the system they supported would lead to more consolidated royal authority, it conversely prevented power from being concentrated in one favorite or faction; in this way they advocated for the kind of traditional kingship practiced by Charles V. Tradition also acted as a powerful check to unbridled royal authority and tyranny in early modern Castile, since the king had to take it (along with justice and the general well-being of the monarchy) into consideration before making decisions. *Santiaguistas* like Quevedo and Losada invoked tradition as a way of claiming that the king had no jurisdiction over patron sainthood; thus they were justified in their refusal to comply with the royal order to celebrate Teresa's patron sainthood. They believed both that Santiago's patronage belonged to the Spanish nation, which predated the Habsburg dynasty, and that the king had no right to alter traditions with such deep cultural, historical, and religious meanings.

Teresianos posited a vision of the monarchy in line with current royal policies—plurality in government backed by plurality in heaven. By doing so, they legitimated Olivares's power and provided a dynamic new patron to represent the monarchy. This "newness" reinforced the reform programs initiated by Olivares, both of which were seen as performing the same function: a jump start to help Spain out of its current state of stagnation. In addition, they insisted that Teresa would struggle on Spain's behalf against its contemporary enemies, particularly Protestants in England and the Low Countries. Teresa's role as the spiritual leader of Spain created a powerful new way for Castilians to represent themselves and their nation, at home and abroad.

4

THE GENDER OF FOREIGN POLICY

Internal political issues such as economic policies, the role of the favorite, and the limits of royal authority were not the only pressing issues of
the 1620s that Castilians considered integral to the monarchy's future. As
Antonio Casuallo de Parada advised Olivares in 1628, "We must consider
that Republics have two types of enemies: external and internal."[1] While
internal enemies (a populace riddled with sin) could be threatening,
Casuallo believed that external enemies presented the greater danger.
He claimed that the Spanish monarchy found itself in a period of height-
ened peril, which he traced back to the reign of Philip II and the conquest
of the Americas and Portugal. These conquests had brought great power
and prosperity, but also new threats; as Spain reached its peak of power,
enemies began lurking outside its borders. Such enemies included every
Protestant kingdom as well as France, since they all envied and feared
Spain and lay in wait for any opportunity to act against it. Nevertheless,
Casuallo argued that divine providence had provided help for the monarchy: "This supernatural help was the birth of the glorious mother Saint
Teresa." The timing of Teresa's birth was not a coincidence, according
to Casuallo, who argued that God had given her to Spain when it needed
her miracles and protection most. Thus Teresa's patron sainthood was a

1. Casuallo de Parada, "Discurso Apologetico de dichosa Patrona."

divine gift sent to remedy the urgent problems Spain faced in the new global politics of the seventeenth century.[2]

Casuallo agreed with a group of *teresianos* who insisted that the crises the nation confronted at the beginning of the seventeenth century required a new patron. He and other *teresianos* argued that because Spain's enemies had changed, the nation required a new protector who would defend them from not from the enemies of the past (the Moors) but from the new threat of the Protestant heresy. The focus on heresy was more than ideological; it reflected the primary foreign policy concern of the day—maintaining Spain's hegemonic role in Europe. Teresa's supporters thus interrupted the traditional Spanish historical narrative of Santiago's devotees to create what was for the most part a new historical and spiritual narrative. This narrative was bound to recent events and to the new spiritual, political, and cultural problems the nation now faced. Even those who argued that Teresa would in no way usurp Santiago's place as traditional patron took part in this profound alteration by suggesting that ancient tradition was no longer sufficient to meet present circumstances. The new narrative—and new saint—put forth by supporters of co-patronage created the need for new ways of representing the nation.

This new narrative was in keeping with the new policies being formulated by Olivares and his faction, for they supported a more aggressive approach to maintaining Spain's reputation and impressing foreign enemies with its power. Other political thinkers debated in the royal court and provincial cities whether Castile would be financially able to maintain multiple military engagements. While Olivares's policies yielded a series of successes in 1625 (the so-called *annus mirabilis*), by the end of the decade Spain had suffered a string of defeats, notably the progress of the United Provinces of the Netherlands toward complete independence.[3] France, moreover, long distracted by years of bloody internal religious wars, was beginning to emerge as a powerful new threat to Spanish hegemony, particularly in Italy.

In addition to these concrete political challenges, Spain faced a broader shift in the geopolitical realities of the day, most especially the gradual movement away from the crusade against Islamic North Africa and the Ottoman Empire and toward responding to the changes in the

2. Ibid. According to Casuallo, Teresa's intercession with God fortified the monarchy against external enemies, while her monasteries purified it from within.

3. Elliott refers to the years 1627–29 as a "turning-point in the history of . . . Habsburg Spain to retain its European primacy." Elliott, "Foreign Policy and Domestic Crisis," in *Spain and Its World*, 125. See also Elliott, *Richelieu and Olivares*.

balance of power in Europe. The great era of Spain as the crusading enemy of Islam had ended; after the final expulsion of all *moriscos* (Muslims who had converted to Christianity and their descendants) from the Spanish kingdoms, a process begun in 1609, the descendants of Muslims no longer lived within Spanish borders. The battle of Lepanto (1571) between the Spanish-led Catholic League and the Ottomans marked a period of withdrawal of the giant navies on the Mediterranean and an end to Ottoman naval expansion. At the same time, several European nations, notably France, England, and the Netherlands, reached new levels of prosperity and military might and stood ready to challenge Spain in Europe, the Mediterranean, and the Atlantic. Spain thus looked increasingly to Europe as its primary focus for foreign policy. Spanish monarchs naturally remained concerned about Islamic enemies, particularly the Maghribi pirates who ravaged the Spanish coast and attacked Spanish ships in the Mediterranean. But the early seventeenth century saw a rapid increase in military engagement in Europe and, more significantly, new concerns about maintaining Spanish hegemony there.

It is no coincidence that the same years that witnessed a shift in Spain's place in the European balance of power also gave rise to heated debate over the choice of the nation's patron saint. As Spanish power began to wane, some wondered whether Spain's traditional patron, the Moorslayer, was failing them. Many argued that a new national patron would provide the Spanish with more effective intercession in heaven, as well as a strong new image for the struggling monarchy. Thus, beyond being objects of veneration, national patron saints served other important purposes: As defenders of the nation, they embodied concrete foreign policies and represented Spain's military might and spiritual superiority to the outside world; thus they could help preserve Spain's international reputation. Although a patron saint's role as national representative might have escaped the notice of other European powers, Castilians exhibited almost obsessive concern over how foreigners might view the issue and thus influence Spain's international reputation. The issue of national reputation consumed political thinkers of the early seventeenth century, as they became increasingly convinced that it constituted a key method of maintaining Spain's international holdings.[4] The political theory of reputation in the early modern era held that states that kept their neighbors and subjected territory—whether

---

4. For an excellent discussion of the role of reputation in Spanish foreign policy, see Elliott, "Foreign Policy and Domestic Crisis," 114–36. See also José Alcalá-Zamora and Queipo de Llano, "Zúñiga, Olivares y la política de reputación," in *La España del Conde-Duque de Olivares,* ed. John H. Elliott and Angel García Sanz (Valladolid: Universidad de Valladolid, 1987), 103–8.

friendly or hostile—consistently aware of their power could forestall serious challenges to their hegemony. It was a foreign policy of preemptive deterrence, critically important to the Spanish monarchy, especially at a time when its position as the preeminent European power was being challenged.

Teresa's supporters were quick to fashion an image of their saint as the ideal choice to defend and sustain Spain, but they were not unanimous in their approach to this goal. One group worked to transform Teresa from a saint renowned for her femininity, obedience, and humility into one who embodied strength and military might. For these *teresianos,* the new patron required a complicated gendering that neither denied her femaleness nor equated it with weakness. A second group took a more radical approach, celebrating rather than minimizing Teresa's femininity. This group described her virtuous traits (piety, eloquence, humility, love) as feminine and insisted that such qualities would be key to increasing the strength and reputation of the nation. Those who opposed Teresa's elevation immediately seized on her sex as a primary reason for her ineligibility. Opponents viewed the idea of a female patron as a threat to their collective virility and a sign of weakness on an international scale; they interpreted *teresiano* challenges to Santiago's masculinity as aspersions on their collective masculinity as Spaniards. To these *santiaguistas,* Teresa's patronage (and gender) came to embody all of the dangers of economic decline and international humiliation the monarchy faced at this crossroads in its history. A fierce debate ensued; fueled by Spain's new geopolitical position, the debate seamlessly integrated fears about national decline and gender (dis)order.

In order to present an image of Teresa as a fierce and powerful new protector of the Spanish people, her supporters connected her to two key elements of Spanish messianism—its defense of the Catholic faith and its rejection of Protestant heresy.[5] While these were traditional images of Spain, they also mirrored the monarchy's foreign policy concerns. In the first half of the seventeenth century, Europe was convulsed by its final war of religion, the Thirty Years' War (1618–48). At the same time, the English continued their aid to the Protestant United Provinces in their bid to escape completely from Spanish suzerainty. *Teresianos* seized on their saint's crucial role in the defense of the faith against

---

5. Elliott, "Self-Perception and Decline," in *Spain and Its World,* 246–47. This dynamic was not unique to Spain—France, England, and Portugal all developed strains of messianism that positioned their nations as the new "chosen people."

Lutheran enemies as a central strategy for aligning her with Spain's self-representation as the last upholder of the true faith.

From the beginning, one of the primary motivations for elevating Teresa to national patron sainthood had been her special dominion over eradicating heresy and maintaining orthodoxy. The opposition between Teresa and Luther had been established a decade earlier, during her beatification proceedings, when her supporters had crafted an eschatological vision in which the saint played a central role in aiding the church militant in its struggle against Lutheranism. The primary purpose of such efforts was to portray Teresa as an essential asset to Tridentine reform.[6] The connection between Teresa and the eradication of heresy drew inspiration from the work of the saint herself; in *The Book of Her Life,* she explained that she had founded her monasteries in order to stop the infestation of heresy.[7] Preachers eagerly seized on this theme and made it part of every sermon given in honor of her beatification in 1614.[8] These sermons claimed that Teresa had provided two main forms of spiritual aid: First, she acted as an exemplum of orthodoxy and the miraculous powers of God, and second, she served as a spiritual warrior in the eternal battle against the devil (in this context, Luther and Lutheranism).[9]

The ancient spiritual metaphor of the embattled soul—echoed in Teresa's own *Interior Castle*—was embodied in the sixteenth century by the literal and very bloody battles between religious sects throughout the heart of Europe.[10] In response to these battles, Teresa's supporters described their saint's contribution to the church in the language of armies and soldiers. Alonso de Villegas, a canon from Toledo, described Teresa's gifts of chastity, poverty, obedience, and prayer as "arms,"

6. For an excellent example of the same phenomenon in another attempted canonization, see Sara T. Nalle, "A Saint for All Seasons: The Cult of San Julián," in Cruz and Perry, *Culture and Control,* 25–50. "While much of the focus of the Counter-Reformation was on the suppression of heterodoxy, enormous effort was also directed toward creating new cults that would carry forward the emerging Tridentine ethic. Particularly favored were cults that explicitly defended points of doctrine legitimating the religious regime that the Protestants hoped to overthrow" (25).

7. Teresa de Jesús, "Libro de su vida," in *Obras completas,* 32.

8. José de Jesús María, *Sermones predicados en la Beatificacion.*

9. The notion of Christian people locked in a struggle against the forces of evil is one of the oldest themes in Christian theology, beginning with the desert fathers and exemplified by the life of Saint Anthony (d. 356). In the desert, Anthony was beset by demons, which he combated with both brutal asceticism and occasional physical fights in which he was greatly wounded. Athanasius, *Life of Antony and Letter to Marcellinus,* trans. Robert C. Gregg (New York: Paulist Press, 1980), 38–39. Both martyrs and ascetics were commonly described throughout the Middle Ages as "athletes of Christ" and "soldiers of God."

10. Teresa de Jesús, "El castillo interior, o Las moradas," in *Obras completas,* 834–997. *The Interior Castle* describes the soul's journey to God through the metaphor of a soldier's perilous struggle to scale various castle walls.

"munitions," and "fortifications." He insisted that, unlike other spiritual battles, the one Teresa was waging with the forces of evil was epic and eschatological, lasting as long as the church itself.[11] Despite the presence of real confessional warfare, the metaphors connected to Teresa described spiritual rather than literal combat.

Although they described Teresa exultantly as both weapon and war-rior, preachers nevertheless took pains to justify the idea of a woman's active role in war, even spiritual war. One way of doing so was to invoke the *topos* of the manly woman as a legitimate form of spiritual transfor-mation. The idea of a woman taking on male attributes had deep roots in Christian theology.[12] Early theologians, such as Saint Augustine and Saint Ambrose, developed the idea of women who transcended their female (bodily) weakness to acquire manly virtue; this theme continued throughout the Middle Ages, and hagiographical accounts of holy women often contained spiritual manly women as well as descriptions of women cross-dressing as men for the better fulfillment of spiritual life.[13] During Teresa's beatification sermons, preachers frequently depicted her as a manly woman. One Dominican preacher reminded his listeners that it was hardly a new thing for a woman to be transformed into a man, "leaving behind her weak feminine self, to be considered a robust man and given masculine attributes."[14] In Teresa's 1622 canoniza-tion bull, Pope Gregory XV called her "the new Deborah," exulting in the saint's ability to overcome her feminine weakness and to lead spiri-tual battles.[15]

During the co-patronage debate, *teresianos* appropriated the lan-guage and style of beatification and canonization sermons but adapted them to the specific needs of national patron sainthood. In a 1627 ser-mon, Tomás de San Vicente explained that Teresa had been named

11. His exact words were "armas," "municiones," and "pertrechos." Alonso de Villegas, "Ser-món predicando en la fiesta de la Beatificación de la Beata Teresa de Iesus, en Toledo, por el Doctor Alonso de Villegas, Canonigo Doctoral en la Santa Iglesia de aquella Ciudad," in José de Jesús María, *Sermones predicados en la Beatificacion de la Beata Madre Teresa de Iesus Virgen*, fol. 91r–v.

12. See, for example, Saint Perpetua's (d. 203) vision, in which she was transformed into a man in order to slay her (pagan) enemy. "The Passions of Sts. Perpetua and Felicity," in *Readings in Medieval History*, ed. Patrick Geary (Peterborough, Ont.: Broadview Press, 1997), 61.

13. For background on the martial language of the early church, see Valerie Hotchkiss, *Clothes Make the Man: Female Cross Dressing in Medieval Europe* (New York: Garland, 1996), 17–21.

14. Pedro de Herrera, "Sermon que predico el PMF Pedro de Herrera de la orden de Sancto Domingo, Catedratico de Prima de Teología en la Universidad de Salamanca," in *Relacion de las fiestas de la ciudad de Salamanca en la beatificacion de la S. Madre Teresa de Iesus, Reformadora de la Orden de N. Señora del Carmen*, ed. Fernando Manrique de Luján (Salamanca: Diego Cusio, 1615), 209–10.

15. "Bulla Canonizationis Sanctae Teresiae Virginis Carmelitarum Discalceatorum Fundatricis a Santimisimo Gregorio Papa XV factae," in *Liber secundus actorum pro canonizatione*, fol. 161r.

defender of orthodoxy, an honor that had been revealed in a vision to Antonia del Espíritu Santo, one of the first nuns to join the Discalced Carmelite reform. After her death, Teresa purportedly appeared at Antonia's convent in Granada to recount to her daughter how God had made her patron of the conversion of the unfaithful.[16] Tomás used this story to illustrate how Teresa's role as patron saint of conversion made her the ideal choice as patron for Spain, a bastion of orthodoxy in a Europe lost to heresy and rebellion. Teresa thus came to embody Spain's messianic pretensions in Europe.

Francisco Cueva y Silva made this argument more explicit, claiming "that since these Kingdoms are the principal opponents of the infidelity of the Lutheran rebels, and since God conceded the protection and rule of this matter to our Saint Teresa, he also gave her patronage of these same Kingdoms, which principally fight for the Faith and sustain its defense and strength."[17] His argument centered on a simple syllogism: Teresa was the patron saint against heresy; Spain was the only country pure in faith and entrusted with the task of eradicating said heresy; therefore Teresa's patronage of Spain was given by God to expedite this task. Like plagues of disease, the "infestation" of heresy was seen by Spaniards as requiring divine assistance to overcome; Luther was the plague, Teresa the antidote sent by God. Her supporters thus carefully created causal links between the monarchy's chief goals and aims, Spanish identity, and Teresa's strengths as saint.

The preacher Francisco de Jesús was even more direct: While Santiago had been a useful patron against ancient enemies (Muslims), a new patron was required to deal with contemporary enemies.[18] Francisco recognized that the new, more pressing enemy came from Protestant Europe to the north, not from the Islamic Ottoman Empire to the east; he insisted accordingly that the Spanish elevate a new patron who was specifically endowed with powers against the new enemy. As such, Teresa would provide badly needed protection to Spain at a critical time in its history. In addition to shoring up Spain's defenses against its hostile

16. Tomás de San Vicente, *Sermon predicado por el padre fray Thomas de San Vicente, Religioso Descalço de la Orden de Nuestra Señora del Carmen, en su Conuento de S. Hermenegildo el dia quinto de las Octauas, que el Rey Don Felipe IIII nuestro Señor celebró a una de los dos Conuentos de Carmelitas Descalços, y Descalças de Madrid, a la fiesta del Patronato de la gloriosa Virgen Santa Teresa Fundadora desta Reformacion, Patrona de los Reynos de España Corona de Castilla* (Madrid: Pedro de Madrigal, 1627), fol. 10v.

17. Cueva y Silva, *Informacion en derecho sobre el titulo de Patrona destos Reynos,* fol. 175r.

18. Francisco de Jesús, *Sermon que predico el dia primero de la octava,* 54–55: "y que supuesta la mayoria que tiene en Santiago, se quede con la defensa que antes le tocaba contra nuestros enemigos antiguos, y la que fuere menester contra los que se nos han levantado de nuevo sea de nuestra nueva Patrona."

neighbors, Teresa's elevation would present a new image of Spain. Francisco proposed that the Spanish nation update its medieval image by casting off the crusading knight in favor of the post-Tridentine heresy fighter.

The political and ideological conflict between Spain and its Protestant enemies led *teresianos* to forge Spanish identity (as seen through its patron saint) in opposition to its confessional rivals, particularly England. Francisco Morovelli de Puebla, for example, saw England as Spain's darkly mirrored twin. He reminded his readers sharply that Spain could not rest on its laurels as pure in faith, and he insisted that Teresa was integral to the monarchy's continued preservation in its traditional role as pure of faith. It was clear, he argued, that historical allegiance to the church in Rome was not enough to guarantee faithfulness, and he reminded his readers of the ugly example of Henry VIII of England, "whom we saw yesterday writing against Luther, and the next day he had become his defender, he who had used the seal of the Church as his coat of arms!"[19] Morovelli stressed that Spain's status as defender of the faith could not be maintained solely through tradition. He stressed that collective Spanish piety required vigilance, which could only be provided by Teresa, whom he credited with preventing Lutheranism from taking root in Spain. Morovelli's argument preserved Christianity as the key element of Spanish identity, as Santiago's adherents had done. The difference was Morovelli's emphasis on maintaining internal purity of faith, rather than military action against Christianity's enemies (as in the case of reconquest). Thus Teresa could embody a new style of spirituality—post-Tridentine inner purity.

Co-patronage preacher Basilio Ponce de León created another comparison between England and Spain as mirror forces aligned against each other. He compared Teresa's foundation of her first monastery in 1569 to the church's pronouncement, the following year, that Elizabeth was a schismatic for proclaiming herself head of the Church of England. "When Queen Elizabeth of England lost all fear of God and the world and declared herself head of the Church, destroying temples and persecuting the faithful, God raised up our holy Teresa of Jesus. . . . Just as God placed holy ancient Elias in the world during the time of an evil Jezebel in order that he could face her and oppose her fury; in these times, this daughter of Elias was sent to us from divine providence in

19. Morovelli de Puebla, *Defiende el patronato de Santa Teresa*, fols. 29v–30r.

order to oppose the ferocity of Elizabeth, and to repair the harm she has caused."[20]

The metaphor worked beautifully: Teresa, who traced her spiritual ancestry from Elijah and Elias on Mount Carmel, assumed the role she inherited from these progenitors by opposing the reign of a tyrannical and ungodly queen. In Spanish, the names Isabella (Elizabeth) and Jezebel are also sonorous, heightening the interchangeability of the two rulers. The gender dynamics of the example are also telling: Elizabeth/Jezebel embodies corruption, weakness, and sinfulness through femininity (emphasized by repetition of the words "fury" and "ferocity"), while Teresa is endowed with the spiritual masculinity of her virtuous male ancestor. Ponce de León transformed Teresa into the protector of Spanish interests abroad, the essential element not only in Spain's protection but in its restoration. The opposition of Spain and England was a crucial element in Spanish identity formation; since an "us" always requires a "them," the English provided a chilling example of what could happen should the Spanish fall prey to heresy. The choice of a new "them" in the guise of the English could not be more telling of the profound shift that was taking place in the Castilian understanding of the Spanish nation.

But Teresa represented more than internal reform and piety to her supporters, many of whom linked her not just to a metaphorical struggle against heretics but to war. Such a shift was critical for a national patron saint, since such patrons were often soldier-saints, mirroring the military prowess that medieval kings had to exhibit. Discalced Franciscan and royal preacher Diego del Escurial insisted that Teresa could and should be depicted as the military protector of Spain. "We ought to paint [Teresa]," he declared, "with a sword in her hand, shield on her arm, helmet with a crest and plume on her head . . . because of the help she is always giving us, because she fights our battles, defends our side, and crowns our victories."[21] The image of Teresa in the trappings of the Roman goddess Minerva appeared solely for the purpose of representing her as a patron saint; through this metaphor, Diego emphasized that the central role of every patron saint was to protect and defend the nation

20. Basilio Ponce de León, "Sermon predicado por . . . el dia de la Santa Madre Teresa de Iesus, en el Monasterio de las Descalças Carmelitas de Toledo, a 5 de Octubre de 1620," in *Sermones de la Purissima Concepcion de la Virgen, y de la S M Teresa de Iesus, y del Santo F. Thomas de Villanueva* (Salamanca: Antonia Ramírez, 1620), 23.

21. Diego del Escurial, *Sermon Predicado en el Convento de las Carmelitas Descalças de Madrid, en la Octaua que sus Magestades hizieron a la Santa Madre Teresa de Iesus, al nueuo titulo de Patrona de España* (Madrid: La Viuda de Alonso Martín, 1627), fol. 16v.

through aid in battle, just as Santiago was purported to have done. It also reflected the strong and warlike image that Spain needed to project to other European powers.

As part of building the case for Teresa as defender of the nation, her supporters began to attribute military victories to her.[22] The most important of these was a battle that took place in Bahía, Brazil, and came to occupy a place of central importance to the monarchy of the 1620s, as it produced a memorable and heartening victory at a time of political uncertainty. In 1624 the Dutch seized the Portuguese city of Bahía, striking a blow against Spanish supremacy in South America. The Spanish monarchy responded quickly, sending a fleet of Spanish and Portuguese ships under the command of Fadrique de Toledo at the beginning of 1625, which successfully drove out the Dutch the following summer.[23] The victory at Bahía represented a moment of triumph for the Spanish monarchy and provided rich material for polemicists, including the royal chronicler Tomás Tamayo y Vargas, who published an account of the victory in 1628.[24]

The victory at Bahía began to be attributed to Teresa's intervention early in the co-patronage debate. Fadrique de Toledo wrote to the count of Lemos, declaring that Teresa was the protector of his armada.[25] Tamayo explained in his account of the battle that the king had ordered the armada to sail under the standards of the Immaculate Conception and Saint Teresa (to whom he referred as "a particular honor to the name of Spain"), declaring that the victory had been won with the help of these holy women.[26] The choice of Teresa as co–standard bearer on this important mission has been overlooked by historians of the event, even though the attribution of the victory of Bahía to Teresa marked a critical moment in the development of her cult, as this was the first time that anyone had claimed that the saint had protected the monarchy in a military engagement. *Teresianos* jumped on this connection, making

---

22. Carmelite historian José de Santa Teresa provides the examples of the battles of Lepanto, Perpignan, Ambers, and Bahía, Brazil. José de Santa Teresa, *Reforma de los Descalzos de Nuestra Señora del Carmen, de la Primitiva Observancia*, vols. 3 and 4 (Madrid: Julian de Paredes, 1683–84), 4:756–57. José wrote the third and fourth volumes of a history of the order begun by one of the order's historians—and a supporter of Teresa's co-patronage—Francisco de Santa María, who wrote the first two volumes.

23. Elliott, *Count-Duke of Olivares*, 215–36.

24. Tomás Tamayo y Vargas, *Restauracion de la ciudad del Salvador, i Baía de Todos-Sanctos, en la Provincia del Brasil por las armas de Don Philippe IV el Grande, rei Catholico de las Españas i Indias, etc.* (Madrid: La Viuda de Alonso Martín, 1628), fols. 1v–2v.

25. José de Santa Teresa, *Reforma de los Descalzos de Nuestra Señora del Carmen*, 4:756–77.

26. Tamayo y Vargas, *Restauracion de la ciudad del Salvador*, fols. 60r–v, 135r. It is interesting to note that both Lope de Vega and Tirso de Molina, in their respective plays celebrating the Brazilian victory, attribute it to Santiago.

frequent references to it in their co-patronage treatises and sermons and promoting Teresa as the physical embodiment of the monarchy's victorious foreign policy.

The image of Teresa as Spain's Minerva was both an innovation in the saint's iconography and crucial to the *teresiano* cause. Since a patron saint had to be on hand to aid the monarchy in its military engagements, Teresa needed a military moniker. In order to fashion this image, many co-patronage preachers drew on the idea of the manly woman, but rather than use it in its more strictly theological model, they began to employ Renaissance and popular imagery. Such imagery of the manly woman had exploded onto the cultural landscape of the early modern world; from Shakespeare's cross-dressing Rosalind to Lope de Vega's Amazon queens, early modern audiences were often faced with images of manly women, particularly as soldiers, sometimes leading and commanding troops.[27] Renaissance fascination with antiquity permitted comparisons of female saints to such figures as Minerva and the Amazons to become as widely popular as those to the biblical manly women Judith, Deborah, and Jael.[28] Queen Isabel, for example, was frequently lauded during her lifetime as an Amazon queen, and compared to Judith, Dido, and Diana.[29] Historians have often tied these popular images of women warriors to times of instability, crisis, and war, endemic in the Europe of the late sixteenth and early seventeenth centuries.[30] The extensive cultural presence of manly women, both fictive and real, provided a wealth of theological and popular images from which Teresa's

27. The historiography on this subject is quite large. For a few important works on the topic, see Natalie Zemon Davis, "Women on Top," in her *Society and Culture in Early Modern France* (Stanford: Stanford University Press, 1975), 124–51; Dianne Dugraw, *Warrior Women and Popular Balladry, 1650–1850* (Cambridge: Cambridge University Press, 1989); and Mary Elizabeth Perry, "The Manly Woman: A Historical Case Study," *American Behavioral Scientist* 31, no. 1 (1987): 86–100.

28. Moshe Sluhovsky, *Patroness of Paris: Rituals of Devotion in Early Modern France* (Leiden: Brill, 1998). In this study of the evolving cult of Saint Geneviève in Paris, Sluhovsky argues, "The growing popularity of the warrior-maid Sainte Geneviève in this period coincided with a cultural fascination with the legendary Amazons, who intrigued (and threatened) the minds and symbolic system of early modern French people. Amazon imagery and speculation about the existence of an Amazonian social order abounded in literature, political pamphlets, plays, engravings, and novels. The discovery of new continents and civilizations with unfamiliar and non-Christian social systems contributed to this vogue" (50).

29. Elizabeth Teresa Howe, "Zenobia or Penelope? Isabel la Católica as Literary Archetype," in *Isabel la Católica, Queen of Castile: Critical Essays*, ed. David A. Boruchoff (New York: Palgrave Macmillan, 2003), 91–102. Howe points out, however, that while Isabel was compared to warrior queens during her lifetime, by the seventeenth century her image had become "domesticated," and she was invariably used as an example of faithfulness or traditional feminine virtues (97–98). In keeping with this observation, I should say that not once is Isabel used as an example of a female leader in a *teresiano* text.

30. For two examples of the representation of women warriors tied to crisis and war, as well as to New World discoveries, see Perry, "Manly Woman," 93; and Sluhovsky, *Patroness of Paris*, 49.

followers could draw in their efforts to explain how it was possible, even glorious, for a woman to play a crucial role in spiritual battle.

Spiritual metaphors of femininity, even when they ascended to masculinity, could not provide co-patronage preachers with military rhetoric strong enough to demonstrate that a woman could be a patron saint. The Spanish national saint required martial characteristics; a patron saint was not only a national symbol but a type of public office charged with defending Spanish borders from enemies. The preacher Jerónimo de Pancorbo used the Amazons to bolster his claim that invoking Teresa in war was nothing new but rather the continuation of a long tradition of women taking up arms in defense of their countries.[31] Another writer claimed that histories were full of accounts of women who, in times of crisis, left behind their "more proper" arms of distaff and needle to take up the sword and lance; he included Amazons, Roman matrons, queens, princesses, and "other women of valor" as evidence, citing specifically only Judith and Deborah. He also described how ancient stories of Minerva often discussed her great skill at spinning, but observed that spinning had not hampered her from fighting in battle or prevented her from being named goddess of wisdom.[32] Thus femininity and strength were not mutually incompatible, and Teresa, no less than a traditional male soldier-saint, was capable of protecting her nation. In fact, accounts of the co-patronage festivals in Avila included the exhortation "Teresa, i cierra Espana!"[33] This phrase was traditionally associated with Santiago and his protection of Spain. In appropriating Santiago's battle cry, Teresa also appropriated his role as military commander.

The association of Teresa with a classical manly woman had additional polemical and allegorical uses. The Spanish nation was represented during the early modern era allegorically as a woman. Titian's painting *Religion Succoured by Spain* (1572–75) depicts Spain, represented by a classical warrior woman, with an army of female warriors behind her, rushing to aid an exhausted and ragged Faith (also a woman). Although the allegory of nation as woman is not unique to Spain, it is worth noting that *España* is a feminine noun. Gendering a nation as

31. Jerónimo de Pancorbo, "Sermon predicado en la muy noble y muy leal Ciudad de Jerez de Frontera, en la fiesta que se hizo en el Convento de nuestra Señora del Carmen a la gloriosa Madre Teresa de Jesus, recibiendola por Patrona de España, 7 noviembre 1627," in Pancorbo, *Sermones varios* (Cádiz: Juan de Borja, 1627), fol. 6v.

32. Sebastián de San Agustín, *Sermon a la inclita Virgen Santa Teresa de Iesus, Patrona de España. En la Solemnidad, que al nuevo Patronazgo celebró la insigne Villa de Lora, Bayliasgo del Orden de San Iuan* (Seville: Juan de Cabrera, 1628), fols. 9r–v, 10r.

33. "Teresa, and strike for Spain!" "Una carta de una relación de las fiestas se celebró Ávila por el patronato de Teresa de Jesús" (1627), BNM, MS 9140, fol. 274r.

feminine had polemical benefits, especially in artworks that included the sovereign. In these cases, a sovereign depicted next to the (female) nation produced a couple; the king could be said to be wedded to the nation. For example, Philip IV was depicted alongside an allegorical Spain (as a woman) in Madrid's Plaza Mayor during the festivals celebrating the canonization of four Spanish saints in 1622. In the plaza—the heart of the royal capital—the decorations were arranged in gendered pairs, the newly canonized Saint Isidro (the patron saint of the city) with his wife, Saint María de la Cabeza, and Philip IV together with Spain. Here, as in Titian's painting, Spain was depicted as his lady, sumptuously dressed and crowned.[34] The elevation of a female patron saint, therefore, had an added benefit of aligning the saint with allegorical—and gendered—representations of Spain. Teresa *became* Spain in a way that Santiago could and did not.

Some *teresianos* saw co-patronage itself as producing the ultimate gendered pair—Teresa and Santiago together could be reimagined as a classical duo, most commonly Mars and Minerva. One broadsheet advertising a poetry contest in Granada for the 1618 co-patronage celebrations included a description of Santiago and Teresa as gods, this time as Mars and Thresa. The poster claimed that the latter figure was an alternate translation of Bellona (the Roman goddess of war, sometimes another name for Minerva). Bellona was the sister of the god Mars, and the two were often depicted together, Mars with sword unsheathed and Thresa holding a flaming torch. This is indeed how the poster depicted the two in an engraving at the top, one of the only surviving images of Teresa and Santiago as co-patrons. In this case the flaming torch had two meanings, one connecting Teresa to the goddess Thresa and the other associating her with the Carmelite founder Elijah. "From this we understand how well defended Spain will be between Mars and Thresa," the poster proclaimed, "with the sword of Santiago and the fire of Teresa; both are threatening the enemies of the Catholic faith and of Spain with sword and fire."[35] The poster provides a fusion of spiritual and classical readings of Teresa's sanctity—on one hand, she was Thresa; on the other, she remained the daughter of Elijah (that is, a Carmelite).

One of the altars decorated for this festival in honor of Teresa in Granada presented a more literal and classical depiction of the saint as soldier. This altar contained a painting of Jesus as a child, dressed in

34. Lope de Vega Carpio, "Relación de las fiestas que la insigne villa de Madrid hizo en la canonización de su bienaventurado hijo y patron San Isidro," in *Colección escogida de obras no dramáticas de Frey Lope Felix de Vega Carpio*, ed. Cayetano Rosell (Madrid: Ediciones Atlas, 1950), 150.

35. "Iusta Poetica en el Convento Real de los Santos Martires," fol. 288r.

secular clothing and holding a lance, which he was handing to a figure kneeling before him. The figure, Teresa, was holding a shield. Beneath the painting someone had written, "So that you might defend Spain / against the pagans / I choose you as *Capitana*." The copyist of the piece added below, "Those are appropriate weapons for a woman even if she is a saint = [that is] spear and shield,"[36] thereby underscoring the message that nothing in the image transgressed contemporary gender norms. The choice of arms evoked classical mythology, as these are also the arms traditionally associated with the goddess Minerva. The exchange taking place also invoked the feudal ceremony of investiture. Symbolically, Jesus was investing Teresa with Spain in return for her use of military arms against the enemies of the church. The combination of the classical, feudal, and spiritual created a powerful argument justifying and glorifying Teresa's role as protector of Spain. Despite the allusion to Elijah, the classical imagery provided the bridge needed to fashion Teresa both as woman and as warrior.

But Teresa as patron saint had weightier duties than military protection; her role as the national patron gave her special political authority and significance. Her supporters thus had to insist that women were capable of holding positions of authority, in spite of Saint Paul's injunction against women preachers. Carmelite preacher Cristóbal Avendaño replied to the Pauline injunction with the blithe explanation that to every rule there was an exception, and he produced some biblical examples, including the sinless state of the Virgin Mary.[37] The preacher Rodrigo Niño also celebrated the very aspects of Teresa's life and career that ran counter to the Pauline prohibition, exulting, "O new miracle and rare prodigy, not keeping quiet, but speaking, teaching, and writing; not only obeying, but also ordering, commanding, ruling; not staying enclosed, but walking, traveling; not spinning, but fighting in war alongside Santiago!"[38] Here Niño rejected the most common female virtues—silence, obedience, staying inside, and spinning—and proclaimed that Teresa's sex did not prevent her from participating in any aspect of public life.

36. Ibid.

37. Cristóbal Avendaño, *Sermones para algunas festividades de las mas solenes de los santos, predicadosen en la Corte de Madrid* (Valladolid: Juan de Rueda, 1628), fols. 180v–181r. For one example of Paul's prohibition against teaching in a *santiaguista* treatise, see González Guijelmo, *Discurso en derecho*, 24.

38. Rodrigo Niño, *Sermon que predico el padre Rodrigo Niño . . . a la Octava que su Magestad mandó celebrar de la Santa Madre Teresa de Iesus, Patrona destos Reynos, en el Conuento de S. Hermenegildo de los Padres Carmelitas Descalços desta villa de Madrid, a 7 de Octubre del año 1627* (Madrid: Juan González, 1627), fols. 8v–9r.

Other *teresianos* refuted the notion that women could not be inter-cessors or advocates, citing secular and biblical precedent for women's acting as judges. One author sought to provide a historical basis for Teresa's appropriation of a male role, claiming that there had been women judges in the past in spite of the prohibition against it. He then provided some examples of noblewomen performing judicial functions, among them countesses, duchesses, and queens.[39] It is important to note that his examples consisted of women of the highest nobility, who were sometimes powerful landholders who took on roles, in their capacity as "lords," generally deemed masculine.[40] The nobility, like the saints in heaven, were therefore allowed certain exemptions from routine, tem-poral law. Along similar lines, Discalced Carmelite León de Tapia lashed out against the poor theology of those who suggested that sex ought to be considered in matters of intercession at all, calling this division of heavenly labor "a bad and perverse doctrine."[41] The saints, according to Tapia, transcended gender.

To most *teresianos,* it was vital to demonstrate that Teresa could uphold the military and political responsibilities of patron sainthood in spite of her sex. They did so largely by masculinizing Teresa, either by portraying her as a literal soldier or as a warrior in the spiritual combat against heresy, or by simply insisting that women could perform leader-ship roles. Their efforts, built largely on classical images, aimed to prove that a female patron saint would not feminize the Spanish people, either at home or in the eyes of foreign nations. They also created something of a middle ground in the cultural reconceptualization of the nation. On the one hand, they forged a new vision of the nation by eschewing the Moorslayer for the heresy fighter, who would maintain purity of the faith and combat the new Lutheran, European enemy. On the other hand, they maintained the outward trappings of the traditional model of patron sainthood, in which the saint performed military tasks as a sol-dier, and the saint was gendered male, even if a woman.

Still, as we have seen, not all of Teresa's supporters felt that a national patron saint needed to be gendered as male. Some constructed

39. "Por la conservacion del patronato de la gloriosa virgen Santa Teresa," fols. 42v–43r.

40. For an example of early modern noblewomen doing just this, see Helen Nader, ed., *Power and Gender in Renaissance Spain: Eight Women of the Mendoza Family, 1450–1650* (Urbana: University of Illinois Press, 2004).

41. Tapia, *Examen y refutacion de los fundamentos,* fol. 37r. "Novedad es muy escandalosa, que . . . se haga tanto caso de la distinccion de los sexos, dando occasion al vulgo ignorante, a que piense que Santiago, por ser hombre y poder ponerse a caballo, es mas a propositio para ser invocado en las batallas, que santa Teresa por ser muger. Esta mala y perversa dotrina, tambien excluye a la reina de los angeles."

a new way of envisioning a representative of the nation in a far more radical fashion, by emphasizing Teresa's femininity. They often glorified the complementary relationship that would exist between Teresa and Santiago as co-patrons, which they believed would ensure the most thorough protection of the Spanish monarchy. Authors often represented the complementary duality of the two saints through the symbols of Santiago's sword and Teresa's pen, or prayer. They used these symbols to demonstrate that Santiago's ability to protect Spain and its interests abroad militarily was strengthened by Teresa's contemplative and purifying powers to improve Spanish souls from within. The dualities authors used to represent co-patronage—sword/prayer, arms/letters, exterior/interior, active/passive, masculine/feminine—drew on early modern ways of defining pairs in terms of gender. In appropriating such dualities for the co-patronage debate, *teresianos* demonstrated that femininity and masculinity offered the nation equal value. While traditional narratives of the nation always included the hypermasculinity of Santiago's military prowess, the introduction (and valorization) of Teresa's feminizing influence added a new dimension to Spanish identity.[42]

Teresiano preacher Diego del Escurial claimed that since Spain had a divine Mars in the patronage of Santiago, God wanted Spain to have a spiritual Pallas (Minerva) to accompany him. Having two patrons fulfill two distinct purposes, Diego continued, would parallel the dual functions of Christ: the first, to strike fear into people, and the other, to reconcile them to him through love.[43] Although Diego compared Teresa to Minerva, who was usually invoked as an example of a manly woman, here he associated her with the feminine role of inspiring love, while leaving the traditionally masculine role of inspiring fear to Santiago. In discussions that glorified dual patronage, then, Santiago retained his masculinity and role as a soldier, while Teresa more commonly was associated with prayer, love, internal reform, and letters.

Authors who emphasized Teresa's femininity made good use of the wealth of metaphors available to them in Renaissance rhetoric. All dualities lent themselves to masculine and female attributions in the early modern period, since male and female represented the most obvious of all dual variations of a single form found in nature. The preacher

---

42. While Spanish scholars have noted an identity crisis in Spain being played out through fears of gender disorder, most emphasize fears of femininity, or the idea of femininity as a shaming device for men (in contrast to what I have discovered in co-patronage); see, for example, Donnell, *Feminizing the Enemy*. See also Elizabeth A. Lehfeldt, "Ideal Men: Masculinity and Decline in Seventeenth-Century Spain," *Renaissance Quarterly* 61, no. 2 (2008): 463–94.

43. Diego del Escurial, *Sermon predicado en el Convento de las Carmelitas Descalças*, fol. 16r.

Domingo Cano claimed that the dual patronage of Santiago and Teresa reflected the universe as ordered by God, comparing rule by the two to the sun and the moon, "which are in their genders male and female."[44] Cano asserted that because God ordered the universe to be ruled partially by the movements of the sun and partially by the moon, it was perfectly in line with natural law to designate a male and a female as co-patrons (co-rulers) of Spain.

Natural dualities such as sun and moon, unsurprisingly, led to human examples of complementarity and the inherent strengths of the whole created by the union of male and female, echoing earlier comparisons to classical pairs. The introduction of human examples proved especially crucial to *teresianos,* who hoped to silence critics who retorted that if Santiago did need a co-patron, the new helper should be male.[45] The most ready human model available to *teresianos* was the one supplied in Genesis: that of Adam and Eve. Bishop Cristóbal de Lobera explained that a reading of the book of Genesis demonstrated clearly that there was nothing at all new in God's supplying a man with a female helper: "God did not give Adam another man as a helper, but a woman, and he did not say that he gave her in order to multiply humankind, but in order to help him."[46] Lobera insisted that this critical event, in which God deliberately created a second human being, a female, proved that God wished men to be helped by women and, therefore, that Teresa was the most appropriate choice for co-patron to aid Santiago in his work on Spain's behalf.

The notion of Teresa and Santiago uniting in a spiritual marriage grew out of ideas about the meaning and nature of marriage at play in the Renaissance. Metaphors about marriage echoed visions of order, harmony, nature, and divine providence.[47] Teresa's supporters frequently invoked the biblical injunction from Genesis 2:18: "It is not good for man to be alone" (*Non est bonum hominem esse solum*).[48] The *Non est*

44. Cano, *Sermon que en la Fiesta de la gloriosa Santa Teresa,* fol. 9v.

45. This idea recurred in many *santiaguista* treatises. For one example, see Jerónimo de Ceballos's letter to the town council of Toledo, urging it to reject Teresa's co-patronage. Ceballos enumerated the glories Santiago had bestowed on Spain, emphasizing his role in battles and military actions, then suggested that Saint Dominic would be a more worthy companion to Santiago than a woman. "Parecer contra el patronazgo de España," 379.

46. Lobera, *Iusta Cosa a sido eligir por Patrona de España,* fol. 4v.

47. For one example, see the work of Fray Luis de León, in *A Bilingual Edition of Fray Luis de León's "La Perfecta Casada" (1583): The Role of Marriage and Women in Sixteenth-Century Spain,* ed. John A. Jones and Javier San Lera (Lewiston, Maine: Edwin Mellen Press, 1999). "And, with a marvelous skill and as is done in music with different strings, God produced out of such different natures a profitable and sweet harmony" (47).

48. Cerdán also noted this aspect of the 1627 sermons, commenting, "Todos insisten en este punto, que Santiago y Santa Teresa se complementan." "Santa Teresa en los sermones," 607.

bonum passage, for example, was the main theme of Sebastián de San Agustín's sermon celebrating Teresa's co-patronage.[49] Another preacher, Domingo Cano, explained that it was strange that Santiago had been left alone for so long without a female companion, and that it was appropriate that he be given one, especially as women were "more devout than men and more given to prayer."[50] Hortensio Félix Paravicino invoked Santiago and Teresa as Spain's new Adam and Eve, sent by God to repair the damage wrought on Spain by Rodrigo and Florinda, who had been responsible for Spain's fall into slavery and Islamic rule in the eighth century.[51]

The strength of Teresa's prayer and pen was seen as providing Spain with increased protection. The preacher Cristóbal de Torres proclaimed, "And I do not know who kills more enemies, Santiago with his sword, or Teresa with her pen." He went on to describe Santiago's killing as the taking of lives (implicitly, Spain's external enemies), whereas Teresa killed like a ray of light, burning the vices of the human body into the ash of humility.[52] While Torres emphasized the value of both types of action against enemies, the poetry and passion with which he described Teresa's purification of the human soul suggests that he privileged this spiritual rebirth over Santiago's temporal slaying. Some *teresianos* thus used such images not only to reshape the way in which patron saints were imagined but also to provide commentary on the proper goals and directions of the monarchy. Some clergy used this rhetoric to convey measured criticism of royal policy in the United Provinces by pointing out that the useless slaughter of so many Protestants and Catholics affirmed that spiritual reform ought to supersede military action when confronting the problem of heresy.[53] Teresa herself had expressed some veiled criticism of Philip II's foreign policy by suggesting that prayer

49. Sebastián de San Agustín, *Sermon a la inclita Virgen Santa Teresa de Iesus.* Sebastián's choice of theme was rather unorthodox; liturgically speaking, he ought to have taken the passage arranged for Teresa's feast day. Celebrated liturgically as a "virgin," her theme was a passage from the Gospel of Matthew on the ten virgins (Matt. 25).

50. Cano, *Sermon que en la Fiesta de la gloriosa Santa Teresa,* fols. 9v–10r.

51. Paravicino, *Oracion Evangelica,* fol. 35r–v.

52. Cristóbal de Torres, *Sermon al Dignissimo Patronazgo de sus Reynos, que fundo el inclito monarca Felipe IIII. Rey de España, en cabeça de la gloriosa virgen santa Teresa de Iesus* (Madrid: Alonso Martín, 1627), fol. 21v.

53. For one particularly acerbic example of this by a co-patronage author, though not in a co-patronage text, see Juan Balboa de Mogrovejo, *El dean y cabildo de la santa Iglesia de Salamanca, por el estado Eclesiastico al Rey nuestro Señor* (1623), BNM, VE 207/67, 75–76. After a vitriolic attack on reason-of-state advocates like Machiavelli, Balboa lamented, "Peligrosa cosa es emprobecer la Iglesia en España, y cercenar sus rentas: que muy poco aprouechan contra los rebeldes las armas temporales, ni gruesos exercitos, aunque hagan rios de sangre, como ha tantos años que se experimenta en Flandes; pues alcabo el principal sustento de todo, nace de las armas espirituales de la Iglesia."

offered a more effective solution to heresy than warfare.[54] Teresa's spiritual weapons could replace the violence represented by Santiago.[55] Thus Teresa's elevation had the potential, at least according to a few of her supporters, to offer an entirely new vision of Spain—of what it valued, how it represented itself, and which policies it pursued. Rather than portray Teresa as the Spanish Minerva, Torres insisted on her utter femininity, and in this femininity he saw a new ideal and a new path for the nation. Rather than preserve cultural gender standards, he transformed them.

Many preachers, however, agreed that attendance to both spiritual reform and military aggression, as embodied by Teresa and Santiago, constituted necessary defenses for the monarchy. For Tomás de San Vicente, for example, Santiago remained the captain who fought against the Moors and infidels, while Teresa had been made patron in order to continue her spiritual battle against heretics.[56] This language of complementarity allowed *teresiano* authors to argue for the necessity of a new patron while maintaining Santiago in his traditional role. Nevertheless, the introduction of Teresa and her femininity reshaped the national narrative, much as discussions of her "modernity" had done. It permitted *teresianos* to posit both a new type of national patron saint—a feminine woman (as opposed to a manly woman)—and a contemporary update of the national narrative. In these dual portraits of Santiago and Teresa, one finds both masculine and feminine, and it is the equal importance of both elements that is strikingly new.[57] The bitter debate over co-patronage, therefore, reveals that a nation could be imagined in multiple ways by its members, who clashed over collective ideas of being and belonging. Moreover, a national community represented by both arms and letters, by military strength and moral purification, ancient and modern, male and female, opened up new possibilities for the valorization of the feminine in the early seventeenth century, and a new way of imagining Spain and Spanishness.

For their part, *santiaguistas* rejected both models of co-patronage—Teresa as Minerva, and Teresa and Santiago as a perfect union. They saw

---

54. Bilinkoff, *Avila of Saint Teresa*, 134. Bilinkoff points out that this remark by Teresa was censored out of some editions of *The Way of Perfection* (134n69).

55. The sixteenth and early seventeenth centuries were a time in which effective (and legal) methods of conversion were debated vigorously, largely in response to atrocities committed by Spaniards against the indigenous populations of colonial Latin America.

56. San Vicente, *Sermon predicado por el Padre Fray Thomas de San Vicente*, fol. 15r–v.

57. It is worth remarking again that most scholars who have noted gender anxiety in the Spanish empire focus almost exclusively on a crisis in masculinity in which feminization was perceived as dangerous and undesirable.

metaphors like Paravicino's as devastating alterations to the story of spiritual origins that the apostle's devotees had been expounding for centuries. Moreover, they denounced angrily the image of Teresa as a warrior defending Spain. They did not hesitate to point out the inappropriateness, even monstrosity, of naming a woman to a position of leadership for a military monarchy during a time of war. Bemoaning the ridicule to which the monarchy would be subjected when outsiders realized that the powerful nation was hiding behind the skirts of a woman, they struck back against their opponents' attempts to construct a new model for national patron sainthood and the nation. While the *teresianos* attempted to describe Teresa's gender positively, Santiago's faction denied that spiritual representation by a woman could have any other than shameful results.

Teresianos' use of the marriage metaphor drew particular fire from their opponents, who rejected mystical or allegorical understandings of marriage and framed their counterarguments solely in terms of the prosaic and temporal aspects of the union. By rejecting theological metaphors involving spiritual marriage (e.g., nuns as brides of Christ), *santiaguistas* could emphasize the unsuitability of having a *wife* at all—in this context, a woman whose gender is understood negatively as embodying weakness and passivity. Reginaldus Vicencius found the image of Santiago and Teresa as a placid domestic couple particularly distasteful. He proposed a satirical image of Santiago as the good husband, picking up his sword and going off to war to kill the Moors, while Teresa, like a good wife, stayed at home with distaff and needle. Like other *santiaguista* authors, Vicencius ignored the spiritual metaphor of marriage as two parts coming together to create one whole in favor of a more negatively gendered and domestic one. Mocking not only the *teresiano* authors but also female enterprise generally, Vicencius cited Thomas Aquinas's dismissal of women: "Women are helpers to men only in procreation; because it is better for men to be helped by men, than to be helped by women."[58] He concluded by asserting that Santiago had many worthy (male) disciples who could help him more effectively than Teresa, adding sarcastically that no one had ever felt the lack of a woman. Whereas in the *teresiano* marital metaphor, Teresa's gender also contained a *value*, as it was her difference that enabled her to balance and complement Santiago, the opponents of co-patronage worked to portray femaleness (not just femininity) as a negative, an obstacle to equality.

It is clear from the ways in which *santiaguistas* formulated gendered arguments that the idea of having a woman serve as the spiritual leader

58. Vicencius, *Respuesta al papel de Morovelli*, fol. 19r–v.

of Spain provoked deep revulsion. Nearly every denunciation of Teresa's elevation involved a corresponding assertion of women's unworthiness, which was often tied to discussions, both metaphorical and literal, of the distaff. The use of the specific term "distaff" (*rueca*) by Vicencius reflected a particularly evocative use of language, as spinning constituted the quintessential representation of femininity in the early modern period. Like many symbols of femininity, the distaff held both positive and negative associations: that of womanly industry and modesty and also that of feminine weakness and sexuality.[59] The distaff functioned as a symbol of the helplessness implicit in traditional female roles and legal rights; the one holding the distaff was denied access to both arms and letters. Whether used to condemn or to praise women, the distaff often appeared in contrast to the sword, representing passivity versus activity, powerlessness versus force.

By choosing the word "distaff," *santiaguista* authors took Teresa out of the realm of sanctity and into a traditional Spanish household. With this move, Teresa's sanctity was also downplayed; she was now more woman than saint. For example, Quevedo applied the term in a scathing attack on the presumption that Teresa could take over Santiago's defense of Spain. Addressing the Carmelites, Quevedo wrote contemptuously, "And you take the sword from Santiago's altar, snatching it from his hand, in order to give it to Saint Teresa, who has been depicted even by her own children with a distaff?"[60] He suggests that the Carmelites themselves were aware of Teresa's unfitness, as they were the ones who had portrayed her with the distaff in the first place.[61]

Joan Salgado de Aráujo likewise fixated on Teresa's inability to be a patron saint because of her sex; he described the idea of a female patron as "indecorous," a strike against the saint's modesty, good manners, and natural order. He also insisted that Teresa's renowned (feminine) humility would lead Teresa herself to reject her election as patron, made on

59. For examples of the *topos* of sewing equipment, see Lisa Vollendorf, ed., *Recovering Spain's Feminist Tradition* (New York: Modern Language Association of America, 2001), particularly the essays by M. I. Barbeito, Lisa Vollendorf, and Anne J. Cruz. For primary evidence, see María de Zayas y Sotomayer, "La fuerza del amor," in Sotomayer's *Novelas amorosas y ejemplares*, ed. Agustín G. de Amezúa y Mayo (Madrid: Real Academia Española, 1948), 241–42.

60. For two more examples of the deployment of the term *rueca* with derisive and prohibitive intent, see *Memorial a su Magestad en nombre de la Iglesia de Sanctiago*, BNM, VE 211/46, fol. 12v; and "Memorial de las raciones que prometio el Reino a su Magestad que la madre Theresa no puede ser patrona de Hespaña" (1617), BNM, MS 1167, fol. 360r–v.

61. Quevedo's claim is accurate. Carmelite engravings and paintings of Teresa sometimes portrayed her with a distaff, although the distaff was usually on the floor, near the writing desk where the saint was working. These works emphasized the saint's femininity, symbolized through the distaff, perhaps as an attempt to mitigate the masculine activity of writing.

her behalf by the Carmelites. In conclusion, he reminded his readers that early Christians had been condemned as heretics by Saint Epiphanius of Salamis (d. 403) for the "defect" of allowing women to sacrifice publicly to God, an act that Salgado described as a "manly office."[62] In this way Salgado created a parallel example of gender disorder as heresy, which implied that having a female national patron likewise constituted spiritual gender disorder and was therefore heretical.

The same themes of gender and disorder were repeated throughout *santiaguista* treatises. Pedro González Guijelmo claimed that because of Teresa's natural modesty (as a woman) she was not only incapable of preaching and leading but unable to take military command, because "manly actions are contrary to feminine modesty."[63] Here modesty acted not as a device used to shame a woman into correct behavior but as something inherent in a true woman's nature, part of her biology that would almost physically prevent her from taking part in such actions. *Santiaguista* Francisco de Lucio Espinosa penned a detailed analysis of the 1627 papal brief that attacked the idea of manly women as contrary to divine and natural law, proclaiming that the papal brief ought to be revoked in order to "conform to divine and human law, which excludes women from these offices, because manly actions are contrary to the modesty of her sex, like a monstrosity and disharmony."[64] The emphasis on prohibitions in divine and human law against women's taking public office provided a key argument for the illegality and nullity of Teresa's patron sainthood (though it is also interesting to note that Lucio felt comfortable proclaiming a papal brief contrary to divine and human law).

Other opponents of co-patronage provided more specific arguments against women's taking on men's roles. Both Mera and Quevedo emphasized the inability of a woman to intercede in battles, in the process ignoring the tradition of invoking the Virgin Mary as a battle commander.[65] Jerónimo de Ceballos focused on women's inability to hold

---

62. Salgado de Aráujo, *Memorial, informacion, y defension apologetica*, 109–11.

63. González Guijelmo, *Discurso en derecho*, 29.

64. Francisco de Lucio Espinosa, *Memorial y informacion en derecho, que don Francisco de Lucio Espinosa hizo a instancia de los Cardenales de Santiago, en fauor de su Patronazgo. Dando el sentido literal a las palabras del Breue de la Santidad de nuestro Santo Padre Urbano Octauo* (Madrid, [ca. 1627]), BNM, VE 215/90, fol. 2r.

65. Mera Carvajal, *Informacion en derecho, por el estado eclesiastico*, fol. 30r; and Quevedo y Villegas, "Memorial por el patronato de Santiago y por todos los santos naturales de España," in *Obras de don Francisco de Quevedo Villegas*, ed. Aureliano Fernández-Guerra y Orbe, BAE 23 (Madrid: Rivadeneira, 1852), 225. Maximilian of Bavaria dubbed the Virgin Mary "generalíssima" after her intercession led to a victory against Protestant forces at White Mountain in 1618. Robert Bireley, *The Refashioning of Catholicism, 1450–1700: A Reassessment of the Counter-Reformation* (Washington,

office when he argued that Teresa was not eligible to be patron. He used the example of the Crown of Aragón, which, he explained, called its governor *el justicia mayor,* not *la justicia,* even though the Spanish "justicia" is gendered feminine and would grammatically take "la," not "el."[66] The masculinity of the role precluded a feminine gender, and proper grammar must give way to proper gender order. To all of these men, patron sainthood clearly functioned as a different category from other types of saints, even from civic patrons. No one could deny the large number of local female saints throughout the Catholic world. The angry reaction to Teresa's elevation centered on the concept of national patron sainthood as a type of public office, a role of crucial political and symbolic importance that simply could not be performed by a woman. Violation of the prohibition against women in public office would result in the collective shaming of Spanish men and masculinity, delivering a great blow to their identity.

Unsurprisingly, given *santiaguista* hostility to the idea of a woman as patron saint, images of Teresa as a goddess and battle commander did nothing to placate them. Instead, defenders of Santiago attacked such images as exemplifying everything they despised about female patron sainthood and as a direct attack on their apostle's traditional prerogatives as Spain's military defender. They insisted that Santiago needed no help in his role as the origin of Spain's greatness, past, present, and future. Any assertion that a military battle had been led by a saint other than Santiago was interpreted as a charge that the apostle had become old and weak and required Teresa's help, even in military matters. This was all the evidence the cathedral of Santiago de Compostela needed to persist in its belief that its enemies were attempting to use co-patronage to undermine the apostle's entire cult. Decades later, a *santiaguista* pamphlet recounted bitterly that its opponents had insulted the apostle by asserting that Santiago had only killed a few Moors in battle, whereas Teresa had destroyed thousands of heretics. The cathedral authorities ended this diatribe by claiming that the contentions by Teresa's supporters had grown so offensive that the Inquisition had to be brought in to stop them.[67] It was not only the characterization of Santiago as old and weak that they found troubling, but the new patron's theft of the old

---

D.C.: Catholic University of America Press, 1999), 89–109. In addition, the Virgin was occasionally invoked as a "conquistadora" in the Middle Ages and in the New World. For an excellent look at this phenomenon, see Remensnyder, "Colonization of Sacred Architecture."

66. Ceballos, "Parecer contra el patronazgo de España," 379.

67. *Defensa de la unica proteccion y patronazgo de las Españas perteneciente al Gloriosa Apostol Santiago el Mayor, que su Apostolica Iglesia dio a la Magestad del Rey, nuestro Señor* (ca. 1640), BNM, VE 211/56, fol. 23v.

one's qualities. They clearly saw this as a sign that regardless of what Teresa's adherents claimed, their ultimate purpose was to displace Santiago completely.

In response to *teresiano* depictions of Santiago as obsolete, *santiaguistas* provided a passionate defense of Santiago's great feats of conquest and war in a global context. Melchor Alfonso Mogrovejo y Escovar repeated *santiguista* claims that Santiago not only liberated Spain from the "yoke of the Africans"; he also allowed the Spanish to conquer "many cities and provinces in the Orient, converting many idolatrous nations to the Faith. Our Castilians went forth with their swords in their hands into an unknown world, guarded and helped by this glorious Patron. . . . God gave guardianship [of these provinces] to the Spanish nation, who subdued their natives and chained them to the sweet yoke of Evangelical law."[68] Mogrovejo understood his opponents' view that Santiago was responsible for all Spanish conquests and larger messianic destiny. *Santiaguistas,* like their opponents, viewed the world as a stage for the dramatization of Spain's special relationship to church and heaven. For them, Santiago continued to play an integral role in the successful completion of God's work in expanding the Christian world and battling unbelievers. Beyond rejecting the need for a co-patron, *santiaguistas* also enlarged Santiago's role from a relatively narrow one (as the Moorslayer) to international conqueror and evangelist. In this way they glorified their patron and justified the Spanish imperial enterprise throughout the world.

Santiaguistas, as we have seen, expressed outrage at the gender inversions implied by the introduction of a female patron saint. Dominican Juan de Almogábar provided an aggressive and flamboyant attack on the idea of female leadership in war and the potentially catastrophic results this could entail. "Already in Spain," he began, "men are women, and women are men; already women take up arms and armor, and men long locks of hair like women, and for these types, a woman would be a good captain."[69] Female military leadership could occur only in a context in which gender norms were hopelessly mixed up and men were as effeminate as women. A female leader was also a sign, visible to all, that Spanish society had gone off the rails and descended into effeminacy and

---

68. Mogrovejo y Escovar, *Don Melchor Alfonso Mogrovejo y Escovar,* fols. 193v–194r. For a similar panegyric on Santiago's role in conquest, see Rodríguez de León, *Carta a su Magestad,* 9–12.

69. Juan de Almogábar, *Sermon predicado en la catolica Iglesia de Santiago, en la fiesta que haze octaua de S. Estauan Protomartir, en hazimiento de gracias, de la conquista de Granada, por las Magestades de los Santos Reyes, D. Fernando y doña Isabel, en defensa del unico Patronato del gran Apostol Santiago* (Santiago: Juan de León, 1630), 52–53.

ineffectuality. Almogábar then described another type of soldier, one who never put down his weapons, day or night; he declared that these virile, energetic, powerful soldiers were the proper followers of Santiago.

It is important to note that Almogábar's sermon was preached during a commemoration of the conquest of the city of Granada by the Catholic Kings in 1492. In honor of this event, the preacher dedicated the next section of his sermon to glorifying the past victories of Spain. Almogábar juxtaposed his critique of present-day soldiers—manly women and womanly men—to the glorious days of the Catholic Kings. The conquest of Granada officially ended the reconquest of Spain, symbolized the ultimate defeat of the Moors, and reaffirmed Santiago's patronage; these glories were possible because Spanish military might was untainted by feminine weakness. The sermon reflected general fears that Spain was becoming increasingly feminine, fears that had been expressed in various writings since the end of the sixteenth century, particularly after the humiliating defeat of the Spanish Armada in 1588. Just after this defeat, the Jesuit historian Pedro de Ribadeneira wrote a treatise explaining why he believed God had visited this disaster on Spain. Chief among the reasons for this catastrophe was the rise of leisurely activity that made men "effeminate and womanly." He suggested that men practice military exercises, which would preserve good customs, benefit the republic, and keep men strong.[70] Thus, decades before the co-patronage controversies, political commentators and moralists had connected military failures with the loss of God's favor, which they attributed to sinful and shameful conduct, including anything that resembled gender play.

Joan Salgado agreed with Almogábar and denounced representations of Teresa as "a papal goddess, Artemisia, Semiramis, and a Virago," all of which referred to *teresiano* depictions of the saint as a female warrior (Artemisia and Semiramis were ancient queens who led armies). Salgado added, "or maybe God will permit this to punish us . . . just as God saw the elevation of Deborah and Judith as patrons as a punishment and an affront, as we read in divine Scripture . . . [he] punished them for the insult of placing something that reeks of femininity in a man's office, as we see in the book of Isaiah."[71] Salgado's exegesis of the biblical stories of Deborah and Judith took the opposite view from most mainstream early modern commentators, who viewed the two women as holy saviors of their

70. Ribadeneira, "Tratado de la Tribulación," 380. "Pero no solamente se estragan las costumbres y se arruinan las repúblicas, como dicen estos santos, con esta manera de representaciones; pero hácese la gente ociosa, regalada, afeminada, y mujeril . . . pero que no es Buena recreacion la que es dañosa a las buenas costumbres y destruidora del vigor y esfuerzo varonil."

71. Salgado de Aráujo, *Memorial, informacion, y defension apologetica*, 112.

people. According to Salgado, God's entire purpose in promoting Deborah and Judith to positions of authority was to shame and punish the Hebrew people, whose (male) leaders had been incapacitated in the face of danger. He supported this reading of the Old Testament with a citation from the book of Isaiah, where the prophet denounced feminine/effeminate rulers as an affront to God, who would destroy those who served them.[72] Thus, for Salgado, any form of female leadership constituted divine punishment and symbolized humiliation, weakness, and failure.

Salgado was not the only *santiaguista* to provide this commentary on the book of Judges. Pedro de Losada y Quiroga also compared Spain's current situation to the story of Deborah (Judg. 4–5), when the prophet-judge took charge of the Hebrew army. Rather than quote the biblical account of the battle, he turned to Sulpicius Severus's fourth-century *Chronicle,* which described the events in this way: "Therefore, having no hope at all left in their leaders, they were defended with the help of a woman."[73] Losada believed that Europe would see Teresa's election as a sign that Spaniards, like the Hebrews, had lost faith in their leader and were in a state of crisis, and that this would lead to widespread rejoicing at Spain's decline.[74] Losada's words resonated with that part of Castilian society that feared the monarchy's downward spiral in reputation and international power.

In addition to deriding Teresa's qualifications for patron sainthood, the apostle's supporters had to affirm Santiago's continued miraculous presence as the protector of Spain. *Santiaguistas* took one of two positions on the issue of Santiago's contemporary efficacy, claiming either that Spain faced no new troubles or that, if it did, Santiago was perfectly capable of interceding to eliminate them. Fernando de Mera Carvajal, a professor at the University of Valladolid and governor of the bishopric of Cuenca, angrily attacked his opponents for portraying Santiago as an "old soldier" whose age rendered him no longer able to fight. On the contrary, Mera claimed, "it is clear that this patron who has taken care of this Spanish Province for so many years and defended her from so many and such dangerous predicaments when our strength was less and that of our

72. Ibid., 112. Salgado's reference here is to Isa. 3:12. A modern translation reads: "My people—a babe in arms will be their tyrant, and a women will rule them! O my people, your leaders mislead, they destroy the paths you should follow."

73. Sulpicius Severus, *Chroniques,* ed. Ghislaine de Senneville-Grave (Paris: Les Éditions du Cerf, 1999), 148. "Adeo nihil spei in eorum ducibus erat ut muliebri auxilio defenderentur" (1.23.3). It is interesting that Losada uses this passage in an attempt to disparage female leadership; the next line of Severus's text makes it clear that he understood Deborah's leadership as prefiguring the victory of the church over slavery and idolatry: "Quamquam haec in typum ecclesiae forma praemissa sit, cuius auxilio capituitas depulsa est."

74. Losada y Quiroga, *Al illustrissimo y reverendissimo Señor Arzobispo,* fols. 69v–70r.

enemies greater; and [he did] all of this without the help of a co-patron, so he does not need one now, *when this Monarchy is more powerful than ever* and the dangers fewer" (emphasis added).[75] Mera, like others who defended Santiago, took exception to the idea that the older saint might not be doing his job properly. At the center of this argument stood the idea that Spain was the most powerful monarchy in the world; it had no enemies it could not defeat, it needed no aid, and it was stronger than it had ever been. No changes were necessary either to patron sainthood or to the national narrative; staying the course was all that was required.

Preserving Spain's international reputation was vital, according to Losada, because "everyone knows that every other country, Christian or not Christian, envies greatly the happiness and glory of Spain. Everyone knows we have this glory because of Santiago's help. . . . Therefore, those who wish to diminish Spain have no other method of doing so than robbing us of Santiago's defense."[76] In Losada's account of political theory, the "envy" of foreign nations played a key role in maintaining a country's international reputation. The nation that was envied the most was thus the most powerful and feared. In addition, Losada connected the loss of Santiago with envious nations, implying that *teresianos* and their supporters were actually performing the work of—or even working on behalf of—the monarchy's enemies. Other *santiaguista* authors begged the monarch repeatedly to reconsider any action that might reflect poorly on Spain in the eyes of the world. Martín Añaya Maldonado called the preservation of Santiago's singular patronage a "reason of state," in that Spain's appeal to a new patron indicated a position of weakness and would lead foreign countries to think Spain in a state of crisis.[77]

The Jesuit preacher Juan Fernández Saavedra warned his parishioners about the dangers of upsetting the traditional role of Santiago. He pointed to the current political situation in the world, in which the Spanish monarchy found itself continually losing battles: "We fight in Flanders, we fight in Italy, we fight on the sea, we fight in the Indies. God sees this . . . allowing it to consume our wealth and lose thousands of people. We have deserted the Apostle and offended God."[78] The continuing losses and humiliations suffered by the Spanish monarchy throughout the latter half of the 1620s, which eclipsed the brief joy of the 1625

75. Mera Carvajal, *Informacion en derecho por el unico y singular Patronato*, fol. 10v.

76. Losada y Quiroga, *Al illustrissimo y reverendissimo Señor Arzobispo*, fols. 69v–70r.

77. Martín Añaya Maldonado, *Discurso, en que se prueba que el Apostol Santiago ha sido, y deve ser unico Patron de España, y se declara el Breve de la Santidad de Urbano VIII que a petition de los Procuradores destos Reynos concedio a Santa Teresa de Iesus* (ca. 1627), BNM, VE 201/61, fol. 7v.

78. Juan Fernández Saavedra, *Sermon del P. Iuan Fernandez Saavedra Predicador de la Compañia de Iesus, que predicó en defensa del Patronato del unico Patron de las Españas Santiago, en la Iglesia del mismo S. Apostol, el dia de su gloriosa Translacion, treinta de Diziembre de 1629* (Santiago de Compostela: Juan de León, 1630), 51.

victories, were a sign to the *santiaguistas* of what exactly was at stake for the monarchy in its choice of co-patron. The choice was clear—Spain could choose to return to Santiago and preserve its history of victory and glory, or it could turn its back on its traditional patron and risk losing everything the Spanish nation had become.

Through lively debates over patron sainthood and international reputation, the seemingly disconnected problem of gender was catapulted to the center of the controversy. Each side drew on a variety of preexisting tropes concerning women and gender to bolster its own position. From marriage, to distaffs, to Deborah, gendered language remained deeply ambivalent in the early seventeenth century, open to contest and interpretation. The clash over Teresa's gender provides the most poignant example of the co-patronage debate as an impassioned conflict over identity. While both sides expressed the desire for the same end in terms of concrete policies—defeat of the heretics and enemy nations, maintenance of purity of religion domestically, and firm control over the Indies—they articulated different visions of how to achieve these results. *Teresianos* used co-patronage to argue the need for change, declaring that Teresa's protection would fortify weakening Spanish defenses and give new strength to the monarchy, in concert with the foreign policy aims of the Olivares regime. They saw the older policies of the monarchy as increasingly irrelevant in the shifting political scene of the early seventeenth century. Other *teresianos* agreed that Spain required a new representative, but they put forward a more radical vision, in which Teresa's womanhood both feminized Spain *and* strengthened it. Opponents of co-patronage, by contrast, turned to the past as the source of Spain's future revitalization and cried out against the loss of their traditional symbol and patron. They felt, as keenly as the *teresianos* did, that Spain was in need of both internal moral reform and external military defense, but they argued that moral reform could come only from Spain's traditional values and customs— most obviously martial culture and masculinity—as symbolized by Santiago. The new realities of the seventeenth-century world called into question traditional models of self-understanding in Spain; patron sainthood sparked vitriolic debate precisely because such a change in spiritual representation would mark the new religious and political landscape not as a passing aberration but as a permanent reality.

5

MAPPING SACRED GEOGRAPHY

While those involved in the co-patronage debate agreed that a patron saint's job was to protect and serve the nation, the question of what exactly was the "nation," and who belonged to it, requires further examination. We have seen that the participants used the term "Spain" to mobilize a specific shared cultural, geographical, and religious history. Yet early seventeenth-century Castilians were just as aware as we are today that "Spain" was an unstable concept, since a memory of a shared past (Hispania) coexisted with the concrete reality of distinct kingdoms, each with its own laws and customs. Thus the category "national patron saint" could have multiple meanings in a context in which "Spain," in a political or juridical sense, did not exist. Because patron saints represented a concrete space as well as an imagined place, participants had to confront potential gaps between the two. They grappled with a basic question: Over what territory exactly had Teresa been made patron saint? In fact, Castilians exhibited a surprising amount of confusion and disagreement over the physical boundaries of Teresa's patron sainthood; such disagreement illuminates the challenges facing early modern attempts to create a national patron.

Was Teresa a "national" patron? What made a saint national, as opposed to regional? Who had the power to make such a decision? Attempts to answer these questions led to frank discussions about the exact meaning of "Spain" and about Castile's relationship to the other Spanish kingdoms. They also revealed multiple layers of jurisdiction and identity *within* Castile, since Castile was in its own right a composite kingdom. This chapter assesses the relationship between national, regional, local, and individual jurisdictions and identities. A detailed analysis of some of the key figures in the debate is necessary here; the chapter thus ends with a specific case study—Andalusia—that will allow us to trace the motivations of individual participants in detail. A microhistorical examination of these individuals reveals the fluid movement of Castilian identities through the porous boundaries of the personal, local, regional, and national.

The bishop of Córdoba, Cristóbal de Lobera, recognized the uncertainty many people felt over the question of Teresa's spiritual jurisdiction, and in his third *teresiano* pamphlet he addressed "pious people who still doubt whether Teresa is or is not, the patron of all Spain, or only of Castile."[1] Doubts about the extent of Teresa's jurisdiction could have arisen only in an environment in which the demarcation between Castile and Spain exhibited some degree of slippage. How could there be any doubt as to Teresa's jurisdiction? The papal brief naming Teresa co-patron stated that the Apostolic See "approved and confirmed, with apostolic authority, the said election."[2] Here "the election" referred to the vote by the delegates of "the kingdoms of the crown of Castile," or the Castilian Cortes. A case could be made, therefore, that the brief ratified Teresa's election only in Castile. The Castilian secular authorities also expressed a clear delineation of the territories conceded to Teresa's patronage by focusing solely on Castile. The election in the Cortes, for example, specified Teresa's patronage in "these kingdoms," meaning the ones represented in the Cortes.[3] The kingdoms specified by the Cortes were those of Castile, which had been gradually joined to one another (Asturias, Galicia, León, Castile, and Andalusia). Philip IV also restricted Teresa's jurisdiction to Castile alone; in a letter to his ambassador in Rome, the king explicitly described Teresa as patron of Castile.[4]

1. Cristóbal de Lobera, *Respuesta a los largos papeles, que han salido contra el Patronato de Sancta Theresa* (1628), BNM, MS 9140, fol. 104v.

2. "Breve del papa Urbano VIII declarando el patronato de Santa Teresa en España," in *Escritos de Santa Teresa,* 425–26.

3. *Copia de un decreto de las Cortes de Castilla, en que reciben a la gloriosa madre santa Teresa de Iesus por Patrona destos Reynos* (1627), BNM, VE 18/9.

4. Philip IV to the City of Jaén, 27 September 1627, BNM, MS 9140, fol. 6r; and Philip IV to Urban VIII, 7 April 1629, ACSC, IG 301 (38): "he deseado el que estos mis Reynos de Castilla tengan por Patrona a Sta Tersea natural dellos."

For their part, the official Carmelite documents also declared Teresa patron of Castile. The jurist Juan Balboa de Mogrovejo articulated this official position in a lawsuit (*pleito*) on behalf of the order against the cathedral of Santiago for its refusal to celebrate Teresa as patron. In this lawsuit, Balboa asserted that the papal brief made Teresa patron saint only of Castile. While such a limitation of her patronage to Castile might have resulted in some loss of prestige for the saint, it also provided her supporters with a strategy for winning the lawsuit and affirming Teresa's patronage. The title of patron of Castile permitted the Carmelites to claim that her elevation in no way impinged on Santiago's historical title of "unique patron saint of Spain." "Santiago is the universal patron, and unique of the Spains," Balboa declared. "Teresa is the particular patron of only Castile, and not principal, like Santiago, but less a principal and minor patron."[5] It is impossible to tell whether or when the Carmelites consciously decided to eschew "Spain" in favor of Castile, but the history of acrimonious objections to Teresa's patron sainthood might have played a role in their subsequent decision to circumscribe her jurisdiction in order to preserve her patronage.

The Carmelites drew inspiration for this strategy from the example of another Spanish kingdom—Navarre. Balboa emphasized the Navarrese example in his lawsuit, pointing out that a few years earlier Navarre had elected Francis Xavier as its second patron, alongside Santiago. The Navarrese election had prompted no objection from the archbishop of Santiago. If co-patronage in Navarre was inoffensive to Santiago, Balboa asked, how could co-patronage in Castile be any more harmful?[6] Discalced Carmelite Gaspar de Santa María employed the same example, pointing out acidly that when Francis Xavier had been made co-patron of Navarre in 1624, its Cortes had acted without an order from the king or papal confirmation. He explained that Xavier had been chosen co-patron of Navarre because he was a native Navarrese, just as Teresa had been chosen because she was Castilian.[7] The example of Navarre thus provided ammunition for the *teresianos* on several levels: It cited the precedent of an election by parliament without papal interference; it was an uncontested co-patronage; and it emphasized the legitimacy of choosing a second patron saint who was a native of the region. Popular

---

5. Juan Balboa de Mogrovejo, *Por la Sagrada religion de Carmelitas Descalços, con la Santa Iglesia Metropolitana de Santiago, y demas consortes, sobre el Patronazgo destos reynos de Castilla, que a instancia de su Magestad concedio la Santidad de nuestro santissimo Padre Urbano VIII* (ca. 1627), BNM, MS 9140, fol. 156v.

6. Ibid., fol. 162r.

7. Tapia, *Examen y refutacion de los fundamentos*, fol. 5r–v.

devotion to a regional saint, *teresianos* argued, could have no deleterious effects on Santiago's primacy as Spain's only patron.

Cristóbal de Lobera, an ambitious Castilian prelate, had been bishop of Pamplona (Navarre) when Francis Xavier was named Navarre's patron. As a supporter of the election, he had been present in the Navarrese Cortes for the declaration of Xavier's patronage. By 1627, Lobera, now the bishop of Córdoba, provided vocal support for Teresa's patronage—but this time he placed himself in a different camp by insisting that she was the patron not just of Castile but of all Spain. He claimed that both the king and the pope wanted Teresa's jurisdiction to extend throughout the Spanish kingdoms, emphasizing particularly the king's role in the election. According to the bishop, the king's direct involvement in the matter meant that he wished his decision to apply to all his dominions.[8] In contrast to the Carmelite position laid out by Balboa, Lobera argued that royal involvement in Teresa's election changed the nature of her patron sainthood. The Navarrese example represented an individual region or kingdom spontaneously electing a native son to a local post, whereas in this case the king had chosen Teresa to act as patron to all the territories he ruled. It is important to note, however, that Lobera limited Teresa's patron sainthood to Spain and did not argue for her patron sainthood over the entire monarchy. Members of the Spanish nation, therefore, held a special and distinct relationship to one another not shared by other members of the monarchy.

In addition to arguing that the king desired Teresa for a Spanish patron, Lobera also argued that the pope agreed. The bishop quoted from the papal brief that Teresa had been declared patron "in uniuersa Hispaniarum Regna"—that is, throughout the kingdom of Spain—thereby extending the jurisdiction endorsed by the Cortes, which had voted for Teresa as the patron of Castile alone. He also quoted a reference in the brief to Teresa as patron of the kingdoms of the Crown of Castile, rather than of the kingdoms of Castile. The distinction was significant, according to Lobera, because while the "kingdoms of Castile" referred only to the kingdoms that made up Castile, the "kingdoms of the Crown of Castile" implied additional kingdoms. He insisted that Navarre, Aragón, and Portugal would also have to be included under this heading, for "they are subject to it [the Crown of Castile]."[9] The ease with which Lobera made this claim glosses over its enormous significance, since the ties that bound Castile to Aragón and Portugal consisted solely of joint loyalty to one sovereign. Both kingdoms maintained

8. Lobera, *Respuesta a los largos papeles*, fol. 105r.

9. Ibid., fol. 105r–v. Lobera appears to be engaged in a willful misreading of the papal brief, which clearly names Teresa as patron of Castile only.

separate governments, customs, coinage, and laws, none subject to the other. Rather than reflect political reality, then, Lobera was asserting that Castile was the most powerful member of the monarchy and could dominate the others. Thus we can trace two main ideas about Spain embedded in Lobera's argument: first, that Castile maintained the place of dominance among Spanish kingdoms; and second, that the Spanish kingdoms maintained a relationship as a nation, distinct from the other members of the monarchy (the Netherlands, Naples and Sicily, and the American colonies).

The end of peripatetic courts in the reign of Philip II and the king's quasi-permanent settlement in Madrid (in spite of the brief move to Valladolid during the reign of Philip III) had led to a gradual process of what historians have sometimes termed "Castilianization" within the monarchy.[10] While Castilian intellectuals often complained about bearing the greatest share of the burdens of monarchy, particularly fiscal ones, such disproportionate burdens originated in Castile's preeminent position as home to the monarchy's capital and the nearly constant physical presence of the king. Thus Castile's glory was in many ways a reflection of royal power, an idea that permeated Lobera's treatises on co-patronage. His stance on Teresa's election was clear: The king had chosen her as patron; therefore, such patronage extended to all his (Spanish) kingdoms. Lobera's privileging of Castile as head of the Spanish monarchy thus espoused royalist as well as Castilianist sentiments. His insistence on Teresa as patron saint of all Spain, for example, does not appear to have derived from the ideological motive of bringing Castile and Aragón together as the true historic Spain. Rather, the bishop used the term "Spain" because he associated Teresa's jurisdiction with royal jurisdiction; he, like other *teresianos,* believed that patron sainthood was a type of public office.

Lobera's insistence on Teresa's jurisdiction over "Spain" was far from unique, in spite of the contrasting opinions on the subject put forward by the papal brief, the king, and the Carmelite lawsuit. In fact, all *santiaguistas* and most *teresianos* agreed with Lobera. *Santiaguistas,* keenly aware of the Carmelites' attempt to win their lawsuit by limiting Teresa's jurisdiction, insisted that it was ludicrous for their opponents to pretend that Teresa had been made patron only of Castile.[11] Alonso Rodríguez de León agreed with Lobera that Castile's election meant that

---

10. See Thompson, "Castile, Spain, and the Monarchy."

11. For one example of this, see the response to Balboa in Pedro González Guijelmo, *Discurso en derecho,* 47. He contested the points made by Balboa, beginning with number 98 in Balboa's text: Balboa de Mogrovejo, *Por la Sagrada religion de Carmelitas Descalços,* fols. 156v–159r.

her patronage extended to all of Spain. He argued that Castile acted as the "head" of the Spanish monarchy; as such, Aragón, Navarre, and Portugal were under the authority of the Crown of Castile. As the Carmelites suspected, agreeing with Lobera gave *santiaguistas* a stronger position from which to reject her patron sainthood—if Teresa were the patron saint of Spain, then her patronage would *necessarily* diminish Santiago's, rendering the papal brief invalid. In addition, only the extension of her patron sainthood to all of Spain would invalidate the Cortes's election as an overreaching of its authority. For example, one *santiaguista* argued, "How can the kingdoms of Castile and León, which are the only ones that come together in the Cortes, oblige all the rest that comprise 'the Spains' [Aragón, Catalonia, Valencia, Navarre, Portugal, and the rest] to have a new patron?"[12] Rejecting Lobera's vision of the "Spains" bound together by the unity of the king's will, these *santiaguistas* emphasized the composite nature of the monarchy and the inability of any part to speak for the whole. While this argument might seem hypocritical, given that Santiago himself was something of a Castilian saint, it is important to remember that *santiaguista* authors dated the apostle's patron sainthood to his evangelization of Iberia before its political fragmentation.

Pedro González Guijelmo broke down the Cortes's representative ability even more minutely, claiming that even the cities and provinces allegedly represented by the *procuradores* had not consented to co-patronage. He described such "defects in consent" as a result of the gap between what the cities authorized their representatives to do and what the representatives had done.[13] The Cortes was a system of representation for the major Castilian cities (between eighteen and twenty-two in this period) that met primarily to vote on the allotment of funds, via taxation, to the Crown.[14] In the period of the co-patronage debate, the cities' representatives to the Cortes lacked independent power. Rather, they attended the Cortes with specific instructions from the cities themselves; any new business compelled the representative to return to his city council for consultation.[15] González argued that the representatives

12. *Memorial a su Magestad en nombre de la Iglesia de Sanctiago*, BNM, VE 211/46, fol. 9v. This argument was repeated in another anonymous treatise, the *Memorial de Advertencias al papel que Don Francisco Morovelli*, fols. 2v–3r.

13. González Guijelmo, *Discurso en derecho*, 54. The specific context of this excerpt is the deception he claimed was practiced on the pope to extort the brief of 1627 from him. He believed that the Cortes willfully misrepresented itself to Urban. Quevedo also stressed this point in "Su espada por Santiago," 435.

14. Thompson, "Crown and Cortes in Castile, 1590–1665," in *Crown and Cortes*, 32–36.

15. The power and importance of the Cortes has been the subject of great interest to scholars in recent decades. See, for example, Juan Luis Castellanos, *Las Cortes de Castilla y su diputacion*

had failed to do this and thus had overstepped their allotted powers and voted independently of the will of their respective cities. Even an institution like the Cortes could not sustain a true representative function in a decentralized kingdom.

If *santiaguistas* rejected the Cortes's ability to choose a patron saint for all of Spain, then the question remains why (and how) they also refused to concede Teresa's patronage in Castile only. One answer may be that *santiaguistas* understood that no matter what the Carmelites claimed, any patron of Castile probably would also be considered the patron saint of Spain (within Castile). Such anxiety might have been logical, considering that Santiago's own claim to the title "patron saint of Spain" had limited salience outside Castile—the apostle in fact was primarily a Castilian saint, made national by his associations with the Crown and royal policies. Fear of Teresa gaining ground as Castilian patron prompted Francisco de Villafañe to assert that neither Spain nor Castile was an appropriate territory for Teresa's spiritual jurisdiction. He reported from Rome that his attempts to persuade some cardinals to nullify the papal brief included a lesson in Spanish geography. He informed his listeners that, while the "Crown of Castile" might seem like a small region, it in fact "included almost all of Spain." He suggested that the Carmelites had been greedy in their geographical reach and hinted that it might be more appropriate to give Teresa Old Castile alone.[16] Were Teresa patron only of Old Castile, then the potential problem of conflating Castile and Spain would be resolved.

There are ironies in the positions espoused by both sides. Many *teresianos* promoted an aggressively Castilianist agenda, but they did so by using the rhetoric of the Spanish nation. On the *santiaguista* side, the cathedral and archbishop exhorted men to support their cause as "true and legitimate Spaniards," while operating largely out of local concerns, such as the desire to protect ecclesiastical privilege or the cult of a local saint.[17] Nevertheless, most members of both groups, consciously or

---

(1621–1789): *Entre pactismo y absolutismo* (Madrid: Centro de Estudios Políticos y Constitucionales, 1990); Charles Jago, "Habsburg Absolutism and the Cortes of Castile," *American Historical Review* 86, no. 2 (1981): 307–26; and Thompson, *Crown and Cortes*.

16. Francisco de Villafañe to the Compostelan cathedral chapter, 9 January 1629, ACSC, IG 301 (32), fol. 5r. "Hemos les satisfecho con que la corona de Castilla yncluye la mayor parte casi toda España, como es a Castilla la viexa al reino de León al Toledo al de Granada al de Seuilla al de Jaén al de Murcia al de Galicia al principado de Asturias etc. y parece juzgaron que era mucho lo que pedian los padres."

17. This particular example, although it is not an isolated use of the phrase, comes from a letter to the bishop of Zamora, which reads, "Y cada dia mas que a nra persuasion y por mostrarse uerdaderos y legitimos españoles y gratos al Apostol de quien han recibido tantos beneficios, quieren correr la misma fortuna." Compostelan cathedral chapter to the bishop of Zamora, 28 November 1627, ACSC, IG 940, fols. 268r–269r.

unconsciously, implicitly or explicitly, understood Castile and its relationship to the larger monarchy in similar ways. Those who weighed in
on the question, like Lobera and Rodríguez, viewed Castile as the most
important kingdom in the monarchy and the focal point of all the other
Spanish kingdoms, which were dependent upon it. This attitude had the
potential to unify them as Castilians, whether they were from Andalusia,
Old Castile, or Galicia. Yet, although Castilians described a vision of
Spain from a Castilian perspective, they usually did not use "Spain" as
another way of saying "Castile." Even if some *santiaguistas* described
"Spain" largely in terms of absence—by insisting that the various kingdoms that made up Spain were fragmented and distinct—they still
understood "Spain" as an entity encompassing all the Spanish kingdoms.
And, more important, they continued to view Spain as a living cultural
presence rather than as a mere historical memory.[18] The key difference
between the two sides centered on divergent understandings of
Spain—in the arguments of the *teresianos,* we see a legal and political
case for the power of the king and the superior position of Castile with
respect to other kingdoms. For many *santiaguistas,* by contrast, Spain
remained largely cultural and historical, distinct in some ways from the
vagaries of royal authority.

While Castilians might have viewed themselves as "Spaniards" ideologi-
cally or culturally, the debate nevertheless remained almost entirely a
Castilian affair. Whatever Teresa had been made patron saint of, the fact
remained that she was celebrated as patron only within the Crown of
Castile; in addition, almost every author or preacher involved in the
debate was Castilian, and nobody outside Castile seemed particularly
interested in the event.[19] Two important exceptions came from Portugal,
which had been integrated into the Spanish monarchy for nearly five

18. In "Castile, Spain, and the Monarchy," Thompson discusses a growing sense of "Spanishness" among Castilians and Aragonese by the mid-seventeenth century. Thompson recognizes the
multilayered identity issues involved in the debate when he describes the movement as a struggle
between anti-Hispanists (*teresianos*) and Hispanists (*santiaguistas*); he uses these categories to denote
Castilian political thinkers who believed that the various kingdoms should have nothing to do with
one another (retaining their older composite model) and those who believed the various units
should be integrated more fully into a "Spain," even though they might retain different customs
and laws.

19. One possible exception may be Mexico, which seems to have elected Teresa as co-patron
with the royal decree in 1618. What came of this decision, if anything, is not clear, and has not yet
been studied, to my knowledge; for a brief discussion of Teresa's election as patron saint of Mexico,
and a description of what were clearly co-patronage images of Teresa and Santiago in the church of
the Carmelite convent of San José, see Elisa Sampson Vera Tudela, *Colonial Angels: Narratives of
Gender and Spirituality in Mexico, 1580–1750* (Austin: University of Texas Press, 2000), 17–18.

decades. The first, Antonio de Casuallo de Parada, was a *teresiano* priest; little can be discerned about Casuallo personally, although his treatise was dedicated to Olivares. The second, Joan Salgado de Aráujo, was an author of a lengthy *santiaguista* treatise and a native of Braga.[20] Salgado was an abbot in the Portuguese town of Pero when he wrote his defense of Santiago's patronage (in *castellano*); soon after finishing his treatise, in October 1628, he appealed to the Compostelan cathedral to help him publish it in Galicia. He explained that the archbishop of Lisbon had blocked attempts to grant him a printing license.[21] The chapter declined to print Salgado's treatise, whereupon the abbot proceeded to Salamanca, where he made a secret contract with a printer and published his 112-folio treatise without a license.[22] Despite the Compostelan cathedral's lukewarm response to Salgado's overtures, the chapter had previously attempted to garner some support for its cause within Portugal. In October 1627 the chapter sent letters to Cardinal Albernoz, the archbishop of Lisbon, the archbishop of Coimbra, the archbishop of Braga, and the University of Coimbra.[23]

In addition to searching for allies in Portugal, *santiaguistas* looked to Aragón for support by emphasizing the two kingdoms' shared history and indebtedness to the apostle's evangelization. Both kingdoms were drawn together by the presence of an important shrine to Our Lady of the Pillar in Zaragoza, where the Virgin Mary had appeared to Santiago and encouraged him in a moment of despair to continue his work evangelizing Spain. The pillar marking the spot where the Virgin had appeared remained one of the most important devotional sites in Aragón. The apparition created mutually reinforcing ties between the two kingdoms, and provided a basis for potential devotional unity between them, since they shared the historical, cultural, and religious effects of

20. Casuallo de Parada, "Discurso Apologetico de dichosa Patrona." This is the only edition of this work that I am aware of, and it is in manuscript. Perhaps others were printed in Portugal and can be found in archives there. See also Salgado de Aráujo, *Memorial, informacion, y defension apologetica.*

21. Salgado to the Compostelan cathedral chapter, October 1628, ACSC, IG 301 (89), unpaginated. It is possible that the archbishop of Lisbon did not wish to approve a treatise for publication that might anger Olivares or Philip IV.

22. Compostelan chapter to Salgado, 26 October 1628, ibid.; and Salgado to cathedral chapter, 27 November 1628, ACSC, IG 310, unpaginated. Salgado's treatise demonstrated great loyalty to the cathedral of Santiago; it provided a lengthy and spirited defense of *santiaguista* traditions in Spain, including a refutation of Baronius and Loaysa, and advocated the protection of the *voto.*

23. Compostelan chapter to University of Coimbra, 26 October 1627, ACSC, IG 940, fol. 243r. The university seems to have eventually made a declaration in favor of Santiago. Cathedral chapter to Cardinal Sandoval, 26 March 1628, ACSC, IG 941, fols. 39v–40r. The chapter assured the cardinal that "las uniuersidades de Coimbra, Alcala, y Valladolid . . . concurren a la defensa del Patronazgo de nro Apostol."

Santiago's evangelization of Spain. The connection between the two was so strong that the cathedral of Santiago claimed, in a 1618 letter to Philip III, that the Virgin Mary already held the place as patroness of Spain, manifest through her intervention in Spain's conversion.[24] The earliest attempts to garner support in Aragón on Santiago's behalf were undertaken by Pedro de Castro, archbishop of Seville, who tried to elicit the archbishop of Zaragoza's support on the grounds of Teresa's threat to the apostle's cult. He wrote to the archbishop in September 1618, alerting his fellow prelate to the temerity of the Discalced Carmelites and encouraging him to join his voice to the *santiaguistas*'. The letter ended with a reminder of what the cult of the Virgin of the Pillar in Zaragoza owed to Santiago.[25] The archbishop of Zaragoza, however, was not swayed by this unified devotional vision of Spain. His response reminded Castro tartly that the laws of Castile did not apply to Aragón, that the royal letters ordering the celebration of Teresa's patronage had not arrived, and furthermore that Castro ought to remember that it was Saint George and not Santiago who appeared in Aragonese battles to defend them against infidels.[26]

Two conclusions may be drawn from the cathedral's attempts to find support in Aragón, Portugal, and Navarre.[27] First, the response from non-Castilian officials and churches must have been lukewarm at best; none seemed particularly interested in jumping into the fray, and there is little or no evidence to suggest an outburst of interest in co-patronage in any of these places. Second, the Compostelan cathedral itself demonstrated very little interest in these places. While it did send letters urging support outside Castile, they were few and far between. Such lack of activity provides a striking contrast to the hundreds of letters it sent to every prelate in Castile, most cities, and the most important universities,

24. It was not, interestingly, an argument that gained any ground. Compostelan chapter to Philip III, 30 September 1618, ACSC, IG 940, fol. 149r.

25. Pedro de Castro to the archbishop of Zaragoza, 18 September 1618, BNM, MS 18647 (66), fol. 1r–v.

26. Archbishop of Zaragoza to Pedro de Castro, 28 September 1618, ibid., fol. 2r–v: "porque como este Reyno no se gouierno por lo que haze el de Castilla, no han venido las cartas con tanto prisa a sus Ciudades, y lo que alla es Santiago es aca San Jorge que les ha favorecido en sus batallas con tan grandes milagros y tan continuos, que pudieron con tan poca gente hechar tan inmemorables numero de infieles como salieron de su tierra" (fol. 2r). Subsequent attempts by *santiaguistas* to enlist the aid of the Aragonese were no more successful. Compostelan chapter to the *diputados* of the kingdom of Aragón, 2 November 1627, ACSC, IG 940, fols. 250v–251r. The cathedral chapter also wrote to the Church of the Pillar in Zaragoza, from which it received a somewhat more favorable reply. Cathedral chapter of Santiago to the Church of the Pillar, 17 May 1628, ACSC, IG 941, fol. 62r.

27. Compostelan chapter to the *diputados* of Navarre, 29 May 1628, ACSC, IG 941, fol. 65r–v.

which in some cases devolved into unrelenting nagging of those who did not respond swiftly enough. Despite the appeal provided by the vision of ancient Hispania united under the banner of the unique and singular patronage of Santiago, the reality of such a vision could not match the cathedral's rhetoric. Indifference to Santiago's plight outside Castile suggests that the apostle's cult did not in fact have much salience elsewhere, and that the other kingdoms—not included in the royal mandate to celebrate co-patronage—could not rouse much interest in a controversy that had nothing to do with them. The limitation of symbolic reach reveals that despite the passionate rhetoric about "Spain," the national dimension of *both* saints' patronage remained elusive. If the patron saint of Castile could potentially be called the patron saint of Spain, the patron saint of Spain nevertheless remained Castilian.

But even Castile itself cannot be viewed as a monolithic whole. It was permeated by local identities that operated alongside any national agenda, and few things aroused local pride and loyalty more intensely than local sacred geography. The cult of Santiago, for example, was local as well as national. Despite the apostle's significance throughout the Iberian Peninsula, his relics rested in Galicia, where the local population was invested in his shrine in a way that other Castilians were not. In addition to local loyalties, a variety of circumstances could affect the way a specific city reacted to the new patron saint; for example, some celebrated Teresa's feast day as patron because the king asked them to. Yet it is important to remember that a city's dutiful compliance with the 1627 royal letter mandating the celebration of the feast day does not prove that the city was "for" Teresa's elevation. In fact, many cities expressed embarrassment over their compliance with the royal mandate. They occasionally wrote the cathedral that the feast had been celebrated only out of loyalty to the king, and they promised never to celebrate it again. One example comes from the bishop of Badajoz, Juan Roco Camposio, who responded to the cathedral of Santiago with a letter of regret, explaining that the cathedral had been "obligated" by the royal order and the insistence of the town council.[28] Scarcely two months later, in mid-January 1628, the cathedral chapter of Badajoz printed a letter to the king in which it protested Teresa's elevation.[29] It is difficult to tell

28. Bishop of Badajoz to the Compostelan cathedral, 13 November 1627, ACSC, IG 301 (93), unpaginated.

29. "Copia de la carta que la santa Iglesia de Badajoz." On 6 February 1628 the cathedral of Santiago wrote to the cathedral of Badajoz, congratulating it on its "valiant" letter to the king. ACSC, IG 941, fol. 26r.

whether the cathedral of Badajoz had succumbed to the pressure of the cathedral of Santiago or had gained confidence to resist the king from the examples of other cathedral chapters.[30]

Most of the detailed information for a mapping of support for or resistance to co-patronage relates to cathedral chapters. The emphasis on these chapters, rather than on towns or even bishops, could potentially distort our understanding of the geographical distribution of support for Santiago, since the chapters were overwhelmingly opposed to co-patronage. Although this problem is discussed in more detail in the next chapter, it must be remarked here that the unified *santiaguista* position of the most powerful and wealthy cathedral chapters—Toledo, Burgos, Seville, Santiago—suggests strongly that many cathedral chapters might simply have closed ranks behind these powerful archbishops. The cathedral of Santiago, in particular, proved relentless in its attempts to persuade, bribe, or coerce all other Castilian chapters into supporting its apostle. In one early letter to the archbishop of Santiago, the chapter confided that "we offer with great pleasure our livings and lands in defense of our sacred Apostle."[31] The cathedral spent much of its time on its vast letter-writing offensive, and much of its revenue on printing, distributing, and, most probably, rewarding the authors of favorable treatises. Several of these authors were themselves members of the chapter, including Pedro Astorga de Castillo, Benito Méndez de Parga y Andrade, and Alonso Rodríguez de León, all of whose treatises must have been financed by the cathedral and were printed by the same publisher in Santiago de Compostela, Juan Guixard de León.[32] Many authors not officially connected with the cathedral attempted to gain the chapter's attention by sending it a copy of their work in the hopes of gaining patronage, including (with the dates of their letters, all but

30. Town councils, especially those that elected representatives with votes in the Cortes that had unanimously voted for Teresa's elevation, had a different agenda from the cathedral chapters. The tensions between municipal and ecclesiastical authorities are discussed in chapter 6.

31. "Nuestras uidas, y haçiendas que con mucho gusto ofreçemos en defensa deste sagrado Apóstol." Cathedral chapter of Santiago to the archbishop, 10 October 1627, ACSC, IG 940, fol. 238r–v.

32. Pedro Astorga de Castillo, *Informacion por el Dean y Cabildo de la Santa Iglesia Apostolica y Metropolitana de Santiago, unico Patron de las Españas; con la religion sagrada del Carmen Descalço* (Santiago de Compostela: Juan de León, 1631); Méndez de Parga y Andrade, *Discursos del unico patronazgo de España;* Benito Méndez de Parga y Andrade, *Respuesta a un papel que escrivio el Dotor Balboa de Mogrovejo . . .* (Santiago de Compostela: Juan Guixard de León, 1628); Benito Méndez de Parga y Andrade, *Alegatio iuris pro unico hispaniarum Patrono Diuo Iacobo Zebedeo* [Santiago: Juan de León, ca. 1628], ACSC, IG 301 (9); and Rodríguez de León, *Carta a su Magestad.* For more on Méndez and his role in the cathedral, see Fermín Bouza Brey, "Dos obras desconocidas de Méndez de Andrade, famoso defensor de las prerrogativas de la Iglesia Compostelana," *Compostellanum* 11, no. 4 (1966): 615–20.

the last from 1628) Pedro de Losada y Quiroga (22 February), Francisco Melgar (6 March), Fernando Mera Carvajal (22 June), Alonso de Serna (22 August), Pedro González Guijelmo (1 November), Joan Salgado de Aráujo (27 November), and Andrés de Torres (1 August 1629).[33]

The cathedral of Santiago played a vital role not only in encouraging and financing *santiaguista* partisans but also in distributing their works. One *teresiano* author complained loudly about the number of treatises flying from Galicia to the rest of Castile.[34] Most *santiaguista* authors sent an early copy to Santiago de Compostela, which in turn circulated them throughout Castile. The diversity of cities in which various treatises were printed (including Cuenca, Málaga, Cádiz, and Barcelona) posed no impediment to their far-flung dissemination. The cathedral often included *santiaguista* treatises in letters that tried to persuade other churches to come to its side; it also sent such treatises to churches already loyal, perhaps in an endeavor to keep them agitated and on board.[35] In addition, cathedral representatives in Madrid spread pamphlets around the court.[36] All of this activity on the cathedral's part is one explanation for the rapid and widespread distribution of the texts. The printing and distribution of treatises constituted a critically important aspect of the debate, as it enabled the quick spread of ideas across vast tracts of land and allowed anyone in a populous Castilian town to have access to at least one of the major treatises.

The *teresiano* faction, by contrast, was less unified than its opponents and lacked a geographical center. The best source available for tracking Carmelite correspondence to supporters comes from two letters destined for Rome, both of which contained lists, compiled in Italian, of co-patronage supporters, the first dated March 1628 and the second, April of the same year. In March 1628, Juan Ortiz de Zarate, a royal secretary, compiled a list of twenty-seven cities that had written to verify their conformity to the royal order to celebrate Teresa as patron: Toledo, Burgos, Palencia, Cartagena, Salamanca, Badajoz, Cadiz, Astorga, Ciudad-Rodrigo, Guadix,

33. All of these letters can be found in ACSC, IG 310, unpaginated.

34. Ahumada y Tapia, "A Don Francisco Tamariz" (1628), HSA, unpaginated: "y es ansi que la repugnancia que ay en algunos es nacida de la inundacion de cartas y memoriales de que Galicia a llenado a Espana."

35. The cathedral of Tuy, for example, acknowledged receipt of a work written in the name of the archbishop of Santiago on 2 December 1627, Méndez's treatise on 20 July 1628, Pedro de Losada's on 5 October 1628, and Rodríguez de León's on 1 January 1629. The cathedral of Jaén likewise received a copy of Méndez's treatise on 8 August 1628. ACSC, IG 301 (49), unpaginated.

36. Compostelan cathedral chapter to its representatives at court, 5 March 1628, ACSC, IG 941, fol. 31r–v. This letter refers to the cathedral's sending a number of copies of Méndez's treatise for distribution in Madrid.

Oviedo, Sigüenza, Valladolid, Calzada, Tudela, Ubeda, Plasencia, Segovia, Murcia, Cuenca, Soria, Coria, Ecija, Trujillo, Lucena, Vitoria, and Lorca (see map 3).[37] The next letter included a notarized list of letters supporting co-patronage collected by the papal nuncio in Madrid; their authors included the bishop of Córdoba; cathedral chapters of Salamanca, Avila,

Map 3   Cities celebrating Teresa's patron sainthood, 1627

37. ACSC, IG 301 (38), unpaginated.

and Calahorra; and the cities of Vitoria, Segovia, Avila, Málaga, Córdoba, Valladolid, Granada, Baeza, Andújar, Ciudad-Real, Antequera, Medina del Rioseco, and Berlanga.[38] Similar lists, with small variations, can also be found in Carmelite collections.[39] It is not surprising to note the presence of many cities with monasteries founded personally by Teresa, including Baeza, Segovia, Soria, Burgos, Palencia, Valladolid, Salamanca, and Avila. The mapping of the cities from these two letters presents a widely dispersed landscape of initial supporters for Teresa's elevation in Old and New Castile, Andalusia, León, and Asturias; the geographical diversity reflects both general conformity to the royal order mandating the celebration of her feast day and the widespread presence of Carmelite religious houses dotting Castile's sacred landscape.

On the opposing side, analysis of the cathedral of Santiago's intense letter-writing campaign leaves a more detailed trail of information than the Carmelite evidence, largely owing to the fact that the cathedral's strategy included updating its list of supporters, which grew longer over time. Palencia, León, Burgos, Lugo, Oviedo, Orense, and Astorga all received a special letter from the cathedral of Santiago in November, preserved under the title "Letter to the churches who do not receive the patronage of Teresa," indicating that these churches emerged quickly as staunch *santiaguista* cathedral chapters.[40] By January 1628 the cathedral could boast of an increased number of allies who had written notarized letters declaring their opposition to co-patronage, among them Toledo, Santiago, Seville, Granada, Burgos, Córdoba, Cuenca, Cartagena, Coria, Palencia, León, Astorga, Orense, Lugo, and Mondoñedo. It added that it hoped soon to receive letters from Jaén, Málaga, Cádiz, and Zamora (see map 4).[41] By the middle of March the cathedral claimed that only Valladolid, Avila, and Salamanca remained

38. Ibid. Although this postdates the previous list, it precedes it in the legajo.

39. Juan Ortiz de Zarate's list can also be found in Antonio de San Joaquín, *Año teresiano, Diario Histórico, panegyrico moral, en que se descriven las virtudes, sucesos, y maravillas de la Seraphica, y Mystica Doctora de la Iglesia, Santa Teresa de Jesús, asignadas a todos los dias de los meses en que sucedieron*, 7 vols., vol. 2 (Madrid: Manuel Fernández, 1735), 149–50. Testimony collected by the royal Cámara and the Carmelite order can be found at RAH, Col. Salazar y Castro, MS 9/1042, fol. 224r. Each includes slight variations when compared to the Italian list at the ACSC.

40. Compostelan cathedral chapter to churches not receiving Teresa's patronage, 21 November 1627, ACSC, IG 940, fol. 261r–v.

41. Compostelan cathedral chapter to Fernando Brandamo, 23 January 1628, ACSC, IG 941, fol. 21r–v: "que dando solamente por la parte de los Frailes Auila, donde nacio, Salamanca donde murio y está su sagrado cuerpo, Valladolid, Siguença, Plasencia, Callahorra, y Badajoz." Twelve core supporters of the *santiaguista* cause (Toledo, Seville, Burgos, Palencia, Cuenca, Córdoba, Jaén, Calahorra, Sigüenza, Cádiz, Lugo, and Almeria) banded together in the summer of 1629 and wrote a letter to the pope in the name of the Castilian clergy. "Twelve churches of the Crown of Castile to His Holiness the pope," 23 July 1629, ACSC, IG 301 (38), unpaginated.

Map 4   Cities staunchly opposed to co-patronage, 1627–1630

on the *teresiano* side.[42] Patterns of support for the cathedral of Santiago from either cathedral chapters or bishops throughout Castile show dense clusters of support for the apostle in Galicia and Andalusia, north and south, the oldest and most recent parts of Spain, respectively. The Compostelan cathedral proved particularly relentless at forcing its

42. Cathedral chapter to its representatives at court, 5 March 1628, ACSC, IG 941, fol. 31r–v; and cathedral chapter to Pedro Sanz de Castillo, 12 March 1628, ibid., fol. 36r–v.

suffragan churches into loyalty to its apostle and obedience to its will. Yet the number of cities appearing on both the *teresiano* and *santiaguista* lists suggests that the cities' responses to co-patronage tended to be varied; they did not reflect a black-and-white demonstration of loyalty or opposition but sometimes hedged or flip-flopped, no doubt as a result of complicated internal politics and devotional patterns.

One mainstay of *santiaguista* support in the heartland of Castile was the cathedral chapter of Cuenca. Fernando Mera Carvajal, the governor of the bishopric, wrote two treatises in defense of Santiago's patronage, one in 1628 and one in 1631, both of which were printed in Cuenca.[43] He received a warm letter of thanks and congratulation from the cathedral of Santiago for his first treatise in the spring of 1628, to which he replied with gratitude and humility.[44] In addition, the cathedral chapter of Cuenca appears to have been heavily involved in writing letters in support of Santiago, particularly to Rome. It assured the cathedral of Santiago that its agent in Rome, Pedro de Alarcón y Granada, was working actively to help Santiago's agents at the papal curia.[45] It is possible that the cathedral of Cuenca's staunch defense of Santiago originated in its ties with the priory of Uclés, within the bishopric of Cuenca, which was the head of the Order of the Knighthood of Santiago.[46]

Staunch support for Teresa, on the other hand, centered in the cities of Avila, Salamanca, and Valladolid. These cities formed what we can think of as the Teresian heartland, her native land. She was born in Avila, where she passed most of her life and began the Discalced reform, founded important monasteries in Salamanca and Valladolid, and died in the town of Alba de Tormes in the archdiocese of Salamanca, where her sepulcher is housed. She also maintained close ties with several powerful noble families in the area, who acted as patrons to her foundations— namely, the dukes of Alba and the Mendozas.[47] The ducal seat of the Alba family was Alba de Tormes, where Teresa took ill and died while on a visit to the duchess. In Valladolid, María de Mendoza sponsored the foundation of a Discalced convent by providing land on which it could

43. Mera Carvajal, *Informacion en derecho por el unico y singular Patronato.*

44. Compostelan cathedral chapter to Fernando de Mera Carvajal, 16 May 1628, ACSC, IG 941, fol. 61v. The cathedral proclaimed, "Ha de empeñado Vm las prendas quede su gran caudal teniamos, y ha mostrado quien por naturaleza y por gracia, pues como español sigue a su Patron Santiago, y como sabio jurisconsulto le defiende."

45. ACSC, IG 301 (49), unpaginated.

46. The prior of Uclés naturally raised his voice loudly in defense of his saint. See Jorge de Oreo Tinco, *Una carta del prior de Uclés al Rey Felipe IV* (1627), BNM, VE 60/37.

47. For an overview of Teresa's patrons and her relationships with them, see Weber, "Teresa's Problematic Patrons," 357–80. On the powerful Mendoza women, see Nader, *Power and Gender in Renaissance Spain.*

be built; María's early interest in Teresa's reform is not surprising, given that her brother, Alvaro de Mendoza, was the bishop of Avila who championed Teresa's first foundation, San José.[48]

Both Avila and Salamanca regularly celebrated Teresa's feast day; details about the celebrations are scanty, although the account of the feast in Avila gushed euphorically about the festivities and named the well-known Carmelite Cristóbal de Avendaño as one of the preachers for the event.[49] As early as Teresa's beatification, the city of Salamanca vowed to celebrate her feast day "perpetually," as the city's particular *abogada,* because of the presence of her relics in the bishopric, her personal foundation of a Discalced Carmelite convent, and her intercession for the city during her lifetime and after her death.[50] One anonymous *teresiano* proudly pointed out that it was fitting for Teresa to be patron of Salamanca, a renowned university city filled with many great men, since Teresa was the mother of wisdom.[51] Valladolid also manifested lively devotion to Teresa and enduring support for her patron sainthood. In the city's celebration of Teresa's canonization (1622), decorations included a reference to Teresa as patron saint—one of the banners proclaimed her patron of Spain.[52] This banner is the only surviving reference that I have uncovered to Teresa as patron during the lull in the co-patronage debate, a clear sign that Teresa's supporters in that vibrant city had not lost hope that she would regain the title promised her in 1617–18. Sermons for this canonization festival were preached by Cristóbal de Avendaño (again) and Francisco Pimentel, who was the brother of the bishop of Valladolid, Enrique Pimentel. Francisco also appeared in Madrid for the 1627 festivities for Teresa's patron sainthood, where he preached a sermon dedicated to the count-duke of Olivares.[53] The Discalced convent in Valladolid also housed two prominent poets, sisters

---

48. Bilinkoff, *Avila of Saint Teresa,* 148–49. For more on the foundation in Valladolid, see Juan Luis Rodríguez and Jesús Urrea, *Santa Teresa en Valladolid y Medina del Campo* (Valladolid: Caja de Ahorros Popular de Valladolid, 1982), 117–64.

49. "El voto de la ciudad de Salamanca a Santa Teresa en 1618," *Basilica Teresiana* 3, no. 16 (1899): 214–15; and "Una carta de una relación de las fiestas se celebró Ávila por el patronato de Teresa de Jesús," BNM, MS 9140, fol. 274r–v.

50. Manrique de Luján, *Relacion de las fiestas de la ciudad de Salamanca,* 59–60.

51. "Por la conservacion del patronato de la gloriosa virgen Santa Teresa," fol. 38v.

52. "Y por porla alrededor de las palmas en el friso del escudo, dezia así, *Theresiae Matris, Viriginis almae, Hispaniae Patronae, Stemata praeclara.* Las tres palmas en significación de Virgen, Mártir, y Doctora con sus coronas, laureolas de su gloria accidental, y la imperial, en significación de la essencial." *Relacion de la fiesta que se hizo en el convento del Carmen Calçado de Valladolid, en la canonicaçion de Santa Teresa de Iesus, por un deuoto suyo* (1622), fols. 5v–6r.

53. The Pimentel brothers were connected to royal power and patronage at the highest levels. They were of the house of the Counts of Benavente; another brother, Domingo, became a Dominican who was eventually sent by Philip IV to Rome as an ambassador extraordinaire in 1633. Quintín

who gained some celebrity for their involvement in poetry contests connected to feast day celebrations. One of the sisters, María de San Alberto, wrote a cycle of poems celebrating Teresa's patron sainthood, which ranged from simple rejoicing to sharper commentary addressing the controversy more directly.[54]

Not only did these three cities represent the heartland of Teresian devotion, they were also the only cities not included in the cathedral of Santiago's letter-writing campaign. The cathedral believed that Avila and Salamanca in particular had what it called a "natural interest" in electing Teresa as their patron; the cathedral of Santiago therefore viewed these cities' celebration of her as their patron saint as separate from the issue of national patron sainthood.[55] This perspective reflected the Castilian understanding of devotional practices, which privileged local saints, particularly those who were born and died in a given place. The cathedral's neglect of these cities led ironically to their relative silence throughout the debate—they were not included; therefore they did not participate, at least not in any way that has left traces. It appears that they remained satisfied with the local devotion to Teresa.

The cathedral of Santiago demonstrated great sensitivity to local loyalties and local cults on several occasions; it often attempted to woo churches into opposition to co-patronage by tapping into pride about local cults. It would point out the potential destruction of a local cult (as in the case of Zaragoza) or by hinting that a local favorite saint had just as much right to be patron as Teresa. The cathedral employed the latter tactic in a letter to the chapter of Osma, in which it cleverly inserted a reference to Osma's local canonized bishop, San Pedro, into the list of renowned Spanish holy people who were as suitable as Teresa to be patron.[56] Such appeals to local pride tapped into the rising popularity of local distinctions throughout the late sixteenth and early seventeenth centuries.[57] Jerónimo de Ceballos, an *arbitrista* and native Toledan, wrote

Aldea Vaquero, Tomás Marín Martínez, and José Vives Gatell, eds., *Diccionario de la historia eclesiástica de España,* 4 vols. (Madrid: CSIC, 1972), 3:1982.

54. "Es santa Teresa / patrona de España / a pesar de Gallegos / y bien de su patria." María de San Alberto, *Viva al siglo, muerta al mundo,* ed. and trans. Stacey Schlau (New Orleans: University of the South Press, 1998), 98 (the whole cycle can be found on pp. 93–124). On the two sisters, María de San Alberto and Cecilia del Nacimiento, see Electa Arenal and Stacey Schlau, *Untold Sisters: Hispanic Nuns in Their Own Words,* translations by Amanda Powell (Albuquerque: University of New Mexico Press, 1989), 122–63.

55. For one example of many, see Compostelan cathedral chapter to the churches of Zamora, Salamanca, and Badajoz, 19 December 1627, ACSC, IG 941, fols. 12v–13r.

56. Cathedral chapter to chapter of Osma, 16 October 1627, ACSC, IG 940, fols. 241v–242r. One of the canons in the cathedral of Osma, Pedro González Guijelmo, wrote a popular *santiaguista* treatise.

57. For studies that address the issue of local identity in early modern Castile, see especially Kagan, "Clio and the Crown," 73–99; and Thompson, "Castile, Spain and the Monarchy," 137.

the town council in 1618, urging it to reject Teresa's co-patronage. One of his arguments stressed the great number of Catholic saints worthy of patron sainthood, among which he gave precedence to the numerous saints from Toledo, pronouncing twelve Toledan saints "worthy of this title."[58] Ceballos's argument suggests that it was not so much that he doubted Teresa's worthiness to be patron as that he harbored a regional complaint against the unfair favoring of one city over another. Rather than view the elevation of Teresa as the election of a popular saint to patron of Spain, authors like Ceballos saw the matter as a privilege granted to Avila; any privilege granted to one city alone had the potential to harm the rest, and thus provided ample motivation for rejecting co-patronage.

Both Teresa and Santiago can be read as local and national saints simultaneously. Despite its rhetoric of Spanish identity, the cathedral of Santiago's main motivation in rejecting co-patronage was to maintain the integrity, celebrity, and wealth of its local cult, in the same way that the Discalced Carmelites had initiated Teresa's election at least partly to promote and strengthen the cult of their founder. Yet I do not wish to suggest that co-patronage rhetoric or national patron sainthood was a cynical scheme to mask selfish interests. While local loyalties sometimes lay at the heart of individual motivations, shared historical, devotional, personal, and ideological concerns forged ties between places. "España" served as a rallying cry and ideological focus for both sides of the co-patronage debate. Center and periphery, nation and region, stood in tension with each other, but they were also deeply intertwined; sometimes they nourished, and sometimes they repelled each other.

In order to see all these forces at work with and against one another, a more narrowly focused discussion is required. Andalusia provides a fascinating example of the collision (and collusion) of regional, particularist, royal, and national interests in the co-patronage debate. The fiercest battles of the controversy occurred in this southernmost province of the Crown of Castile, largely as a result of its thriving intellectual community, strong Carmelite presence, and unique historical circumstances. Andalusia had been integrated relatively late into the Christian kingdoms of Spain after many centuries of Islamic rule; even its name, Andalusia, reflects its Islamic ties—from the Arabic *al-Andalus*. Early modern Andalusians displayed anxiety about their imperfectly Christian past, which often led to attempts to erase Islam from their imaginary

58. Ceballos, "Parecer contra el patronazgo de España," 378.

historical landscape as much as possible.[59] This desire manifested itself in a variety of ways, one of which involved reclaiming and emphasizing Andalusia's early Christian past, manifested in various "discoveries" of the relics of early Christian martyrs, along with the forged *plomos* outside Granada in 1585. As Katie Harris has astutely remarked, "For Granada's Old Christian majority, however, the finds [the *plomos*] became key elements in the process by which Granada, the emblematic city of Spanish Islam, was transformed into a model Christian city. The relics and the writings of their patron saint enabled Granadinos to imagine themselves as the legitimate heirs to an ancient and now restored Christian heritage."[60] The discoveries, and the transformation they entailed, rested firmly on the foundation of Santiago's evangelization in the first century.[61] While all Castilian local histories wished to tie their town's conversion to the apostle, Andalusians felt the strongest impulse (outside Galicia) to validate Santiago and his cult.[62]

Granada provides an obvious example of a city indebted to Santiago and his cult. But its role in the co-patronage debate was conflicted, partially owing to a lively Discalced Carmelite presence in the city. In 1617 sumptuous celebrations were prepared in honor of Teresa's feast day, mandated by the archbishop, Felipe de Tarsis.[63] One of the sermons preached during this event by a well-known Andalusian Discalced Carmelite, Agustín Núñez Delgadillo, was eventually printed.[64] The city

59. Andalusian cities have been the subject of numerous recent works on devotion and identity. See, for example, David Coleman, *Creating Christian Granada: Society and Religious Culture in an Old-World Frontier City, 1492–1600* (Ithaca: Cornell University Press, 2003); Heather Ecker, "'Arab Stones': Rodrigo Caro's Translation of Arabic Inscriptions in Sevilla (1634), Revisited," *Al-Qantara* 23, no. 2 (2002): 349–401; and Harris, *From Muslim to Christian Granada*.

60. A. Katie Harris, "The Sacromonte and the Geography of the Sacred in Early Modern Granada," *Al-Qantara* 23, no. 2 (2002): 518.

61. Justino Antolínez de Burgos, *Historia eclesiástica de Granada,* ed. Manuel Sotomayor (Granada: Universidad de Granada, 1996), 653–54. For more on Antolínez's life and career, see Sotomayor's introduction to the *Historia Eclesiástica,* xiii–xxii. Antolínez died the bishop of Tortosa (Catalonia) in 1637.

62. On local histories and their interest in discovering connections to conversion by the apostle, see Kagan, "Clio and the Crown," 89. Other cities, like Avila, boasted the relics of Santiago's disciples, although such relics did not attain the importance that Andalusia's did.

63. During the procession, an image of Teresa was taken from the Discalced Carmelite convent of San José to the church, where the Discalced Carmelite monks donated it. This description of the festival comes from Francisco Henríquez de Jorquera, *Anales de Granada,* ed. Antonio Marín Ocete, 2 vols. (Granada: Universidad de Granada, 1987), 2:615. The *Anales* make no other reference to Teresa or to co-patronage.

64. Agustín Núñez Delgadillo, *Sermon de la gloriosa Sancta Teresa de Iesus, predicado en el Conuento de las Carmelitas descalcas de Granada, lunes de su octaua* (Granada: Juan Muñoz, 1617). Núñez had also preached a sermon in honor of Teresa's beatification in Granada: "Sermón predicado en la misma solenidad, y convento de Granada, por el Padre Maestro Fr. Agustin Núñez Delgadillo, Carmelita, Regente, y Lector de Prima de Teologia, en el Convento de nuestra Señora de la

prepared the next year for Teresa's feast day with events that included a literary contest, for which an advertisement still survives, depicting Teresa and Santiago as co-patrons.[65] Prominent Carmelite Gaspar de Santa María appears on the advertisement as one of the judges. Gaspar was a Granadino and the author of a vitriolic defense of Teresa's right to be patron saint of Spain, which was published under the pseudonym León de Tapia. A history of the Carmelite Order singled Gaspar out as one of the most noteworthy Carmelites of the early seventeenth century, calling him "most learned in Greek and Hebrew, great in Scripture, theology, poetry, and all letters. . . . His health was very poor; therefore, he could not enter into leadership, nor publish as much as he could have."[66] It must have been the leadership of local Carmelites like Gaspar who insisted that the festivals honoring Teresa as co-patron ought to proceed despite the complaints of local cathedral chapters.

During the second phase of the debate (1627–30), the new archbishop, Cardinal Agustín Spinola, suspended Teresa's feast day in the city until the co-patronage controversy had been decided in Rome.[67] Although the cathedral of Santiago was wont to claim Granada as an ally, in a 1628 letter to its representatives in Rome it confessed that Granada would remain neutral on the issue of co-patronage, despite its frequently expressed desire to defend the prerogatives of Santiago. The chapter speculated that because the cathedral in Granada remained under the direct patronage of the king, it might not wish to go against the king's desire.[68] In the need to prevent the king's anger while simultaneously maintain close ties with Santiago's cult, the archbishop established a middle territory in which he expressed unconditional loyalty to the apostle, while refraining from playing a high-profile role in the debate.

Support for Teresa's patronage cropped up in other Andalusian towns and villages, particularly in the early years of the debate. Málaga

---

Cabeça," in José de Jesús María, *Sermones predicados en la Beatificacion de la Beata Madre Teresa de Iesus.*

65. The poster can be found folded and tucked neatly into a volume of works primarily on the Immaculate Conception at the BNM. "Iusta Poetica en el Convento Real de los Santos Martires," fol. 288r.

66. José de Santa Teresa, *Reforma de los Descalzos de Nuestra Señora,* 4:923.

67. Francisco Bermúdez de Pedraza, *Historia eclesiástica de Granada* (1638), ed. Ignacio Henares Cuéllar (Granada: Universidad de Granada, 1989), fol. 280v.

68. "Aunque Granada nos ha escrito tener muchos desseos de concurrir con nosotros, no ha tomado resolucion quiça por ser aquella Sta Igla de Patronazgo de su Magd de derecho, y querer con esta neutralidad cumplir con esse respeto." Compostelan cathedral chapter to its representatives, 19 March 1628, ACSC, IG 941, fols. 36v–37r. For a discussion of the development of royal patronage and its effects on the cathedral chapter and archbishopric of Granada, see Coleman, *Creating Christian Granada,* 82–90.

(1618), Andújar (1618), and Antequera (1627) all celebrated feasts for the saint's elevation; Málaga also elected Teresa patron saint of the city.[69] Carmelite strength must have been at least partially responsible for such strong local support for Teresa's patronage. Many of the most highly respected Carmelites of the century were Andalusian; in addition to Gaspar, another of the great Discalced Carmelites of the early seventeenth century was a Granadino, Francisco de Santa María (1567–1649). Francisco wrote a *teresiano* pamphlet, became the official historian of his order, and acted as the Discalced Carmelite provincial for Andalusia in the 1630s.[70] Before becoming a religious, his secular name was don Fernando Pérez de Pulgar y Sandoval, which tied him to the powerful Sandoval family. Two members of the Sandoval family were in the prelacy at the time of the co-patronage debate: Melchior Moscoso y Sandoval, bishop of Segovia, and Melchior's brother, Cardinal Baltasar Moscoso y Sandoval, bishop of Jaén (Andalusia).[71] The brothers were the nephews of Francisco Gómez Sandoval y Rojas, the duke of Lerma and chief minister to Philip III. Francisco de Santa María, a relative of one of Spain's noble families and a highly placed Carmelite, is a good example of the strength of the *teresiano* movement in Andalusia.

Francisco and Baltasar Moscoso y Sandoval were connected by more than a family tree; Francisco wrote a treatise on behalf of the cardinal and his cathedral of Jaén, verifying the authenticity of a set of relics discovered in Arjona, a small village outside Jaén.[72] Yet in spite of the cathedral of Jaén's close ties to the Carmelite community, it rejected co-patronage and maintained a close alliance with the Compostelan cathedral. The first of a copious correspondence flowing back and forth between Jaén and Compostela was a letter from the cardinal himself, dated 2 November 1627, which began: "I have always venerated the cult

69. Enrique Gómez Martínez, "Las Carmelitas y fiestas que en la ciudad de Andújar se hacen en honor de Santa Teresa," in Criado de Val, *Santa Teresa y la literatura mística hispánica,* 629–35; and *Traslado y Relacion a la Letra a de las Solemnidades.* See also Francisco López Estrada, *Fiestas por Santa Teresa de Jesús en Málaga y en Antequera (1618 y 1627)* (Madrid: Schlesinger, 1982).

70. Francisco de Santa María, *Defensa del Patronato;* and Francisco de Santa María, *Reforma de los Descalzos de Nuestra Señora del Carmen, de la Primitiva Observancia,* vols. 1 and 2 (Madrid: Diego Díaz de la Carrera, 1644, 1655).

71. The position of the cathedral chapter of Segovia is unknown, but its bishop, Melchior Moscoso y Sandoval, supported co-patronage. A treatise—*Al illustrissimo y Reverendissimo senor Don Melchior de Moscoso, y Sandoual, Obispo de Segouia, del Consejo de su Magestad* (ca. 1628), HSA—was dedicated to the bishop, urging him to change his mind. Part of the anonymous author's argument is an exhortation to follow the example of his brother, Cardinal Moscoso y Sandoval, the bishop of Jaén and a defender of Santiago.

72. José de Santa Teresa, *Reforma de los Descalzos de Nuestra Señora del Carmen,* 4:921. Francisco de Santa María is also discussed in the *Diccionario de la historia eclesiástica de España,* 2:960. On the relic finding, see Olds, "'False Chronicles' in Early Modern Spain."

of our holy Apostle Santiago." The rest of the epistle pledged Jaén's support to the apostle's cause, offering to "tell his Majesty that it would be good not to make such a decision without hearing from the prelates and cathedral chapters."[73] The cardinal's two motivations—personal devotion to Santiago and the defense of ecclesiastical immunity—came together as mutually reinforcing impulses. The prior of the Discalced Carmelite monastery in Jaén, Alonso de San Hilarion, wrote a long letter to the cardinal, laying out the reasons why Moscoso ought to accept the 1627 brief and Teresa's patronage.[74] In spite of this Carmelite effort, the cardinal remained a stalwart defender of Santiago.[75]

Throughout 1628, Jaén and Compostela maintained close communication. Their alliance was strengthened by Jaén's production of an *auto capitular*, which declared the cathedral's loyalty to Santiago.[76] One of the cathedral canons, Pedro de Losada y Quiroga, eventually emerged as one of the greatest stars of the co-patronage debate. While not much is known about Losada beyond his involvement in Santiago's defense, he must have played a prominent role in the cathedral chapter. His signature appeared with that of two other canons on the 31 December 1627 letter to the cathedral of Santiago, written to announce the cathedral's *auto capitular*. The author of the *auto* was the chapter's secretary, Diego José de Mata, who explained that the chapter planned to write letters to the cathedral of Santiago as well as to the king and to Olivares. He added that the letters were to be handed over to Losada for delivery.[77] Losada's role in the *auto* and with the aforementioned letters earned him a personal message from the cathedral of Santiago, praising him for the high quality of his work.[78] Sometime in 1628, Losada wrote his own treatise, an extended defense of Santiago's singular patronage that remained one

73. Cardinal Moscoso y Sandoval to the Compostelan cathedral, 2 November 1627, ACSC, IG 301 (49), unpaginated.

74. Alonso de San Hilarion, "Una carta del prior de los descalzos carmelitas de Jaén, a S. Cardenal D. Baltasar de Moscoso y Sandoval, obispo de Jaén sobre el patronato de Santa Teresa" (ca. 1627), BNM, MS 9140, fols. 258r–263v.

75. Evidence suggests that Andalusian Carmelites did not hold this against the cardinal; Discalced Carmelite Jerónimo de Pancorbo, a native of Jaén and resident of Seville, wrote an epitaph honoring the cardinal upon his death in 1646. Balbino Vélasco Bayón, *Historia del Carmelo Español*, vol. 3 (Rome: Instititum Carmelitanum, 1994), 493.

76. *Copia del auto Capitular que hizo la santa Iglesia de Jaén en 31 de Deciembre de 1627 tocante de la defensa de la singularidad del patronazgo del Apóstol Santiago* (1628), ACSC, IG 301 (57). The cathedral archive of Santiago has preserved thirteen letters from either the bishop of Jaén or its cathedral between November 1627 and October 1628, an unusually high volume of surviving letters. All of them can be found in the original at ACSC, IG 301 (49), unpaginated.

77. *Copia del auto Capitular que hizo la santa Iglesia de Jaén*, fol. 71r–v. The 31 December letter can be found in ACSC, IG 301 (49). Losada also wrote to several cardinals at the papal curia in the name of the chapter. Archivo Diocesano de Jaén, Autos capitulares, libro 22 (1628), fol. 176r.

78. Compostelan cathedral to Pedro de Losada, 6 February 1628, ACSC, IG 941, fol. 25r.

of the most widely read treatises of the debate and was printed in two separate editions.[79] Two Carmelites wrote treatises directly refuting Losada, and their angry and insulting tone reflect the passion the canon's treatise provoked.[80] Not surprisingly, both Carmelite authors were Andalusians; the first was Gaspar de Santa María and the second, an anonymous Calced Carmelite whose work was printed in Cádiz.

Despite Losada's prominent role in the debate and the controversy his writings caused, the most dramatic conflict over co-patronage occurred in Seville, a city of great commercial and cultural vitality. Seville held a privileged position in the Indies trade, which ensured that the wealth flowing from the colonies traveled through its port on the Guadalquivir River. This wealth supported a thriving community of artists and men of letters; it was the home of some of baroque Spain's most famous painters, including Francisco Pacheco, Diego de Velázquez, and Bartolomé de Murillo. Its cathedral chapter was one of the wealthiest and most powerful in the Spanish kingdoms, and it duly took center stage in the debate beginning in 1617. Indeed, during this first stage, the archbishop of Seville, Pedro de Castro, played a larger role in defending Santiago's patronage than did the archbishop of Santiago.[81] Castro had a particular interest in the cult of Santiago, as he had been the archbishop of Granada during the discovery of the *plomos* and organized a tireless campaign to have the findings there verified.[82] The archbishop's letter to Philip III protesting Teresa's elevation was printed and circulated widely, provoking bitter responses from opponents.[83] In his *Ecclesiastical History of Granada* (1638), Francisco Bermúdez de Pedraza attributed the victory

79. Losada y Quiroga, *Al illustrissimo y reverendissimo Señor Arzobispo;* and Losada y Quiroga, *Defensa del unico y singular Patronazgo.* The editions are identical, except that the second was printed by a license in Santiago, most probably at the archbishop's behest.

80. *Respuesta a los Papeles en forma de memorial, que el Licenciado Pedro de Lossada, Canonigo de Iaen, embió a el Arcobispo de Santiago, en defensa de el Patronato de el Santo Apostol; y en opposicion de el de la Gloriosa Santa Teresa* (Cádiz: Gaspar Vezino, [ca. 1628]) (dedicated to the Discalced nuns of Córdoba); and Tapia, *Examen y refutacion de los fundamentos.* The anonymous author refers to Losada's "lo torpe y feo de tal pluma" (fol. 164r).

81. Castro also urged the members of Seville's municipal council to reject Philip III's call to celebrate Teresa as patron. Pedro de Castro to the town council, 25 September 1618, Archivo Municipal de Sevilla, sección XI, tomo 7, no. 57, fol. 74r–v. The paucity of information from the Compostelan cathedral for 1617–18 provides a strong contrast with the avalanche of surviving letters and treatises from 1627–30. This could have been the result of the lack of interest of the archbishop, Juan Beltrandus de Guevara (d. 1622), during the first phase, or a lack of organization on the part of the cathedral. The Actas capitulares from Santiago for the years 1617–18 (vol. 24) make only two references to fighting against the Carmelites: ACSC, IG 562, fols. 297v and 299v (autumn of 1618).

82. Bermúdez de Pedraza, *Historia eclesiástica de Granada,* fol. 274r.

83. BNM, MS 1749, fol. 421r–v, preserves a manuscript copy of Castro's letter, while a printed version can be found in BNM, MS 20711 (5). In addition, BNM, MS 9140, fols. 106r–111v, includes a manuscript copy of the letter, followed by a treatise responding to it point by point.

of Santiago's unique patronage almost solely to the forcefulness and intelligence of Castro's letters. "He [Castro] wrote the king," Bermúdez insisted, "and his reasons were so vigorous, his authority so great, that the king suspended Saint Teresa's festivals . . . in spite of the learned and subtle treatises written in favor of Teresa by her supporters."[84] In Bermúdez's glorified account, Castro's wit outshone his opponents' attempts to confound his arguments.[85]

By the second phase of the debate, Castro had died and a new arch-bishop, Diego de Guzmán, had been elected. Guzmán followed his pre-decessor and played a vocal role in resisting co-patronage. While he never assumed the centrality that Castro did, Guzmán and the church of Seville played a prominent role in the debate. The cathedral of Seville wrote its counterpart in Compostela a letter in November 1627, offering all its support and aid in the cause. It claimed that its deepest desire was to follow the great example of its former archbishop, Castro, by joining in the apostle's defense. As part of this defense, the cathedral pledged the aid of one of its canons, Manuel de Sarmiento. Sarmiento was at the time residing in court as the chapter's representative and was instructed to be of any assistance possible to Santiago's representatives in Madrid.[86] Later on, the cathedral of Seville extended the same orders to its repre-sentative in Rome, Juan Federigui, admonishing him to aid the two rep-resentatives of Santiago in the papal curia to the best of his ability.[87] In addition to these actions by the Sevillian chapter, some of its canons leapt into the fray individually. Juan González Centeno and Francisco de Melgar both printed attacks on Teresa's patronage, although the former's treatise was printed without a license.[88] Melgar's work, commissioned

84. Bermúdez de Pedraza, *Historia eclesiástica de Granada*, fol. 280r–v.

85. Later Sevillian historians quoted Bermúdez's account of Castro and the debate verbatim. Diego Ortiz de Zúñiga, *Anales eclesiásticos y seculares de la muy noble y muy leal ciudad Sevilla (1246–1671)*, 5 vols. (Seville: Guadalquivir, 1988), 4:289.

86. Cathedral chapter of Seville to Compostelan chapter, 16 November 1627, BCC, 1.13.489, fol. 22v. Shortly thereafter, the chapter of Seville wrote to Sarmiento in Madrid with orders to help the *santiaguista* cause. Cathedral chapter of Seville to Manuel de Sarmiento, 23 November 1627, ibid., fol. 23r. It is unclear how well Sarmiento completed the tasks assigned to him by his chapter in aiding the representatives of Santiago at court; he appeared in the accounts of the 1627 festivals for co-patronage in Madrid, celebrating one of the masses in honor of Teresa (*Relacion sencilla y fiel de las fiestas*, fol. 6v). The Carmelite historian Silverio de Santa Teresa claimed that Sarmiento had particularly close ties to the Discalced Carmelites, a partiality confirmed by his presence at the 1627 festivals and at Teresa's 1615 beatification celebrations, for which he also preached a sermon. Manuel de Sarmiento, "De Don Manuel Sarmiento canonigo magistral de Sevilla, predicado en el Colegio del Angel de la guarda de Carmelitas Descalços de la misma ciudad," in José de Jesús María, *Sermones predicados en la Beatificacion de la Beata Madre Teresa de Iesus*.

87. Cathedral chapter of Seville to Juan Federigui, 12 September 1628, BCC, 1.13.489, fol. 37v, and 12 January 1629, fols. 43v–44r.

88. González Centeno, *Tres Puntos*; and Melgar, *Proposicion, y discurso*. Both men are listed officially as cathedral canons as early as 1616 in BCC, 8.7.59 (1).

by Diego de Guzmán and dedicated to him, was circulated widely, and was printed a second time in a slightly different edition.[89]

Other Sevillians took up the standard of Santiago's defense as well, among them Martín Añaya Maldonado, a canon from the Real Convento de la Espada de Santiago (Seville's Royal Convent of Santiago's Sword), and Alonso de Serna, whose treatise remains remarkable for its vitriolic rhetoric.[90] Añaya's rhetoric was heavily infused with a militaristic flavor. He dedicated his work to don Enrique de Guzmán, who was the marques of Pobar, a knight of the Order of Alcantara, and the president of the Royal Council of Orders, which oversaw the Spanish military orders, including the Order of Santiago. Añaya produced an extensive defense of the history of Santiago's cult in which he declared that San Fernando, the medieval Castilian king who freed Seville from the Moors and whose relics remained in that city, was a more appropriate choice for co-patron than Teresa.[91] Añaya's agitation for San Fernando was more than a random expression of pride in a local cult. At the same time he was writing, a group of Sevillians, with the support of Archbishop Guzmán, began a movement to have King Fernando officially canonized.[92] The glorification of Fernando's cult celebrated Seville's reconquest as the most important moment of its history and identity.[93] Devotion to the king-saint mirrored the cult of Santiago, as both saints were liberators and "Moorslayers." Añaya's rejection of Teresa's elevation in favor of a patron who was male, military, and local speaks to the devotional priorities among some Andalusians, who wished to keep spiritual emphasis on the most glorious moments of its history.

But *santiaguistas* in Seville faced spirited resistance from the vibrant Carmelite presence there. Two highly respected Discalced Carmelites renowned throughout Castile for their erudition and eloquence, Jerónimo de Pancorbo and Agustín Núñez Delgadillo, lived much of their

89. I located eight copies of Melgar's work: RAH, 9/3691 (4); BNM, VE 211/47; BNM, MS 9140 (fols. 10r–25v); BNM, MS 4011; Biblioteca Universitaria de Sevilla, 111/151 (28) and 109/88 (17); BCC, 9.147.6 (2) and 63/6/24, fols. 1v–11r; and BNM, VE 141/15, the last of which is the second printing.

90. Añaya Maldonado, *Discurso, en que se prueba que el Apostol Santiago ha sido;* and Serna, "Carta al Rey sobre el patronato." Serna traded letters with the cathedral of Santiago in the late autumn of 1628 regarding his treatise, which he sent to them, and their thanks. Serna to the Compostelan cathedral chapter, 22 August 1628, ACSC, IG 310, unpaginated; and Compostelan chapter to Serna, 24 September 1628, ACSC, IG 941, fol. 78r.

91. Añaya Maldonado, *Discurso, en que se prueba que el Apostol Santiago ha sido,* fols. 5r–v, 8v.

92. Juan de Pinedo, *Memorial de la excelente santidad y heroicas virtudes del señor rey don Fernando tercero deste nombre, primero de Castilla, i de León . . .* (Seville, 1627).

93. Amanda Jaye Wunder, "Search for Sanctity in Baroque Seville: The Canonization of San Fernando and the Making of Golden Age Culture, 1624–1799" (PhD diss., Princeton University, 2002).

lives in Seville.[94] Another Sevillian Discalced Carmelite, Francisco de Jesús, preached a sermon in honor of Teresa's elevation to co-patron in the royal festivities in Madrid. Although other preachers addressed the controversy in their sermons, Francisco's engagement in the debate was the most direct and spirited, and he argued painstakingly that Teresa's patronage did not diminish Santiago's but complemented it.[95] The friar took a middle position rarely achieved in the debate: His impassioned defense of Teresa in no way affected what appears to have been a genuine devotion to the apostle.[96]

The cathedral and archbishop's campaign on behalf of Santiago and the Carmelites' defense created the perfect conditions for an electric storm of wills in Seville. Ironically, the spark that ignited a miniature conflagration drew inspiration from the north: Francisco de Quevedo's work on behalf of Santiago provoked the irascible Sevillian Francisco Morovelli de Puebla to jump into the fray with a sharp-tongued treatise he bragged he had written in only a week.[97] Morovelli was a native of Seville, a man of letters, and apparently something of a professional troublemaker. In addition to Quevedo's work, which prompted Morovelli's treatise, the Sevillian author recounted the list of authors whose co-patronage works he had read: *teresiano* authors Pedro de la Madre de Dios and Juan Balboa de Mogrovejo, and *santiaguista* writers Pedro de Losada, Añaya (for whom he had particularly harsh words), Melgar, and González Centeno. Morovelli's reading list contained both local and national works: Sevillians had access to treatises such as Quevedo's as well as to works by local authors, and local authors were read throughout Castile.

Although the co-patronage debate had begun in Seville before Morovelli became involved, his work seems to have catalyzed the opposition, in part, no doubt, because of the nastiness of his attacks on fellow Sevillians Melgar and Añaya. One Sevillian, Antonio Moreno, wrote to

94. Jerónimo de Pancorbo, "Sermon predicado en la muy noble y muy leal Ciudad de Jerez de Frontera."

95. Francisco de Jesús, *Sermon que predico el dia primero de la octava.* On Francisco de Jesús, see also Miguel Rodríguez Carretero, *Epytome historial de los Carmelitas de Andalucía y Murcia* (1807) (Seville: Ediciones de la Provincia Bética, 2000), 278–79; and Vélasco Bayón, *Historia del Carmelo Español,* 181.

96. In addition to his participation in the co-patronage movement, Francisco also wrote a treatise defending Santiago's evangelization of Spain. Francisco de Jesús, *Cinco discursos con que se confirma la antigua tradición que el Apostol Santiago vino y predicó en España* (Madrid: Imprenta Real, 1612).

97. Morovelli de Puebla, *Defiende el patronato de Santa Teresa.* Morovelli had a history of conflict with the cathedral, including one altercation that landed him in prison. See his *Linaje de Morovelli y otros ilustres de Sevilla* (1619), ed. Santiago Montoto (Seville, 1918). In the introduction, Santiago Montoto tells an anecdote about Morovelli's ongoing trouble with the cathedral (p. 13).

his friend Rodrigo Caro, "Everyone thought [Morovelli's] treatise on Saint Teresa was bad."[98] The resulting scandal generated at least four treatises refuting Morovelli, by Juan Pablo Mártir Rizo, Torivio González, Reginaldus Vicencius, and one anonymous writer.[99] Of these four, Mártir Rizo stands apart as a native of Madrid, although his work was dedicated to the cathedral of Seville and included a request to be put under its protection.[100] The other three were anonymous works (the first two names have been identified as pseudonyms), but they all were most probably the work of Sevillians.[101] José Antonio Maravall has identified Reginaldus Vicencius as a Sevillian doctor named Simón Ramos through some distinguishing features on one of the original printings of the document; Ramos's involvement in the co-patronage debate was further demonstrated by his authorship of a Latin poem in defense of both Quevedo and Santiago. The poem was printed under a pseudonym, Moran Sminos, which Maravall points out is an anagram of Simón Ramos.[102]

Morovelli's works sparked such vitriolic counterattacks that one of his allies, Sancho de Ahumada y Tapia, declared that "the head of one of

98. Moreno to Caro, 2 June 1628, BCC, 58–1-9 (251).

99. Toribio González, "Censura contra Don Francisco de Morovelli de la Puebla, en la defensa del patronato de Sancta Theresa de Jesus, respuesta de lo que escriuio contra Don Francisco de Quevedo, y don Francisco de Melgar, canonigo de la doctoral de Sevilla, y otros" (1628), BNM, MS 4278; Juan Pablo Mártir Rizo, *Defensa de la verdad que escrivio D. Francisco de Quevedo Villegas, Cavallero professo de la Orden de Santiago, en favor del Patronato del mismo Apostol unico Patron de España. Contra los errores, que imprimio don Francisco Morovelli de Puebla, natural de Sevilla, contradiziendo este unico Patronato* (Málaga: Juan René, 1628); *Memorial de Advertencias al papel que Don Francisco Morovelli;* and Vicencius, *Respuesta al papel de Morovelli.*

100. Mártir Rizo to cathedral chapter of Seville, 26 June 1628, BCC, 1.147.6 (2). For more on Mártir Rizo's life and career, see *Diccionario de la historia eclesiástica de España*, 3:1439–40. Mártir Rizo's refutation of Morovelli sparked a bitter feud between the two authors that continued beyond co-patronage. See Juan Pablo Mártir Rizo, *Historia de la Muy Noble y Leal Ciudad de Cuenca* (1629), Biblioteca de Historia Hispánica: Historias Regionales y Locales (Barcelona: Ediciones El Albir, 1979); Morovelli, "Apología por la Ciudad de Sevilla Cabeça de España que se muestra y defiende la lealtad constante que siempre á guardado con sus Reyes contra Juan Pablo Mártir" (1629), in the Biblioteca de Historia Hispánica series; and Mártir Rizo, *Respuesta de Iuan Pablo Mártir Rizo, a las calumnias de don Francisco Morouelli de Puebla, a la historia de Cuenca* (Zaragoza: Juan de Lanaja y Quartanet, 1629).

101. The identity of Toribio González remains the most controversial; his treatise has occasionally been attributed to Quevedo himself by such scholars as Aureliano Fernández-Guerra y Orbe, who includes this treatise in his edition of the *Obras de don Francisco de Quevedo y Villegas.* The González treatise is full of harsh attacks on Morovelli's scholarship, as well as some personal insults. The Sevillian Antonio Moreno commented in a letter to his friend Rodrigo Caro that a fellow Sevillian, Juan de Torres, was writing a treatise against Morovelli "en venganza de lo que dice del," so Torres could be the author. Moreno to Caro, 13 July 1628, BCC, 58–1-9.

102. José Antonio Maravall, "Introduction," in Mártir Rizo, *Norte de Príncipes*, xxxii. The Latin poem, "Oratio pro nobili Francisco de Quevedo Villegas . . . Pro defensione indivisibilis Patronatus Hispaniarum Divi Iacobi," can be found together with Vicencius's work in BNM, R/11465.

the most important cathedral chapters in Spain had affirmed that it was a mortal sin to read it [one of Morovelli's treatises]."[103] The quarrel became so widely known in Seville that a nun from a local convent, Catalina Alonso, wrote to a friend in another convent to excoriate Morovelli's treatise, professing her loyalty to Santiago and demonstrating that she had also read co-patronage pamphlets by Quevedo and Melgar.[104] Participating in such a controversy was not without its risks; one important Sevillian author, Juan de Robles, published his treatise in defense of Santiago anonymously. While the letter itself circulated without the author's name, Robles included it in a later work.[105] One hypothesis is that Robles did not wish to provoke the ire of someone in Seville, most probably the dukes of Medina Sidonia, who were the benefactors of his benefice as well as relatives of the count-duke of Olivares.[106] Once the co-patronage debate was over, Robles published *El culto sevillano,* a celebration of the greatness of Sevillian letters and rhetoric, which included the co-patronage work, dedicated to fellow Sevillian intellectual Rodrigo Caro, as an exemplum of high rhetorical style. Following the reprint of Robles's co-patronage work was a letter from Francisco de Castro, which praised Robles for his brilliant rhetoric, particularly his use of syllogism.[107] Both Robles's use of syllogism and the reprinting of his letter suggest that the topic of co-patronage was occasionally appropriated by literary figures for exercises in high rhetorical style. The involvement of such authors as Quevedo, Morovelli, Pacheco, and Mártir reflects the small world of intellectual and literary activity in early seventeenth-century Spain.

Although most Sevillian works opposed Santiago's sole patronage, some prominent men, like Morovelli, sided with the Carmelites. Perhaps the best known of these is Francisco de Pacheco (d. 1644), the famous Sevillian painter and theorist. He wrote a letter, probably circulated in manuscript, in defense of Teresa's elevation to co-patron, which briefly

103. "Apenas huuo la Santa tomando su possession, quando começaron a llouer por toda España papeles harto mal parecidos, y llenos de siniestras relaciones. Las satyras de don Francisco de Queuedo, en prosa y en verso, hasta en las gazetas aduuieron." Ahumada y Tapia, *Carta apologetica,* fols. 25v–26r.

104. Catalina Alonso to Ana Pérez, n.d., RAH, Col. Jesuita, MS 9/3681, fols. 32r–33v.

105. Juan de Robles, *Carta escrita por un sacerdote natural de Sevilla a un amigo suyo a cerca del Patronato de la gloriosa Santa Teresa de Iesus* (ca. 1628), RAH, Col. Jesuita, 9/3680 (74); and Robles, *El culto sevillano* (1631), ed. Alejandro Gómez Camacho (Seville: Universidad de Sevilla, 1992), 196. Despite the anonymity of the first work, it seemed common knowledge in Seville that he had written it. Moreno to Caro, 13 July 1628, BCC, 58–1-9 (255).

106. For Robles's relationship with the dukes of Medina Sidonia, see Gómez Camacho's introduction in Robles, *Culto sevillano,* 14.

107. Ibid., 208–9. Rodrigo Caro was most probably a supporter of Santiago; in 1627, he had just finished a defense of the Flavius Dexter history. Ecker, "'Arab Stones,'" 348–49.

refuted some of Quevedo's major points.[108] Among Pacheco's many friends and acquaintances one finds distinguished Carmelites, including Jerónimo de Pancorbo and Agustín Núñez Delgadillo.[109] In addition, Pacheco figured at the center of an influential humanist school of arts and letters in the city, which connected him intellectually and socially to some of the local *santiaguista* authors.[110]

One can delineate at least three circles of involvement in the co-patronage debate in Seville: the cathedral of Seville and those related to it, the Carmelites, and men of letters. These groups were interrelated and included men who were friends and acquaintances of those in other circles. The large number of humanists involved in Seville (Pacheco, Morovelli, Robles) was a reflection of the vibrancy of Sevillian cultural and intellectual life at the beginning of the seventeenth century.[111] In addition, authors obviously felt that the debate over Teresa's elevation might be an area that could result in lucrative patronage. The cathedrals of Santiago and Seville offered generous financial incentives to authors who wrote on behalf of Santiago. At the same time, royal patronage was available to *teresianos,* particularly through the count-duke of Olivares, who loomed large in Seville, his native city.[112]

Sevillian reaction to the co-patronage controversy reflected a broad array of motivations and inspirations: desire for patronage (from either the count-duke or the cathedral); literary notoriety or competition; devotion to Santiago, firmly rooted in regional devotion to Andalusia's early Christian past; or devotion to Teresa, inspired by the vibrant Carmelite presence. The complexity of individual reaction that we see in Seville mirrored larger patterns throughout Castile. The multiplicity of influencing factors—devotion, personal animosity, financial gain—

108. Francisco de Pacheco, "En fabor de Santa Teresa de Jesus" (1628), BCC, 85-4-2, fols. 282r–288v. For a modern reprint of Pacheco's treatise, see Ismael Bengoechea de Santa Teresita, "El pintor Francisco de Pacheco por el patronato de Santa Teresa," *Monte Carmelo* 64 (1956): 182–89.

109. The link between Pacheco, Núñez, and Pancorbo can be found in Pacheco's *libro de retratos* (book of portraits), which combined portraits of distinguished men with poems or epitaphs by well-known men of letters. The brief description of Núñez's life ended with an epitaph by Pancorbo. Francisco Pacheco, *Libro de descripción de verdaderos retratos de ilustres y memorables varones,* ed. Pedro Piñero Ramírez and Rogelio Reyes Cano (Seville: Diputación Provincial, 1985), 191–97. I would like to thank Tanya J. Tiffany for pointing out this connection to me.

110. For more on this topic, see Jonathan Brown, *Images and Ideas in Seventeenth-Century Spanish Painting* (Princeton: Princeton University Press, 1978).

111. For information on intellectual life in Seville, see Guy Lazure, "To Dare Fame: Constructing a Cultural Elite in Sixteenth-Century Seville" (PhD diss., Johns Hopkins University, 2003).

112. Many historians have remarked on Olivares's eagerness to bestow patronage on his fellow Sevillians; the most obvious example is that of Diego Velázquez (Pacheco's son-in-law and pupil), whom Olivares brought from Seville to Madrid to be the court painter. Elliott, *Count-Duke of Olivares,* 176; and Wright, *Pilgrimage to Patronage,* 13.

helped to intensify the debate and expand its scope. While devotion to one or the other saint could certainly lie at the heart of an author's participation, it was only when devotion combined with these other factors that the debate took on such broad geographical and emotional dimensions. Patron sainthood was simultaneously a national and local issue, both communal and individual. The cults of both saints could unify the nation while being deployed by a specific group for particular (or personal) ends. Devotion to Santiago tied the cities and regions of Castile together, even as each region could use its relationship with the apostle to make specific claims regarding its individual and particular importance. Teresa's cult, naturally, lacked such a dense history, but its intensity and novelty, combined with the ambition and popularity of the Discalced Carmelites and the support of Philip and Olivares (and the patronage at their disposal), created a centralizing force. The evolution of the debate on both sides, then, reveals the essential fluidity between local and national in the early modern period. One can say that the two sides in the debate created each other, in the sense that the establishment of particular local identities and sacred geographies relied on a larger national narrative, while that larger narrative could not persist without its transmission and acceptance at the local level.

6

KING, NATION, AND CHURCH IN THE HABSBURG MONARCHY

While the sacred could act as a unifying force in seventeenth-century Spain, the role of the clergy in the co-patronage debate proved anything but uniform. *Teresianos* were firm in their insistence that recognition of co-patronage by the highest secular and ecclesiastical authorities should compel the rebelling cathedral chapters to comply. Discalced Carmelite preacher Jerónimo de Pancorbo declared in a 1627 sermon, "The Cortes, the king, the [Carmelite] order, the Pope and the Cardinals all together and each one individually has examined and considered [the issue] and arrived at the same opinion, in accordance with one another."[1] To Pancorbo, the concordance of the highest authorities—multiple votes in the Castilian Cortes (1617, 1626, and 1627), Philip IV's avid promotion, and the 1627 papal brief—constituted an unassailable position. Yet the cathedral chapters continued to resist; neither royal mandates, nor papal confirmation, nor the desires of their city councils proved powerful enough to stop their opposition.

From a certain perspective, then, the co-patronage debate appears to fall along secular versus ecclesiastical lines. The *teresianos* boasted the support of the highest secular authorities—the king and the Cortes—as well as the cities with representatives in the Cortes. Tensions simmering

---

1. Jerónimo de Pancorbo, "Sermon predicado en la muy noble y muy leal Ciudad," fol. 8v.

between ecclesiastical and secular authorities in Castilian cities often erupted into full-fledged conflict over the celebration of public religious festivals, since festivals marked key sites of intersection between the sacred and the civic.[2] Both municipalities and churches sponsored feast day festivals; beyond honoring a specific devotional cult, festivals often brought the community together in celebrations of civic pride and identity. In the case of co-patronage, many municipalities supported festivals for Teresa's patron sainthood against the objections of their cathedral chapters. In contrast, the cathedral chapters viewed the celebration of a patron saint as a spiritual and liturgical matter, an ecclesiastical privilege that could have no legal force without the support of the Spanish prelacy, even when endorsed by the papacy.

While on the surface such divisions appear to support the *santiaguista* claim that the "Spanish church" stood firmly against co-patronage, the reality was more complex. Although almost all the cathedral chapters rallied behind the apostle's cause, the bishops and the religious orders played more ambivalent roles in the debate. Castilian bishops in particular found themselves in an unpleasant position—subject to pressure from their chapters, on one side, and from the king, on the other. Bishops often had contentious relationships with their chapters, largely because chapters tended to be composed of local clergy, whereas bishops moved from see to see and were almost always "foreigners." In addition, Spanish kings held the power to appoint bishops; thus all prelates relied on royal goodwill for their careers. A close examination of clerical responses to the co-patronage issue reveals tension and division.

The two sides in the debate presented differing views of authority, clerical privilege, and patron sainthood. *Santiaguistas* understood patron sainthood as firmly under ecclesiastical jurisdiction and an issue of clerical privilege. Supporters of co-patronage, especially those associated with the Castilian Cortes, advocated a secular, communicentric patron sainthood that resisted ecclesiastical efforts to control what many saw as a matter of the common good. Even though a patron saint acted as a spiritual representative, many still saw Teresa as primarily representing the nation; thus they believed that the choice of patron derived from the civic community rather than the Castilian churches. Through nuanced examination of these complicated (and sometimes contradictory) facets of the controversy, it is possible to arrive at a clearer picture of the

---

2. Jesús Bravo Lozano, " 'El que de vosotros quisiere ser el primero . . .': Iglesia, sociedad y honor en las postrimerías del XVII," in *Política, religión e inquisición en la España moderna: Homenaje a Joaquín Pérez Villanueva,* ed. Pablo Fernández Albaladejo, José Martínez Millán, and Virgilio Pinto Crespo (Madrid: Ediciones de la Universidad Autónoma de Madrid, 1996), 129–46.

Castilian ecclesiastical estate, its place in the larger Castilian society, and the spiritual dimensions of Castilian national consciousness. The Castilian clergy, no less than civic officials, could shift between multiple relational identities: They could see themselves by turns as members of a transnational spiritual republic, as upholders of local power as part of a specific community, as loyal subjects of the monarch, and, occasionally, as Spaniards.

It has often been remarked that Spaniards during the early modern era held their confessional identities as integral to their sense of self; to borrow from Pablo Fernández Albaladejo, they viewed themselves as Catholics rather than as Spanish citizens.[3] We have seen in the discussion of co-patronage and international reputation that the view of Spain as the last guardian of the true faith was central to many Spaniards and to the monarchy's foreign policy. Yet the messianism demonstrated by Castilians did not necessarily reflect the priority of universal Catholicism over national sentiment. On the contrary, such messianism was in its essence deeply tied to Spanishness, to Castilians' separation from (and implicit superiority to) their Protestant *and* Catholic neighbors. It marked the Spanish as special and different, a nation chosen, as the Hebrews had been chosen, to do God's work. In the larger context of a national identity inextricably intertwined with religion, the clerical response to co-patronage requires careful attention. In spite of endemic conflict between church and state in early modern Castile, the clergy were central to the co-patronage polemic, where they helped to fashion the historical, mythical idea of Spain and of what it meant to be Spanish.

Teresa's elevation exacerbated long-standing tensions between the Castilian churches and the royal government. The emergence of more powerful and centralized states beginning in the sixteenth century brought new challenges for harmonizing secular and ecclesiastical authorities, as monarchs attempted to wrest as much control as possible from competing authorities, including the church. Such conflict traditionally centered around one basic question: When did the church have the right to maintain its privilege of immunity from royal interference? Jurisdictional boundaries between church and state had been a source of tension (even violent conflict) from the investiture controversy on, but as early modern monarchies began creating more powerful bureaucratic states and more centralized control, such issues gained increasing intensity. All

3. Pablo Fernández Albaladejo, "Católicos antes que ciudadanos: Gestación de una 'política española' en los comienzos de la edad moderna," in Fortea Pérez, *Imágenes de la diversidad,* 103–27.

monarchs strove to retain the greatest power they could achieve over their subjects, yet they faced continual jurisdictional and legal challenges from the Catholic Church, which political writers of the day sometimes described as a distinct republic. The church, for its part, maintained its medieval status as a major landowner, holder of immense wealth, and professional home to a healthy minority of the population. At the same time, some clergy worked closely with royal government, often in royal posts, while fulfilling (or neglecting) their obligations to the church.

Monarchs of Spanish kingdoms, like almost all early modern princes, had traditionally demonstrated marked hostility to ecclesiastical interference. The pious language of the "Catholic monarchs" and their consistent assertion of loyalty to the papacy and its defense have sometimes obscured the more pragmatic royal agenda.[4] Ferdinand and Isabel ensured that the papal bull granting them permission to establish an Inquisitorial tribunal in their kingdoms left the majority of control over the new Holy Office in royal hands; it was overseen by one of the royal councils, the *Suprema*.[5] Spanish monarchs consistently resisted papal intervention in Inquisitorial affairs, even attempting to block appeals to Rome.[6] In addition, they successfully brought much of the ecclesiastical hierarchy under royal control by winning the right to appoint bishops, a crucial power in maintaining the loyalty of the prelacy to royal causes.[7] Yet early modern Spanish monarchs did not perceive their persistent attempts to place churches under their control as contradictory to or inconsistent with their advocacy on behalf of the papacy and universal Catholicism in international affairs.

At the same time that Spanish monarchs made efforts to curtail papal influence inside their kingdoms, prelates became increasingly powerful and active members of the royal government, often working in harmony with monarchs.[8] But many members of the clergy, including

4. For an excellent discussion of the rhetorical strategies employed by Queen Isabel, see Boruchoff's introduction in *Isabel la Católica*, 1–23.

5. For all the relevant documents in Spanish and Latin regarding the establishment of the Inquisition under Ferdinand and Isabel, including early conflict between monarchy and papacy, see Gonzalo Martínez Díez, ed., *Bulario de la Inquisición española (hasta la muerte de Fernando el Católico)* (Madrid: Editorial Complutense, 1997).

6. Henry Kamen, *The Spanish Inquisition: A Historical Revision* (New Haven: Yale University Press, 1997), 44–50, 140–62.

7. H. E. Rawlings, *Church, Religion, and Society in Early Modern Spain* (New York: Palgrave, 2002), 52.

8. On the subject of powerful prelates in various Habsburg regimes, see H. E. Rawlings, "The Secularisation of Castilian Episcopal Office Under the Habsburgs, c. 1516–1700," *Journal of Ecclesiastical History* 38, no. 1 (1987): 53–79.

some bishops, zealously attempted to limit royal intervention in ecclesiastical matters. Most of the conflict between local churches and monarchies stemmed from the church's traditional privilege of exemption from almost all forms of taxation; such conflict became endemic as the monarchy's need for revenue reached a crisis in the late sixteenth century, as a result of governmental bankruptcies and financial disasters.[9] The Spanish Crown began to levy three taxes on its churches: the *cruzada* (a tax on papal indulgences), the *subsidio* (a subsidy on clerical incomes), and the *excusado* (a tithe from the richest estate in each parish). The papacy permitted the Crown to levy these taxes with the understanding that they would be used for wars against nonbelievers (North African pirates, the Ottoman Empire, and Protestants).[10] Clerical opposition to taxation increased with the advent of the *milliones* tax, established in 1590 as a direct tax on wealth that did not discriminate between laity and clergy.[11]

While the connection between ecclesiastical struggles with the royal government over taxation may seem far removed from the conflict over the appointment of a co-patron saint, Teresa's elevation occurred during a particularly intense period of church-state conflict. Aldea Vaquero argues that 1628–31 was a period of strife between the Spanish episcopacy and the royal government over issues of taxation.[12] Yet arguments over taxation were only a part of a much larger and more complex political discourse on the proper relationship between secular and clerical powers in a Catholic monarchy.[13] Resistance to the king on the matter of co-patronage was one element of a larger pattern of ecclesiastical resistance to royal authority. Clerical anger at the government's interference in the

9. For more information regarding ecclesiastical resistance to royal authority, see Quintín Aldea Vaquero, "Política interior: Oposición y resistencia—la resistencia eclesiástica," in Elliott and García Sanz, *España del Conde-Duque de Olivares*, 404–14; Pablo Fernández Albaladejo, "Iglesia y configuración del poder en la monarquía católica (siglos XV–XVII): Algunas consideraciones," in *Etat et eglise dans la genèse de l'etat moderne,* ed. Bernard Vincent (Madrid: Bibliothéque de la Casa de Velázquez, 1986), 209–16; and Sean T. Peronne, "Clerical Opposition in Habsburg Castile," *European History Quarterly* 31, no. 3 (2001): 323–51.

10. Rawlings, *Church, Religion, and Society*, 135.

11. Peronne, "Clerical Opposition in Habsburg Castile," 331–33. In reference to the 1591 papal brief, Peronne asserts that "the key difference between this papal concession and previous concessions for the subsidy and *excusado* was that the clergy were being taxed as vassals, not as an estate" (332).

12. Aldea Vaquero, "Política interior," 404–10.

13. For an overview of opposing theories on state power vis-à-vis the Castilian church, see Quintín Aldea Vaquero, "Iglesia y estado en la época barroca," in *Historia de España: La España de Felipe IV, el gobierno de la monarquía*, ed. Ramón Menéndez Pidal et al., 43 vols. (Madrid: Espasa Calpe, 1982), 25:525–633.

matter of patron sainthood must be seen in the context of a church zealously committed to guarding its own privileges in a period of increased threat.[14]

At the same time that Castilian clergy were trying to limit royal taxation, the church (and its wealth) was coming increasingly under fire owing to the ongoing fiscal crisis. Some prominent Castilian thinkers began to see Castilian churches and monasteries as withholding vast reserves of needed money. Many *arbitristas,* for example, wondered how a Castile struggling under crippling financial burdens could ignore the enormous fiscal resources of the church. They criticized the ecclesiastical state for hoarding wealth and for promoting superfluous religious foundations, which diverted people from the workforce and acted as a drain on the struggling economy.[15] Jerónimo de Ceballos loudly decried the overabundance of monasteries and urged the Castilian government to make a full account of the church's temporal goods in order to tax them more comprehensively.[16]

In addition, the sheer number of feast days exacerbated the tension between ecclesiastical and secular authorities, and supplied another source of outrage for *arbitristas.*[17] Pedro Fernández Navarrete, an *arbitrista* as well as an emissary for the cathedral of Santiago, lamented that in some places a full third of the calendar year was spent celebrating saints' festivals. He cited the cessation of work, the excessive expense of the celebrations, and the gluttony and vice to which they led as serious drains upon the economy and the moral health of the people. "Even though there are many important reasons to celebrate the solemnities of the saints with exterior acts, which awaken interior devotion," he wrote, "I warn you that these feasts ought not be harmful to the people, or expensive to the poor."[18] He also pointed out that the clutter of festivals on the annual calendar in Spain was much worse in August, September,

14. Tarsicio de Azcona, "Estado e iglesia en España a la luz de las asambleas del clero en el siglo XVI," in Egido Martínez, García de la Concha, and González de Cardedal, *Actas del Congreso Internacional Teresiano,* 1:297–330. Azcona provides a helpful elaboration on the term "ecclesiastic immunity": "Pero ya no sólo como doctrina canónica, sino como expresión estamental y como divisa de clase privilegiada" (300).

15. Lucía Carpintero Aguado, "La congregación del clero de Castilla: Un organismo mediatizado por la fiscalidad," in Fernández Albaladejo, Martínez Millán, and Pinto Crespo, *Política, religión e inquisición,* 153–54.

16. Ceballos, *Arte real para el buen gobierno,* fols. 123r–132v. For an excellent analysis of Ceballos's views on the Castilian church, see Aranda, *Jerónimo de Ceballos,* 200–218.

17. The pope eventually intervened, reorganizing the festival calendar for the Spanish church and suppressing nineteen festivals held annually in various parts of the kingdom. José Deleito y Piñuela, *También se divierte el pueblo* (Madrid: Alianza Editorial, 1988), 11n2.

18. Fernández Navarrete, *Conservación de monarquías,* 105.

and October, the months of harvest.[19] Navarrete targeted the overabundance of festivals largely because of their excessive expense, which included the cost of the procession; the "expense" of providing all workers with a holiday (including the negative productivity that holidays entail); the price of elaborate decorations needed for both churches and public landmarks along the procession route; and additional lavish entertainments such as fireworks displays, poetry contests, theater performances, bullfighting, and other games. Navarrete issued a plea for moderation, advocating greater balance between piety and economic necessity.

In the case of Teresa's elevation to co-patron, the king stipulated that every town in Castile had to celebrate an additional annual feast day with an octave—that is, eight days of processions and services, which constituted an enormous burden to the cathedral chapters in a kingdom already faltering under an economic crisis. The city of Avila, for example, simply could not afford lavish celebrations in honor of its native daughter in 1617.[20] Concerned Castilians like Navarrete thus opposed the celebration of Teresa's feast day both as *santiaguistas* who resented the insult to the apostle's honor and as *arbitristas* who felt that the multiplicity of feast days was bad for the moral well-being of peasants and a burden on Castile's economy. In addition, the cathedral chapters bore the brunt of the organization and expense of religious festivals. Thus economic concerns over the celebration of co-patronage intensified the fear of loss of ecclesiastical privilege and unified clerical opposition to Teresa's elevation in the chapters.

Despite its importance to Castile's economic situation, the practical problem of the octave's expense remained in the background of the debate. The issue of ecclesiastical immunity and the Castilian churches' role in the monarchy's political and economic life took center stage. Many *santiaguistas* argued that the secular government could not interfere in a religious matter without the permission of the clergy. Supporters of co-patronage, by contrast, argued fiercely that the permission of the episcopacy was superfluous and unnecessary—as Juan Balboa de Mogrovejo put it, the will of the king was sufficient to establish Teresa's patronage. He challenged his opponents to provide specific texts from canon law, popes, or councils that declared the communal will insufficient authority for a city, province, or kingdom to elect a patron. He

19. Ibid., 13–15.

20. Jodi Bilinkoff discusses the economic crisis in Avila in the same time period that forced the city to cancel the 1616 Corpus Christi celebrations for lack of funds. In 1617 the city was forced to cut back drastically on the sumptuous feast day for Teresa for the same reason. Bilinkoff, *Avila of Saint Teresa*, 158–59.

also called attention to the abundance of votive festivals that had been established by secular authorities.[21] Thus Balboa, himself a cleric and staunch defender of the church's freedom from royal taxation, argued passionately in this context that patron sainthood originated with an individual, city, or nation, not with a bishop.

Several other *teresiano* authors claimed that the church's obligation to comply with the king's decision lay in its obligation as a member of the republic. They stressed the civic nature of patron sainthood to claim that the church was obliged to accede to the will of the secular republic. One *teresiano* declared that because the purpose of the patron saint was to pray for the good of the republic, clergymen were compelled to support and uphold the choice of patron, as they were also members of the republic and beneficiaries of the saint's intercession. Moreover, he argued, the clergy ought to comply because church and nation should be one, in harmony with each other.[22] These authors presented a unified image of the republic in which the secular and ecclesiastical estates were fused in a balanced whole. But the idea of balance implied that the clergy should follow the will of the nation. Discalced Carmelite Pedro de la Madre de Dios reinforced this position with explicit references to the Spanish bishops as the king's "faithful vassals,"[23] which placed them squarely under royal authority and secular jurisdiction. While some authors, like Balboa, explicitly cited the will of the king, overall they tended to speak of Teresa's elevation as originating in the will of the nation (*España, república, nación,* and occasionally *el pueblo*).[24]

Santiaguistas, naturally, refused to acknowledge that their status as vassals applied to co-patronage or any ecclesiastical matter. One author railed against the attempt to secularize patron sainthood: "It is completely contrary to ecclesiastical immunity and the respect and obedience due to his Holiness and the Holy Apostolic See, and a dishonor to all the prelates of this kingdom."[25] The significance of this author's choice of

21. Balboa de Mogrovejo, *Por la Sagrada religion de Carmelitas Descalços,* fols. 149v–150r. Balboa's argument here becomes even more important when compared to his 1623 defense of the ecclesiastical exemption from taxation, in which he claimed that the ecclesiastical state had the right to tell the king when his decisions were harmful to the republic or repugnant to the laws of conscience. "Porque es mas estrecha y mayor la obligacion de obedecer a Dios que a los Reyes." Balboa de Mogrovejo, *El dean y cabildo de la santa Iglesia de Salamanca,* 5.

22. *Acerca del Patronato de la gloriosa santa Teresa de Iesus,* fol. 209r.

23. Pedro de la Madre de Dios, *Memorial que Dio a su Magestad el padre F. Pedro de la Madre de Dios,* fol. 136v. "Los obispos de España son fieles vasallos de VM y tan ajustados a su seruicio y gusto . . . que no se de ninguno, que por lo menos al descubierto, se aya opuesto a VM."

24. Melchor Alfonso Mogrovejo y Escovar insisted that the people (*el pueblo*) of a republic should choose as patron the native saint whom they loved the most. *Don Melchor Alfonso Mogrovejo y Escovar,* fol. 205r–v.

25. "Memorial de las raciones que prometio el Reino a su Magestad," fols. 358v–359r.

the word "dishonor" suggests the clerical fear of loss of status that would follow such dishonor. Ecclesiastical immunity was more than a principle in seventeenth-century Castile; it was a jurisdictional privilege, and its loss equaled a loss of power and status, ensuring that more catastrophic losses would follow. The cathedral of Santiago, for example, drew a firm line between the clerical and secular estates, commenting that the clerical estate in fact constituted a distinct republic, with a different head and different laws, although it also referred to clergy as "citizens" of the secular republic.[26] At the same time, *santiaguista* authors remained adamant that co-patronage did not qualify as a secular matter, governable by secular law. It was, they argued, improper for the king to order the churches to choose a patron or to celebrate religious festivals, which were clearly spiritual matters to be decided by the Spanish church.[27] Not only did *santiaguista* clergy stress their exclusive right to determine patron sainthood, they argued that it was the *king's* obligation to defend the church and the apostle. Thus they posited that spiritual power was greater than secular, and that the king should acknowledge that the future of the monarchy's well-being lay not with him (or his decisions) but with God and the church.

Given this fundamental position, it is not surprising that many of the key opponents of co-patronage were powerful clergy famous for their defenses of ecclesiastical immunity; some of them seem to have been drawn into the debate precisely over this issue. The best example is the archbishop of Seville, Pedro de Castro, who was a central figure in the first phase of the co-patronage debate. As we have seen, he was a widely respected and venerated prelate, renowned for his outspoken defense of ecclesiastical prerogatives. The seventeenth-century historian Gil González Dávila described Castro in glowing terms: "Such was the life, deeds, and death of archbishop Pedro—he was venerated by our kings like Saint Ambrose was by Emperor Theodosius in Milan, and respected by the popes of his time for the singular zeal that he demonstrated in defending the immunity of the churches."[28] In the *Ecclesiastical*

26. *Memorial a su Magestad en nombre de la Iglesia de Sanctiago*, fols. 6v–9r. "El Estado Ecclesiastico es Republica distincta de la secular, con distincion de cabeça, i leies: I aunque en quanto a lo civil son Ecclesiastico, i seculares son ciudadanos i estan obligados los Ecclestiasticos a guardar las leies civiles justas i necesarias" (fol. 9r).

27. Questions of authority and approval are argued passionately in Miguel Pedro de Azpeitia, *Informacion en derecho, sobre que el titulo de Patrona deste Reynos, que se da a la gloriosa santa Madre Teresa de Iesus, no lo pueden hazer los Procuradores de Cortes por si, sin decreto y confirmacion de los Prelados Eclesiasticos* (ca. 1618), BNM, VE 184/66, fols. 3v–8v.

28. Gil González Dávila, *Teatro Eclesiástico de las iglesias metropolitanas, y catedrales de los Reynos de las dos Castillas*, 4 vols. (Madrid: Pedro de Horna y Villanueva, 1645), 2:112. In the fourth century, the Roman emperor Theodosius had ordered a massacre during the course of a battle; Ambrose

History of Granada, Antolínez de Burgos included a more specific panegyric to Granada's most famous archbishop that detailed the prelate's conflicts with Philip II and Philip III over issues of ecclesiastical taxation.[29] Thus many contemporaries viewed Castro as a prelate who had won the respect of monarchs through his principled resistance to their infringement of ecclesiastical prerogatives. His vocal and influential opposition to Teresa's elevation, therefore, can be understood more clearly in light of his larger advocacy of clerical privilege.

The greatest ecclesiastical power in Castile resided in Toledo, the primatial see; its sympathies were a crucial factor in cementing ecclesiastical resistance to co-patronage in Castile. Toledo did not seem to play a large role in the debate, but it did side with the archbishop of Santiago from the beginning, and it maintained this support throughout the controversy. This is perhaps surprising given the long-standing feud between Toledo and Santiago over the primatial see, which culminated in Loaysa's covert attacks on the legend of Santiago's evangelization of Spain in the sixteenth century. It is likely that Toledo supported Santiago because it viewed co-patronage as a secular violation of ecclesiastical immunity; as the head of the church in Castile its main responsibility was to uphold ecclesiastical prerogatives.[30] The cathedral of Santiago was careful to emphasize that co-patronage would endanger the entire ecclesiastical state, not just the apostle's cult.[31]

As the primatial see, the cathedral of Toledo was also the head of the Congregation of the Clergy (Congregación del Clero), which provided centralized defense of ecclesiastical immunity. In some ways an ecclesiastical counterpart to the Cortes, the Congregation provided the cathedral chapters with a unified voice by establishing an assembly of Castilian clergy who met to discuss issues affecting the Castilian church, starting in the fourteenth century. Generally the Congregation concerned itself

---

insisted that the emperor do penance for this, which Theodosius eventually did. The conflict between Saint Ambrose (d. 397) and Emperor Theodosius (d. 395) is a quintessential example of the church compelling secular authority to recognize its superior claims over moral and spiritual issues.

29. Antolínez de Burgos, *Historia eclesiástica de Granada,* 397–417. In addition, the abbot of Labanza and secretary for the Congregation of the Clergy in 1618 wrote Castro a letter during the congregation of that year, in which he stressed Castro's great contributions to ecclesiastic liberty: "En comendar a Dios a VSI y que nos le guarde para exemplo y dechado del gouierno espiritual y defensa de la inmunidad eclesiastica tan cayda por tantos caminos por no auer quien asi ponga el hombro a todas estas materias su divina Mgd." Juan Alonso de Córdoba to Pedro de Castro, 13 November 1618, BNM, MS 4011, fol. 280r.

30. Cathedral chapter of Toledo to Compostelan chapter, 1627, ACSC, IG 301 (43), unpaginated.

31. Compostelan cathedral chapter to chapter of Toledo, 16 April 1628, ACSC, IG 941, fol. 46r–v.

with the monarchy's attempts to tax the clergy and the defense of ecclesiastical prerogatives. By the sixteenth century, it consisted solely of representatives from every cathedral chapter in the kingdom.[32] The restriction of participants to the cathedral chapters reduced its representative nature; the exclusion of prelates also hinted at a potential rift within the clergy. Nevertheless, the Congregation remained central to ongoing efforts to defend clerical prerogatives, even though it could not assemble without royal permission.[33] The Congregations of 1618 and 1628—both of which discussed the issue of co-patronage—convened only after months of arduous negotiations with the royal government, as royal officials and some clergy complained bitterly about the unnecessary expense the Congregation entailed.[34]

The Congregation's unilateral rejection of Teresa's elevation acted as an ecclesiastical counterweight to the Cortes's unanimous election of the new patron. One of the *santiaguista* authors claimed that the Congregation's vote against co-patronage in 1618 explained in large part Philip III's eventual withdrawal from the controversy.[35] The events of the 1618 Congregation are murky, as the sections of its minutes dealing with co-patronage have been lost.[36] But we know that the Congregation remained in session all autumn, including the crucial month of November, which was the same month the Inquisition sent out its decree authorizing silence on co-patronage and demanding that all related treatises be confiscated.

32. Sean T. Peronne, "The Castilian Assembly of the Clergy in the Sixteenth Century," *Parliaments, Estates, and Representation* 18 (1998): 54–62.

33. Although generally understudied, good work on the subject of the Congregation of the Clergy can be found in Azcona, "Estado e iglesia en España"; Carpintero Aguado, "Congregación del clero de Castilla," 147–60; Sean T. Peronne, *Charles V and the Castilian Assembly of the Clergy: Negotiations for the Ecclesiastical Subsidy* (Leiden: Brill, 2008); and Peronne, "Castilian Assembly of the Clergy," 53–70.

34. In 1618 a canon in the cathedral of Toledo and a key figure at court, Álvaro de Villegas, wrote a long response to a printed treatise that demanded an assembly of the Congregation. *Lo que el señor Doctor Aluaro de Villegas, Canonigo de la santa Yglesia de Toledo respondio al memorial, y papel incluso, que se dio a su majestad por parte del Estado Eclesiástico, suplicando no se impidan las Congregaciones, y diziendo del efeto que son* (1618), ACC, sec. IX, fols. 117r–184v.

35. Rodríguez de León, *Carta a su Magestad*, 23. "Al [tiempo de] Religiosissimo y Catholisissimo Señor Phelipe III que auiendo le reclamado el año 18 todo el Estado Eclesiastico, junto en su Congregacion y presentado memoriales cerca deste mismo punto . . . dando su Real palabra que no se haria nouedad, por estas," he wrote, then addded this citation: "Li. Cong. Ecl. Hispan. Año 18."

36. Unfortunately, the edition of the minutes for the Congregation of 1618 housed in the BNM is incomplete. It is interesting to note, however, that the *procurador* from Santiago for the year was Francisco de Villafañe, the same canon charged with representing the *santiaguista* position in Rome in 1628. For the partial account of this Congregation, see *Congregacion que celebraron las santas Yglesias Metropolitanas, y Catedrales de los Reynos de la Corona de Castilla, y León* (1618), BNM, VE 277/113.

The venerable Archbishop Castro took a great interest in the Congregation of 1618 and worked assiduously behind the scenes to make sure that it rejected Teresa's patronage. The archbishop was informed of the progress of the Congregation by Bernardo de Aldrete, a canon in the cathedral of Córdoba and its representative in the Congregation that year. Castro told Aldrete that he had sent a few writings on Santiago's behalf for Aldrete to present to the Congregation in Castro's name.[37] A week later, Aldrete replied to Castro, acknowledging the archbishop's letter and announcing that the Congregation was fighting hard to prevent co-patronage.[38] Castro received two letters, one from Aldrete and the other from the abbot of Labanza (the Congregation's secretary), dated the same day as the Inquisitorial decree (13 November), in which both men assured Castro of the successful end to the matters in which he held an interest at the Congregation.[39] Castro evidently approved of the Inquisition's involvement in silencing proponents of Teresa's elevation, which he considered the final word on the matter. One week after the issuance of the decree, the archbishop wrote a stern letter to the archbishop of Santiago, rejecting a plan by the Compostelan prelate to call a general meeting of prelates to discuss co-patronage further; instead, Castro strongly advised that the only way to close the door on the debate was through silence.[40] In the 1617–18 phase of the co-patronage controversy, then, the Congregation played a key role in bringing Teresa's election to a halt, with the help of a powerful prelate and the Inquisition; neither king nor Carmelites could counter these combined forces.

37. Castro to Aldrete, 6 November 1618, BNM, MS 4011, fol. 274r. He added: "[Y] yo escribi largo en este negocio y en otros para la Congregacion dos renglones remitiendo me a VM en 23 del pasado . . . y e recebido carta del Obispo de Cuenca. Parece me que le veo inclinado a favor de la beata en todo por titulo de abogada e intercesora no por Patrona y os digo que ni uno ni otro por Reyno."

38. Aldrete to Castro, 13 November 1618, ibid., fol. 282r. Unfortunately, while the ACC houses letters sent by Aldrete from the Congregation in its *Correspondencia de los Procuradores,* the entire months of October and November—the ones critical for co-patronage—are missing. The alliance between Castro and Aldrete stemmed from a preexisting bond forged when Aldrete wrote a treatise on behalf of the *plomos* in Granada, dedicated to the archbishop. Bernardo de Aldrete, *Varias antigüedades de Espana* (Antwerp, 1614).

39. Juan Alonso de Córdoba to Castro, 13 November 1618, BNM, MS 4011, fol. 280r. Castro had previously written Aldrete to acknowledge receipt of a resolution by the Congregation from 16 October 1618 against Teresa's patronage. Castro to Aldrete, 6 November 1618, ibid., fol. 274r. Aldrete sent Castro a comprehensive response on 13 November 1618, ibid., fol. 282r.

40. Castro to the archbishop of Santiago, 20 November 1618, ibid., fol. 283r–v. "Parecele a VSI que aya junta de Prelados y que se espere lo que su Sd mandare. Yo sr digo que no es negocio este para junta ni para disputarse que ahora aya escriben y imprimen informaciones por la Madre Teresa. Digo que esta puerta se cierre de manera que en Hespaña no oye nadie hablar en ello y el camº no para esto seria castigar."

The Congregation came out vocally against co-patronage for a second time during its 1628 session, in response to a petition brought forward by the representative from Compostela.[41] It assigned several members the task of producing a second treatise urging the king to reject Teresa's patronage. It furthermore sent representatives to the court to give copies of this treatise to the king, Olivares, and the cardinal-infante; these representatives included the cathedral of Toledo, as well as those from Santiago, Seville, and Cuenca, the three most vociferous opponents of co-patronage.[42] But this time, without the involvement of a prelate as powerful as Castro, and after the 1627 papal bull, the Congregation found itself in a tenuous position. Philip IV and Olivares were not going to waver as Philip III had, and the Congregation's new difficulties are apparent in the next reference to the controversy in its records, which notes the failure of the mission to persuade the king. The representatives had been given an audience with Olivares, where they received a firm rejection of their petition and a vaguely menacing suggestion that they rethink their own stand on the matter.[43] Some members of the Congregation considered brokering a compromise with Olivares—to restrict Teresa's patron sainthood explicitly to Castile, or even Old Castile—but the cathedral of Santiago rejected this idea forcefully.[44]

Although the king's and Olivares's support for co-patronage continued to present a major obstacle to *santiaguista* efforts, most opponents declined to criticize the king directly in their blistering attacks on co-patronage. Instead, they often targeted the Castilian Cortes as being responsible for Teresa's election. This line of attack was simple: The election of a patron saint was a liturgical matter; therefore, it lay outside

41. *Assientos de la congregacion que celebraron las santas iglesias metropolitanas y catedrales de los reynos de la Corona de Castilla y León* (1628), fol. 30r–v.

42. Ibid., fol. 66v. I was able to locate one copy of this printed treatise: "Memorial de la Congregación contra el patronato de la Santa Teresa, de Assientos de 1628," HSA.

43. *Assientos de la congregación*, fol. 86r. The record for 12 December reads: "Este dia los señores Diputados para dar el memorial a su Magestad sobre el patronato del glorioso Apostol Santiago, refirieron como su Magestad le auia recebido, y dicho que lo mandaria ver, y que passando a la audiencia del señor Conde Duque, dieron a su Excelencia el memorial, y le informaron de las rezones aduertidas en las sesiones passados, y respondio, que por lo mucho que su Magestad deseaua que no se contradizese por la santa Congregacion el Patronato de la santa madre Teresa por la gran deuocion que tenia a esta Santa, seria bien que la Congregacion lo mirase muy bien." The HSA also houses a letter preceding the Congregation's treatise, dated 24 January 1629, from don Mauricio de Alzedo to an unknown person, detailing the Congregation's efforts to dissuade the king from promoting Teresa's elevation, including references to attempts to persuade the cardinal-infante, archbishop of Toledo, to intercede with his brother, the king.

44. Gaspar Ortega de Villar to cathedral chapter of Jaén, 29 January 1629, Archivo Diocesano de Jaén, Correspondencia (1629), unpaginated. I would like to thank Katrina Olds for sharing with me her wealth of information from the cathedral of Jaén.

the authority of the Cortes. Opponents of co-patronage such as Benito Méndez de Parga y Andrade argued at length that the Cortes's involvement in a liturgical question was inappropriate. "How can twenty or thirty gentlemen," Méndez asked snidely, "who have never studied, except military games or to read books about chivalry, oblige all of Spain to accept Teresa as patron?"[45]

Santiaguistas argued that the Cortes, as a secular body, could not decide a devotional issue without the support of the prelacy. Juan González Centeno stated simply that, because the Cortes had exceeded its authority in designating Teresa co-patron, the election was null and void.[46] Fernando Mera Carvajal compared the co-patronage situation to Moses' election of Joshua as governor of Israel. Moses, Mera pointed out, had asked the assistance of God in choosing a governor before calling the Hebrew people together to confirm the decision.[47] The Cortes, analogously, had failed to follow the correct procedure, as they had first called the assembly to confirm a decision and had left God— represented by the Spanish church—out of the loop. But Mera did not rely on biblical precedent in making his case; he also drew on Plato and Cicero, declaring that "even if one part of the republic approves of a law, if another feels the opposite, it ought not to be proclaimed, and if it has been proclaimed, it ought not to be executed."[48] Mera concluded that a law that was controversial in one part of the republic would foment discord in the entire republic. Furthermore, he argued, in this case it was more precise to say that the law had not been ratified by *either* estate, for the Cortes could not be considered representative of the entire secular estate, since it only reflected the will of the major cities.[49]

The question of exactly who had consented to co-patronage provided a key element of *santiaguista* arguments because they asserted that patron saints were made by vows, not laws. According to Benito Méndez de Parga y Andrade, a vow was not a law but a "promise made to God. . . . And even though a vow can be from all the people, it cannot be obliged with the force of a law, but only the force of a promise, which only obliges the one who has vowed, or those who have consented."[50]

45. Méndez de Parga y Andrade, *Respuesta a un papel que escrivio el Dotor Balboa de Mogrovejo,* 27–34.

46. González Centeno, *Tres Puntos,* fol. 119r.

47. Mera Carvajal, *Informacion en derecho por el unico y singular Patronato,* fol. 3r. The biblical reference is to Num. 27:18–23.

48. Ibid., fols. 27v–28r.

49. Ibid., fol. 28v. Regarding the cities with votes in the Cortes, Mera wrote, "las ciudades de voto en Cortes, ni han venido en ello, ni dieron orden, ni para tal cosa; y asi no se puede dezir, que el Estado secular ha consentido, sino tan solamente los treinta particulares que lo votaron."

50. Méndez de Parga y Andrade, *Respuesta a un papel que escrivio el Dotor Balboa de Mogrovejo,* 32.

A vow derived its legitimacy from the consent of the person who made it; thus it constituted a "free act." Méndez's argument stressed the difference between a secular act (a law) and a religious one (a vow); unlike a law, which could be enacted by a legislative body or king without the consent of the people, the authority of a vow originated in a person's own conscience. He denied that a vow could be forced on an unwilling person; consequently, each individual had the right to refuse such a vow.

In addition to arguing that vows required the consent of the prelates and cathedral chapters and could not be foisted on an unwilling party, *santiaguistas* claimed that the Cortes could not produce a legitimate vow because it lacked authority to promulgate the vow throughout Castile or Spain. In the process of attacking the Cortes's role in the co-patronage controversy, *santiaguistas* insisted that the national representative assembly had no ability to speak for the entire republic; it could not even represent the entire secular estate. Rather than imagine a republic in which the estates worked together in harmony and sympathy, *santiaguistas* revealed a system of decentralized and limited authority in which no individual or institution could speak for everyone in every situation. The idea that promulgating an unpopular law would result in disruption suggested that success and stability within a republic stemmed from collaborative and popular sovereignty. In their bid to maintain the singularity of their patron saint, *santiaguistas* insisted on Spain's diversity and pluralism, supporting both the cities' right to refuse royal commands and the absolute integrity of ecclesiastical privilege.

Teresianos, on the other hand, advocated stricter obedience to the king and a broader understanding of the Cortes's authority. In addition, they posited a communicentric understanding of patron sainthood free of exclusive clerical control, which claimed to overcome all particularist divisions. The Cortes itself played a strong role in asserting its right to elect Teresa as patron and upholding the legitimacy of its vote. Even after the suspension of co-patronage in 1618, the Cortes struggled gamely on, reaffirming their vote in favor of Teresa. The representatives justified their role in Teresa's election by claiming that the Cortes had never intended to insult ecclesiastical prerogatives by ordering a religious festival or by obliging the churches to celebrate masses to her. The vote had declared only their desire to have Teresa as their patron.[51] In this way

---

51. *Actas de las Cortes de Castilla,* 32:376–81, 414–19. Juan de Trillo (Granada) vocally opposed the Cortes in its continued support for Teresa.

the Cortes attempted to create a clear distinction between the prerogatives of the ecclesiastical state (celebrating feast days) and the powers of
the Cortes (to make a vow in the name of the kingdom).

Most *teresiano* authors agreed with the Cortes that its vow to Teresa
did not violate ecclesiastical prerogatives. Cueva, for example, made the
case for the validity of the Cortes's vote by tracing the history of electing
public patrons along classical and historical, rather than ecclesiastical,
lines. He declared that the practice of patronage had been instituted by
Romulus at the dawn of the Roman Empire, and he insisted that Romulus "made this patronage from the beginning to be voluntary and
optional, to demonstrate that the name 'patron' applies to the person
one wishes to ask for intercession, and that other formalities are not
necessary."[52] Cueva cited Plutarch's *Lives* in his description of how
Romulus organized the Roman state. Plutarch claimed that Romulus
chose the most eminent citizens to act as counselors. They were called
patricians rather than lords because one of their main duties was to act
as "fathers" (patrons) to the main body of people (clients). This structure
in turn created love and friendship between patrons and their clients,
because the patrons advocated for and advised their clients.[53] In Cueva's
view, a patron saint, like a Roman patrician, helped and protected the
weak and powerless; no formal ceremony or declaration was necessary
to create the bond between the two—one had only to request the saint's
intercession.

By emphasizing the classical origin of patronage, Cueva reinforced
the public and civic nature of patron sainthood, which stemmed from
the patron's position as the community's protector. In this analogy, a
patron's primary duty was to protect and intercede for the weak and
troubled; thus the powerless (and in particular the laity) were central to
the patronage system, not ancillary to it. "The word patron signifies an
intercessor before the Divine Majesty," he asserted, "on behalf of the
pious who offer themselves to the protection of the saint they elected."[54]
In his view, the Cortes had made a public vow to make Teresa the
nation's intercessor, an action wholly consistent with its role as a public,
secular assembly. The Cortes mandated no specific liturgical practices;
how to celebrate Teresa's patronage was outlined in the breviary and
missal, not by the Cortes. Cueva thus preserved the church's traditional
right to control and oversee liturgical practices, while simultaneously

---

52. Cueva y Silva, *Informacion en derecho sobre el titulo de Patrona destos Reynos*, fols. 169v–170r.

53. Plutarch, "Romulus," in *The Lives of the Noble Grecians and Romans* (Chicago: Encyclopaedia
Britannica, 1952), 20.

54. Cueva y Silva, *Informacion en derecho sobre el titulo de Patrona destos Reynos*, fol. 177v.

insisting on the right of secular involvement (even its primacy) in the matter of choosing patrons.[55]

Other *teresiano* authors also emphasized the public, communal nature of patronage in defending the Cortes's involvement in Teresa's election. One anonymous author insisted that the Cortes functioned as a true representative body for the kingdom of Castile, that it in some fashion "spoke" for the Castilian people in conjunction with the king. In addition, he elaborated on Cueva's distinction between a public patron elected on behalf of all members of the larger community and an individual's choice of personal, private intercessor. "A patron is elected in order to remedy communal problems," he wrote, "particularly in matters of war; therefore, just as in as far as warfare is concerned, only the king and kingdom declare war or try to avert it, so in the election of patron saints, everybody must subject themselves to the will of those in charge."[56] The patron's duties—protecting and defending the kingdom—were predominantly civic and thus fell under the provenance of secular authorities. This author asserted that the Cortes's election of Teresa grew not out of personal choices but rather from its role as the voice of the community. Since the Cortes acted as the community's representative in the co-patronage vote, all members of the community were obliged to participate. He ridiculed his opponents' notion that every member of the community needed to consent if the vow were to be valid. This would be impossible, he declared, and a source of endless confusion and conflict; no community, whether village, city, or kingdom, would be able to achieve the agreement of every member. He concluded, citing Thomas Aquinas, that all theologians agreed that universal consent for communal patronage was unnecessary.[57]

Another anonymous author explained the relationship between the power of the Cortes and royal authority: "It is clear that the representatives of the Cortes, apart from being persons like don Juan and don Pedro, embody the community and the kingdom, and they are universal people who represent the communities subject to the king, who is the head."[58] The specific duties and responsibilities of the representatives,

---

55. Ibid., fol. 180r.

56. *Acerca del Patronato de la gloriosa santa Teresa de Iesus*, fol. 208r.

57. He cited Aquinas's *Summa theologica*, 2.2.q.98.ar.2.ad.4: "Quai iuramentu^m est actio personalis, ille qui de nouo sit ciuis, non obligatur, quasi iuramento ad obseruanda illa, quae ciuitas se ser natura^m, iurauit, tamen tenetur ex quada^m fidelitate, ex qua obligatur, ut sicut sit socius bonoru^m ciuitatis, ita etiam fiat particeps oneru."

58. "Breve resumta, en que se dize la asignacion que las Cortes hizieron, de la Gloriosa Virgen Santa Teresa de Iesus en Patrona de España; y se aduierte la estrecha obligacion, que todos tienen, assi seculares, como Eclesiasticos de admitirla, y celebrarla por tal en toda esta Monarquia" (1627), BNM, MS 9140, fol. 228r–v.

therefore, elevated them beyond mere individuals expressing personal preference; rather, representatives in the Cortes spoke for the entire kingdom. In addition, the Cortes had merely followed the pattern previously established by cities. Clearly the obligation to celebrate a civic patron saint was communal, not "personal," and therefore applied to everyone. Furthermore, vows to local patrons did not apply only to the generation in question but to subsequent ones, since vows bound the community, which transcended individual life spans. The enduring nature of the vow was proof that it was public and communal rather than private and individual.[59]

In addition to furthering communicentric notions of patron sainthood, many *teresiano* clergy rejected the charge that they were weakening clerical privilege. In fact, as we have seen, the prominent *teresiano* Juan Balboa de Mogrovejo had written a treatise a few years before becoming involved in Teresa's elevation that argued against *arbitristas* who thought the church was too wealthy and ought to be taxed. Instead, he insisted, a rich church would be Spain's salvation: "It is a dangerous thing to impoverish the Church and to cut its rents. Temporal arms and terrible battles have achieved little against the rebels, even when rivers of blood flow, as we have seen these many years in Flanders. The sustaining principle of everything is the spiritual arms of the Church!"[60] According to Balboa, the secular world of taxation, military maneuvers, and bloodshed would avail the monarchy little without the foundational strength of the church behind it. He also provided a caustic analysis of the prevailing military situation, disagreeing that the solution to the monarchy's woes could be found in increased taxes and military expenditures. Balboa understood the church as playing a vital role in the maintenance of the nation's strength and continued success, and he clearly viewed patron sainthood as an additional protection that the church could offer Spain.

By stressing communal interests over personal ones, *teresianos* made strong claims for the civic and national importance of patron sainthood and the involvement of secular government in choosing Teresa to stand

59. Ibid., fols. 228v–229r. "No ay obligacion mas personal, ni que mas dependa de la voluntad del que a de quedar obligacion, que el juramento, y con todo basta el de la Ciudad, y sus cabeças, y antecessores, para que quede el pueblo, y sucessores obligados, luego la eleccion de Patron para esta comunidad, no siendo personal, como no lo es, sino publica, como se ha visto, puede, y deue obligar a los subditos, aunque ellos personalmente no la elijan" (fol. 229r).

60. Balboa de Mogrovejo, *El dean y cabildo de la santa Iglesia de Salamanca*, 75–76. This treatise defending ecclesiastic prerogatives was denounced to the Inquisition. The Inquisitorial file on the treatise can be found at Archivo Histórico Nacional, Madrid, leg. 4467 (1).

alongside Santiago. They continued to build on the idea of patron saint-hood as a public office in emphasizing that national patrons played an essential civic role. While they made no attacks on clerical privilege or control over liturgy, they insisted that patron saints ought to be chosen by their people, not by bishops or cathedral chapters. The Cortes and the municipal councils that voted in it stood strongly behind Teresa's elevation and upheld their jurisdiction over the choice of patron. The presence of staunch defenders of ecclesiastical immunity like Balboa in their camp indicates that not all clergy viewed the Cortes's election of patron as an act of hostility against the Spanish church or a threat to its privilege. Thus, despite the cathedral chapters' nearly unanimous rejec-tion of co-patronage, the debate did not divide neatly between secular and clerical interests. In fact, the majority of participants on both sides of the debate were clergy.

While so far we have focused on the role of canons of cathedral chapters in the co-patronage debate, we need to address two additional clerical groups: the religious orders and the prelacy. The role played by religious orders in the co-patronage debate is one of its most obscure aspects. The orders constituted a diverse group, frequently quarreling among themselves. In addition, they had a vested interest in saints, since reli-gious orders were the greatest organizational force behind the canoniza-tion of new holy people; naturally, each order's campaign promoted a saint from its own order, and each jealously guarded the prerogatives of its own saints. Apart from the obvious Carmelites, there is little evidence of the involvement of religious orders in the co-patronage controversy, except in surviving sermons. Representatives of at least eight different religious orders appeared in the sixteen sermons for the 1627 festivals for Teresa held in Madrid. It is difficult to discern any broad pattern of support for co-patronage among the various orders in such a small sam-ple. An additional complication in analyzing the limited data is that the existing sample comes from the sermons preached for the festivals in Madrid; almost all the preachers for this event were royal preachers whose motives were thus complicated by the desire for patronage or by professional obligations.

The Carmelites' advocacy of Teresa's elevation was a natural exten-sion of their support for her as their beloved mother.[61] They clearly

---

61. The Calced Carmelites naturally did not have the same relationship to Teresa as the Dis-calced, and the two branches of the order were embroiled in a series of fierce quarrels in the early seventeenth century. Yet there is limited evidence of Calced Carmelite support for Teresa's co-patronage, largely through sermons preached by Calced friars.

played a central role in the advancement and election of Teresa as Spain's patron saint, just as all orders tended to be aggressive promoters of their own saints. In this case, however, the controversy generated a venomous backlash against the Carmelites; *santiaguistas* accused them of pressuring, bribing, and deceiving in their campaign for Teresa. Francisco Tamariz denounced the Carmelites for the worldliness of their arrogance and ambition, which he considered unsuitable for an order dedicated to poverty. He condemned the Carmelite elevation of Teresa as a "desire for gold and silver."[62] Méndez likewise classified the Carmelites' interest in Teresa's elevation as "ambition" and "an excessive appetite for the dignity of honor." Méndez took his attack a step further, adding, "The Carmelite fathers try to put themselves before all the other orders, even though there are so many notable ones in Spain."[63] Here Méndez cleverly reminded the other religious orders that the Carmelite efforts to elevate Teresa placed her above the saints of all other orders. By launching direct assaults on the order's integrity, *santiaguistas* destabilized Carmelite claims that their pursuit of co-patronage was a disinterested quest for the benefit of all Spain and denounced it as naked ambition and self-interest.

While *santiaguista* authors occasionally spread ugly rumors about the Carmelites' role in Teresa's elevation, conflict between the religious orders does not appear to have played a major role in the controversy. More dramatic intraclerical conflict occurred in a few cases where a prelate and his cathedral chapter went to war over the celebration of Teresa's feast day. Prelates, like royal preachers, had ample motives for refusing to side with the cathedral chapters against the king, since Philip was responsible for all episcopal appointments as well as for elevating some bishops and archbishops to high positions in the royal government.[64] Closeness between prelates and kings frequently generated hostility between prelates and their cathedral chapters, although acrimonious power struggles could result from a variety of local conflicts as well.[65] The clash over Teresa's elevation was no exception. Although opponents of co-patronage often claimed that the bishops and chapters

---

62. Tamariz, *A mi padre Fr. Pedro de la Madre de Dios*, fol. 4r. Ahumada caustically fired back, "Quanto mejor se dirá eso de la parte contraria, que tantas millaradas de ducados ha metido en Roma?" *Carta apologetica*, fol. 3v.

63. Méndez de Parga y Andrade, *Respuesta a un papel que escrivio el Dotor Balboa de Mogrovejo*, 38.

64. For a discussion on the king's use of bishoprics as a form of patronage, see Rawlings, *Church, Religion, and Society*, 55–66.

65. Carpintero Aguado describes the cathedral chapter's attitude toward bishops as "suspicious," in the context of collaborating with the king. "Congregación del clero de Castilla," 150.

had joined forces against Teresa's elevation, one anonymous *teresiano* asserted vehemently that all the bishops except one had accepted co-patronage.[66] Whatever the accuracy of this author's claim, he exposed the lack of cohesion in attitudes toward co-patronage among the secular clergy.

As part of its opposition to co-patronage, the cathedral of Santiago engaged in an extensive letter-writing campaign to find out where each chapter and bishop stood on the issue; of particular interest was whether they had celebrated the 1627 festivals for Teresa as the king had ordered. In response to queries from Compostela, the cathedral chapter of Tuy (one of Compostela's suffragan churches in Galicia) admitted that it had celebrated the feast day. The cathedral expressed shame for having done so, but a separate letter from the bishop, Pedro de Herrera, proved more defiant.[67] The bishop declared himself "extremely obligated" to Teresa above all saints, and announced that he did not believe that the king's desire to have Teresa as a particular intercessor could in any way diminish Santiago's patronage.[68] Herrera's defiance appears to have annoyed the Compostelan chapter, which sent three additional letters to Tuy between the end of November and the middle of December, chastising it for its support of Teresa and reminding it of its particular obligation to Compostela as its suffragan.[69] By early February 1628 the cathedral chapter had capitulated to the demands of its archbishop, sending a letter dated 6 February to the king asking him to suspend co-patronage. It is possible that the chapter felt pulled between its bishop and archbishop; in the end, it sided with the archbishop, on whom it depended. The bishop, on the other hand, maintained some of his loyalty to Teresa's cause; the last record of correspondence between Herrera and the Compostelan chapter revealed his sour obedience.[70]

The most dramatic confrontation between a cathedral chapter and its bishop occurred in Córdoba. The cathedral chapter of this city, like

66. For the *santiaguista* side: "pero contra la voluntad de todas las Catedrales, y de los Prelados, y hombres desapasionados, que miran esta causa con los ojos se le deuen." Losada y Quiroga, *Al illustrissimo y reverendissimo Señor Arzobispo*, fol. 56v. The *teresiano* countered, "Diez y nueve iglesias catedrales an recibido el patronato de la Santa, todos los obispos y prelados exceptos seis, todas las ciudades exceptas dos." Ibid., marginalia.

67. ACSC, IG 301 (49), unpaginated. The letter from the chapter was dated 4 November and that of the bishop 10 November.

68. Ibid.

69. Compostelan cathedral chapter to churches that had received Teresa's patronage, 21 November 1627, ACSC, IG 940, fols. 260v–261r. It listed these churches as Valladolid, Tuy, and Mondoñedo. The Compostelan chapter sent the cathedral another letter of chastisement on 12 December, which can be found in ACSC, IG 941, fols. 7v–8v.

70. The collection of letters from the chapter and bishop of Tuy from 1627–30 can be found in ACSC, IG 301 (49), unpaginated.

most Andalusian cathedrals, had traditionally been deeply devoted to the apostle Santiago. The bishop of Córdoba during the first phase of the co-patronage debate, Diego de Madrones (d. 1624), was described by one local historian as "most bitter in defending the unique patronage of Spain for the Apostle Santiago." The truculent Madrones went so far as to erect a niche in the main chapel with a figure of the apostle on horseback and an inscription in black jasper, calling him "the most certain, ancient, singular, and unique patron," obviously a direct slap at the 1618 co-patronage attempt.[71]

By the second phase of the debate, however, Córdoba had acquired a much different bishop. Cristóbal de Lobera (d. 1633) was born of a noble family in Plasencia and had quickly gained the patronage of the duke of Lerma. Lerma's patronage evidently served Lobera quite well, a fact never forgotten by the bishop, whose loyalty to Lerma never faltered even after the cardinal-duke's fall from power.[72] Apparently unhampered by Lerma's fall, Lobera had a typically mobile career as a bishop, moving from the bishopric of Badajoz (1615–18) to Osma (1618–23), and thence to Pamplona (1623–25), before reaching Córdoba in 1625. Each of these moves represented small upward shift in the wealth and prestige of the prelacies.[73]

An ambitious ecclesiastic, possibly wishing to curry the same favor with the count-duke that he had found with Lerma, it was not surprising that Lobera would take the king's side in the co-patronage question. His support of Teresa's elevation began in the fall of 1627, when Lobera requested permission from the chapter to celebrate her feast day with a pontifical mass and all solemnities at the Discalced Carmelite convent, Santa Ana.[74] The cathedral chapter initially agreed, as the first reference to the celebration made no mention of honoring Teresa as patron. The

71. "Havia sido nuestro Obispo acérrimo defensor del Patronato unico de España por el Após-tol Santiago; y habiéndose acabado el nicho del lado del Evangelio en la Capilla mayor, colocó en el Sagrado Apóstol a caballo, y en una lapida de Jaspe negro puso la inscripcion siguiente: *B. Jacobo Hispaniarum Dei dono singulari, unico certiss. Antiquiss. Que Patrono, trriumph. Hostium invictiss. D. Fr. Dieg. Mardons. Epis. Cord. DD anno CICDCXX.*" Juan Gómez Bravo, *Catálogo de los Obispos de Córdoba, y breve noticia histórico de su Iglesia Catedral y obispado*, 2 vols. (Córdoba: Juan Rodríguez, 1778), 2:596.

72. Ibid., 2:606.

73. For calculations of the wealth of each bishopric, see Konrad Eubel, ed., *Hierarchia catholica medii aevi, sive summorum pontificum, S.R.E. Cardinalium, Ecclesiarum Antistitum Series*, 6 vols., vol. 4, 1910–14 (Monasterii: Sumptibus et Typus Librariae Regensbergianae, 1914); and Rawlings, *Church, Religion, and Society*, 62–63. Rawlings's figures for the income from bishoprics for 1570 rank Lobera's prelacies, from poorest to richest, as Pamplona, Badajoz, Osma, and Córdoba. Eubel lists them in the same order (poorest to richest) in which Lobera was appointed to them.

74. ACC, Actas capitulares, lib. 44, fol. 179r–v, 3 October 1627. A pontifical mass is celebrated by a bishop, garbed in full episcopal insignia, including his pastoral staff and miter.

bishop then proceeded to publicize the mandatory celebration of Teresa's feast day as patron saint throughout the bishopric. He shifted the celebration to patron sainthood without asking the permission of either the chapter or the town council, both of which were necessary before augmenting a feast day.[75] After the celebrations occurred, the bishop printed an account that provided details of several paintings produced for the feast day, two of which depicted co-patronage. One showed Teresa taking a bloodied sword from a hand coming down from the sky. Another pictured Spain as a woman dressed in armor, together with a lion in the habit of Santiago on one side and a bee with a rosary on the other, and an inscription lauding Spain's great protection from its two patrons.[76] While the second image depicted co-patronage allegorically, with the lion symbolizing Santiago and the bee Teresa, the first invoked a more powerful (and controversial) image of Teresa as a battle commander. Far more than representing dual patronage, it suggested that Teresa's patronage superseded Santiago's. Lobera later bragged that in the bishopric of Córdoba, Teresa's feast day had been celebrated as solemnly as if it had been Easter.[77] This kind of excess most likely galled the members of the cathedral, who no doubt felt they had been tricked into celebrating Teresa's patron sainthood.

While Lobera's decisive move might have cost him much with his own chapter, it earned him the gratitude of the king, who wrote to the cathedral on 16 October.[78] Despite words of encouragement from the king, the chapter took matters into its own hands almost exactly a month later and issued a public statement of its opinion, called an *auto capitular,* declaring its loyalty to Santiago's cause. It included its intention to send one of its canons, Andrés de Rueda Rico, to the royal court to argue the chapter's position to the king and his ministers. It also announced that it planned to send a delegation of canons to the bishop to let him know in no uncertain terms that the celebration of Teresa's feast day as patron of Spain would not be accepted in the bishopric of Córdoba or entered as such into the official book of prayer.[79] The battle lines between bishop

75. Gómez Bravo, *Cátalogo de los Obispos de Córdoba,* 2:610.
76. *Relacion de las fiestas que se celebraron en la Ciudad de Cordova a la gloriosa Santa Teresa de Iesus, Reformadora de la Recolecion y descalça del Carmen con occasion del Nuevo Titulo que Nuestro muy Santo Padre Urbano Octavo a Peticion de SM y de sus Cortes le a dado de Patrona de España* (Córdoba: Salvador de Cea Tesa, 1627). The bee, a symbol of wisdom, was frequently used as part of Teresa's iconography.
77. Lobera, *Iusta Cosa a sido eligir por Patrona de España,* fol. 6v.
78. Philip IV to the cathedral of Córdoba, 16 October 1627, RAH, Col. Salazar y Castro, MS 9/1042, fol. 230r.
79. *Copia de un Auto en pleno Cabildo, hecho por los Señores Dean y Cabildo de la santa Iglesia de Córdoba, martes 16 de noviembre 1627* (Córdoba, 1627). The printed copy circulated widely, as did the

and chapter were drawn. It is unclear, of course, which came first: the chapter's outrage over Lobera's neglecting to ask proper permission or its anger over the insult to Santiago. Each affront probably fed off the other; the chapter's ire may also have been exacerbated by the imposition of a "foreign" idea by a nonnative bishop.

The appointed cathedral canons dutifully made their way to see the bishop three days after issuing the *auto*.[80] Although the cathedral's accounts do not record the bishop's reaction, Lobera's response came swiftly enough. Obviously not one to back down, the bishop proceeded to print a brief pamphlet on behalf of Teresa's patronage and in justification of his own actions, the first of three such pamphlets he presented during the course of the debate, probably written in quick succession.[81] Lobera had the first pamphlet delivered to the chapter less than a week after the visit from the canons; it was duly read aloud in the chapter meeting.[82] Lobera's efforts may not have endeared him to his chapter, but he received a hearty letter of praise from Olivares in December 1627.[83]

The chapter pursued its *santiaguista* agenda with vigor throughout late 1627 and 1628. Its representative at court, Andrés de Rueda Rico, received a letter of deep gratitude from the cathedral of Santiago for his strenuous efforts on the apostle's behalf.[84] In addition to such efforts, the chapter in Córdoba enlisted the aid of the city council, claiming that both had had their authority usurped by the overzealous bishop.[85] The quarreling among the three bodies ended in a stalemate that lasted until the end of the co-patronage debate. The end of the controversy did little to soothe the animosity that had erupted between bishop and chapter. In the summer of 1630, one of the most ardently *santiaguista* canons in the cathedral preached a sermon on the apostle's feast day (25 July). During the course of the sermon, Lucas González de León uttered statements that profoundly offended the bishop, who must have been present. It is

---

auto from Jaén. The original can be found in its entirety in ACC, Actas capitulares, lib. 44, 16 November 1627, fols. 189v–190r.

80. ACC, Actas capitulares, lib. 44, 19 November 1627, fol. 190r.

81. Cristóbal de Lobera, *Adicion a la Informacion de derecho, que se hizo en Cordoua el mes passado de Nouiembre, en defensa del Patronato de S. Teresa de Jesus* (1628), BNM, MS 9140, fol. 100r–v; *Iusta Cosa a sido elegir por Patrona de España;* and *Respuesta a los largos papeles.*

82. ACC, Actas capitulares, lib. 44, 27 November 1627, fols. 192v–193r.

83. Olivares to Lobera, 31 December 1627, BNM, MS 9140, fol. 8r.

84. Cathedral chapter of Santiago to Andrés de Rueda, 12 December 1627, ACSC, IG 941, fols. 5v–6r. Rueda responded with modesty and renewed vows of solidarity. Rueda to cathedral of Santiago, 1 January 1628, ACSC, IG 310, unpaginated. The chapter received a similar letter from Compostela, decrying Lobera's support for Teresa. Cathedral chapter of Santiago to the chapter of Córdoba, 16 January 1628, ACSC, IG 941, fol. 20r–v.

85. ACC, Actas capitulares, lib. 44, 24 January 1628, fol. 205v.

impossible to know the content of the speech, but presumably González peppered his sermon with strongly anti-*teresiano* rhetoric. The bishop, in return, attempted to excommunicate him, and the two battled on in acrimonious legal wrangling throughout August, when González was cleared of wrongdoing. Peace was brought to the cathedral of Córdoba only by the timely opening of the bishopric of Plasencia, Lobera's native town, to which he was moved in 1632. A historian of the Cordoban cathedral, Gómez Bravo, remarked sorrowfully a century later that even though Lobera and González had acted out of piety, their behavior had lacked prudence and discretion, resulting in great scandal to the church.[86]

Lobera and his cathedral chapter were not the only participants in the co-patronage debate who lacked prudence and discretion. The outbursts of temper and incivility that marked the controversy reveal how deeply participants cared about the issue. While personalities cannot be ignored, the controversy reached such levels of bitterness and acrimony largely because of the larger jurisdictional and power struggles that lay behind it. The clergy responded with great diversity in the way they viewed Teresa's elevation, patron sainthood, and ecclesiastical privilege. Ambitious clergymen like Cristóbal de Lobera weighed the opportunities of royal patronage against local hostility to Teresa's elevation; others, like Balboa, believed that a national patron saint strengthened Spain by binding it more closely to spiritual purity. They did not view royal involvement in naming a national patron as an affront to clerical privilege; rather, they argued that a king who appointed a patron acted in both the secular and ecclesiastical interests of the Spanish people. A patron saint represented the nation, not the church; as such, Teresa's elevation provided spiritual dimensions to a communicentric vision of the nation.

Yet widespread clerical defiance of Teresa's elevation demonstrates how co-patronage strained already tense relations between the clergy and the king in Castile. For the supporters of Santiago, rejection of co-patronage often stemmed from a desire to protect local as well as clerical privilege. Their staunch defense of what they viewed as Santiago's essential role in Spain's history (and thus in their identities as Spaniards) led them to resist not only the royal mandate to celebrate Teresa's elevation. Resistance to co-patronage reflected the fragility of the concept of unified nationhood by insisting on separation of the estates and on the

---

86. Gómez Bravo, *Cátalogo de los Obispos de Córdoba*, 2:619. Brief references to the quarrel between Lobera and González can also be found in ACC, Actas capitulares, lib. 45, fols. 180v–181r and 188v.

inability of the Cortes to act in the name of the larger community. Failed efforts to change the king's mind, or to achieve a full stop to Teresa's patron sainthood, eventually stalled the co-patronage polemic in Castile. The Compostelan cathedral realized that the king and Olivares would not be swayed. This left one option. In 1628 *santiaguistas* decided to shift the battleground from Madrid to Rome, in an ambitious attempt to coerce the pope into admitting that he had erred in issuing the 1627 brief. All eyes turned toward Rome.

7

Endgame in Rome

Although the cathedral of Santiago had ample resources, support from powerful ecclesiastical friends, and the full backing of the Congregation of the Clergy, it could do little to halt Teresa's patron sainthood in Spain as long as the king and Olivares persisted in their dedication to the cause. The cathedral's efforts to persuade the king and Olivares stalled; in early January 1629, Juan Fedirigui described the situation at court as "not very favorable" to the apostle's cause.[1] Some time after its audience with Olivares, the Compostelan cathedral became convinced that the count-duke was intractable on the subject of Teresa's election. Only one avenue remained to achieve a revocation of the 1627 papal brief. A letter from the cathedral to its representatives reflected this tactical change. "We have seen clearly who supports the Carmelite interests [presumably Olivares]," it read, "which is reason enough that we ought to turn to the source, which is Rome."[2] The stalemate at court had made it obvious to both sides of the debate that the controversy would be won or lost not in Castile but in Rome.

1. Fedirigui to cathedral chapter, 12 January 1629, BCC, 1.13.489, fols. 43v–44r. "Que se compongan las cosas de manera que no padezian los negocios por falta de auisos el que nos da VM de el estado que tiene la causa de el patronazgo de el glorioso Apostol Santiago nos dexa algo cuidadoso que ser la gran lastima obrasen dilegencias ni afectos para que esta materia llegue a tener la menor duda. Los efectos que se ban experimentado despues que se trata son poco faborables."

2. Compostelan chapter to legates in Madrid, 23 February 1628, ACSC, IG 941, fols. 21v–22v.

The movement of the debate from Castile to Rome added new layers to the conflict. The papal curia had long been the last court of appeal for the most acrimonious disagreements between royal authority and ecclesiastical jurisdiction. The papacy's mediating role, however, was far from simple. Papal decisions about Spanish churches had complex motivations, including (but not limited to) the desire to leverage a given issue for the purpose of gaining a separate concession from the Spanish king; the need to protect ecclesiastical jurisdiction from secular predation; or a willingness to work with the king against obstreperous local churches, which sometimes clashed with the pope over the implementation of Tridentine reforms. Therefore, the dynamic between the Spanish monarchs and their clergy cannot be understood fully without taking into account relations between monarchy and papacy.[3] At the same time, local churches did not always move in harmony with the papacy. Instead, they occasionally put forward their own agendas, based on local concerns and interests that could be at odds with the pope's theological or political aims.

One major source of strife between the papacy and local churches in the early modern period was the liturgical celebration of local cults, which the papacy was working to streamline and universalize.[4] At the same time, devotions to certain saints became increasingly integrated into civic and national identities. The tension between these two impulses—the universal power of the church and the association of saints with specific places and peoples—intensified during the seventeenth century, resulting in frequent conflicts over saints throughout Catholic Europe. Although it built on older devotional styles and patterns, the seventeenth century saw new ways of fashioning and understanding patrons, pitting native saints against nonnatives, new against old, secular against ecclesiastic, and local against papal jurisdiction. In the case of co-patronage, the king and pope worked together to establish a legitimate cult for an important Catholic Reformation saint, while local cathedral chapters united against the perceived harm being done to their traditional (though historically dubious) patron. At the same time, the pope became increasingly alarmed at the escalating encroachment of royal authority on papal prerogatives. Patron sainthood provided fertile ground for the growth of such disputes, for it existed at the nexus of

3. This point is made aptly by both Peronne and Aldea Vaquero. See Aldea Vaquero, "Política interior," 402; and Peronne, "Clerical Opposition in Habsburg Castile," 336–38.

4. Conflict was not, of course, inevitable. For a discussion of local churches working to fit their local cults into Tridentine reform and liturgical conformity, see Ditchfield, *Liturgy, Sanctity, and History in Tridentine Italy.*

spiritual and political, liturgical and communicentric. In an effort to explain the nuances of such conflict, this chapter examines the endgame of Castile's co-patronage battle in Rome. The movement of the debate out of Spain and into Rome also supplies an opportunity to examine patron sainthood in the larger European context and to illuminate the complexity of early modern sanctity in the era of emergent nations and a papacy determined to maintain its hold over liturgy.

While most *teresianos* articulated a vision of patron sainthood that was deeply national and communicentric in nature, they did not hesitate to use papal support for Teresa's elevation as key evidence for the righteousness of their cause. When *santiaguistas* persisted in their defiance of the mandate to celebrate Teresa's feast day, *teresianos* responded with incredulity. Sancho de Ahumada y Tapia, for example, wrote sarcastically, "You say that whoever is against Santiago is against God, country, religion, and faith. So the king and the pope are against God, country, religion, and faith?"[5] Ahumada's jab succinctly punctured his opponents' argument that all "true and legitimate" Spaniards defended the apostle's cause. Another *teresiano* contended that the pope's decision to ratify Teresa's election (after consulting his cardinals) constituted a legitimate use of his power, which was the same as the will of God; since the pope was the vicar of God on earth, everyone was obligated to obey him.[6] These authors struck at the heart of the challenge *santiaguistas* faced: It was one thing for a group of ecclesiastics to denounce the secular authorities for interfering with clerical matters, quite another to suggest that the pope had no right to designate a patron saint.

Santiaguistas quickly realized the need to convince the pope and cardinals to repeal the co-patronage brief. But they could not use the same argument they had previously employed with the king—that the papal brief constituted an illegitimate violation of Spanish traditions—because of the pope's clear and inarguable right to determine such questions. Like many local churches in disagreements over saints and the liturgy throughout early modern Europe, they needed to establish a balance between their own view of Santiago's patron sainthood as inviolable and the larger structure of the church's prerogatives. A close examination of the cathedral of Santiago's careful efforts to justify its refusal to accept Teresa's elevation reveals a two-pronged effort: a mainstream legal effort centered on the fine print of issuing briefs according

5. Ahumada y Tapia, *Carta apologetica*, fol. 21v.
6. "Por la conservacion del patronato de la gloriosa virgen Santa Teresa," fol. 39v.

to canon law, on the one hand, and behind-the-scenes political intrigue, on the other.

First, *santiaguistas* worked to establish legal justification for nullifying the papal brief by pointing out that it had been issued conditionally, as it contained the disclaimer that Santiago's cult could not be harmed in any way. More precisely, the brief stated that Teresa's elevation to co-patron could not prejudice Santiago's status (which the participants referred to as the *sine preiudicio* clause). Pedro de Losada y Quiroga claimed, "It is certain that the clause '*sine preiudicio*' confers conditional grace." As a result, violation of the conditional grace provided would lead to the brief's nullification. He went on to argue that this clause meant that Santiago's permission was needed before the brief could be validated.[7] Implicitly, such permission could only be granted by the archbishop, as the keeper of the apostle's relics and thus his representative. Most of Losada's partisans, however, restricted themselves to pointing out that Teresa's elevation did in fact constitute prejudice to Santiago and caused his cult grievous harm.[8] Of course, the basis of their argument lay in understanding Teresa's co-patronage as in fact causing harm to Santiago, even though the clause was clearly designed to act as a blanket assurance that Santiago's patron sainthood would be preserved. The *santiaguista* reading of the clause proved absurd, since it ultimately amounted to an assertion that the pope had issued a brief that nullified itself, because (in their view) it was not possible for Teresa's patron sainthood to exist without harming Santiago's.

Precisely for this reason the *sine preiudicio* clause did not provide sufficient grounds for nullifying the brief. Thus *santiaguistas* were compelled to seek additional legal recourse against the brief, which they eventually discovered. According to the code of canon law, an individual or group could petition for the nullification of a papal brief by proving that the brief had been issued improperly because its issuance had originated out of one of the following conditions: "obreption" (*obreptio* in Latin), defined as "statements of falsehood," or "subreption" (*subreptio*), "concealment of truth."[9] The term "subreption" in particular echoed throughout *santiaguista* treatises, which provided the beginning of a legal

7. Losada y Quiroga, *Defensa del unico y singular Patronazgo*, 37.

8. See, for example, Robles, *Carta escrita por un sacerdote natural de Sevilla*. "Mas que (bien mirado) no conviene ser recebida por Patrona General; porque dello parecer, que resulta un modo de agravio al Gloriosismo Apostol Santiago, y a los demas Santos Españoles, y puede resultar asi mismo algun perjuicio al sosiego, honor y reputacion del nombre Español" (fol. 1v).

9. *Code of Canon Law, Latin-English Edition* (Washington, D.C.: Canon Law Society of America, 1983), 18–19 (canon 63). For the entire section on papal rescripts, see 13–29 (canons 18–75).

case for the brief's nullity. Nicasio Philaleto, one of the most gifted *santi-aguistas* on questions of canon law and theology, explained his position succinctly: "His Holiness gave [the brief] conditionally, and as a result of the subreption and obreption . . . it is of no value."[10] *Santiaguistas* generally made subreption their principal complaint, arguing that the Carmelites had employed secrecy with an intent to deceive when obtaining the brief. In this version of events, the Carmelites had pushed the brief through ratification so quickly and quietly that the Compostelan cathedral did not know was happening and therefore had no opportunity to present a counterargument to the pope. The *santiaguistas* insisted that if the pope had been informed of all the harm that would result to Santiago's cult, he would not have issued the brief.

The *teresiano* faction reacted to this charge with outrage. One anonymous author wrote a blistering condemnation of his opponents that included an extensive retelling of the events that had led up to the 1627 papal brief. He referred to the 1617 vote in the Cortes, the small-scale elections of Teresa as civic patron in a handful of cities that year, the king and Olivares's request that the Cortes vote a second time in 1626, and the Cortes's second unanimous vote. "And afterwards the kingdoms received the brief with public demonstrations," he continued. "Following this, there was a most solemn procession, in which his Majesty participated even though he was convalescing, with all his councils, accompanied by his nobles. And this is a 'secret' brief in the opinion of the most prudent cathedral chapter!"[11] In each part of his chronology, the author stressed the public nature of the events and the visible participation of the king and his courtiers. While the celebratory processions occurred after the fact, the multiple votes in Cortes could hardly be defined as clandestine.

Although the Compostelan cathedral hurled the accusation of subreption against the Carmelites from the beginning of the debate, their efforts to quash Teresa's patronage remained focused primarily on Castile until the spring of 1628. But that spring the cathedral received news from an ally at the papal curia that dramatically altered its plans and strategy: The Carmelites in Rome were in the process of petitioning for

---

10. Nicasio Philaleto, *Por el Apóstol Santiago, unico y singular patron de las Españas. Advertencias a la información de derecho de los padres Carmelitas Descalcos, que firmó el Doctor don Juan de Balboa Mogrouejo, Canonigo de la Santa Iglesia de Salamanca, Catedrático de prima de su universidad* (ca. 1628), HSA, fol. 15r. Sancho de Ahumada y Tapia declared Philaleto to be a pseudonym for Francisco Tamariz, to whom he addressed his own treatise, *Carta apologetica*, fols. 12v–13r.

11. "Traslado de una carta que el cabildo de la santo Yapostolica Iglesia de Santiago embio al de la santa Iglesia de Granada, con aduertencias sobre esta" (1627), BNM, MS 9140, fol. 78r–v.

a *perinde valere*.[12] The Carmelites were evidently responding quickly to the accusations of subreption flying back in Castile. Under canon law, a party wishing to defend the legitimacy of a brief against the objection of *subreptio* could do so. In order to reaffirm the legitimacy of the original rescript, one could petition either that the *subreptio* did not exist or that it did not affect the legitimating parts of the brief. Papal acceptance of this defense would result in a document declaring that notwithstanding the objection of *subreptio,* the brief retained its force of law "just as strongly"; this attachment was therefore called a *perinde valere*.[13] In the spring of 1628 Philip IV sent instructions to the count of Oñate outlining his desire for his Roman ambassador to intensify the struggle against the *santiaguistas*. Having heard that his opponents were attempting to nullify the papal brief, Philip instructed Oñate to work for a *perinde valere* that would stop the dissension.[14]

A successful bid for a *perinde valere* would herald the ultimate defeat of all the cathedral's efforts to protect its patron. The news sent shock-waves of panic through the cathedral chapter, which fired off a desperate letter to the archbishop of Toledo begging for help and another to Francisco Brandano, its envoy at the papal curia, instructing him to do all in his power to obstruct the *perinde valere*.[15] Brandano was already working alongside Cardinal Pedro de Peralto to try to win other cardinals to their side.[16]

News of the *perinde valere* changed everything for the Compostelan cathedral. The authorities there decided that their only recourse was to instigate a full-scale campaign at the papal curia against the Carmelites. Dissatisfaction with Brandano's progress led the cathedral to dispatch two additional envoys to Rome in the autumn of 1628, cathedral canons

12. Cathedral chapter to envoys in Madrid, 16 April 1628, ACSC, IG 941, fols. 45v–46r.

13. *The New Catholic Encyclopedia,* 17 vols. (New York: McGraw-Hill, 1967), 7:783–84. Information regarding *perinde valere* is found under the subject "rescripts."

14. Philip IV to Count of Oñate, n.d., BNM, MS 9140, fol. 2r. Philip instructed, "le suplicareis [su Santidad] con muchas veras, que para que cese la contradicion de algunas Iglesias que le refusan, tenga por bien de conceder segundo breue en forma de *perinde valere* confirmando el primero para que se guarde, y cumpla y execute sin embargo de qualquier replica, que a el se aya opuesto." Philip sent another letter, repeating his request for a rescript confirming the 1627 brief. Philip IV to the Count of Oñate, 17 May 1628, MAE, leg. 59, fol. 72r.

15. Cathedral chapter to archbishop of Toledo, 16 April 1628, ACSC, IG 941, fol. 46r–v; cathedral chapter to Francisco Brandano, 30 April 1628, ibid., fol. 48r–v.

16. The cathedral of Santiago wrote to Peralto asking for help at the inception of the debate. Cathedral chapter to Pedro de Peralto, 26 October 1627, ACSC, IG 940, fols. 247v–248r. Previously, Brandano's main task had been to deliver to the secretary of briefs, Monsignor Maraldo, notarized letters collected from the Castilian cathedral chapters in March 1628, which declared their opposition to Teresa's patron sainthood. Cathedral chapter to Monsignor Maraldo, 19 March 1628, ACSC, IG 941, fol. 38r–v.

don Francisco de Villafañe and don Pedro Astorga de Castilla; their sole task would be to plead the cathedral's case and to work against the *perinde valere*.[17] In addition to the two canons and Luis de las Infantas, the agents for the Castilian Congregation of the Clergy in Rome, other *santiaguista* churches pledged that their agents in Rome would also work tirelessly for the apostle's cause.[18] The ultimate goal of these envoys was to entreat the pope to have the brief reassessed by a panel that would listen to the cathedral's case and decide whether or not to nullify the brief.[19]

While the pope was naturally the most powerful figure at court, as with any monarch it was difficult to gain access to his presence. Surrounding the pope were his courtiers the cardinals, an influential body of potential enemies and friends; they also staffed the powerful curial congregations, including the Congregation of Sacred Rites.[20] In addition, the papal curia, like all early modern courts, teemed with ambassadors and envoys lobbying for individual churches, religious orders, and various monarchs. The presence of so many determined (and moneyed) petitioners intensified factional conflict among members of the curia. The various factions at the curia represented a multilayered blend of local (Roman), Italian, and international interests, all competing for privileges and power. For example, each cathedral chapter might have an envoy at the curia, to lobby for specific issues on an ad hoc basis or more permanently. The convergence of quarrelsome envoys from local churches on Rome proved problematic not just for the papacy; monarchs were acutely aware that the pope's role as intermediary in all conflicts—both intrachurch and between church and secular authorities—could have a potentially destabilizing effect on royal authority at home.[21]

17. Cathedral chapter to Pedro Sanz de Castillo, 13 September 1628, ACSC, IG 941, fol. 77r–v. In this update to its envoy in Madrid, the chapter noted, "no respondimos a VMs por . . . estar ocupado en el despacho de los legados para Roma que finalmente partieron a los 6 deste." A complaint regarding Brandano's service can be found in Compostelan chapter to Cardinal Sandoval, 26 March 1628, ibid., fols. 39v–40v.

18. These two churches were the cathedral of Cuenca and its agent, Pedro de Alarcán, and the cathedral of Jaén and its agent, Pedro de Contreras. These pledges can be found in ACSC, IG 301 (49), unpaginated. One example of many referring to Luis de las Infantas can be found in cathedral to Fernando Brandano, 16 November 1627, ACSC, IG 941, fols. 2r–4v.

19. Villafañe to cathedral of Santiago, ACSC, IG 301 (32).

20. On the inner workings of the papal curia during this period, see Antonio Menniti Ippolito, *Il governo dei papi nell'età moderna: Carriere, gerarchie, oganizzazione curiale* (Rome: Viella, 2007).

21. Philip IV's instructions to his ambassador, the count of Oñate, included specific instructions that the count shut down any squabble that might cause scandal, disorder, or prejudice to the common good back in Spain. "Ynstruccion prudente y politica del Rey Phelippe IV al Conde de Oñate embaxdoe Ordinario en Roma," July 1625, MAE, leg. 58, fols. 273v–274r.

The politics and factions of the papal curia were therefore matters of great importance to Spain's monarchs, who sought to maintain a pro-Spanish faction among the cardinals to shore up Spanish influence against French incursions. In the early 1630s the secretary to the Spanish ambassador in Rome, Diego de Saavedra Fajardo, assessed the loyalty of various cardinals, beginning with the Barberini, Urban VIII's influential relatives.[22] He described Cardinal Francesco Barberini, the powerful cardinal-nephew, as "well intentioned" and "affectionate to Spain," while his brother Antonio "has shown himself more French than Spanish." The two Barberini cardinals were also rivals for political power; Francesco in particular demonstrated marked unease over his brother's acquisition of the red hat.[23] An additional member of the papal family, the pope's brother-in-law, Magalotti, was described as both "inclined toward France" and Antonio's enemy.[24] In addition to the personalities and proclivities of individual cardinals, money played a large role in papal politics through the establishment of lines of patronage and client-age. For example, Saavedra described Monsignor Maraldo (the secretary of briefs) as a man who had invented prejudicial rumors against Spain for personal gain, whereas Cardinal Borghese was "obligated to Spain by gifts."[25] Saavedra ultimately recommended to the ambassador that the best course of action for the Spanish in Rome would be to provoke divisions and quarrels among various factions at the curia, particularly among the Barberini—a basic divide-and-conquer strategy.[26]

An additional source of competition and acrimony at the papal curia were the religious orders, which also built factions and lines of clientage in order to strengthen and enrich their respective orders. The Carmelites

22. For an excellent discussion of the role of Urban's family in the curia, and particularly of the significance of the cardinal-nephew in papal tradition, see Wolfgang Reinhard, "Papal Power and Family Strategy in the Sixteenth and Seventeenth Centuries," in Asch and Birke, *Princes, Patronage, and the Nobility,* 329–56.

23. On the rivalry between the two brothers, see Torgil Magnuson, *Rome in the Age of Bernini,* vol. 1 (Stockholm: Almquist and Wiksell International, 1982), 220–21.

24. Monsignor Lorenzo Magalotti was Urban VIII's secretary of state; he eventually became a cardinal. For further information on Magalotti and the position of secretary of state, see Antonio Menniti Ippolito, "The Secretariat of State as the Pope's Special Ministry," in *Court and Politics in Papal Rome, 1492–1700,* ed. Gianvittorio Signorotto and Maria Antonietta Visceglia (Cambridge: Cambridge University Press, 2002), 145–47.

25. Diego de Saavedra Fajardo, *España y Europa en el siglo XVII: Correspondencia de Saavedra Fajardo,* ed. Quintín Aldea Vaquero, vol. 1 (Madrid: CISC, 1986), 7–9. For more on Saavedra Fajardo, see Manuel Fraga Iribarne, *Don Diego de Saavedra y Fajardo y la diplomacia de su época* (Madrid: Centro de Estudios Políticos y Constitucionales, 1998).

26. Saavedra Fajardo, *España y Europa en el siglo XVII,* 11–12. For a discussion of fomenting discord as Spanish policy in Rome, see also Maria Antonietta Visceglia, "Factions in the Sacred College in the Sixteenth and Seventeenth Centuries," in Signorotto and Visceglia, *Court and Politics in Papal Rome,* 99–131.

had a powerful presence in Rome, with many friends and allies at the papal curia. Teresa's Discalced reform had appeared early in Italy; only two years after her death, the first Discalced Carmelite convent, Santa Ana, was constructed in Genoa. By the end of the century Rome had its own Discalced convent, Santa Maria della Scala.[27] Shortly after the completion of Santa Maria, an Italian edition of Teresa's spiritual autobiography appeared in Rome.[28] An official life of Teresa circulated in manuscript just before her canonization, written by fellow Discalced Carmelite and Spaniard Alfonso Manzanedo de Quiñones, who had been a deacon in the Sacred Rota and a driving force behind Teresa's canonization.[29] He may even have drafted her canonization bull.[30] Urban VIII demonstrated personal devotion to Teresa as well, not only by promulgating the first brief for her patron sainthood but by including her among a group of saints for whom he personally wrote hymns to be included in their festal offices.[31] In addition to showing great favor to Teresa, Urban had promoted the beatification of fellow Florentine and Discalced Carmelite Maria Maddalena de' Pazzi (d. 1607), renowned for her mysticism, much as Teresa had been, to whom he was deeply devoted.[32]

Thus Urban's close ties to the Carmelites and to Teresa in particular probably encouraged the pontiff's favorable response to Philip IV's request for the initial 1627 brief ratifying her election. The brief also provided the pope with an easy way to perform a service on behalf of the king of Spain, during a time of tense relations between the two.[33]

27. Elisabetta Marchetti, "Il carmelo scalzo e gli oratoriani a Roma," *Archivio della Società di Storia Patria* 123 (2000): 105–6.

28. For a complete history of early translations of Teresa's work in Italy, see Elisabetta Marchetti, *Le prime traduzioni italiane delle opere di Teresa de Gesù, nel quadro dell'impegno papale post-tridentino* (Bologna: Lo Scarabeo Editrice, 2001).

29. Manzanedo's life of Teresa circulated in manuscript and also exists partially in print; it was finished many years later by another author. Filippo Lopezio, *Compendio della Vita, et atti Heroici della Serafica VS Teresa di Giesu, Gloria dell'antica Religione della Madonna del Carmine, e Fondatrice de' Padri, e Monache Scalze del medemo Ordine* (Rome: Vitale Masxardi, 1647).

30. Irving Lavin, *Bernini and the Unity of the Visual Arts*, vol. 1 (New York: Pierpont Morgan Library, 1980), 80–81.

31. Quoted in ibid., 116–17. A poem attributed to Urban VIII in praise of Teresa also appears in Lopezio's *Compendio della Vita* (unpaginated). For more on Urban's poetry, see Peter Rietbergen, *Power and Religion in Baroque Rome: Barberini Cultural Policies* (Leiden: Brill, 2006), 95–142.

32. Pamphilio made sure to mention in his dispatches to the papal curia that the court in Madrid had celebrated Maria Maddalena's beatification with a three-day festival (one of the only references he made to religious festivals). Nuncio Pamphilio to the secretary of state, 24 July 1627, ASV, Segreteria di Stato, Spagna, vol. 67, fol. 266v.

33. Popes often beatified or canonized holy people as a method of getting into the good graces of monarchs. See, for example, the discussion of Diego de Alcalá's canonization as a gesture of thanksgiving for Spanish efforts against the British in 1588, in L. J. Andrew Villalon, "San Diego de Alcalá and the Politics of Saint-Making in Counter-Reformation Europe," *Catholic Historical Review* 83, no. 4 (1997): 713–14.

Urban VIII, born Maffeo Barberini, had ascended to the papal throne in
1623 after a successful career that included a four-year appointment as
papal nuncio to France (1604–8), during which time he had been elevated
to cardinal at the French king's request.[34] When Barberini was elected
pope, the Spanish were not happy with the choice; they consistently
complained that Urban hated the Spanish and supported the French
because of his previous experience as the French nuncio. Part of the
Spaniards' agitation stemmed from the rivalry developing between Spain
and France during this period, and their fears of losing Rome to French
influence.[35] Since the beginning of the seventeenth century, new stability
in France's internal political situation had allowed the king to turn his
attention to larger geopolitical concerns. Not surprisingly, the French
were particularly concerned with reducing Spanish hegemony in
Europe. As part of these efforts, the French worked to forge tighter
bonds with the papacy, enabled in part by the friendship between Urban
and the previous French king.[36]

Urban's apparent sympathy for the French provoked great hostility
among the Spanish; even so, the ease with which later historians have
repeated Spanish assertions that the pope loved France and hated Spain
represents something of an oversimplification. In 1631 Diego de Saavedra
Fajardo described the situation in Rome in this way: "[The pope] loves
the French and hates the Spanish; but he does not want either in Italy."[37]
Saavedra's observation was astute: While he noted the pope's personal
inclination (from the Spanish perspective), such inclination did not seem
to deter Urban from his main goals—freeing Italy from foreign domination and asserting papal authority throughout the Catholic world. Thus
Urban's main concerns focused on expanding papal power during a time
of increasing political and religious challenges from secular monarchies.
Urban's position between France and Spain grew increasingly difficult as
the hostility between the two nations verged ever closer to full-scale
war. While Urban tried to use French support as leverage with which to
break apart Spanish dominance, he also clearly understood that the
Spanish could not be alienated from the papacy.[38] The Spanish pursued

34. Magnuson, Rome in the Age of Bernini, 1:215–16.

35. For more on sixteenth-century Spanish relations with Italian states, and the papacy in
particular, see Thomas Dandelet, Spanish Rome (New Haven: Yale University Press, 2001); and
Michael Levin, Agents of Empire: Spanish Ambassadors in Sixteenth-Century Italy (Ithaca: Cornell University Press, 2005).

36. Dandelet, Spanish Rome, 190–99.

37. Saavedra Fajardo to the secretary Pedro de Arce, 1631, in Saavedra Fajardo, España y Europa
en el siglo XVII, 6–7.

38. For Urban using France as leverage against Spain, see A. D. Wright, The Early Modern
Papacy: From the Council of Trent to the French Revolution, 1564–1789 (London: Longman, 2000), 176–77.

their own political goals, often regardless of what the papacy thought, but they were a staunch papal ally against heresy and the Ottoman Empire, for which Urban expressed gratitude.[39] Yet the political realities of Spanish claims to universal sovereignty brought the pope and the Spanish monarch into increasing conflict throughout the late 1620s and 1630s.

During the years in which the issue of Spain's patron sainthood was being fought over in Rome, the Spanish monarchy and the papacy were engaged in a particularly tense political standoff regarding a series of political and military events that unfolded in northern Italy beginning in 1628. The conflict began in the duchy of Mantua (which included the strategically vital Monferrat) over a dynastic dispute when the last Gonzaga duke of Mantua, don Vicenzio, died late in 1627. The Gonzagas had traditionally been allied with the Spanish Habsburgs, and this had helped to sustain the monarchy's control of northern Italy, since both Mantua and Monferrat bordered on the Spanish-controlled duchy of Milan. The duke had no direct heir; there were several claimants, including the French duke of Nevers, whose claim threatened the Spanish and the Austrian Habsburg position in the region.[40] It was clear to all politicos in Madrid that the duke of Mantua's death boded ill for Spain's position in northern Italy and was a blow to its Austrian cousins. The Spanish sent an army to the region after Nevers arrived to claim the dukedom. Intermittent military conflict dragged on until 1631, when the Spanish were eventually forced into a humiliating peace.[41]

Urban VIII, for his part, had kept careful watch over the political scene in Italy and became increasingly alarmed over the deteriorating situation. He feared that much blood would be spilled if the Spanish persisted and the French army arrived. In April 1628 he sent a series of letters to key figures in Madrid in an attempt to persuade them (and have them persuade the king) to alter Spain's apparent course.[42] From this point on, the conflict in Mantua took center stage in the papacy's dealings with Spain—nearly every piece of correspondence in late 1628 and 1629 between the nuncio in Madrid and the secretary of state in

39. Urban's letters to Philip IV often remarked on the great services the Spanish monarchy had accomplished on behalf of the church; for one example, see Urban VIII to Philip IV (ca. 1627), ASV, Ep. ad Princ., registra, vol. 41, fols. 72v–73r.

40. R. A. Stradling, *Philip IV and the Government of Spain, 1621–1665* (Cambridge: Cambridge University Press, 1988), 72–73.

41. Elliott, *Count-Duke of Olivares*, 400–403.

42. Letters were sent to Philip IV, Olivares, and influential women in Madrid, including Queen Isabel, the Countess of Olivares, and the king's aunt, Margaret of the Cross. ASV, Ep. ad Princ., registra, vol. 42, fols. 144r–153r.

Rome discussed the situation in Italy (and Madrid's response to it).[43] Urban's interests here appear to be motivated largely by a desire for peace, and the avoidance of warfare within Italy more specifically. In the larger context, the pope wished to use his influence to broker a peace between two hostile Catholic nations, as he believed they should be working together against Protestant and Islamic enemies rather than warring with each other.

Urban's frantic efforts to prevent violence in northern Italy between two Catholic powers failed. This failure presaged both the full-scale war that would shortly break out between France and Spain and the gradual decline of papal influence on the foreign policies of secular monarchies in Europe. The Thirty Years' War showed no signs of abatement. The Spanish viewed Urban as an enemy, while the French pursued their own foreign policies in Europe, largely heedless of what the pope might think.[44] While Urban continued to try and influence the Catholic monarchies of Europe, his failure portended worse to come; as Peter Rietbergen has observed, "Economic, political, and intellectual developments in the world at large simply could not be controlled any more by the Church's representatives."[45]

This larger political context complicated attempts by Compostelan envoys to navigate their way through the curia in the years 1628–29. They had to contend with the unpopularity of the Spanish faction, on the one hand, and with the hostility of the royal ambassador, several cardinals, and the Carmelite order, on the other. Of the potential obstacles they faced, the envoys quickly focused on the Spanish royal ambassador as one of the most difficult to overcome or circumvent.[46] Villafañe reported to the cathedral chapter at length about his attempts to convert the count of Oñate to the *santiaguista* position.[47] The count of Oñate, ambassador for the Spanish monarchy, had already received explicit instructions from the count-duke of Olivares, affirming his and the king's deep devotion to Teresa and her patron sainthood.[48] The *santiaguista* envoys realized that they needed either to persuade Oñate to join their side or to find a way of preventing him from fulfilling his duties. Rather than move against Oñate in a clandestine manner, Villafañe went to the

43. See ASV, Segreterio di Stato, Spagna, vols. 68 and 69.
44. Wright, *Early Modern Papacy*, 176–78.
45. Rietbergen, *Power and Religion in Baroque Rome*, 424.
46. Aldea Vaquero, "Política Interior," 403. Aldea claims that relations between the Spanish ambassadors and the Roman representative of the Castilian Congregation of the Clergy were often contentious.
47. Villafañe to the archbishop of Santiago, 1629, ACSC, IG 301 (32), unpaginated.
48. Olivares to Oñate, 27 March 1627, in Teresa de Jesús, *Escritos de Santa Teresa*, 425.

ambassador directly, giving him a letter from the archbishop and discussing with him the possibility of working together. In his report to the chapter, Villafañe remarked sadly, "Today, the count of Oñate has left this court; this is hard for us because in him we would have a favorable enemy. Wednesday, the count of Monterrey arrives to occupy this post."[49] Monterrey would prove to be an unfavorable enemy: He was not only an agent of the king but Olivares's brother-in-law.[50]

In addition to the royal ambassador in Rome, the envoys from Compostela had to contend with the powerful Carmelite presence in the curia. The Carmelites had allies among the cardinals, including Cardinal Colona, whom Villafañe described as actively working with the friars to obtain the *perinde valere*. Villafañe claimed that the cardinal's loyalty to the friar stemmed from a family connection—his sister was a Discalced Carmelite nun.[51] In a letter to the cathedral of Seville, Villafañe and Astorga confided that they faced mounting difficulties, because once the Carmelites had felt "the first blow" to block the *perinde valere*, they worked to shut out the Galician envoys through "a multitude of favors."[52] For their part, the *santiaguista* agents worked to instigate opposition to the Carmelites throughout the curia. First they attempted to ally themselves with members of the curia known to be hostile to the friars. Then they sought the support of the other religious orders by reminding them that the Carmelites had maneuvered to elevate one of their own saints over other equally prestigious saints among the Dominicans, Franciscans, and Jesuits.[53]

The envoys' decision to involve the other religious orders in the battle against the Carmelites was highly strategic. *Santiaguistas* knew they could use jealousy between the orders to their advantage, especially once they learned about another patronage scandal that had erupted a few years earlier in the kingdom of Naples. Sometime in the 1620s, the viceroy of Naples, Antonio Álvarez de Toledo, duke of Alba (viceroy 1622–29), encouraged by his Discalced Carmelite confessor, had spearheaded an attempt to have Teresa named patron and protector of the kingdom of Naples.[54] The viceroy's interest in such a measure is not

49. Villafañe to the archbishop of Santiago, 1629, ACSC, IG 301 (32), unpaginated.

50. Monterrey also received strict instructions to continue agitating against the cathedral of Santiago's envoys in Rome. Philip IV to the Count of Monterrey, 7 April 1629, MAE, leg. 59, fol. 68r–v.

51. Ibid.

52. Villafañe to the cathedral of Seville, 25 February 1630, BCC, 9.147.6 (2).

53. The cathedral detailed this strategy in the autumn of 1627. Cathedral to Fernando Brandano, 16 November 1627, ACSC, IG 941, fols. 2r–4v.

54. For an eighteenth-century description of this event, including excerpts from the original resolution translated into Spanish, see José de la Encarnación, *Apuntos, documentos y cartas para su obra Año benigno teresiano*, BNM, MS 12318, 959–60.

surprising, given that the seat of the dukes of Alba, Alba de Tormes, housed Teresa's relics.[55] Villafañe related the events that unfolded in Naples to Santiago de Compostela: The Carmelites won the viceroy's support, yet at the same time the Jesuits lobbied to have their own saints, Ignatius of Loyola and Francis Xavier, named the kingdom's patrons. The kingdom approved a decree that conceded the honor to all three saints; this compromise did not please the viceroy, who wanted Teresa to be the sole patron, not one of three. The viceroy therefore told Philip only that Teresa had been elected, so that when the royal agent arrived in Rome to request papal approval of the election, only Teresa's name would appear.

Somehow the Jesuits got wind of the viceroy's machinations and had the kingdom of Naples issue another decree naming only the two Jesuits saints as patrons. The Jesuits also hurried to the pope to gain approval for the measure, which was duly given, so that when the royal envoy arrived with the decree naming only Teresa, the pope, having just named the two Jesuits, refused. The royal agent persisted, insisting that no patron saint could be elected without the approval of the king, who wished the honor to go to Teresa. The pope begrudgingly handed the matter over to the Congregation of Sacred Rites, which complied with Philip's request. But when this body sent the brief ratifying Teresa's election to the pope, he apparently refused to sign it.[56] The confrontation between the pope and the royal envoy revealed starkly different attitudes about national patron sainthood. As we have seen, in Philip's view (and that of many teresianos), a national patron functioned as a public office. Because the patron's responsibilities centered on representing the nation and working for its well-being, the king insisted that it was within his rights to choose the saint who would fulfill that role, in much the same way that Spanish kings chose bishops for their sees.

The pope, for his part, agreed with the Castilian cathedral chapters that national patron sainthood remained firmly within the ecclesiastic domain. As a liturgical matter, it fell squarely within the jurisdiction of the Congregation of Sacred Rites. By attempting to force the pope to accept a specific patron, Philip had overstepped his bounds and angered Urban in the process. The pope therefore decided to draw up a motu proprio—a papal decision reached by the pope alone, without the cardinals—regarding the election of patrons. The purpose of the decree was to assert papal jurisdiction over national patron sainthood, to establish

55. ACSC, IG 301 (32), unpaginated.
56. Ibid.

clear norms for the election of patrons, and to avoid unseemly conflict over such elections in the future. It included provisions mandating the consent of the clergy and establishing only one major patron, although other patrons could be named, provided they were classified as "minor" (which stipulated a lower degree of liturgical formality). Villafañe heard about the specific contents of the *motu* and confided to the cathedral, "It has not been published because some phrasing required more deliberation; we think that the Carmelite Fathers prevented it from being published, out of fear that it might have bad consequences for them if it were to be."[57] Villefañe's account can be read in at least two ways: On the one hand, the Carmelites had mustered the power to prevent the unfavorable *motu proprio* from being issued. On the other hand, the attempt to have Teresa made patron of Naples had failed, largely because the pushy claims of the viceroy had insulted papal prerogatives.

Villefañe's close attention to the story of Naples reveals his acute sense that the precedent could be used to the cathedral of Santiago's advantage. Whatever devotion the pope might have felt personally toward Teresa, he could hardly ignore another Spanish infringement on papal authority. He also may have viewed the controversy as an opportunity to promulgate his *motu*. If this was Villefañe's assessment of Urban's reaction, he was correct: In 1629, Urban agreed to reconsider Teresa's elevation. Allowing a meeting to consider the legality of the brief was the first step toward its nullification; the Compostelan envoys must have felt that victory was near once they were granted this concession. Late in the autumn of 1629, the pope appointed a council of cardinals and other learned men to consider the issue. An ambassadorial report between the Spanish secretary and Monterrey revealed that representatives from all the complaining cathedral chapters were present, along with Villafañe and Astorga. Together they protested the novelty of Teresa's election, the harm done to Santiago's cult as a result, the interference of the secular state in ecclesiastical affairs, and the subreption of the brief.[58] The meeting resulted in the complete nullification of the 1627 brief and the reaffirmation of Santiago's right to the singular patronage of Spain. Cardinal Caetano, the papal nuncio in Spain, issued a copy of the papal revocation of co-patronage. Caetano's brief announcement included the following version of the events:

His Holiness committed the examination of this business to a certain assembly of prelates, which met before the illustrious and most

57. Ibid.
58. Diego Saavedra to the Count of Monterrey, 14 February 1630, MAE, leg. 59, fol. 69r–v.

reverend Cardinal Caetano. On the second of December [1629], the members of this assembly heard the different positions many times, and considered them with much prudence. . . . They decided that the aforementioned Brief was not valid. But owing to a request from the king of Spain, a new grace has been granted, that those who ask in the name of whatever city or diocese, with the approval of its bishop, clergy, and people, may have Saint Teresa as patron.[59]

Despite the second concession, the *santiaguista* victory was complete. The attempt to appease the king by allowing Teresa to be named a local patron hardly counted as a compromise, since she was already being celebrated as such throughout Castile. The decision completely quashed any possibility of Teresa's attaining nationwide status, or even patron sainthood throughout Castile alone. The ambassador's secretary made it clear to Monterrey that the king should be advised that no further protestations in favor of Teresa's patron sainthood should be made; Philip could say what he liked, but the decision was final.[60] A second brief, dated January 1630 and issued by the monsignor in charge of briefs, Maraldo, formalized the earlier decision.[61] Villafañe and Astorga returned in triumph to Galicia, where they were immortalized in poetry during the sumptuous celebrations held in honor of Santiago's renewed singularity.[62]

Shortly after issuing the new brief, Urban VIII quickly proclaimed his previous *motu proprio*, which established the correct procedure for the election of patron saints. Printed in March 1630, it included reforms aimed at ending disagreements that might arise over such elections. For example, it stipulated that there must be consensus over the choice of a patron between the bishop, clergy, and the people of a city or province. It also mandated that the ultimate approval of the election of a patron

59. *Translado de un Decreto de nuestro Santissimo Padre Urban VIII, en fauor del unico, y singular Patronazgo de Santiago Apóstol* (2 December 1629), BNM, MS 9140, fol. 286r.

60. Diego Saavedra to the Count of Monterrey, 14 February 1630, MAE, leg. 59, fol. 70r: "Esto es lo que a pasado y el estado en que se halla este negocio, y parece conven(te) concluir la carta representandole a su Magd que aviendo llegado este negocio a terminos de justicia y estando ya resulto no sera bien que su Magd se empeñe revolviendo sobre el, porque no tendran effetto sus instancias."

61. "Breve del papa Urbano VIII sobre elegir en patrona universal de España a Teresa de Jesús" (1629), RAH, Col. Salazar y Castro, MS 9/1032, fols. 16r–17v.

62. Antonio Gayoso Figueroa y Moscoso, "Regozijo de la muy noble, y leal ciudad de Santiago de Compostela, y de su ilustrissimo Cabildo, en la noticia que despues de medio dia, jueues 21 de Hebrero de 1630 tuuo de la declaracion que hizo nuestro santissimo padre Urbano VIII del unico patronato de las Españas en favor de Santiago Zebedeo" (1630), in ibid., fols. 43r–51v. Villafañe went on to be appointed bishop of Mondoñedo (Galicia).

saint rested in the hands of the Congregation of Sacred Rites, which oversaw canonization processes and liturgical practices.[63]

The decision to nullify Teresa's co-patronage was motivated in large part by a desire to end the scandals created by acrimonious disputes over patron saints. That such disputes arose during this period suggests the growing significance of regional and national patrons; previously, the policy had not been necessary, in part because such saints had been handled on a local level. But the large-scale clashes that had erupted in Castile and in Naples over patron sainthood could be neither contained nor dismissed as a local problem. From the papal perspective, Teresa might very well have seemed a more appropriate national patron than Santiago; she was a model Tridentine saint who promoted papal goals like the continuing struggle against heresy. Ironically, the pope was put in the position of defending the prerogatives of Santiago, even though the Spanish legends regarding the apostle's evangelization of Spain had fallen into disrepute in Rome. The decision to nullify Teresa's patron sainthood, therefore, did not constitute a rejection of Teresa in Rome. The central problem was *how* she had been elected and the uproar this had caused throughout the Castilian church. Urban's decision to over-turn Teresa's co-patronage provided him the opportunity to issue a sharp rebuke to the Spanish monarchy for overstepping its bounds and encroaching on territory that properly belonged to the church. A patron saint might be national, but she could never be *secular*.

Yet Urban's view of patron saints failed to keep up with changes in the political and religious culture of the seventeenth century, an era in which the symbolic association between saints and nations was becoming more firmly established. At the same time, the rapid proliferation of civic patrons and religious feast days provided a logistical as well as a spiritual problem for the church, which Urban finally took a firm hand in controlling. While the proliferation of new civic and national patrons had begun in the late Middle Ages, the cult of the saints experienced a profound revival in the early modern period; from the local to the national level, patrons multiplied rapidly. There were several possible reasons for this new vitality. First, the long hiatus in "saint-making" that had persisted throughout most of the sixteenth century finally came to an end.[64] The late sixteenth and early seventeenth centuries saw the

---

63. *Decretum super electione Sanctorum in Patronos* (23 March 1629), BNM, VE 67/74, 1630. For more on the decretal, see Jean-Michel Sallmann, "Il santo patrono cittadino nel '600 nel regno di Napoli e in Sicilia," in *Per la storia sociale e religiosa del mezzogiorno d'Italia*, vol. 2, ed. G. Galasso and C. Russo (Naples: Guida, 1982), 188–90.

64. Peter Burke, "How to Become a Counter-Reformation Saint (1984)," in *The Counter-Reformation: Essential Readings*, ed. David Luebke (Oxford: Blackwell, 1999), 130–42.

introduction of many new saints, some of whom—like Ignatius of Loy-ola and Teresa herself—proved tremendously popular. Second, the Prot-estant Reformation caused an increasing focus on the cult of the saints as a major line of confessional demarcation.[65] At the same time, emer-gent nation-states and powerful interest groups within nations (including cities) expressed their new political power through religious symbols in much the same way that Italian city-states had done four centuries earlier.[66]

Patron saints increased rapidly throughout the early modern world. While those who opposed Teresa's election in Spain often claimed that electing more than one patron was an aberration and an unwelcome departure from standard devotional practice, in fact nothing could be further from the truth. Historian Ricardo Fernández Gracia has noted that "the seventeenth century in Spain was, without a doubt, the century of patron sainthoods."[67] The same can be said for wider Catholic Europe. Nations, like cities, usually had more than one patron saint. Francisco de Santa María detailed the fact that England had several patrons in addition to Saint George, including Saint Joseph of Arimathea, while France honored Saint Denis as national patron but did not exclude Clovis, Saint Louis, and others.[68] In fact, many cities and kingdoms elected more patrons than ever before during the sixteenth and seven-teenth centuries. Jean-Michel Sallmann gives the following figures for early modern Naples: Between 1630 and 1750, 225 towns elected 410 patrons. Of these towns, the city of Naples led the way, designating Agrippino, Aniello, Aspreno, Athanasius, Eusebius, Severus, and Januar-ius as patrons.[69] Sallmann concludes that this rapid multiplication of patron saints actually had the effect of reducing the individual power of the saints while reinforcing the central and universal power of the

65. Eire, *From Madrid to Purgatory*, 507.

66. "And its [the commune's] lay government, far from being 'secularized' by its separation from the cathedral and bishop, came to express and understand itself through ever more explicitly religious rhetoric and symbols." Thompson, *Cities of God*, 3.

67. "El siglo XVII en España fue, sin duda, el de los patronatos. . . . El fenómino lo resume Lafuente en esta famosa frase: 'a cada tribulación se discurría un nuevo patronato.' A la cabeza de todo aquel fenómino hay que situar, a más alto nivel, el enfrentamiento entre los partidarios de Santa Teresa y Santiago aunque se repitió en muchos lugares con otros santos." Ricardo Fernández Gracia, *San Francisco Javier, Patrono de Navarra: Fiesta, religiosidad e iconografía* (Pamplona: Gobierno de Navarra, 2006), 31.

68. Francisco de Santa María, *Defensa del patronato*, fol. 253r–v. To Francisco's list of English patrons we could also add the medieval national patrons Saint Edmund and Saint Edward, who were often depicted alongside Saint George. Riches, *St. George*, 102.

69. Jean-Michel Sallmann, *Naples et ses saints a l'âge baroque (1540–1750)* (Paris: Presses Universitaires de France, 1994), 66.

church.[70] But in spite of multiple patrons in a civic pantheon, cities and nations tended to focus exclusively on one or two as their main symbol(s). As nations and saints became more closely connected, the universal church appears to have been the overall loser, because communities were beginning to see themselves as the originators of the meanings and roles of patron saints. The diminishment of papal authority outside Rome in this period lent new political and spiritual force to this claim.

Throughout the early modern period, then, new saints provided spiritual inspiration for cities, kingdoms, and nations. The newest and most important of these developments was the increasingly powerful association between saint and nation. The medieval idea that a native patron would be the best spiritual representative for a city began to be expanded to national patrons, even if this meant supplanting a more ancient, nonnative saint. Jean-Marie Le Gall has contended that in the early modern period, blood or birthplace became the primary identity marker for an individual and that this process affected the saints as well, who could be either replaced by a native (as in the case of Santiago and Teresa) or occasionally retroactively made a native (as in the case of Saint George in England).[71]

Another example of this trend worth examining in some detail occurred in the Iberian kingdom of Navarre when a move was made to elevate Francis Xavier (d. 1552) to co-patron saint alongside Navarre's traditional patron, San Fermín. Fermín bore many similarities to Santiago in Castile: Both were ancient saints, evangelizers, and martyrs. Neither was a native of the kingdom he had been chosen to represent, but both played key roles in bringing Christianity to these regions (Fermín was Pamplona's first bishop). And both had their status as patrons potentially disrupted by the popular election of two additional patrons in the 1620s: Francis and Teresa, both sixteenth-century figures, newly canonized, and natives of their respective kingdoms. Clearly, then, the motivation that led to Teresa's election was not an isolated Castilian impulse; rather, it reflected a trend that affected other regions as well.

The first talk of elevating Francis Xavier as patron saint of Navarre began soon after his beatification in 1619, in much the same way that efforts began for Teresa. Anticipating Francis's impending canonization, the Cortes of Navarre elevated Francis to patron saint in 1621.[72] The act of naming a patron saint in Navarre thus moved along the same path

70. "La multiplication des saints patrons conduisait à la dissolution de cette relation exclusive entre le patron et ses client. L'inflation provoquiat une dévalorisation." Ibid., 95.

71. He cites the Spanish example specifically. Le Gall, *Mythe de Saint Denis*, 519.

72. Ibid., 40.

that the process did in Castile. Both kingdoms waited only until their saint had been beatified, and in both cases a vote was taken in the Cortes. The presence of the viceroy and the bishop of Pamplona at the event solemnizing the ratification of the Cortes's decision in 1624 highlighted the legitimacy of this process of electing a patron saint.[73] The reasons for the outpouring of devotion to Francis mirrored the Castilian Cortes's justifications for Teresa's elevation: "He will fulfill the office of intercessor and advocate with the obligations that he owes this kingdom as having been born there."[74]

But the Cortes of Navarre, much like the Cortes of Castile, underestimated the controversy it would provoke with this decision, particularly from the powerful bishopric and city of Pamplona, which already recognized and celebrated San Fermín as Navarre's patron saint. Unlike Teresa's situation, however, the controversy over the co-patronage of Francis and Fermín did not boil over until decades later, with a series of cultic changes that occurred in the 1640s. The kingdom of Navarre then separated its own offices for the saints from those of the rest of Spain; as part of this declaration, a new book of divine offices for Navarre was issued, which referred to Francis as the patron saint of the kingdom, to be celebrated with a double octave. At the same time, it diminished Fermín's office to a festival in the city of Pamplona only. The decision to elevate one patron over the other actually originated in Rome, where Urban VIII was involved in yet another attempted reorganization of the festal calendar. He was motivated this time primarily by the desire to reduce the excessive number of feast days celebrated in Catholic nations. But the shift in celebrating Francis as the "unique patron saint of Navarre" sparked an agitated response from the bishop of Pamplona and devotees of San Fermín.[75] Thus, in contrast to Castile, people manifested little concern, let alone outrage, about having two patron saints; the two saints worked in harmony with each other until Francis was lifted above Fermín.

The cities and bishoprics of Navarre quickly fell in line behind one saint or the other, the majority of them behind Francis. Although the specific political, personal, and spiritual context for the controversy in Navarre must have been as complicated as that in Castile over Teresa and Santiago several years earlier, it is possible to generalize about the two foundational arguments for the partisans. Most important, of

---

73. *Actas de las Cortes de Navarra (1530–1829)*, 19 vols. (Pamplona: Servicio de Publicaciones del Parlemento de Navarra, 1991–96), 2:130.

74. Quoted in Fernández Gracia, *San Francisco Javier*, 41.

75. Ibid., 44–45.

course, Francis was a native son of Navarre. In addition, he represented the highest of Catholic Reformation values; his missionary work in India and seminal role in the earliest days of the Society of Jesus rendered him internationally famous. As a native of Navarre, his international acclaim and prodigious missionary work had brought glory and honor to his kingdom. On the other side, supporters of San Fermín emphasized the bishop's role in evangelizing the kingdom. First loyalty, they argued, was owed to the saint who first brought the faith to the city. The wrangling in Navarre continued until 1657, when Pope Alexander VII finally declared that both saints would be celebrated as principal patrons, in an effort to quash a controversy that was bringing scandal upon the church.[76]

When comparing the co-patronage controversies of Castile and Navarre, the two most striking characteristics of the new patrons are that both had recently achieved sainthood and both were natives of their respective kingdoms. This new seventeenth-century focus on national patrons and on reserving that position for natives marks a new impulse in national patron sainthood, born of the new political and spiritual context. Teresa's and Francis's supporters understood the close bond between saint and nation as the most suitable relationship between a native and his or her home. The connection between a national patron and a people (derived from sharing the same place of birth) enhanced the growing idea that the nation, not a lesser locality, should be viewed as the primary site of loyalty. While Francis, during his life, lacked the same close relationship with his nation that Teresa had with hers (Francis spent most of his life outside Navarre), the fame that his sanctity brought to Navarre smoothed over his abandonment of his home. The Navarrese, then, adopted as a national symbol a saint who would represent their claims to importance in a political context in which Navarre was marginalized and partially subordinate to the larger Spanish monarchy. Thus patron sainthood became increasingly communicentric in its orientation—that is, patrons were increasingly appropriated by civic and national leaders as symbols that were no longer exclusively, or even primarily, theological, even while they retained their spiritual importance. The early modern refashioning of patron saints as bound to their native lands transformed the relationship between the nation and the holy.

76. Ibid., 45–50. Fernández Gracia includes a list of the breakdown of partisans in the controversy on p. 48. The book also contains several beautifully reproduced paintings and engravings of the two saints as co-patrons.

Of course, not all patrons were natives. Birthplace was not a necessary qualification for the office, as we have seen in the examples of
Santiago and Fermín. These saints resonated deeply as national symbols
primarily because they were embedded in long-cherished historical narratives of the nation. The saint's active participation in the life of his
place of residence over the course of several centuries could have the
same emotional impact and symbolic importance as a native saint's
could do. Central to the cults of these two saints, and to their significance
as national patrons, was their relationship to their nations; both lived in
these lands and brought the Christian faith to them. During the early
modern period we see an increasing need to establish a preexisting relationship between saint and nation, privileging a tie that bound the two
together *during the saint's lifetime,* as in the case of an evangelizing saint.
This need is particularly striking in the example of Santiago, who, as we
have seen, had been an important national patron in the Middle Ages,
even though his medieval cult downplayed his journey to Spain in favor
of his relics and apparitions. In addition, ancient patrons demonstrated
an established and provable pattern of aid. It is thus not surprising to
see in Sallmann's research on early modern Naples that throughout the
seventeenth century ancient saints remained the most popular choice for
new patrons, followed by medieval saints, with modern saints coming
in last.[77] Modern saints lacked a demonstrable track record (though they
were also far fewer in number). But modern saints could transcend this
shortcoming through their birth in a specific land—the tie between a
native saint and her nation was sufficient for proving her future loyalty
and dedication to her people. The presence of the saints' relics, while
sometimes included as a gift from the saint to her nation, did not play
an essential role in forging a tie between a native saint and the nation.

   One of the most important patron saints in the history of the Catholic Church is the Virgin Mary. Holding a special place in the church
particularly from the twelfth century on, Mary has the highest number
of shrines and churches dedicated to her. While her eminence was a
reflection of her universal importance to Catholic and Orthodox Christians, she also demonstrated a nearly limitless ability to adapt to the
needs of local cults, which eagerly adopted her as their particular
patron—Our Lady of Guadalupe, Our Lady of Montserrat, Our Lady of
Paris. A quick look at a list of national patron saints today reveals that
the Virgin Mary still holds a place of prominence; she remains the
national patron of at least half of all nations with patron saints, often in

77. Sallmann, *Naples et ses saints,* 76.

conjunction with other saints (who had a more immediate connection to the nation in question) but occasionally on her own, particularly in the case of more recently converted nations.[78]

When and how the Virgin Mary became associated with individual nations is difficult to determine, largely because scholars have not addressed this question. The case study of Mary is particularly interesting for national patron sainthood, because her universal importance to the church had the potential to militate against the kind of particular relationship between saint and nation that we see, for example, between Spain and Teresa, or England and George. During the Spanish co-patronage debate, supporters of Santiago sometimes claimed that the Virgin was already the co-patron, alongside Santiago. This is not a surprising claim given the intensity of devotion to the Virgin in early modern Spain;[79] what is fascinating, however, is that this argument did not gain much traction, though we do see occasional references to the Virgin as the patron saint of the Spanish throughout the seventeenth century.[80] This pattern suggests that in the early modern era of "nationalizing" saints through patronage, the Virgin might have been too universal a saint to be mobilized effectively for national representation.

There is, however, at least one early modern example of the Virgin Mary's being transformed into a potent "national" symbol: Our Lady of Guadalupe in Mexico. While a comprehensive analysis of this important cult is not possible here, the development of the cult in the seventeenth century does bear some comparison to larger trends involving national patrons in Europe, and therefore is worth a brief review. The cult of the Guadalupe arose in the sixteenth century, following the apparition of

78. While no "official" or definitive list of national patron saints exists (largely because such patrons are often held by tradition rather than by decree, and because they change over time), one such list can be found at http://www.catholic-saints.info/patron-saints/patron-saints-countries.htm (accessed 14 July 2009). (Under Spain, note that the Virgin Mary and Saint James are listed; other lists I have found also include Teresa of Avila and John of Avila.)

79. One of the most vital cults to Mary in early modern Spain was that of the Immaculate Conception. Also understudied, a good account of this devotional movement can be found in Suzanne L. Stratton, *The Immaculate Conception in Spanish Art* (Cambridge: Cambridge University Press, 1994).

80. For one example, see Hernando Cano de Montoro, *Al Illustrissimo y reverendissimo Señor Don Diego de Guzmán, Arçobispo de Sevilla . . . Dedica y Consagra estos Discursos, Predicados en su Sancta Yglesia, en defensa de el unico Patronato de nuestro grande Apostol Sanctiago el Mayor, hijo de Zebedeo* (Seville: Juan de Cabrera, [ca. 1628]). "Mas, que se debe ponderar mucho el respeto, digase así, que la Virgen Sanctissimia a tenido siempre en esta parte a Sanctiago, pues siendo Patrona, y Protectora de España, así la llama el Illustrissimo Arçobispo Don Rodrigo y dize que en la batalla de las Navas, salieron los nuestros con su favor vencedores" (fol. 7r). It is interesting to note here that Cano reminds readers of the crucial role the Virgin played in a reconquest battle and the Spanish cult dedicated to that victory (Our Lady of Las Navas).

the Virgin to an indigenous man, Juan Diego, in the Mexican countryside; the cult became increasingly prominent as the seventeenth century
progressed.[81] Although today the Guadalupe is often connected to indigenous devotion, the earliest group to take up the cult was the Creoles,
when two Creole priests, Miguel Sánchez and Luis Laso de la Vega,
supplied the first written accounts of the apparition in the 1640s.[82]

One of the most important functions that the apparition of the Virgin of Guadalupe served for seventeenth- and eighteenth-century Creoles was to provide them with a myth of spiritual foundation for their
nation. This new spiritual foundation allowed Mexican Creoles to legiti-
mize their own messianic destiny. It also permitted a rejection of the
myths of spiritual conquest sometimes elaborated by peninsular Spaniards, who proclaimed that New Spain had been conquered with the
spiritual assistance of Santiago.[83] As Stafford Poole argues, Sánchez's
work in particular put Mexico City "on par with the great religious
centers of the Catholic world."[84] By placing Mexico City within a larger
Catholic context, Creoles claimed for Mexico spiritual equality with the
old Catholic homeland, and for themselves a way to challenge their
political oppressors, peninsular Spain. The Mexican Guadalupe supplies
an important example of how a medieval European cult was trans-
planted to a new country, culture, and context; there it was fashioned in
new ways to meet the needs of an emerging nation. Thus it was possible
for the Virgin Mary to be transformed into a national patron, though she
did not materialize fully as such in Mexico until the eighteenth century.

Whether the connection forged between nation and saint evolved
out of a tradition of reciprocity or birthplace, the early modern phenomenon of electing new and more numerous saints became particularly
significant when associated with expanding and centralizing nations.
Saints throughout early modern Europe became allegorical representations for their nations in a way that reflected new ways of imagining the
nation. Samantha Riches has demonstrated that it was common in
England for political commentators to use saints as allegorical representations of nations in political dialogues and polemics beginning in the

81. Stafford Poole, *Our Lady of Guadalupe: The Origins and Sources of a Mexican National Symbol,
1531–1797* (Tucson: University of Arizona Press, 1995).

82. Ibid., 100–126. Poole credits Sánchez in particular with fusing Guadalupe "with Mexican
identity."

83. For more on the Guadalupe as a foundation myth, see D. A. Brading, *Mexican Phoenix, Our
Lady of Guadalupe: Image and Tradition Across Five Centuries* (Cambridge: Cambridge University Press,
2001).

84. Poole, *Our Lady of Guadalupe*, 106.

middle of the seventeenth century. A poem allegorizing England's conflicts with Ireland, for example, might present a dialogue between Saints George and Patrick.[85] Thus, while George held a privileged position as one of England's most important patron saints from the Middle Ages, he did not *personify* the nation until the early modern period. A rigorous study of the evolution of national patron saints from the Middle Ages through the seventeenth century would need to be completed in order to understand these changes fully, but it is clear that national patron saints took on a more extensive and elaborate meaning in the seventeenth century as the nations themselves evolved.

One of the more obvious differences between many medieval patrons and their early modern counterparts is the relationship between the saint and the royal family. Medieval national patrons were often promoted by the king and his dynastic branch; the saint gained "national" status primarily through his association with the king.[86] The proliferation and aggrandizing of patron saints in the seventeenth century, therefore, stemmed from more than expanded state power; the nation, like its patrons, did not belong only to the monarch. While monarchs could play powerful roles in the choice of national symbols— particularly by eschewing older ones in favor of new ones more in line with royal aims and contemporary political realities—we see both in Klaniczay's study of Hungary and in this analysis of Spanish co-patronage that the king did not necessarily name the patron. In fact, a national patron could serve as a rallying cry against royal authority in the name of the nation. Thus evolving understandings of nation and holiness resulted in national saints; at the same time, new crises and new ways of envisioning the nation led to corresponding changes in the saints and their meanings.[87]

Thus we see throughout the early modern period a resurgence of devotion to patron saints, and in particular a powerful appearance of national saints. While medieval nations often had their patrons, such patrons tended to be tied to dynastic claims and authority rather than to peoples. In addition, the understanding of the nation itself as a site of primary loyalty (as distinct from the king, though it often comprehended

85. Riches, *St. George*, 188–89.

86. Klaniczay, *Holy Rulers and Blessed Princesses*, 367.

87. One can see a similar pattern in early modern France, where, according to Jean-Marie Le Gall, one of France's traditional patrons, Saint Denis, was systematically being "denationalized." Le Gall argues that from the sixteenth to the eighteenth century, changes in the political and religious realities of France—primarily the increasing strength of the Protestant reform movement as well as the evolution of absolutism—led French kings to abandon Saint Denis, as they increasingly distanced their rituals from their traditional dynastic saint. Le Gall, *Mythe de Saint Denis*, 524.

him) grew out of early modern political thought, particularly in the seventeenth century. The brief survey of cultic devotion I have provided here reveals a shift occurring in the location of spiritual and political authority. This shift created major difficulties for the church, which continued its efforts to maintain control over the regulation and supervision of devotional practices. It had been one of the main projects of the early modern papacy to streamline the process of beatification and canonization, placing them more firmly in the hands of the papal curia. Urban VIII sought to complete these reforms with a variety of his own advances. In addition to the emerging liturgical problem of too many celebrations cluttering the festal calendar, the church faced the challenge of the increasing strength of communicentric understandings of patron sainthood.

While patrons were still deeply embedded in their larger spiritual and theological contexts, they were also appropriated to reflect increasingly secular interests and identities. As a result, cities and nations felt that they should have primary say in the election of their patrons, an attitude that conflicted directly with the church's desire to maintain full authority over liturgical matters. While the medieval church had always claimed some control over the regulation of saints—particularly through efforts at formalizing the process of canonization—patron saints in the Middle Ages had been chosen largely by acclaim. But the increasing challenges to papal authority in the seventeenth century led to an atmosphere in which the pope viewed such popular acclamations as a threat, especially in the case of national patrons. National patron sainthood proved potentially divisive because of the role that national bodies— kings and representative assemblies—played in electing them. These choices could then be forced on unwilling cathedral chapters throughout the nation, reflecting the king's belief that royal authority should extend, as unimpeded as possible, throughout his realms.

The extent to which national patrons could become agents of the nation separate from their spiritual origins is exemplified in the English case. During the early modern period, England transformed itself from a Catholic nation into a Protestant one. Yet Saint George largely maintained his position as allegory for England even though Protestant reforms strictly limited liturgical celebrations of the saints. For their part, Catholic nations worked assiduously to argue for their right to choose their own national representatives, much to the mounting annoyance of Urban, who was increasingly compelled to assert his own jurisdiction over patron sainthood. While sainthood would always be bound up with papal authority, patron saints themselves could move away from the strict control of the church and take on new and expanded lives as representatives and symbols of communities in ways that did not need to meet church standards. Moreover, they began to belong to a nation rather than to the universal church. The idea that each nation should have a native saint as patron can be seen in part as an extension of medieval devotion to local holy people. In some ways, of course, the cult of the saints traditionally had been the part of spiritual devotion most controlled by communities and most outside papal authority. But early modern trends in electing national patrons are more than a manifestation of this older tradition on a national scale; they helped to transform the meaning of the nation for seventeenth-century people. They provided kings and people new symbolic ways to define themselves, contest authority, and draw lines of power and jurisdiction. In short, they helped to forge the concept of the nation itself. A weakening of papal authority in the modern Catholic world, therefore, did not spell the end of national patron sainthood. In some ways, it provided a new beginning.

EPILOGUE

The collapse of Teresa's patronage following the publication of the 1629 papal brief constituted a complete victory for Santiago's supporters. The most ardent *santiaguista* cathedral chapters celebrated festivals of thanksgiving for the revocation of Teresa's patron sainthood. In Santiago de Compostela, this festival was immortalized in a lengthy poem.[1] The Cordoban chapter's desire to celebrate the end of co-patronage with a festival and procession was briefly thwarted by their staunchly *teresiano* bishop, Lobera, although the festival was eventually held during one of the bishop's absences from the city.[2] Seville also responded to the news of the papal brief's revocation with great rejoicing, celebrating the event with a procession and fireworks.[3] Its cathedral chapter also printed a large poster announcing the arrival of the new papal brief and mandating that all members of the clergy, including priests, abbots, canons, and religious of both sexes adhere to its provisions. All insignias representing Teresa as co-patron were to be destroyed and all prayers referring to her as patron were to cease. The poster was then hung on the door of every church and in other public places.[4]

For the next two years the Compostelan cathedral engaged in a series of acrimonious skirmishes with the stubborn remnants of Teresa's

1. Gayoso Figueroa y Moscoso, "Regozijo de la muy noble, y leal ciudad de Santiago de Compostela."
2. Cathedral chapter of Córdoba to chapter of Santiago, 2 July 1631, ACSC, IG 301 (44), unpaginated.
3. A reference to the procession appears in a seventeenth-century account of the events occurring in Seville. Francisco Morales Padrón, ed., *Memorias de Sevilla, 1600–1678* (Córdoba: Monte de Piedad y Caja de Ahorros, 1981), 68. The official account of the festivities, printed by the cathedral, used the occasion to repeat passionately the main points of the *santiaguista* movement. See *Relacion de la solemnidad con que en la santa Iglesia de Sevilla, se publicó el breve de su Santidad, en favor del Patronato, unico, y singular de España del glorioso Apostol Santiago* (ca. 1630), BCC, 8.7.59, fols. 78r–79v.
4. "Un cartel por el Cabildo de Sevilla, por Francisco de Monsalve y Francisco de Melgar—9 May 1630," BCC, 9.147.3. Melgar was named one of the co-executors of the new papal brief.

faction, mostly Discalced Carmelites. It began by systematically forcing all Carmelite convents and monasteries to destroy all insignias, shields, epitaphs, and images depicting their saint as national patron.[5] For the next several years Navarrete continued to send the cathedral chapter updates on the happenings at court and tried to quash various Carmelite attempts to keep co-patronage afloat in the wake of the new papal brief.[6] The debate smoldered in Granada even after the second papal brief revoked Teresa's co-patronage. In the spring of 1630, Gregorio Morillo (a native of Granada) wrote to the archbishop of Santiago, complaining bitterly about the proposed construction of an image of Teresa alongside Santiago for a "triumph" in a public space at one of the entrances to the city. He continued his complaints in another letter to Fernando Dávila, one of the city officials, in April 1630. In both letters he cited the confusion that would be generated among the common people by the presentation of the saints together, especially in light of the recent controversy over co-patronage. He demanded that the image of Teresa be removed, possibly destroyed.[7] While the outcome of Morillo's complaint is unknown, his letters testify to ongoing tensions in the city over co-patronage, and hint that strong support for Teresa continued after the debate's ostensible end.

In 1630 a church in Granada was denounced to the Inquisition for singing a litany to Teresa that included a reference to her as "patron of Spain."[8] By the spring of the next year the cathedral of Santiago was hearing rumors from its agents in Rome that the Discalced Carmelites planned to begin the controversy all over again. The cathedral chapter fired off a scathing letter to the general of the order, who responded politely that the Carmelites were involved in no such scheme.[9] The chapter kept up a constant stream of letters to other cathedral chapters

5. Mera Carvajal, *Informacion en derecho, por el estado eclesiastico*, fols. 284r–293v. The thoroughness of this campaign no doubt explains the paucity of surviving images of co-patronage; I have come across only three (two engravings and one sculpture).

6. There are several more letters from Navarrete to the chapter in this appendix, mostly from the year 1631, describing Carmelite machinations at court. Iglesias Ortega, "Pedro Fernández de Navarrete," 134–36.

7. ACSC, IG 301 (36), fols. 226r–228v. It is likely that the image was removed, in light of the cathedral of Santiago's vigilance in the matter.

8. Archivo Histórico Nacional, Madrid, Sec. Inquisición, leg. 4462 (53), 21 March 1630, unpaginated.

9. Cathedral chapter to general of the Carmelite order, 31 March 1631, BNM, MS 9140, fols. 287r–288r. In the index of MS 9140 (which was compiled by Carmelite Francisco de Santa María), the author noted, "al cabildo de Santiago quejandose de la orden por sospechas sin fundamento de que no guardaba el decreto." For what was most probably the response to this letter from the Carmelite general, see Carmelite general to cathedral of Santiago, 25 June 1631, ACSC, IG 301 (34), unpaginated.

throughout Castile, reminding them of their duty to make sure the Carmelites gave up Teresa's patronage and destroyed their images.[10]

Among those who refused to accept the failure of the co-patronage
attempt was Philip IV. Four years after the retraction of Teresa's co-
patronage, Philip petitioned Urban VIII to put her prayers in the breviary.[11] He also never forgot how new patron saints could bring help in
calamitous times. The 1640s were a disastrous period for Philip, both
personally and politically. During that decade Portugal overthrew the
monarchy and achieved independence, the Catalans rebelled, Naples
revolted, final peace with the United Provinces was made (in terms detri-
mental to Spain), and the king experienced the personal loss of his wife,
brother, and only son. The political and economic failures of those years
also led to Olivares's fall from power and his banishment from court.[12]
As Philip watched his monarchy slip into greater crisis, warfare, and
decline throughout the following decades, the deeply pious king
expressed a sense of personal responsibility and sinfulness. In 1643 he
remarked sorrowfully, "Because I have offended and continue to offend
God so greatly, I deserve the punishment and afflictions that I now
suffer."[13] Alone and adrift, Philip began a correspondence in 1643 with a
Zaragozan nun, Sister María de Ágreda, from whom he sought solace,
spiritual consolation, and political advice. After the death of his heir,
Baltasar Carlos, in 1646, Philip frequently expressed to María his belief
that God was punishing him and, through him, all of Spain.[14]

In 1643 Philip also asked the president of Castile to vote on celebrating the feast day of the Vision of the Archangel Michael (8 May) and to
choose Michael as the "protector" of the monarchy. The Jesuit preacher
Juan Eusebio Nieremberg was charged with writing a treatise announcing the decision, which would be printed and distributed at court.[15] Philip's choice of Michael was telling—the archangel is perhaps preeminent
among all military saints; like Santiago, he is always depicted with a

10. Such letters can be found throughout ACSC, IG 301. It is no doubt owing to Compostelan
vigilance that so few images of Teresa as patron saint have survived.

11. Philip IV to Cardinal Barberini, 30 October 1634, MAE, leg. 158, fol. 175v.

12. For an account of Olivares's fall, see Elliott, Count-Duke of Olivares, 640–51.

13. Quoted in Carlos Seco Serrano, ed., Cartas de Sor María de Jesús de Ágreda y de Felipe IV,
BAE 108 (Madrid: Atlas, 1958), 4.

14. Ibid., 81–82. On 7 and 10 October 1646, Philip described the final illness and death of his
son. Again he described himself as deserving divine punishment but begged Sor María to pray to
God for his son's health (81). He later expressed his feelings about Baltasar Carlos's death: "I remain
in the state which you can imagine, as I have lost my only son. . . . I confess to you that [this blow]
has pierced my heart and transported me to a state where I do not know if I am dreaming or
awake" (82).

15. León Pinelo, Anales de Madrid, 326.

sword in his hand, ready to strike the enemy. Clearly, the 1640s were a time when the Spanish saw themselves in need of increased aid, especially military protection. Richard Stradling claims that "the 1640s, like the 1620s, were years of an attempted moral rearmament."[16] But this time Philip made a more strategic decision when choosing a co-patron: Instead of a female saint, he chose a male; rather than a virgin, an angel.[17] And he replaced the title of "patron" with the more general "protector." Nonetheless, the cathedral of Santiago again leapt into action, printing a treatise in defense of both Santiago's singular patronage and his singular protection.[18] A decade later partisans of Santiago continued to argue against Michael's patronage as an affront to the traditional prerogatives of the apostle.[19]

Philip IV also invoked the Virgin Mary as the patron saint of the Spanish army. In 1645 the preacher Manuel de Nájera referred to the Virgin as the "invincible Bellona," the same rhetoric used to describe Teresa in the 1620s.[20] Such language also resuscitated older ways of imagining Mary as a military saint that had been consistently popular not only in the Middle Ages but in the early modern era.[21] But the triumphal tones of the early decades of the century had disappeared by 1645; rather than invoking the monarchy's might, even in the face of many enemies, Nájera remarked sadly, "I confess that in the disgraces that our kingdom have suffered recently, I see the story of David and Goliath."[22] While the story of David implied victory, it framed Castile's contemporary situation as being confronted by overwhelming odds; Nájera described the kingdom as diminished, beaten down, inferior to its enemies in every practical way.

16. Stradling, *Philip IV and the Government of Spain*, 270.

17. Strictly speaking, angels do not have sexes the way humans do, but they were always gendered masculine.

18. *Defensa de la unica proteccion y patronazgo de las Españas*. More documentation on this second co-patronage attempt, entitled *Patronato del Apóstol Santiago (1643–1671)*, can be found at ACSC, IG 302.

19. Antonio Calderón and Jerónimo Pardo, *Parte Primera y Segunda de las Excelencias del Apostol Santiago (unico y singular Patron de España) entre los demas Apostoles*, 2 vols. (Madrid: Gregorio Rodríguez, 1657–58). The fourth book of this work is dedicated solely to the Michael-Santiago co-patronage issue.

20. Manuel de Nájera, "Sermon de la Concepcion de la Virgen NS, elegida por Patrona de las Armas de España, predicado en la octaua, que por los buenos sucesos de su Magestad, consagró a esta Reina el muy religioso Conuento de las Madres Descalças de la concepcion Dominica," in Nájera, *Sermones varios* (Madrid: María de Quiñones, 1645).

21. Remensnyder, "Colonization of Sacred Architecture." Following a victory claimed for the Virgin against Protestant enemies in 1620, Emperor Maximilian had her declared the "generalissima" of the Catholic army. Bireley, *Refashioning of Catholicism*, 109.

22. Nájera, "Sermon de la Concepcion," 366.

As the political situation in Spain failed to improve throughout the remaining decades of the century, it is unsurprising to see continued efforts to bolster the monarchy's spiritual representation in heaven. Additional assaults on Santiago's unique patronage resurfaced during the reign of Charles II (1665–1700). When the Austrian Habsburgs named Saint Joseph as their patron saint, Charles attempted to follow his cousins' efforts in 1678. Unsurprisingly, the cathedral of Santiago rose up against this effort as well.[23] It is not clear what to make of the attempts to have Saints Joseph and Michael made patrons. Partisans of Santiago claimed credit for defeating these attempts, declaring victories in the apostle's favor.[24] While the king and cathedral of Santiago danced the same steps they had during the earlier co-patronage controversy, no subsequent attempt inspired the same level of intensity that Teresa's elevation had. In part, such a lack of emotional resonance for contemporary Castilians must have resulted from Santiago's continued decline as a meaningful cultural symbol, at least outside Galicia.

While Teresa herself may also have been in decline devotionally and symbolically, by midcentury Charles maintained the same personal devotion to the saint that his father had expressed.[25] In 1681 the king declared his intention to celebrate Teresa's feast day annually in the royal chapel.[26] A decade later he petitioned the Congregation of Sacred Rites to permit him to celebrate Teresa with an octave.[27] Oddly, the king added a codicil to his will requesting that his heirs resolve the conflict over Teresa's patronage and reinstate her as patron saint.[28] As no further references to Teresa's patronage surfaced in the eighteenth century, it is likely that the new Bourbon monarchs ignored the request of the last Habsburg king, no doubt choosing their own saints and symbols instead.

23. *Memorial de la Santa Iglesia de Santiago dado al Rey sobre la Orden que expedio en 29 de noviembre de 1678 . . . que en todos sus Reynos y Señorios recibieron por Tutelar al Glorioso Patriarca Señor San Josef, suplicando se suspendiere la execucion* (1678), BCC, 9.147.6 (2).

24. "Carta circular del deán y cabildo de Santiago [al obispo de Teruel] en defensa del unico patronato de Santiago. 4 febrero 1688," BNM, VE 220/78, fol. 1r–v. Of course, if the attempts to restrict patron sainthood to Santiago had been so successful, it is unclear why the cathedral chapter of Santiago was still harping on the subject as late as 1688.

25. While there is not much work on this issue specifically, later seventeenth-century Carmelite efforts to depict Saint John of the Cross as the founder of the male Discalced Carmelites (thus thrusting Teresa from her role as founder of both) suggest that Teresa's role as a dynamic spiritual powerhouse was waning for the time being. See, for example, Christopher C. Wilson, "Masculinity Restored: The Visual Shaping of St. John of the Cross," *Archive for Reformation History* 98 (2007): 134–66.

26. José de la Encarnación, *Apuntos, documentos y cartas*, fol. 21v.

27. Carlos II to the papal curia, n.d., MAE, leg. 158, fols. 179r–180r.

28. Antonio Domínguez Ortiz, ed., *Testamento de Carlos II* (Madrid: Editora Nacional, 1982).

Yet both Teresa and Santiago remained vital symbols of Spanish national identity. Although neither saint remained constantly in view as a salient figure in Spanish cultural and spiritual life, both were drawn back into public discourse in subsequent centuries. Perhaps the most striking example of the resuscitation of Teresa as national patron saint occurred in the early nineteenth century, when a group of Spaniards met to draw up the nation's first constitution in the wake of the political crisis provoked by the Napoleonic invasion. In the spring and summer of 1812, the convent of Discalced Carmelites in Cádiz formally requested that the delegates of the Cortes of Cádiz, then in the process of drawing up the constitution, reinstate Teresa as Spain's patron saint as an act of thanksgiving to God for his sanctioning of the new constitution. The Carmelites' petition cited Teresa's elevation in the 1620s as a reason why she should be reinstated.[29] The Cortes voted unanimously in favor of renewing Teresa's protection.[30] Teresa thus became the patron saint of the new liberal Spain.

Resistance to the renewal of Teresa's patronage arose immediately from the cathedral of Seville, which launched two attacks on the Cortes's vote in the summer of 1812. Their opposition trotted out the familiar arguments that the Cortes could not vote on what was essentially an ecclesiastical matter and that the vote was not an accurate reflection of the will of the people.[31] Despite Seville's resistance, there was little the cathedral could do against the liberal Cortes. When King Fernando VII returned to Spain from exile in 1814, however, he brought with him the papal nuncio Gravo, who had been exiled in 1812 by the liberals. Teresa's new patronage suffered two blows with the return of these men: First, Fernando refused to ratify the constitution of Cádiz. Second, Gravo quashed an attempt by the cathedral of Toledo to celebrate Teresa's feast day as patron in 1816. The politicians who had originally favored Teresa's

29. Enrique Tierno Galván, ed., *Actas de las Cortes de Cádiz: Antología*, 2 vols. (Madrid: Taurus, 1964), 2:1007–15. Significantly, the Cortes's discussion of the question of Teresa's patronage was followed by a long dispute over whether the *voto* of Santiago ought to be abolished; the heart of this dispute lay in contemporary liberal efforts to force the church and ecclesiastical matters out of the state. Ibid., 2:892–1007. The Cortes abolished the *voto* by a vote of 85–26, in spite of powerful arguments that such an abolition "dividiría los ánimos y disminuiría nuestra fuerza moral, que consiste en la unidad de sentimientos y en la conformidad de nuestros esfuerzos contra el enemigo común" (2:922).

30. Ibid., 2:1025. Another account of the vote in favor of Teresa can be found in *Informe de la Diputación de Ceremonias sobre el copatronazgo* (1812), BCC, sec. 9, leg. 147, no. 3, fols. 1r–2v.

31. "Informe de la Diputación de Ceremonias sobre el copatronazgo," and "Juicio Crítico de los documentos relativos al Patronato de Santa Theresa de Jesús, en España o Disertación histórico-critico por la nulidad de tal patronato acordado por las Cortes generales y extraordinarias el dia 27 de junio de 1812" (1812), BCC, 9.147.4.

re-election insisted that patron sainthood was the nation's business, not the church's. Once again Teresa's patronage provoked a fierce struggle over ecclesiastical versus communicentric understandings of patron sainthood, but this time events unfolded in a very different religious and political context from two centuries earlier. Still, papal control over liturgical matters halted the secular branch of the movement. Teresa could be patron saint in a cultural sense to the secular liberal government, but no matter how deep anticlerical sentiments ran, it proved impossible to elevate a patron saint to whom no priest would pray or any church support. Teresa's patron sainthood, which had never fully taken effect, faded once more into obscurity.[32]

Repeated attempts to name a co-patron saint of Spain, from the early seventeenth century to the early nineteenth, underscore the continuing significance of religious symbolism in the development of national consciousness. The radically different historical contexts for these attempts actually reinforce such continuity. Through careful examination of patronage movements over time, we can arrive at a more complete understanding of the evolution of the concept of nationhood in Spanish history. Though scholars of modern nationalism often acknowledge the indebtedness of national sentiment to religious models, their tendency is to relegate religion quickly to the margins, while focusing on secularist nationalist discourses. A more nuanced approach to the ways in which religious nationalist symbolism could be mobilized both by leaders and by the wider populace is required.[33] Studies of religious symbols like patrons can illustrate the multifaceted ways in which nations could be imagined and states built; such uses of these symbols did not (perhaps could not) go unchallenged, and they could be used just as easily to destabilize or resist state formation. When one symbol clashes with another, the full complexity of such processes can be seen, along with the multiplicity of motivations, identities, and visions that people possessed. Religious symbols, therefore, are not merely "religious"—they frequently comprehend a wide variety of political, ideological, and cultural meanings.

32. For a brief but thorough account of the resurgence of Teresa's patron sainthood in the Cortes of Cádiz and beyond, see Ignacio Lasa Iraolo and Juan María Laboa Gallego, "Santa Teresa de Jesús, patrona de España en las Cortes de Cádiz," *Hispania Sacra* 32 (1980): 265–85.

33. A similar process took place in late nineteenth-century Italy, as devotees began a movement to have Saint Catherine of Siena elevated to patron saint of that country. See Gerald Parsons, *The Cult of Saint Catherine of Siena: A Study in Civil Religion* (Burlington, Vt.: Ashgate, 2008), 43–82. Parsons also comments on the persistence of twentieth-century historians in depicting civil religion in a negative light.

Both Santiago and Teresa remain symbols of deep and tangled significance in Spanish cultural life. In the twentieth century, the famed
pilgrimage route to Santiago de Compostela (known by its popular nick-
name, *el Camino*) had deteriorated, in terms of both infrastructure and
devotional interest. One of the major projects of General Franco's Ministry of Tourism and Propaganda in the mid-twentieth century was to
restore the *Camino;* one of the ministry's most visible achievements was
the construction (or renovation) of a series of high-end luxury hotels
along the route, called *paradores,* most of which were housed in medieval
and Renaissance buildings. To Franco's government, this project
restored the centrality of Santiago as a cultural and ideological symbol;
at the same time, it attempted to reach out to Europeans by reminding
them of their shared heritage of Christianity and pilgrimage.[34] The restoration was a smashing success, reaching its apogee after Franco's death
and the return of republican Spain. But in the last decades of the twentieth century, the route was largely transformed into a center of New Age
spiritualist tourism or ecotourism, rather than Catholic pilgrimage. The
iconography of Santiago also faced new challenges, as many politicians,
artists, and intellectuals became increasingly uncomfortable with the racism of images of the apostle as Matamoros, which were prominently
displayed not only in the cathedral of Santiago de Compostela but
throughout the city and in churches all over Spain. A fierce debate was
sparked over whether such images should be removed; though to date
most have not been taken down, disagreement over the issue reflects
the disgrace into which this aspect of Spanish tradition, so beloved by
Quevedo, has fallen in public opinion.[35]

Teresa, by contrast, has enjoyed a resurgence of scholarly and devotional popularity. In the first half of the twentieth century, Teresa's cult,
like Santiago's, became an important site of veneration. Under Franco's
regime she was proclaimed the "patron saint of the Spanish race," and
it is rumored that the generalissimo himself died holding on to the relic
of the saint's hand.[36] While Santiago's cult has struggled to survive its
associations with fascism and racism, Teresa's has been able to distance
itself from them. In fact, scholars and intellectuals in the late twentieth

34. For more on the restoration of the Camino, see Sasha D. Pack, "Revival of the Pilgrimage
to Santiago de Compostela: The Politics of Religious, National, and European Patrimony, 1879–
1988," *Journal of Modern History* 82, no. 2 (2010): 335–67.

35. For more on this issue, see 15 May 2004 http://www.aciprensa.com/noticia.php?n = 4488
(accessed 7 May 2006).

36. See, for example, a discussion of Teresa and the long history of Spanish imperial messianism in Antonio Pérez-Romero, *Liberation and Subversion in the Writings of Saint Teresa* (Amsterdam:
Rodopi, 1996), 28–31.

century took up her cult as embodying modern liberal ideals of tolera-
tion and individualism. In the autumn of 2006 the Spanish biopic *Teresa,
muerte y vida,* starring the internationally known actress Paz Vega,
opened in theaters throughout Spain. In an interview with *El País,* the
country's most prominent newspaper, filmmaker Ray Loriga commented, "Teresa is a very great figure. She is the Che Guevara, the Bob
Dylan, of women." The reporter concurred in this assessment, responding, "In reality, Teresa could have only existed in Spain. Like Luther in
Germany. Teresa is our past."[37] These statements illuminate the ways in
which some modern Spaniards understand and incorporate the saint. It
is particularly telling that Teresa is desanctified here through comparisons to a political revolutionary and a folksinger, and perhaps this is
fitting in twenty-first-century secular Spain. Yet she has retained her
españolidad, her integral role in Spain's history, culture, and memory.
She is not, however, its patron saint.

---

37. Agustín Díaz Yanes, "Una santa contra los demonios: El cineasta Ray Loriga ahonda en la
lucha heroica y tenaz de Teresa de Jesús," *El País,* 2 March 2007, http://www.elpais.com/articulo/
cine/santa/demonios/elpepucin/20070302elpepicin_1/Tes (accessed 7 May 2007).

BIBLIOGRAPHY

Primary Sources

Archival Sources

Archivio Segreto Vaticano, Vatican City
    Segreterio di Stato, Spagna, vols. 66–70
    Segreterio di Stato, Nunz. Diversi, vols. 120–21
    Epistolario ad Principes, Registra, vols. 41–43
    Fondo Pio, vols. 198–99
Archivo Catedralicio de Córdoba
    Actas capitulares, 1617–19, 1628–30
    Correspondencia, Siglo XVI–XVII: 1617–19, 1623–27
Archivo Catedralicio de Santiago de Compostela
    Actas capitulares, IG 562
    Legs., IG 301–2, IG 310
    Libros de minutario de cartas y exposiciones, IG 940–41
Archivo del Ministerio de Asuntos Exteriores, Madrid
    Archivo de la Embajada, legs. 58–59, 158
Archivo Diocesano de Jaén
    Correspondencia, 1628, 1629
    Actas capitulares, libro 22
Archivo Histórico Nacional, Madrid
    Sección de la Inquisición, legs. 4462 (53), 4467 (1)
    Libro 1255
    Sección del Estado, consejos leg. 7145, exp. 34
Archivo Municipal de Sevilla
    Sección IV, Escribanía de Cabildo, siglo XVII, vol. 35
    Sección XI
    Papeles del Conde de Aguila, vol. 7
    Libros en cuarto, vol. 10
Biblioteca Apostolica Vaticana, Vatican City
    Fondo Barberini, Latini, manuscritti 3334, 8265, 8330–32, 8572,
    8599
    Fondo Barberini, Stampati, Y.VII.119, U.IX.63
Biblioteca Capitular y Colombina de Sevilla
    manuscritos, signatura 26-3-12, signatura 58-1-9, signatura 63-6-24, signatura 84-4-2
    Sección 1 (Secretaría), N. 13 (Correspondencia), libro 489

Sección 8 (varios)

Historia (N. 7), libro 59

Tratados (N. 12), libro 141

Sección 9 (Fondo Histórico General), leg. 147

Biblioteca Nacional de España, Madrid

Manuscritos 1104, 1167, 1749, 1952, 2232, 2260, 2261, 2353, 3706, 4011, 4278, 7326, 9140, 10858, 11262 (15), 12318, 13239 (2), 18647 (66), 20711 (5 and 6)

Hispanic Society of America, New York

Articles with References to St. Teresa's Tutelege of Spain (pamphlet)

Real Academia de Historia, Madrid

Colección Salazar y Castro, manuscritos 9/1032, 9/1042

Colección Jesuita, manuscripts 9/3680–81

Published Sources

Co-Patronage Treatises

Acerca del Patronato de la gloriosa santa Teresa de Iesus, a quien eligieron los Reynos en sus Cortes por Patrona, se han de tratar tres puntos. 1618. BNM, MS 9140, fols. 206r–211v.

Ahumada y Tapia, Sancho de. "A Don Francisco Tamariz." 1628. HSA.

———. *Carta apologetica, en la qual se descubre, arguye y refuta gran numero de falsedades, indignamente supuestas a los padres Carmelitas Descalzos, y a un memorial, que por orden de su Magestad saco a luz el RPF Pedro de la Madre de Dios, difinidor General del dicho orden, por el Patronato de la gloriosa Virgen, y Patriarca, Santa Teresa.* Zaragoza: Antonio Torcido, 1629.

Al illustrissimo y Reverendissimo senor Don Melchior de Moscoso y Sandoual, Obispo de Segouia, del Consejo de su Magestad. Ca. 1628. HSA.

Alonso de San Hilarion. "Una carta del prior de los descalzos carmelitas de Jaén, a S. Cardenal D. Baltasar de Moscoso y Sandoval, obispo de Jaén sobre el patronato de Santa Teresa." Ca. 1627. BNM, MS 9140, fols. 258r–263v.

Almogábar, Juan de. *Sermon predicado en la catolica Iglesia de Santiago, en la fiesta que haze octaua de S. Estauan Protomartir, en hazimiento de gracias, de la conquista de Granada, por las Magestades de los Santos Reyes, D. Fernando y doña Isabel, en defensa del unico Patronato del gran Apostol Santiago.* Santiago: Juan de León, 1630.

Añaya Maldonado, Martín. *Discurso, en que se prueba que el Apostol Santiago ha sido, y deve ser unico Patron de España, y se declara el Breve de la Santidad de Urbano VIII que a peticion de los Procuradores destos Reynos concedio a Santa Teresa de Iesus.* Ca. 1627. BNM, VE 201/61.

Astorga de Castillo, Pedro. *Informacion por el Dean y Cabildo de la Santa Iglesia Apostolica y Metropolitana de Santiago, unico Patron de las Españas; con la religion sagrada del Carmen Descalço.* Santiago de Compostela: Juan de León, 1631.

Avendaño, Cristóbal. "En la fiesta del Patronato de nuestra preciosa Madre Santa Theresa de Jesus." In *Libro Intitulado, otro tomo de sermones, para muchas festividades de los santos,* fols. 173r–190r. Valladolid: Juan de Rueda, 1629.

———. *Sermones para algunas festividades de las mas solenes de los santos, predicadosen en la Corte de Madrid.* Valladolid: Juan de Rueda, 1628.

Azpeitia, Miguel Pedro de. *Informacion en derecho, sobre que el titulo de Patrona deste Reynos, que se da a la gloriosa santa Madre Teresa de Iesus, no lo pueden hazer los Procuradores de Cortes por si, sin decreto y confirmacion de los Prelados Eclesiasticos.* Ca. 1618. BNM, VE 184/66.

Bacelar, Antonio. *Defensa euangelica de la cognacion y parentesco de nuestro glorioso Apostol, y unico patron de España Santiago el mayor, con Christo Redemptor nuestro en quanto hombre.* Santiago de Compostela: Juan de León, 1630.

Balboa de Mogrovejo, Juan. *Por la Sagrada religion de Carmelitas Descalços, con la Santa Iglesia Metropolitana de Santiago, y demas consortes, sobre el Patronazgo destos reynos de Castilla, que a instancia de su Magestad concedio la Santidad de nuestro santissimo Padre Urbano VIII.* Ca. 1627. BNM, MS 9140, fols. 138r–162v.

Boyl, Francisco. *Al Rey Nuestro Señor D. Felipe IIII el Catolico invicto, Magnanimo, Fundador zeloso del nueuo Patronazgo de sus Reynos, en Santa Teresa Virgen, el año de su salud reparada.* Madrid: Los Herederos de Pedro de Madrigal, 1627.

"Breve del papa Urbano VIII sobre elegir en patrona universal de España a Teresa de Jesús." 1629. RAH, Col. Salazar y Castro, MS 9/1032, fols. 16r–17v.

"Breve resumta, en que se dize la asignacion que las Cortes hizieron, de la Gloriosa Virgen Santa Teresa de Iesus en Patrona de España; y se aduierte la estrecha obligacion, que todos tienen, assi seculares, como Eclesiasticos de admitirla, y celebrarla por tal en toda esta Monarquia." 1627. BNM, MS 9140, fols. 227r–232v.

Cano, Domingo. *Sermon que en la Fiesta de la gloriosa Santa Teresa de Iesus, en su convento de Religiosas Descalzas de Madrid predico el Maestro Fray Domingo Cano . . . en el Otavario de Fiestas que el Rey nuestro señor celebró en honor de la Santa, como nueua Patrona de España, y en hazimiento de gracias, por la salud que le alcançó de Dios.* Madrid: Juan González, 1627.

Cano, Rodrigo. "Censura que dio el licenciado Rodrigo Cano al papel de don Francisco de Morobeli." Ca. 1628. BNM, VE 18/2 (2).

Cano de Montoro, Hernando. *Al Illustrissimo y reverendissimo Señor Don Diego de Guzmán, Arçobispo de Sevilla . . . Dedica y Consagra estos Discursos, Predicados en su Sancta Yglesia, en defensa de el unico Patronato de nuestro grande Apostol Sanctiago el Mayor, hijo de Zebedeo.* Seville: Juan de Cabrera, [ca. 1628].

"Carta del Arzobispo de Santiago al Rey." Ca. 1627. BNM, MS 9140, fols. 83r–88v.

"Carta del Cabildo de Santiago pidiendo la anulación del Breve." 1627. ACSC, IG 301 (87).

"Carta del Cavildo de Santiago al Papa contradiciendo la sociedad de Santa Theresa en el Patronato de España." 1618. BNM, MS 1749, fol. 420r–v.

"Una carta de una relación de las fiestas se celebró Avila por el patronato de Teresa de Jesús." 1627. BNM, MS 9140, fol. 274r–v.

"Un cartel por el Cabildo de Sevilla, por Francisco de Monsalve y Francisco de Melgar—9 May 1630." BCC, 9.147.3.

Casuallo de Parada, Antonio de. "Discurso Apologetico de dichosa Patrona de la gloriosa Madre Sta Teresa." 1628. HSA.

Ceballos, Jerónimo de. "Parecer contra el patronazgo de España de la Madre Teresa de Jesús." In *Jerónimo de Ceballos: Un hombre grave para la república,* ed. Francisco J. Aranda Pérez, 378–80. Córdoba: Universidad de Córdoba, 2001.

"Copia de la carta que la santa Iglesia de Badajoz escribió a la Majestad del Rey D. Felipe IIII nuestro Señor, tocante al pretenso Patronazgo de santa Theresa de Iesus." 1628. RAH, Col. Salazar y Castro, MS 9/1032, fol. 70r–v.

Copia del auto Capitular que hizo la santa Iglesia de Jaén en 31 de Deciembre de 1627 tocante de la defensa de la singularidad del patronazgo del Apostol Santiago. 1628.

"Copia de una carta que escribio el Arçobispo de Seuilla don Pedro de Castro, al Rey nro Señor, contra el Patronazgo de la Bienauenturada virgen Santa Teresa, con unas Notas de su deuoto." 1618. BNM, MS 9140, fols. 106r–111r.

Copia de un Auto en pleno Cabildo, hecho por los Señores Dean y Cabildo de la santa Iglesia de Córdoba, martes 16 de noviembre 1627. Córdoba, 1627. ACC, Actas capitulares, lib. 44, fols. 189v–190r.

Copia de un decreto de las Cortes de Castilla, en que reciben a la gloriosa madre santa Teresa de Iesus por Patrona destos Reynos. 1627. BNM, VE 18/9.

Criales y Arze, Gaspar de. Por la santa iglesia cathedral de Cuenca, por si, y en nombre de la Apostolica y Metropolitana de señor Santiago, unico y singular Patron de España, y del Clero de las dos Castillas y León. Con la sagrada religion de Carmelitas Descalços destos Reynos y consortes. 1631. ACSC, IG 301 (6), fols. 107r–138v.

Cueva y Silva, Francisco de la. Informacion en derecho sobre el titulo de Patrona destos Reynos, dado a la gloriosa santa Teresa de Iesus, fundando la eleccion que los Procuradores de Cortes hizieron. Y respondiendo a todas las oposiciones contrarias. Ca. 1618. BNM, MS 9140, fols. 169r–182v.

Defensa de la unica proteccion y patronazgo de las Españas perteneciente al Gloriosa Apostol Santiago el Mayor, que su Apostolica Iglesia dio a la Magestad del Rey, nuestro Señor. Ca. 1640. BNM, VE 211/56.

"Del Patronato de nuestra Santa Madre Teresa de Jesús." 1627. BNM, MS 9140, fols. 233r–241r.

Diego del Escurial. Sermon Predicado en el Convento de las Carmelitas Descalças de Madrid, en la Octaua que sus Magestades hizieron a la Santa Madre Teresa de Iesus, al nueuo titulo de Patrona de España. Madrid: La Viuda de Alonso Martín, 1627.

Discurso en que se muestra que la Beata Theresa de Jesus no puede ser tenida por patrona de estos Reynos, ni los Procuradores de Cortes pudieron admitirla por tal. 1618.

Durán, Agustín. Sermon predicado en el Real Monasterio de Santíspíritus de Salamanca, en el tercer Domingo de Quaresma En la fiesta que celebro del Patronato de Santiago. Salamanca: Antonia Ramírez, 1630.

Fernández Saavedra, Juan. Sermon del P. Iuan Fernandez Saavedra Predicador de la Compañia de Iesus, que predicó en defensa del Patronato del unico Patron de las Españas Santiago, en la Iglesia del mismo S. Apostol, el dia de su gloriosa Translacion, treinta de Diziembre de 1629. Santiago de Compostela: Juan de León, 1630.

Francisco de Jesús. Sermon que predico el dia primero de la octava, con que el Rey nuestro Señor quiso celebrar la Fiesta de la nueva Patrona de sus Reynos de España, NSM Teresa de Iesus. Madrid, 1627.

Francisco de Santa María. Defensa del Patronato de nuestra gloriosa madre Santa Teresa de Jesús. 1627. BNM, MS 9140, fols. 242r–257v.

Gayoso Figueroa y Moscoso, Antonio. "Regozijo de la muy noble, y leal ciudad de Santiago de Compostela, y de su ilustrissimo Cabildo, en la noticia que despues de medio dia, jueves 21 de Hebrero de 1630 tuuo de la declaracion que hizo nuestro santissimo padre Urbano VIII del unico patronato de las Españas en favor de Santiago Zebedeo." 1630. RAH, Col. Salazar y Castro, MS 9/1032, fols. 43r–51v.

González, Toribio. "Censura contra Don Francisco de Morovelli de la Puebla, en la defensa del patronato de Sancta Theresa de Jesus, respuesta de lo que escriuio contra Don Francisco de Quevedo, y don Francisco de Melgar, canonigo de la doctoral de Sevilla, y otros." 1628. BNM, MS 4278, fols. 249v–261r.

González Centeno, Juan. Tres Puntos en que se resuelve lo que a Santiago Apostol compete por Patrono de España. Ca. 1628. BNM, MS 9140, fols. 112r–122v.

González Guijelmo, Pedro. Discurso en derecho, en favor del unico patronazgo del Apostol Santiago. Ca. 1628. BNM VE 211/51.

"Iusta Poetica en el Convento Real de los Santos Martires de la Ciudad de Granada—dia de la gloriosa Virgen Santa Teresa, fundadora del Carmelo Reformado." 1618. BNM, MS 4011, fol. 288r.

Juan de la Asunción. *Sermon que predico el P. F. Iuan de la Assuncion Religioso Descalço de la Orden de nuestra Señora del Carmen. En su Conuento de S. Hermenegildo de Madrid, el dia septimo de las Octauas, que el Rey D. Felipe IIII N. Señor celebró a una en los dos Conuentos de Carmelitas Descalços y Descalças desta Corte. A la fiesta del Patronato de la gloriosa Virgen S. Teresa Fundadora desta Reformacion, Patrona de los Reynos de España, Corona de Castilla.* Madrid: Juan González, 1627.

Juan de San Agustín. *Sermon en la Octava que el Rei Nuestro Señor Felipe IIII celebro a la Santa Madre Teresa de Iesus, nuevamente patrona de España: En el Conuento de las Descalças Carmelitas de Madrid.* Madrid: Pedro de Madrigal, 1627.

Lobera, Cristóbal de. *Adicion a la Informacion de derecho, que se hizo en Cordoua el mes passado de Nouiembre, en defensa del Patronato de S. Teresa de Jesus.* 1628. BNM, MS 9140, fol. 100r–v.

———. *Iusta Cosa a sido eligir por Patrona de España, y admitir por tal, a Santa Teresa de Iesus, y en ello no se hizo perjuyzio alguno al patronato de Señor Santiago Apostol y Patron de España.* 1628. BNM, MS 9140, fols. 92r–98v.

———. *Respuesta a los largos papeles, que han salido contra el Patronato de Sancta Theresa.* 1628. BNM, MS 9140, fols. 102r–105r.

Losada y Quiroga, Pedro de. *Al illustrissimo y reverendissimo Señor Arzobispo y al Dean y Cabildo de la Santa Iglesia Metropolitana del Apostol Santiago.* 1628. BNM, MS 9140, fols. 32r–71v.

———. *Defensa del unico y singular Patronazgo de las Españas, perteneciente al glorioso Apostol Santiago Zebedeo.* Santiago de Compostela: Juan de León, 1628.

Lucio Espinosa, Francisco de. *Memorial y informacion en derecho, que don Francisco de Lucio Espinosa hizo a instancia de los Cardenales de Santiago, en fauor de su Patronazgo. Dando el sentido literal a las palabras del Breue de la Santidad de nuestro Santo Padre Urbano Octauo.* Madrid, [ca. 1627]. BNM, VE 215/90.

Mártir Rizo, Juan Pablo. *Defensa de la verdad que escrivio D. Francisco de Quevedo Villegas, Cavallero professo de la Orden de Santiago, en favor del Patronato del mismo Apostol unico Patron de España. Contra los errores, que imprimio don Francisco Morovelli de Puebla, natural de Sevilla, contradiziendo este unico Patronato.* Málaga: Juan René, 1628.

Mauro de Valencia. *Sermon predicado con assistencia del Reyno en el Conuento de las Carmelitas Descalças desta Corte. El ultimo dia de la real octava que su Magestad dedicó a Santa Teresa de Iesus, nueua Patrona de España.* Madrid: Imprenta Real, 1627.

Melgar, Francisco de. *Proposicion, y discurso, sobre si debe ser admitida por Patrona General de España, juntamente con su antiguo, i unico Patron Santiago, la Bienaventurada Sancta Theresa de Iesus, conforme a lo determinado por los Procuradores de Cortes, i Breve de la Santidad de Urbano octavo.* Seville: Francisco de Lyra, 1628.

Memorial a su Magestad en nombre de la Iglesia de Sanctiago, i del Clero de las de España, por el unico Patronato del Apostol Santiago. 1627. BNM, VE 211/46.

Memorial de Advertencias al papel que Don Francisco Morovelli imprimio derechamente contra don Francisco de Quevedo, y su Memorial en defensa de Santiago, y de recudida contra don Francisco Melgar, doctoral de Sevilla: y los demas. Málaga: Juan René, 1628.

"Memorial de la Congregación contra el patronato de la Santa Teresa, de Assientos de 1628." HSA.

"Memorial de las raciones que prometio el Reino a su Magestad que la madre Theresa no puede ser patrona de Hespaña." 1617. BNM, MS 1167, fols. 358v–366r.

Méndez de Parga y Andrade, Benito. *Alegatio iuris pro unico hispaniarum Patrono Diuo Iacobo Zebedeo.* [Santiago: Juan de León, ca. 1628.]

———. *Discursos del unico patronazgo de España, perteneciente al glorioso Apostol Santiago el mayor.* Santiago: Juan Guixard de León, 1628.

———. *Respuesta a un papel que escrivio el Dotor Balboa de Mogrovejo canonigo doctoral de la sancta iglesia de Salamanca, cathedratico de Prima de aquella Uniuersidad. En razon del Patronato que pretende la Religion del Carmen de estos Reinos, para sancta Theresa de Iesus, despues de nuestro glorioso Apostol, en virtud de un Breue que la Santidad de Urbano VIII le concedio.* Santiago de Compostela: Juan Guixard de León, 1628.

Mera Carvajal, Fernando de. *Informacion en derecho, por el estado eclesiastico de las coronas de Castilla y León, con la sagrada Religion del Carmen descalço, sobre quitar el reço de Patrona de España a gloriosa Virgen santa Theresa de Iesus, y borrar las insignias y blasones deste Patronato.* Cuenca: Salvador de Viader, 1631.

———. *Informacion en derecho por el unico y singular Patronato del glorioso Apostol Santiago Zebedeo, Patron, y Capitan general de las Españas con la sagrada Religion de Carmelitas descalços sobre el nuevo compatronato destos Reynos, que pretende para la gloriosa Virgen santa Teresa de Iesus.* Cuenca: Salvador de Viader, 1628.

Mogrovejo y Escovar, Melchor Alfonso. *Don Melchor Alfonso Mogrovejo y Escovar arcediano de Olmedo y Canonigo en la santa Iglesia de Auila, menor sieruo y deuoto de la Santa Madre Teresa de Iesus, en defensa de su Patronato.* Ca. 1628. BNM, MS 9140, fols. 191r–225v.

Morovelli de Puebla, Francisco. *Defiende el patronato de Santa Teresa de Iesus, patrona illustrissima de España, y Responde a D. Francisco de Quevedo Villegas, Cauallero del habito de Santiago, a D. Francisco de Melgar, canonigo de la Doctoral de Seuilla, y a otros que an escrito contra el.* Málaga: Juan René, 1628.

Niño, Rodrigo. *Sermon que predico el padre Rodrigo Niño . . . a la Octava que su Magestad mandó celebrar de la Santa Madre Teresa de Iesus, Patrona destos Reynos, en el Conuento de S. Hermenegildo de los Padres Carmelitas Descalços desta villa de Madrid, a 7 de Octubre del año 1627.* Madrid: Juan González, 1627.

Oreo Tinco, Jorge de. "Una carta del prior de Uclés al Rey Felipe IV." 1627. BNM, VE 60/37.

Pacheco, Francisco. "En fabor de Santa Teresa de Jesus." 1628. BCC, 85-4-2, fols. 282r–288v.

Pancorbo, Jerónimo de. "Sermon predicado en la muy noble y muy leal Ciudad de Jerez de Frontera, en la fiesta que se hizo en el Convento de nuestra Señora del Carmen a la gloriosa Madre Teresa de Jesus, recibiendola por Patrona de España, 7 noviembre 1627." In Pancorbo, *Sermones varios.* Cádiz: Juan de Borja, 1627.

Paravicino, Hortensio Félix. *Oracion Evangelica del Maestro Fray Hortensio Felix Paravicino, predicador de su Magestad, al Patronato de España, de la Santa Madre Teresa de Iesus.* Madrid: Juan González, 1628.

Pedro de la Madre de Dios. *Memorial que Dio a su Magestad el padre F. Pedro de la Madre de Dios, Difinidor General de la Orden de los Descalços de nuestra Señora del Carmen, en defensa del Patronato de la Santa Madre Teresa de Iesus.* Ca. 1628. BNM, MS 9140, fols. 124r–137v.

Pérez, Antonio. *Un memorial al Rey contra el patronato de Teresa de Jesús.* 1618. BNM, MS 9140, fols. 26r–31r.

Philaleto, Nicasio. *Por el Apóstol Santiago, unico y singular patron de las Españas. Advertencias a la información de derecho de los padres Carmelitas Descalcos, que firmó el Doctor don Juan de Balboa Mogrouejo, Canonigo de la Santa Iglesia de Salamanca, Catedrático de prima de su Universidad.* Ca. 1628. HSA.

Pimentel, Francisco. *Sermon que predico en la Octava, con que el Rey nuestro Señor quiso celebrar la fiesta de la nueua Patrona de sus Reynos de España, Santa Teresa de Iesus.* Madrid: Juan González, 1627.

Ponce de León, Basilio. "Sermon predicado por . . . el dia de la Santa Madre Teresa de Iesus, en el Monasterio de las Descalças Carmelitas de Toledo, a 5 de Octubre de

1620." In *Sermones de la Purissima Concepcion de la Virgen, y de la S M Teresa de Iesus, y del Santo F. Thomas de Villanueva*, ed. M. F. Basilio Ponce de León. Salamanca: Antonia Ramírez, 1620.

"Por la conservacion del patronato de la gloriosa virgen Santa Teresa de Iesus Fundadora de la sagrada familia Descalça de la Virgen del Monte Carmelo." Ca. 1628. RAH, MS 9/3681 (6), fols. 36r–43v.

Quevedo y Villegas, Francisco de. "Memorial por el patronato de Santiago y por todos los santos naturales de España." In *Obras de don Francisco de Quevedo Villegas*, ed. Aureliano Fernández-Guerra y Orbe, 223–34. BAE 23. Madrid: Rivadeneira, 1852.

———. "Su espada por Santiago." In *Obras de don Francisco de Quevedo Villegas*, ed. Aureliano Fernández-Guerra y Orbe, 423–58. BAE 48. Reprint, Madrid: Rivadeneira, 1951.

Relacion de las fiestas que se celebraron en la Ciudad de Cordova a la gloriosa Santa Teresa de Iesus, Reformadora de la Recolecion y descalça del Carmen con occasion del Nuevo Titulo que Nuestro muy Santo Padre Urbano Octavo a Peticion de SM y de sus Cortes le a dado de Patrona de España. Córdoba: Salvador de Cea Tesa, 1627.

Relacion de la solemnidad con que en la santa Iglesia de Sevilla, se publicó el breve de su Santidad, en favor del Patronato, unico, y singular de España del glorioso Apostol Santiago. Ca. 1630. BCC, 8.7.59, fols. 78r–79v.

Relacion sencilla y fiel de las fiestas que el rey D. Felipe IIII nuestro Señor hizo al Patronato de sus Reinos de España Corona de Castilla que dio a la Gloriosa Virgen Santa Teresa de Iesus, año 1627. Madrid: Juan González, 1627.

Respuesta al memorial que escrivió el arçobispo de Santiago, contra el patronazgo de Santa Teresa. Ca. 1627. BNM, MS 9140, fols. 212r–226v.

Respuesta a los Papeles en forma de memorial, que el Licenciado Pedro de Lossada, Canonigo de Iaen, embió a el Arcobispo de Santiago, en defensa de el Patronato de el Santo Apostol; y en opposicion de el de la Gloriosa Santa Teresa. Cádiz: Gaspar Vezino, [ca. 1628].

Ribadeneira, Pedro de. *Sermon en las Octavas que el Catolico Monarca Don Felipe Quarto celebro al Patronazgo de la Santa Madre Teresa de Iesus en sus Reynos de España*. Madrid: Pedro Madrigal, 1627.

Robles, Juan de. *Carta escrita por un sacerdote natural de Sevilla a un amigo suyo a cerca del Patronato de la gloriosa Santa Teresa de Iesus*. Ca. 1628. RAH, Col. Jesuita, 9/3680 (74).

Rodríguez de León, Alonso. *Carta a su Magestad que suplica que cerca del unico y singular titulo de Patron destos Reinos de España*. Ca. 1627. BNM, VE 211/52.

Salgado de Aráujo, Joan. *Memorial, informacion, y defension apologetica del patronato de España por el apostol Santiago*. 1628. HSA.

Sánchez de Ulloa y Puga, Gonzalo. *Apología del singular patronato Santiago*. 1629.

Sebastián de San Agustín. *Sermon a la inclita Virgen Santa Teresa de Iesus, Patrona de España. En la Solemnidad, que al nuevo Patronazgo celebró la insigne Villa de Lora, Bayliasgo del Orden de San Iuan*. Seville: Juan de Cabrera, 1628.

Serna, Alonso de. "Carta al Rey sobre el patronato." Ca. 1627. BNM, MS 9140, fols. 72r–76v.

Tamariz, Francisco. *A mi padre Fr. Pedro de la Madre de Dios, Difinidor General de la Orden de los Descalcos de NS del Carmen—Acerca de un memorial que dio a su Majestad en defensa del patronato de Santa Teresa de Iesus*. HSA.

Tapia, León de. *Examen y refutacion de los fundamentos, con que impugnaban el Licenciado Pedro de Losada, y otros, el Patronato de la gloriosa Virgen santa Teresa. Dado tres vezes por los Reynos de Castilla, y confirmado por la Santidad de Urbano 8 a instancia de la Catolica Magestad del Rey D. Felipe 4*. Barcelona, 1628. BNM, VE 16/63.

Tomás de San Vicente. *Sermon predicado por el Padre Fray Thomas de San Vicente . . . en el Conuento de sus Monjas, el dia sexto de las Octauas, que el Rey Don Felipe IIII Nuestro Señor celebró a una en los dos Conuentos de Carmelitas Descalços y Descalças de Madrid, a la fiesta del Patronato de la gloriosa Virgen Santa Teresa, Fundadora desta Reforma-cion, Patrona de los Reynos de España Corona de Castilla.* Madrid: Pedro de Madrigal, 1627.

———. *Sermon predicado por el Padre Fray Thomas de San Vicente, Religioso Descalço de la Orden de Nuestra Señora del Carmen, en su Conuento de S. Hermenegildo el dia quinto de las Octauas, que el Rey Don Felipe IIII nuestro Señor celebró a una de los dos Conuen-tos de Carmelitas Descalços, y Descalças de Madrid, a la fiesta del Patronato de la gloriosa Virgen Santa Teresa Fundadora desta Reformacion, Patrona de los Reynos de España Corona de Castilla.* Madrid: Pedro de Madrigal, 1627.

Torres, Andrés de. *Por el dotor Don Andres de Torres Abad de Santiago de Peñalba, dignidad y Canonigo de Letura en la Santa Iglesia de Astorga: En defensa del unico Patronato del Apostol Santiago, hijo del Trueno, rayo de los enemigos de la Fe. Luz de la Christiandad de España.* Santiago de Compostela: Juan Guixard de León, 1629.

Torres, Cristóbal de. *Sermon al Dignissimo Patronazgo de sus Reynos, que fundo el inclito monarca Felipe IIII. Rey de España, en cabeça de la gloriosa virgen santa Teresa de Iesus.* Madrid: Alonso Martín, 1627.

"Traslado de una carta que el cabildo de la santo Yapostolica Iglesia de Santiago embio al de la santa Iglesia de Granada, con aduertencias sobre esta." 1627. BNM, MS 9140, fols. 77r–82r.

Traslado y Relacion a la Letra a de las Solemnidades que precedieron a las fiestas que la Ciudad de Malaga hizo, quando juró por Patrona de la misma Ciudad a la Madre Santa Teresa de Jesus. Málaga: Juan René, 1618.

Vega, Francisco de. *Sermon que predico el Maestro Fr. Francisco de Vega de la Orden de San Benito, en la fiesta de Santa Teresa en las Descalzas Carmelitas de Madrid.* Madrid: La Viuda de Alonso Martín, 1627.

Verdugo, Francisco. *Sermon quarto en la octava que la Catolica Magestad del Rey Nuestro Señor mandó celebrar en el Conuento del Carmen Descalço, a la Santa Madre Teresa de Iesus: festiua demostracion de auerla hecho su Santidad Patrona destos Reynos.* Madrid: Imprenta Real, 1627.

Vicencio, Valerio. *Al poema delyrico de don Francisco de Queuedo, contra el Patronato de la gloriosa virgen Santa Teresa, Patrona de los Reynos de Castilla, por nuestro muy Santo Padre Urbano, Papa Octauo.* 1628. BNM, VE 155/59.

Vicencius, Reginaldus. *Respuesta al papel de Don Francisco Morovelli, sobre el patronato de Santa Teresa.* Málaga: Juan René, 1628.

Villafañe, Fernando, and Pedro Astorga de Castillo. *Hispaniarum Unici Patronatus Sancti Iacobi pro Ecclesijs Metropolitanis & Cathedralibus, ac uniuerso Clero Regnorum Coro-nae Castellae & Legionis. Contra Reuerendos Patres Discalceatos de Monte Carmelos. Compendium Facti & Iuris cum Responsionibus.* Rome, 1929. BCC, 9.147.6 (2).

Additional Printed Sources

Abd al-Hakam, Ibn. "Narrative of the Conquest of al-Andalus." In *Medieval Iberia: Read-ings from Christian, Muslim, and Jewish Sources*, ed. Olivia Remie Constable, 32–36. Philadelphia: University of Pennsylvania Press, 1997.

Actas de las Cortes de Castilla. 61 vols. Madrid: Congreso de los Diputados, 1907.

Actas de las Cortes de Navarra (1530–1829). 19 vols. Pamplona: Servicio de Publicaciones del Parlemento de Navarra, 1991–96.

Aldrete, Bernardo de. *Varias antigüedades de Espana*. Antwerp, 1614.

Alfonso X. *Primera Crónica General de España*. 3d ed. Edited by Ramón Menéndez Pidal. 2 vols. Madrid: Editorial Gredos, 1977.

Antolínez de Burgos, Justino. *Historia eclesiástica de Granada*. Edited by Manuel Sotomayor. Granada: Universidad de Granada, 1996.

Antonio de San Joaquín. *Año teresiano, Diario Histórico, panegyrico moral, en que se descriven las virtudes, sucesos, y maravillas de la Seraphica, y Mystica Doctora de la Iglesia, Santa Teresa de Jesús, asignadas a todos los dias de los meses en que sucedieron*. 7 vols. Vol. 2. Madrid: Manuel Fernández, 1735.

Apuntamientos sobre la vida, la canonización, y los milagros de Santa Teresa de Jesús. BNM, MS 2232.

Assientos de la congregacion que celebraron las santas iglesias metropolitanas y catedrales de los reynos de la Corona de Castilla y León. 1628. BNM, Salón General, 2/35599.

Athanasius. *Life of Antony and Letter to Marcellinus*. Translated by Robert C. Gregg. New York: Paulist Press, 1980.

Balboa de Mogrovejo, Juan. *El dean y cabildo de la santa Iglesia de Salamanca, por el estado Eclesiastico al Rey nuestro Señor*. 1623. BNM, VE 207/67.

Bermúdez de Pedraza, Francisco. *Historia eclesiástica de Granada*. 1638. Edited by Ignacio Henares Cuéllar. Granada: Universidad de Granada, 1989.

Botero, Giovonni. *The Reason of State*. 1589. Translated by P. J. Waley and D. P. Waley. London: Routledge and Kegan Paul, 1956.

Boyl, Francisco. *Sermón al san Jorge, patrón de la Corona y Reynos de Aragón*. 1633. BNM, VE 280/22.

"Bulla Canonizationis Sanctae Teresiae Virginis Carmelitarum Discalceatorum Fundatricis a Santimisimo Gregorio Papa XV factae." In *Liber secundus actorum pro canonizatione beatae virginis Teresiae de Iesu Ordinis discalceatorum Reformatae Religionis Beatae Mariae de Montae Carmelo Fundatricis*. 1622. BNM, MS 2261, fols. 160v–167r.

Burns, Robert I., ed. *Las Siete Partidas*. Translated by Samuel Parsons Scott. Vol. 1. Philadelphia: University of Pennsylvania Press, 2001.

Calderón, Antonio, and Jerónimo Pardo. *Parte Primera y Segunda de las Excelencias del Apostol Santiago (unico y singular Patron de España) entre los demas Apostoles*. 2 vols. Madrid: Gregorio Rodríguez, 1657–58.

Castellá Ferrer, Mauro. *Historia del apóstol de Iesus Christo Sanctiago Zebedeo Patron y capitan general de las Españas*. 1610. Edited by José Ma. Díaz Fernández. Santiago de Compostela: Xunta de Galicia, 2000.

Ceballos, Jerónimo de. *Arte real para el buen gobierno de los Reyes, Principes, y sus vasallos*. Toledo: Diego Rodríguez, 1623.

"Chronica Adefonsi Imperatoris." In *Chronica Hispana Saeculi XII*, ed. Antonio Maya Sánchez. Corpus Christianorum: Continuatio Mediaevalis, vol. 71. Turnhout: Brepols, 1990.

Coffey, Thomas F., Linda Kay Davidson, and Maryjane Dunn, eds. *The Miracles of St. James*. New York: Italica Press, 1996.

Congregacion que celebraron las santas Yglesias Metropolitanas, y Catedrales de los Reynos de la Corona de Castilla, y León. 1618. BNM, VE 277/113.

Covarrubias Orozco, Sebastián de. *Tesoro de la Lengua Castellana o Española*. 1611. Edited by Felipe Maldonado. Madrid: Editorial Castalia, 1995.

Díaz del Castillo, Bernal. *Historia verdadera de la conquista de la Nueva España*. Edited by Carmelo Sáenz de Santa María. Madrid: CSIC, 1982.

Diego de San José. *Compendio a las solenes fiestas que en toda España hicieron en la Beatificacion de N. M. S. Teresa de Iesus fundadora de la Reformacion de Descalzos y Descalzas de N. S. del Carmen*. Madrid: Alonso Martín, 1615.

Domínguez Ortiz, Antonio, ed. *Testamento de Carlos II.* Madrid: Editora Nacional, 1982.
———. *Testamento de Felipe IV.* Madrid: Editora Nacional, 1982.
Falque Rey, Emma, ed. *Historia compostellana.* Corpus Christianorum: Continuatio Mediaevalis, vol. 70. Turnhout: Brepols, 1988.
Fernández Navarette, Pedro. *Conservación de monarquías y discursos políticos.* Edited by Michael Gordon. Madrid: Instituto de Estudios Fiscales, 1982.
Francisco de Jesús. *Cinco discursos con que se confirma la antigua tradición que el Apostol Santiago vino y predicó en España.* Madrid: Imprenta Real, 1612.
Francisco de Santa María. *Reforma de los Descalzos de Nuestra Señora del Carmen, de la Primitiva Observancia.* Vols. 1 and 2. Madrid: Diego Díaz de la Carrera, 1644, 1655.
Gascón de Torquemada, Gerónimo. *Gaçeta y nuevas de la Corte de España desde el año 1600 en adelante.* Madrid: Real Academia Matritense de Heráldica y Genealogía, 1991.
Gómez Bravo, Juan. *Catálogo de los Obispos de Córdoba, y breve noticia histórico de su Iglesia Catedral y obispado.* 2 vols. Vol. 2. Córdoba: Juan Rodríguez, 1778.
González Dávila, Gil. *Teatro Eclesiástico de las iglesias metropolitanas, y catedrales de los Reynos de las dos Castillas.* 4 vols. Madrid: Pedro de Horna y Villanueva, 1645.
González de Cellorigo, Martín. *Memorial de la política necesaria y útil restauración a la República de España y estados de ella y del desempeño universal de estos Reinos.* 1600. Edited by José Pérez de Ayala. Madrid: Instituto de Estudios Fiscales, 1991.
Guzmán, Gaspar de. "Gran Memorial." In *Memoriales y cartas del Conde-Duque de Olivares,* ed. John H. Elliott and José F. de la Peña, 48–100. Madrid: Alfaguara, 1978.
Henríquez de Jorquera, Francisco. *Anales de Granada.* Edited by Antonio Marín Ocete. 2 vols. Granada: Universidad de Granada, 1987.
Herrera, Pedro de. "Sermon que predico el PMF Pedro de Herrera de la orden de Sancto Domingo, Catedratico de Prima de Teología en la Universidad de Salamanca." In *Relacion de las fiestas de la ciudad de Salamanca en la beatificacion de la S. Madre Teresa de Iesus, Reformadora de la Orden de N. Señora del Carmen,* ed. Fernando Manrique de Luján, 201–36. Salamanca: Diego Cusio, 1615.
"Iubileo plenísmo en la fiesta de la gloriosa Virgen y Madre Sancta Teresa de Iesus Patrona de los Reynos de la Corona de Castilla." 1629. BNM, VE 197/2.
Jiménez de Rada, Rodrigo. *Roderici Ximenii de Rada Historia de rebus Hispanie, sive, Historia Gothica.* Edited by Juan Fernández Valverde. Corpus Christianorum: Continuatio Mediaevalis, vol. 72. Turnhout: Brepols, 1987.
John of Salisbury. *Policraticus: Of the Frivolities of Courtiers and the Footprints of Philosophers.* Edited by Cary J. Nederman. Cambridge: Cambridge University Press, 1990.
José de Jesús María. *Sermones predicados en la Beatificacion de la Beata Madre Teresa de Iesus Virgen, fundadora de la Reforma de los Descalços de Nuestra Señora del Carmen.* Madrid: Alonso Martín, 1615.
José de Santa Teresa. *Reforma de los Descalzos de Nuestra Señora del Carmen, de la Primitiva Observancia.* Vols. 3 and 4. Madrid: Julian de Paredes, 1683–84.
Juan de Santa María. *Republica y policia christiana para Reyes y Principes; y para los que en el gouierno tienen sus vezes.* Barcelona: Lorenzo Deu, 1619.
León, Luis de. *A Bilingual Edition of Fray Luis de León's "La Perfecta Casada" (1583): The Role of Marriage and Women in Sixteenth-Century Spain.* Edited by John A. Jones and Javier San Lera. Lewiston, Maine: Edwin Mellen Press, 1999.
León Pinelo, Antonio de. *Anales de Madrid (desde el año 447 al de 1658).* Edited by Pedro Fernández Martín. Madrid: Instituto de Estudios Madrileños, 1971.
Liber Sancti Jacobi, "Codex Calixtinus." Translated by J. Feo. Santiago de Compostela: Xunta de Galicia, 1998.
López de Gómara, Francisco. *Historia de la conquista de México.* 1552. Edited by Jorge Gurria Lacroix. Caracas: Biblioteca Ayacucho, 1979.

Lopezio, Filippo. *Compendio della Vita, et atti Heroici della Serafica VS Teresa di Giesu, Gloria dell'antica Religione della Madonna del Carmine, e Fondatrice de' Padri, e Monache Scalze del medemo Ordine.* Rome: Vitale Masxardi, 1647.

Machiavelli, Niccolò. *The Prince.* Edited by Harvey C. Mansfield. Chicago: University of Chicago Press, 1998.

Manrique de Luján, Fernando. *Relacion de las fiestas de la ciudad de Salamanca, en la beatificación de la Santa madre Teresa de Iesus.* Salamanca: Diego Cusio, 1615.

María de San Alberto. *Viva al siglo, muerta al mundo.* Edited and translated by Stacey Schlau. New Orleans: University of the South Press, 1998.

Mariana, Juan de. "De spectaculis, o Contra los Juegos Públicos." In *Obras de Padre Juan de Mariana,* ed. Francisco Pi y Margall, 413–62. BAE 31. Madrid: Atlas, 1950.

———. *Historia general de España.* Edited by Francisco Pi y Margall. BAE 30. Madrid: Atlas, 1950.

Marqués de Careaga, Gutierre. *Respuesta al discurso del licenciado Geronimo de Cevallos regidor de la ciudad de Toledo, que dirigió al señor Presidente de Castilla, persuadiendo a su Señoria Illustrissima, que esta Monarchia de España se yua acabando y destruyendo de todo punto, a causa del estado Eclesiastico, fundacion de Religiones, Capellania y aniuerarios y mayorazgos.* Granada: Martín Fernández Zambrano, 1620.

Martínez Díez, Gonzalo, ed. *Bulario de la Inquisición española (hasta la muerte de Fernando el Católico).* Madrid: Editorial Complutense, 1997.

Mártir Rizo, Juan Pablo. *Historia de la Muy Noble y Leal Ciudad de Cuenca.* 1629. Biblioteca de Historia Hispánica: Historias Regionales y Locales. Barcelona: Ediciones El Albir, 1979.

———. *Norte de Príncipes y Vida de Romulo.* 1626. Edited by José Antonio Maravall. Madrid: Centro de Estudios Políticos y Constitucionales, 1988.

———. *Respuesta de Iuan Pablo Mártir Rizo, a las calumnias de don Francisco Morouelli de Puebla, a la historia de Cuenca.* Zaragoza: Juan de Lanaja y Quartanet, 1629.

Melczer, William, ed. *The Pilgrim's Guide to Santiago de Compostela.* New York: Italica Press, 1993.

Morales Padrón, Francisco, ed. *Memorias de Sevilla, 1600–1678.* Córdoba: Monte de Piedad y Caja de Ahorros, 1981.

Morovelli de Puebla, Francisco. *Linaje de Morovelli y otros ilustres de Sevilla.* 1619. Edited by Santiago Montoto. Seville, 1918.

Nájera, Manuel de. "Sermon de la Concepcion de la Virgen NS, elegida por Patrona de las Armas de España, predicado en la octaua, que por los buenos sucesos de su Magestad, consagró a esta Reina el muy religoso Conuento de las Madres Descal-ças de la concepcion Dominica." In *Sermones varios.* Madrid: María de Quiñones, 1645.

Novoa, Matías de. *Historia de Felipe IV, Rey de España.* Colección de Documentos Inéditos para la Historia de España, vol. 69. Vaduz: Kraus Reprint, 1966.

Nueva Recopilación de las leyes destos Reynos. 1640 facsimile ed. Vol. 1. Valladolid: Lex Nova, 1982.

Núñez Delgadillo, Agustín. *Sermon de la gloriosa Sancta Teresa de Iesus, predicado en el Conuento de las Carmelitas descalcas de Granada, lunes de su octaua.* Granada: Juan Muñoz, 1617.

Ojea, Hernan. *Historia del glorioso apostol Santiago, patron de España: De su venida a ella y de las grandezas de su Yglesia y orden militar.* 1615. Edited by Ignacio Cabano Vázquez. Santiago de Compostela: Xunta de Galicia, 1993.

Ortiz de Zúñiga, Diego. *Anales eclesiásticos y seculares de la muy noble y muy leal ciudad Sevilla (1246–1671).* 5 vols. Seville: Guadalquivir, 1988.

Pacheco, Francisco. *Libro de descripción de verdaderos retratos de ilustres y memorables varones*. Edited by Pedro Piñero Ramírez and Rogelio Reyes Cano. Seville: Diputación Provincial, 1985.

Papeles tocantes a la canonizacion de Teresa de Jesus. Ca. 1622. BNM, MS 7326.

"The Passions of Sts. Perpetua and Felicity." In *Readings in Medieval History*, ed. Patrick Geary, 58–64. Peterborough, Ont.: Broadview Press, 1997.

Pinedo, Juan de. *Memorial de la excelente santidad y heroicas virtudes del señor rey don Fernando tercero deste nombre, primero de Castilla, i de León. Eficaz motiva a la majestad Catolica de Felipo IIII nuestro Senor, para que afectuosamente mande solicitar con al Sede Apostólica la deuida i breue Canonización del Rey Santo, si XIII Progenitor*. Seville, 1627.

Pulgar, Hernando del. *Crónica de los Reyes Católicos: Guerra de Granada*. Edited by Juan de Mata Carriazo. 2 vols. Granada: Editorial Universidad de Granada, 2008.

Quevedo y Villegas, Francisco de. "Epistolario." In *Obras de don Francisco de Quevedo Villegas*, ed. Aureliano Fernández-Guerra y Orbe. BAE 48. Reprint, Madrid: Rivadeneira, 1951.

———. *La epistolario completo de Francisco de Quevedo*. Edited by Luis Astrana Marín. Madrid: Instituto Editorial Reus, 1946.

Relacion de la fiesta que se hizo en el convento del Carmen Calçado de Valladolid, en la canoniçacion de Santa Teresa de Iesus, por un deuoto suyo. 1622. BNM, VE 156/24.

Ribadeneira, Pedro de. "Tratado de la Tribulación." 1589. In *Obras escogidas del Padre Pedro de Rivadeneira*, ed. Vicente de la Fuente, 358–448. BAE 60. Reprint, Madrid: Atlas, 1952.

Ribera, Francisco de. *Vida de Santa Teresa de Jesús*. 1590. Introduction by P. Jaime Pons. Barcelona: Gustavo Gili, 1908.

Robert the Monk. *Robert the Monk's History of the First Crusade: Historia iherosolimitana*. Translated by Carol Sweetenham. Burlington, Vt.: Ashgate, 2005.

Robles, Juan de. *El culto sevillano*. 1631. Edited by Alejandro Gómez Camacho. Seville: Universidad de Sevilla, 1992.

Saavedra Fajardo, Diego de. *España y Europa en el siglo XVII: Correspondencia de Saavedra Fajardo*. Edited by Quintín Aldea Vaquero. Vol. 1. Madrid: CISC, 1986.

Salazar, Juan de. *Política española*. 1619. Edited by Miguel Herrero García. Madrid: Centro de Estudios Políticos y Constitucionales, 1997.

Sánchez, Gaspar. *Gasparis sanctii centumputeolani, e societate Iesu theologi, in collegio complutensi sacrarum literarum interpretis, in libros Ruth, Esdrae, Nehemiae, Tobiae, Iudith, Esther, Machabaeorum Commentarij*. Madrid, 1627. BNM, Salón General, 1/14983.

Seco Serrano, Carlos, ed. *Cartas de Sor María de Jesús de Ágreda y de Felipe IV*. BAE 108 and 109. Madrid: Atlas, 1958.

Severus, Sulpicius. *Chroniques*. Edited by Ghislaine de Senneville-Grave. Paris: Les Éditions du Cerf, 1999.

Silverio de Santa Teresa, ed. *Procesos de beatificación y canonización de Santa Teresa de Jesús*. Biblioteca Mística Carmelitana, vols. 18–20. Burgos: Monte Carmelo, 1935.

Tamayo y Vargas, Tomás. *Restauracion de la ciudad del Salvador, i Baía de Todos-Sanctos, en la Provincia del Brasil por las armas de Don Philippe IV el Grande, rei Catholico de las España i Indias, etc*. Madrid: La Viuda de Alonso Martín, 1628.

Tarsia, Pablo Antonio de. *Vida de don Francisco de Quevedo y Villegas*. 1663. Edited by Felipe B. Pedraza Jiménez. Aranjuez: Editorial Ara Iovis, 1988.

Teresa de Jesús. *Escritos de Santa Teresa*. Edited by Vicente de la Fuente. 2 vols. BAE 53 and 55. Madrid: Atlas, 1952.

———. *Obras completas*. 4th ed. Edited by Enrique Llamas Martínez. Madrid: Editorial de Espiritualidad, 1984.

———. *Obras de Santa Teresa de Jesús.* Edited by Silverio de Santa Teresa. Biblioteca Mística Carmelitana, vol. 2. Burgos: Monte Carmelo, 1915.

Tierno Galván, Enrique, ed. *Actas de las Cortes de Cádiz: Antología.* 2 vols. Vol. 2. Madrid: Taurus, 1964.

Vega Carpio, Lope de. "Relación de las fiestas que la insigne villa de Madrid hizo en la canonización de su bienaventurado hijo y patron San Isidro." In *Colección escogida de obras no dramaticas de Frey Lope Felix de Vega Carpio,* ed. Cayetano Rosell, 148–58. BAE 38. Madrid: Ediciones Atlas, 1950.

———. "27 de septiembre a octubre 1618—Al Duque de Sessa." In *La Epistolario de Lope de Vega Carpio,* ed. Agustín de Amezúa y Mayo, 22–23. Madrid: Real Academia de Española, 1989.

"El voto de la ciudad de Salamanca a Santa Teresa en 1618." *Basilica Teresiana* 3, no. 16 (1899): 214–15.

Zayas y Sotomayer, María de. *Novelas amorosas y ejemplares.* Edited by Agustín G. de Amezúa y Mayo. Madrid: Real Academia Española, 1948.

Secondary Sources

Ahlgren, Gillian T. W. "Francisca de los Apóstoles: A Visionary Voice for Reform in Sixteenth-Century Toledo." In *Women in the Inquisition: Spain and the New World,* ed. Mary E. Giles, 116–33. Baltimore: Johns Hopkins University Press, 1999.

———. *Teresa of Avila and the Politics of Sanctity.* Ithaca: Cornell University Press, 1996.

Alcalá-Zamora, José, and Queipo de Llano. "Zúñiga, Olivares y la política de reputación." In *La España del Conde-Duque de Olivares,* ed. John H. Elliott and Angel García Sanz, 103–8. Valladolid: Universidad de Valladolid, 1987.

Aldea Vaquero, Quintín. "Iglesia y estado en la época barroca." In *Historia de España: La España de Felipe IV, el gobierno de la monarquía,* 43 vols., ed. Ramón Menéndez Pidal et al., 25:525–633. Madrid: Espasa Calpe, 1982.

———. "Política interior: Oposición y resistencia—la resistencia eclesiástica." In *La España del Conde-Duque de Olivares,* ed. John H. Elliott and Angel García Sanz, 401–14. Valladolid: Universidad de Valladolid, 1987.

Aldea Vaquero, Quintín, Tomás Marín Martínez, and José Vives Gatell, eds. *Diccionario de la historia eclesiástica de España.* 4 vols. Madrid: CSIC, 1972–75.

Allen, Paul C. *Philip III and the Pax Hispanica, 1598–1621: The Failure of the Grand Strategy.* New Haven: Yale University Press, 2000.

Alonso Veloso, María José. "La estructura retórica del 'Memorial por el Patronato de Santiago' de Francisco de Quevedo." *Bulletin of Spanish Studies* 79, no. 4 (2002): 447–63.

Amelang, James S. *Honored Citizens of Barcelona: Patrician Culture and Class Relations, 1490–1714.* Princeton: Princeton University Press, 1986.

———. "The Peculiarities of the Spaniards: Historical Approaches to the Early Modern State." In *Public Power in Europe: Studies in Historical Transformations,* ed. James S. Amelang and Siegfried Beer, 39–56. Pisa: University of Pisa Press, 2006.

Anderson, Benedict. *Imagined Communities: Reflections on the Origin and Spread of Nationalism.* 2d ed. London: Verso, 1991.

Aranda Pérez, Francisco J. *Jerónimo de Ceballos: Un hombre grave para la república—vida y obra de un hidalgo del saber en la España del Siglo de Oro.* Córdoba: Universidad de Córdoba, 2001.

Arenal, Electa, and Stacey Schlau. *Untold Sisters: Hispanic Nuns in Their Own Words.* Translations by Amanda Powell. Albuquerque: University of New Mexico Press, 1989.

Asch, Ronald G., and Adolf Birke, eds. *Princes, Patronage, and the Nobility: The Court at the Beginning of the Modern Age, c. 1450–1650.* Oxford: Oxford University Press, 1991.

Astrana Marín, Luis. *La vida turbulenta de Quevedo.* Madrid: Editorial Gran Capitan, 1945.

Azaustre Galiana, Antonio. "La argumentación retórica en la prosa de Quevedo: El 'Memorial por le patronato de Santiago.'" *Edad de Oro* 19 (2000): 29–64.

Azcona, Tarsicio de. "Estado e iglesia en España a la luz de las asambleas del clero en el siglo XVI." In *Actas del Congreso Internacional Teresiano, 4–7 Octubre 1982,* ed. Teófanes Egido Martínez, V. García de la Concha, and O. González de Cardedal, 2 vols. (Salamanca: Universidad de Salamanca, 1984), 1:297–330.

Barreiro Rivas, José Luis. *La función política de los caminos de peregrinación en la Europa medieval.* Madrid: Editorial Tecnos, 1997.

Beaune, Colette. *The Birth of an Ideology: Myths and Symbols of Nation in Late-Medieval France.* Translated by Susan Ross Huston. Berkeley and Los Angeles: University of California Press, 1991.

———. *Naissance de la nation France.* Paris: Gallimard, 1985.

Bell, David A. *The Cult of the Nation in France: Inventing Nationalism, 1680–1800.* Cambridge: Harvard University Press, 2001.

———. "Review: Recent Works on Early Modern French National Identity." *Journal of Modern History* 68, no. 1 (1996): 84–113.

Bengoechea de Santa Teresita, Ismael. "El pintor Francisco de Pacheco por el patronato de Santa Teresa." *Monte Carmelo* 64 (1956): 182–89.

Bibliografía del Camino de Santiago. 2 vols. Madrid: Ministerio de Educación, Cultura y Deporte, 2000.

Bilinkoff, Jodi. *The Avila of Saint Teresa.* Ithaca: Cornell University Press, 1989.

———. "A Saint for a City: Mariana de Jesús and Madrid, 1565–1624." *Archive for Reformation History* 88 (1997): 322–37.

Bireley, Robert. *The Counter-Reformation Prince: Anti-Machiavellism or Catholic Statecraft in Early Modern Europe.* Chapel Hill: University of North Carolina Press, 1990.

———. *The Refashioning of Catholicism, 1450–1700: A Reassessment of the Counter-Reformation.* Washington, D.C.: Catholic University of America Press, 1999.

Bizzocchi, Roberto. *Genealogie incredibili: Scritti di storia nell'Europa moderna.* Bologna: Società Editrice il Mulino, 1995.

Boruchoff, David A., ed. *Isabel la Católica, Queen of Castile: Critical Essays.* New York: Palgrave Macmillan, 2003.

Bouza Brey, Fermín. "Dos obras desconocidas de Méndez de Andrade, famoso defensor de las prerrogativas de la iglesia compostelana." *Compostellanum* 11, no. 4 (1966): 615–20.

Brading, D. A. *Mexican Phoenix, Our Lady of Guadalupe: Image and Tradition Across Five Centuries.* Cambridge: Cambridge University Press, 2001.

Bravo Lozano, Jesús. "'El que de vosotros quisiere ser el primero . . .': Iglesia, sociedad y honor en las postrimerías del XVII." In *Política, religión e inquisición en la España moderna: Homenaje a Joaquín Pérez Villanueva,* ed. Pablo Fernández Albaladejo, José Martínez Millán, and Virgilio Pinto Crespo, 129–46. Madrid: Ediciones de la Universidad Autónoma de Madrid, 1996.

Brown, Jonathan. *Images and Ideas in Seventeenth-Century Spanish Painting.* Princeton: Princeton University Press, 1978.

Brown, Jonathan, and John H. Elliott. *A Palace for a King: The Buen Retiro and the Court of Philip IV.* 2d ed. New Haven: Yale University Press, 2003.

Brown, Peter. *The Cult of the Saints: Its Rise and Function in Latin Christianity.* Chicago: University of Chicago Press, 1981.

Bull, Marcus. *Knightly Piety and the Lay Response to the First Crusade: Limousin and Gascony, c. 970–c. 1130.* Oxford: Clarendon Press, 1993.

Burke, Peter. "How to Become a Counter-Reformation Saint (1984)." In *The Counter-Reformation: Essential Readings*, ed. David Luebke, 130–42. Oxford: Blackwell, 1999.

Carpintero Aguado, Lucía. "La congregación del clero de Castilla en el siglo XVII." PhD diss., Universidad Autónoma de Madrid, 1993.

———. "La congregación del clero de Castilla: Un organismo mediatizado por la fiscalidad." In *Política, religión e inquisición en la España moderna: Homenaje a Joaquín Pérez Villanueva*, ed. Pablo Fernández Albaladejo, José Martínez Millán, and Virgilio Pinto Crespo, 147–68. Madrid: Ediciones de la Universidad Autónoma de Madrid, 1996.

Carrera, Elena. "Writing Rearguard Action, Fighting Ideological Selves: Teresa of Avila's Reinterpretation of Gender Stereotypes in 'Camino de perfección.'" *Bulletin of Hispanic Studies* 79, no. 3 (2002): 299–308.

Castellanos, Juan Luis. *Las Cortes de Castilla y su diputación (1621–1789): Entre pactismo y absolutismo.* Madrid: Centro de Estudios Políticos y Constitucionales, 1990.

Castro, Américo. *España en su historia: Cristianos, moros y judíos.* Buenos Aires: Editorial Losada, 1948.

Cerdán, Francis. "Santa Teresa en los sermones del patronato (1627)." In *Santa Teresa y la literatura mística hispánica: Actas del 1 congreso internacionales sobre Santa Teresa y la mística hispánica*, ed. Manuel Criado de Val, 601–8. Madrid: EDI-6, 1984.

Chartier, Roger. *The Cultural Uses of Print in Early Modern France.* Translated by Lydia G. Cochrane. Princeton: Princeton University Press, 1987.

Christian, William A. *Local Religion in Sixteenth-Century Spain.* Princeton: Princeton University Press, 1981.

Cochrane, Eric. *Historians and Historiography in the Italian Renaissance.* Chicago: University of Chicago Press, 1981.

Coleman, David. *Creating Christian Granada: Society and Religious Culture in an Old-World Frontier City, 1492–1600.* Ithaca: Cornell University Press, 2003.

Colish, Marcia. *Medieval Foundations of the Western Intellectual Tradition, 400–1400.* New Haven: Yale University Press, 1997.

Collins, Roger. *Early Medieval Spain: Unity in Diversity, 400–1000.* London: Macmillan, 1983.

Colmeiro, Manuel. *Biblioteca de los economistas españoles de los siglos XVI, XVII y XVIII.* 5th ed. Madrid: Real Academia de Ciencias Morales y Políticas, 1979.

Correa Calderón, Evaristo, ed. *Registro de arbitristias, económistas y reformadores españoles (1500–1936).* Madrid: Fundación Universitaria Española, 1981.

Criado de Val, Manuel, ed. *Santa Teresa y la literatura mística hispánica: Actas del 1 congreso internacionales sobre Santa Teresa y la mística hispánica.* Madrid: EDI-6, 1984.

Cruz, Anne J., and Mary Elizabeth Perry, eds. *Culture and Control in Counter-Reformation Spain.* Minneapolis: University of Minnesota Press, 1992.

Damon, John Edward. *Soldier Saints and Holy Warriors: Warfare and Sanctity in the Literature of Early England.* Burlington, Vt.: Ashgate, 2003.

Dandelet, Thomas. *Spanish Rome.* New Haven: Yale University Press, 2001.

Davis, Natalie Zemon. "Woman on Top." In Zemon, *Society and Culture in Early Modern France*, 124–51. Stanford: Stanford University Press, 1975.

Deleito y Piñuela, José. *También se divierte el pueblo.* Madrid: Alianza Editorial, 1988.

———. *La vida religiosa española bajo el cuarto Felipe: Santos y pecadores.* Madrid: Espase-Calpe, 1963.

Delooz, Pierre. "Towards a Sociological Study of Canonized Sainthood." In *Saints and Their Cults: Studies in Religious Sociology, Folklore, and History*, ed. Stephen Wilson, 189–216. Cambridge: Cambridge University Press, 1983.

Díaz Fernández, José M. "Quevedo y el cabildo de la catedral de Santiago." In *Estudios sobre Quevedo: Quevedo desde Santiago entre dos aniversarios*, ed. Santiago Fernández Mosquera, 105–18. Santiago de Compostela: Universidad de Santiago de Compostela, 1995.

Díez Borque, José M., and Karl F. Rudolf, eds. *Barroco español y austriaco: Fiesta y teatro en la corte de los Habsburgo y los Austrias*. Madrid: Museo Municipal de Madrid, 1994.

Ditchfield, Simon. *Liturgy, Sanctity, and History in Tridentine Italy*. Cambridge: Cambridge University Press, 1995.

———. "Thinking with the Saints: Sanctity and Society in the Early Modern World." *Critical Theory* 35 (Spring 2009): 552–86.

———. "'Tota regio nil nisi religio': Nations, Nationalisms, and *Historia sacra;* Some Preliminary Reflections." *Annali di Stori Moderna e Contemporanea* 10 (2004): 595–605.

———. "Tridentine Worship and the Cult of the Saints." In *The Cambridge History of Christianity*, vol. 6, *Reform and Expansion, 1500–1600*, ed. R. Po-Chia Hsia, 201–43. Cambridge: Cambridge University Press, 2007.

Domínguez Ortiz, Antonio. *Crisis y decadencia de la España de los Austrias*. Barcelona: Editorial Ariel, 1984.

———. "La defensa de la reputación." In *Arte y saber: La cultura en tiempos de Felipe III y Felipe IV*, 25–54. Madrid: Ministerio de Educación, 1999.

———. *La sociedad española en el siglo XVII*. 2 vols. Granada: Servicio de Publicaciones de la Universidad, 1992.

Donnell, Sidney. *Feminizing the Enemy: Imperial Spain, Transvestite Drama, and the Crisis of Masculinity*. Lewisburg: Bucknell University Press, 2003.

Dugraw, Dianne. *Warrior Women and Popular Balladry, 1650–1850*. Cambridge: Cambridge University Press, 1989.

Ecker, Heather. "'Arab Stones': Rodrigo Caro's Translation of Arabic Inscriptions in Sevilla (1634), Revisited." *Al-Qantara* 23, no. 2 (2002): 349–401.

Egido López, Teófanes. "Introduction." In *El linaje judeoconverso de Santa Teresa*, 9–31. Madrid: Editorial de Espiritualidad, 1986.

———. "Tratamiento historiográfico de Santa Teresa." In *Perfil histórico de Santa Teresa*, ed. Teófanes Egido López, 13–32. Madrid: Editorial de Espiritualidad, 1981.

Egido Martínez, Teófanes, V. García de la Concha, and O. González de Cardedal, eds. *Actas del Congreso Internacional Teresiano, 4–7 Octubre 1982*. 2 vols. Salamanca: Universidad de Salamanca, 1984.

Eire, Carlos M. N. *From Madrid to Purgatory: The Art and Craft of Dying in Sixteenth-Century Spain*. Cambridge: Cambridge University Press, 1995.

———. *War Against the Idols: The Reformation of Worship from Erasmus to Calvin*. Cambridge: Cambridge University Press, 1986.

Elliott, John H. *The Count-Duke of Olivares: The Statesman in an Age of Decline*. New Haven: Yale University Press, 1986.

———. "A Europe of Composite Monarchies." *Past and Present* 13 (1992): 48–71.

———. *Imperial Spain, 1469–1716*. London: Edward Arnold, 1963.

———. *Richelieu and Olivares*. Cambridge: Cambridge University Press, 1984.

———. *Spain and Its World: 1500–1700*. New Haven: Yale University Press, 1989.

Elliott, John H., and L. W. B. Brockliss, eds. *The World of the Favourite*. New Haven: Yale University Press, 1999.

Elliott, John H., and Angel García Sanz, eds. *La España del Conde-Duque de Olivares*. Valladolid: Universidad de Valladolid, 1987.

Ettinhausen, Henry. "The News in Spain: 'Relaciones de sucesos' in the Reigns of Philip III and IV." *European History Quarterly* 14, no. 1 (1984): 1–20.

Eubel, Konrad, ed. *Hierarchia catholica medii aevi, sive summorum pontificum, S.R.E. Cardinalium*. Ecclesiarum Antistitum Series. 6 vols. Vol. 4, *1910–14*. Monasterii: Sumptibus et Typus Librariae Regensbergianae, 1914.

Fernández Albaladejo, Pablo. "Católicos antes que ciudadanos: Gestación de una 'política española' en los comienzos de la edad moderna." In *Imágenes de la diversidad: El mundo urbano en la corona de Castilla*, ed. José I. Fortea Pérez, 103–27. Cantabria: Universidad de Cantabria, 1997.

———. "Iglesia y configuración del poder en la monarquía católica (siglos XV–XVII): Algunas consideraciones." In *Etat et eglise dans la genèse de l'etat moderne*, ed. Bernard Vincent, 209–16. Madrid: Bibliothéque de la Casa de Velázquez, 1986.

Fernández Albaladejo, Pablo, José Martínez Millán, and Virgilio Pinto Crespo, eds. *Política, religión e inquisición en la España moderna: Homenaje a Joaquín Pérez Villanueva*. Madrid: Ediciones de la Universidad Autónoma de Madrid, 1996.

Fernández Gracia, Ricardo. *San Francisco Javier, Patrono de Navarra: Fiesta, religiosidad e iconografía*. Pamplona: Gobierno de Navarra, 2006.

Fernández Mosquera, Santiago. "El sermón, el tratado, el memorial: La escritura interesada de Quevedo." *La Perinola* 2 (1998): 63–86.

Feros, Antonio. "Images of Evil, Images of Kings: The Contrasting Faces of the Royal Favourite and the Prime Minister in Early Modern European Political Literature, c. 1580–c. 1650." In *The World of the Favourite*, ed. John H. Elliott and L. W. B. Brockliss, 205–22. New Haven: Yale University Press, 1999.

———. *Kingship and Favoritism in the Spain of Philip III (1598–1621)*. Cambridge: Cambridge University Press, 2000.

Filgueira Valverde, José. *Historias de Compostela*. Santiago de Compostela: Bibliofilios Gallegos, 1970.

———. "Nuevos documentos para la historia del patronato jacobeo." *Boletín de la Real Academia Gallega* 24–25 (1925): 189–96, 216–22, 240–44, 292–300, 314–18.

Fletcher, Richard. *St. James's Catapult*. Oxford: Oxford University Press, 1984.

Forde, Simon, Lesley Johnson, and Alan V. Murray, eds. *Concepts of National Identity in the Middle Ages*. Leeds: University of Leeds Press, 1995.

Fortea Pérez, José I. "Economía, arbitrismo y política en la monarquía hispánica a fines del siglo XVI." *Manuscrits* 16 (1998): 155–76.

———, ed. *Imágenes de la diversidad: El mundo urbano en la corona de Castilla*. Cantabria: Universidad de Cantabria, 1997.

Fraga Iribarne, Manuel. *Don Diego de Saavedra y Fajardo y la diplomacia de su época*. Madrid: Centro de Estudios Políticos y Constitucionales, 1998.

Fuchs, Barbara. *Passing for Spain: Cervantes and the Fictions of Identity*. Urbana: University of Illinois Press, 2003.

Fuente, Vicente de la. *Historia eclesiástica de España*. 6 vols. 2d ed. Madrid: Compañía de Impresores y Libreros del Reino, 1873–75.

Fumaroli, Marc, ed. *La querelle des anciens et des modernes*. Paris: Gallimard, 2001.

García Cárcel, Ricardo, ed. *La construcción de las historias de España*. Madrid: Marcial Pons, 2004.

García de Enterría, María Cruz, ed. *Las "Relaciones de sucesos" en España (1500–1750)*. Alcalá: Universidad de Alcalá, 1996.

García García, Bernardo José. "Honra, desengaño y condena de una privanza: La retirada de la corte del cardenal duque de Lerma." In *Monarquía, imperio y pueblos en la*

España moderna, ed. Pablo Fernández Albaladejo, 679–95. Alicante: Universidad de Alicante, 1997.

García Morales, José Manuel. "El apóstol Santiago y la monarquía de España." In *Santiago y la monarquía de España (1504–1788)*, 23–32. Madrid: Sociedad Estatal de Conmemoraciones Culturales, 2004.

Geary, Patrick. *Furta Sacra: Thefts of Relics in the Central Middle Ages*. Princeton: Princeton University Press, 1978.

———. *Living with the Dead in the Middle Ages*. Ithaca: Cornell University Press, 1994.

———. "Saints, Scholars, and Society: The Elusive Goal." In *Saints: Studies in Hagiography*, ed. Sandro Sticca, 1–22. Binghamton: Medieval and Renaissance Texts and Studies, 1995.

Gelabert, Juan Eloy. *Castilla convulsa (1631–1652)*. Madrid: Marcial Pons, 2001.

Giles, Mary E., ed. *Women in the Inquisition: Spain and the New World*. Baltimore: Johns Hopkins University Press, 1999.

Gil Pujol, Xavier. "One King, One Faith, Many Nations: Patria and Nation in Spain, Sixteenth–Seventeenth Centuries." In *"Patria" und "Patrioten" vor dem Patriotismus: Pflichten, Rechte, Glauben, und die Rekonfigurierung europäischer Gemeinwesen im 17. Jahrhunder*, ed. Robert von Friedeburg, 105–38. Wiesbaden: Harrassowitz Verlag, 2005.

———. "Spain and Portugal." In *European Political Thought, 1450–1700: Religion, Law, and Philosophy*, ed. Howell A. Lloyd, Glenn Burgess, and Simon Hodson, 416–57. New Haven: Yale University Press, 2007.

Godoy Alcántara, José. *Historia crítica de los falsos cronicones*. Madrid: Colección Alatar, 1981.

Gómez López, Consuelo. "El apóstol Santiago y la corte: Mentalidad, imagen y promoción artística." In *Santiago y la monarquía de España (1504–1788)*, 87–100. Madrid: Sociedad Estatal de Conmemoraciones Culturales, 2004.

Gómez Martínez, Enrique. "Las Carmelitas y fiestas que en la ciudad de Andújar se hacen en honor de Santa Teresa." In *Santa Teresa y la literatura mística hispánica: Actas del 1 congreso internacionales sobre Santa Teresa y la mística hispánica*, ed. Manuel Criado de Val, 629–35. Madrid: EDI-6, 1984.

González López, Emilio, Robert Plötz, Juan Pérez de Tudela, and José Agustín de la Puente, eds. *Galicia, Santiago y América*. Santiago de Compostela: Xunta de Galicia, 1991.

Grafton, Anthony. *Forgers and Critics: Creativity and Duplicity in Western Scholarship*. Princeton: Princeton University Press, 1990.

Greenfeld, Liah. *Nationalism: Five Roads to Modernity*. Cambridge: Harvard University Press, 1992.

Grieve, Patricia E. *The Eve of Spain: Myths of Origin in the History of Christian, Muslim, and Jewish Conflict*. Baltimore: Johns Hopkins University Press, 2009.

Griffen, Clive. *The Crombergers of Seville: The History of a Printing and Merchant Dynasty*. Oxford: Oxford University Press, 1988.

Gutiérrez Nieto, Juan Ignacio. "El pensamiento económico, político y social de los arbitristas." In *El siglo de Don Quijote (1580–1680): Religión, filosofía, ciencia*, ed. Ramón Menéndez Pidal and Jover Zamora, 235–351. *Historia de España*, vol 26. Madrid: Editorial Espasa-Calpe, 1978.

Gutiérrez Rueda, Laurel. "Ensayo de iconografía teresiana." *Revista de Espiritualidad* 23 (1964): 3–168.

Harper, John. *The Forms and Orders of Western Liturgy from the Tenth to the Eighteenth Century: A Historical Introduction and Guide for Students and Musicians*. Oxford: Oxford University Press, 1991.

Harris, A. Katie. "Forging History: The 'Plomos' of Sacromonte of Granada in Francisco Bermúdez de Pedraza's 'Historia Eclesiástica.'" *Sixteenth Century Journal* 30, no. 4 (1999): 945–66.

———. *From Muslim to Christian Granada: Inventing a City's Past in Early Modern Spain.* Baltimore: Johns Hopkins University Press, 2007.

———. "The Sacromonte and the Geography of the Sacred in Early Modern Granada." *Al-Qantara* 23, no. 2 (2002): 517–43.

Hastings, Adrian. *The Construction of Nationhood: Ethnicity, Religion, and Nationalism.* Cambridge: Cambridge University Press, 1997.

Herrero García, Miguel. *Ideas de los españoles del siglo XVII.* Madrid: Editorial Gredos, 1966.

Herrero Salgado, Félix. *La oratoria sagrada en los siglos XVI y XVII.* 3 vols. Madrid: Fundación Universitaria Española, 1996–98.

Herzog, Tamar. *Defining Nations: Immigrants and Citizens in Early Modern Spain and Spanish America.* New Haven: Yale University Press, 2003.

Homza, Lu Ann. *Religious Authority in the Spanish Renaissance.* Baltimore: Johns Hopkins University Press, 2000.

Hossein, Kimberly Lynn. "Was Adam the First Heretic? Luis de Páramo, Diego de Simancas, and the Origins of Inquisitorial Practice." *Archive for Reformation History/Archiv für Reformationsgeschichte* 97 (2006): 184–210.

Hotchkiss, Valerie. *Clothes Make the Man: Female Cross Dressing in Medieval Europe.* New York: Garland, 1996.

Howe, Elizabeth Teresa. "Zenobia or Penelope? Isabel la Católica as Literary Archetype." In *Isabel la Católica, Queen of Castile: Critical Essays,* ed. David A. Boruchoff, 91–102. New York: Palgrave Macmillan, 2003.

Iglesias Ortega, Arturo. "Pedro Fernández de Navarrete, un riojano en la catedral de Santiago." *Berceo* 138 (2000): 91–137.

Ippolito, Antonio Menniti. *Il governo dei papi nell'età moderna: Carriere, gerarchie, oganizzazione curiale.* Rome: Viella, 2007.

———. "The Secretariat of State as the Pope's Special Ministry." In *Court and Politics in Papal Rome, 1492–1700,* ed. Gianvittorio Signorotto and Maria Antonietta Visceglia, 132–57. Cambridge: Cambridge University Press, 2002.

Iturrioz Magaña, Ángel. *Estudio del subsidio y excusado (1561–1808).* Logroño: Instituto de Estudios Riojanos, 1987.

Jago, Charles. "Habsburg Absolutism and the Cortes of Castile." *American Historical Review* 86, no. 2 (1981): 307–26.

Jauralde Pou, Pablo. *Francisco de Quevedo (1580–1645).* Madrid: Castalia, 1998.

Kafadar, Cemal. *Between Two Worlds: The Construction of the Ottoman State.* Berkeley and Los Angeles: University of California Press, 1995.

Kagan, Richard L. *Clio and the Crown: The Politics of History in Medieval and Early Modern Spain.* Baltimore: Johns Hopkins University Press, 2009.

———. "Clio and the Crown: Writing History in Habsburg Spain." In *Spain, Europe, and the Atlantic World: Essays in Honor of John H. Elliott,* ed. Richard L. Kagan and Geoffrey Parker, 73–100. Cambridge: Cambridge University Press, 1995.

———. *Lawsuits and Litigants in Castile, 1500–1700.* Chapel Hill: University of North Carolina Press, 1981.

———. "Nación y patria en la historiografía de la época austriaca." In *Le sentiment national dans l'Europe méridionale au XVIe et XVIIe siècles,* ed. Alain Tallon, 202–25. Madrid: Casa de Velázquez, 2007.

Kagan, Richard L., with Fernando Marías. *Urban Images of the Hispanic World, 1493–1793.* New Haven: Yale University Press, 2000.

Kagan, Richard L., and Geoffrey Parker, eds. *Spain, Europe, and the Atlantic World: Essays in Honor of John H. Elliott*. Cambridge: Cambridge University Press, 1995.

Kamen, Henry. *The Phoenix and the Flame: Catalonia and the Counter-Reformation*. New Haven: Yale University Press, 1993.

———. *The Spanish Inquisition: A Historical Revision*. New Haven: Yale University Press, 1997.

Kantorowicz, Ernst H. *The King's Two Bodies: A Study in Mediaeval Political Theology*. Princeton: Princeton University Press, 1957.

Kendrick, Thomas. *St. James in Spain*. London: Methuen, 1960.

Kennedy, Ruth Lee. "The Madrid of 1617–25: Certain Aspects of Social, Moral, and Educational Reform." In *Estudios hispánicos: Homenaje a Archer M. Huntington*, 275–309. Wellesley: Wellesley College, 1952.

Kitchen, John. *Saints' Lives and the Rhetoric of Gender: Male and Female in Merovingian Hagiography*. Oxford: Oxford University Press, 1998.

Klaniczay, Gábor. *Holy Rulers and Blessed Princesses: Dynastic Cults in Medieval Central Europe*. Translated by Éva Pálmai. Cambridge: Cambridge University Press, 2000.

Kleber Monod, Paul. *The Power of Kings: Monarchy and Religion in Europe, 1589–1715*. New Haven: Yale University Press, 1999.

Lasa Iraolo, Ignacio, and Juan María Laboa Gallego. "Santa Teresa de Jesús, patrona de España en las Cortes de Cádiz." *Hispania Sacra* 32 (1980): 265–85.

Lavin, Irving. *Bernini and the Unity of the Visual Arts*. 2 vols. Vol. 1. New York: Pierpont Morgan Library, 1980.

Lazure, Guy. "Possessing the Sacred: Monarchy and Identity in Philip II's Relic Collection at the Escorial." *Renaissance Quarterly* 60, no. 1 (2007): 58–93.

———. "To Dare Fame: Constructing a Cultural Elite in Sixteenth-Century Seville." PhD diss., Johns Hopkins University, 2003.

Lees, Clare A., and Gillian R. Overing, eds. *A Place to Believe In: Locating Medieval Landscapes*. University Park: Pennsylvania State University Press, 2006.

Le Gall, Jean-Marie. *Le mythe de Saint Denis entre Renaissance et Révolution*. Paris: Champs Vellon, 2007.

Lehfeldt, Elizabeth A. "Ideal Men: Masculinity and Decline in Seventeenth-Century Spain." *Renaissance Quarterly* 61, no. 2 (2008): 463–94.

———. "Ruling Sexuality: The Political Legitimacy of Isabel of Castile." *Renaissance Quarterly* 53, no. 1 (2000): 31–56.

Levin, Michael. *Agents of Empire: Spanish Ambassadors in Sixteenth-Century Italy*. Ithaca: Cornell University Press, 2005.

Llamas Martínez, Enrique. *Santa Teresa de Jesús y la Inquisición española*. Madrid: CSIC, 1972.

López Estrada, Francisco. "Cohetes para Teresa: La relación de 1627 sobre las fiestas de Madrid por el patronato de España de Santa Teresa de Jesús y la polémica sobre el mismo." In *Actas del Congreso Internacional Teresiano, 4–7 Octubre 1982*, ed. Teófanes Egido Martínez, V. García de la Concha, and O. González de Cardedal, 2 vols., 1:637–81. Salamanca: Universidad de Salamanca, 1984.

———. "La fiesta literaria en la época de los Austrias: Contexto y poética." In *Culturas en la edad de oro*, ed. José María Diéz Borque, 181–96. Madrid: Editorial Complutense, 1995.

———. *Fiestas por Santa Teresa de Jesús en Málaga y en Antequera (1618 y 1627)*. Madrid: Schlesinger, 1982.

López Ferreiro, Antonio. *Historia de la Santa A. M. Iglesia de Santiago de Compostela*. 11 vols. Vol. 9. Santiago de Compostela, 1907.

López Ruiz, Antonio. "Algunas reacciones andaluzas ante los escritos santiaguistas de Quevedo." In *Quevedo: Andalucía y otras búsquedas*, 299–317. Almeria: Zéjel Editores, 1991.

Mackay, Ruth. *The Limits of Royal Authority: Resistance and Obedience in Seventeenth-Century Castile*. Cambridge Studies in Early Modern History. Cambridge: Cambridge University Press, 1999.

Magnuson, Torgil. *Rome in the Age of Bernini*. Vol 1. Stockholm: Almquist and Wiksell International, 1982.

Maravall, José Antonio. *La cultura del barroco: Análisis de una estructura histórica*. Barcelona: Editorial Ariel, 1975.

Marchetti, Elisabetta. "Il carmelo scalzo e gli oratoriani a Roma." *Archivio della Società di Storia Patria* 123 (2000): 105–31.

———. *Le prime traduzioni italiane delle opere di Teresa de Gesù, nel quadro dell'impegno papale post-tridentino*. Bologna: Lo Scarabeo Editrice, 2001.

Matias de Niño Jesus. "Indice de manuscritos carmelitanos existentes en la Biblioteca Nacional de Madrid." *Ephemerides Carmeliticae* 8 (1957): 187–255.

McCormick, Michael. *Origins of the European Economy: Communications and Commerce, AD 300–900*. Cambridge: Cambridge University Press, 2001.

McKendrick, Melveena. *Women and Society in the Spanish Drama of the Golden Age: A Study of the Mujer Varonil*. Cambridge: Cambridge University Press, 1974.

Moreno Garbayo, Justa. *La imprenta en Madrid (1626–1650)*. 2 vols. Madrid, 1999.

Nader, Helen, ed. *Power and Gender in Renaissance Spain: Eight Women of the Mendoza Family, 1450–1650*. Urbana: University of Illinois Press, 2004.

Nalle, Sara T. *God in La Mancha: Religious Reform and the People of Cuenca*. Baltimore: Johns Hopkins University Press, 1992.

———. "A Saint for All Seasons: The Cult of San Julián." In *Culture and Control in Counter-Reformation Spain*, ed. Anne J. Cruz and Mary Elizabeth Perry, 25–50. Minneapolis: University of Minnesota Press, 1992.

———. "Spanish Religious Life in the Age of Velázquez." In *The Cambridge Companion to Velázquez*, ed. Suzanne Stratton-Pruitt, 109–29. Cambridge: Cambridge University Press, 2002.

Negredo del Cerro, Fernando. "La capilla real como escenario de la lucha política: Elogios y ataques al valido en tiempos de Felipe IV." In *La capilla real de los Austrios: Música y ritual de corte en la Europa moderna*, ed. Juan José Carreras and Bernardo José García García, 323–44. Madrid: Fundación Carlos de Amberes, 2001.

Nice, Jason A. *Sacred History and National Identity: Comparisons Between Early Modern Wales and Brittany*. London: Pickering and Chatto, 2009.

Nieto Alcaide, Victor, and María Victoria García Morales. "Santiago y la monarquía española: Orígenes de un mito de estado." In *Santiago y la monarquía de España (1504–1788)*, 33–51. Madrid: Sociedad Estatal de Conmemoraciones Culturales, 2004.

Núñez Beltrán, Miguel Ángel. *La oratoria sagrada de la época del barroco: Doctrina, cultura y actitud ante la vida desde los sermones sevillanos del siglo XVII*. Seville: Universidad de Sevilla, 2000.

Nussdorfer, Laurie. "Print and Pageantry in Baroque Rome." *Sixteenth Century Journal* 29, no. 2 (1998): 439–64.

O'Callaghan, Joseph F. *A History of Medieval Spain*. Ithaca: Cornell University Press, 1975.

———. *Reconquest and Crusade in Medieval Spain*. Philadelphia: University of Pennsylvania Press, 2003.

Olds, Katrina B. "The 'False Chronicles' in Early Modern Spain: Forgery, Tradition, and the Invention of Texts and Relics, 1595–c. 1670." PhD diss., Princeton University, 2009.

Olsen, H. Eric R. *The Calabrian Charlatan, 1598–1603: Messianic Nationalism in Early Modern Europe*. New York: Palgrave Macmillan, 2003.

Pack, Sasha D. "Revival of the Pilgrimage to Santiago de Compostela: The Politics of Religious, National, and European Patrimony, 1879–1988." *Journal of Modern History* 82, no. 2 (2010): 335–67.

Parker, Geoffrey. *The Dutch Revolt*. Ithaca: Cornell University Press, 1977.

———. *Europe in Crisis, 1598–1648*. Oxford: Blackwell, 2001.

———. *The Grand Strategy of Philip II*. New Haven: Yale University Press, 1998.

Parsons, Gerald. *The Cult of Saint Catherine of Siena: A Study in Civil Religion*. Burlington, Vt.: Ashgate, 2008.

Pennington, Kenneth. *The Prince and the Law, 1200–1600: Sovereignty and Rights in the Western Legal Tradition*. Berkeley and Los Angeles: University of California Press, 1993.

Pérez-Romero, Antonio. *Liberation and Subversion in the Writings of Saint Teresa*. Amsterdam: Rodopi, 1996.

Peronne, Sean T. "The Castilian Assembly of the Clergy in the Sixteenth Century." *Parliaments, Estates, and Representation* 18 (1998): 53–70.

———. *Charles V and the Castilian Assembly of the Clergy: Negotiations for the Ecclesiastical Subsidy*. Leiden: Brill, 2008.

———. "Clerical Opposition in Habsburg Castile." *European History Quarterly* 31, no. 3 (2001): 323–51.

Perry, Mary Elizabeth. "Beatas and the Inquisition in Early Modern Seville." In *Inquisition and Society in Early Modern Europe*, ed. Stephen Haliczer, 147–68. London: Croom Helm, 1987.

———. "The Manly Woman: A Historical Case Study." *American Behavioral Scientist* 31, no. 1 (1987): 86–100.

Pick, Lucy K. *Conflict and Coexistence: Archbishop Rodrigo and the Muslims and Jews of Medieval Spain*. Ann Arbor: University of Michigan Press, 2004.

Poole, Stafford. *Our Lady of Guadalupe: The Origins and Sources of a Mexican National Symbol, 1531–1797*. Tucson: University of Arizona Press, 1995.

Portela Sandoval, Francisco José. "Santiago, miles Christi y caballero de las Españas." In *Santiago y la monarquía de España (1504–1788)*, 71–85. Madrid: Sociedad Estatal de Conmemoraciones Culturales, 2004.

Pullapilly, Cyriac K. *Caesar Baronius, Counter-Reformation Historian*. Notre Dame: University of Notre Dame Press, 1975.

Rawlings, H. E. *Church, Religion, and Society in Early Modern Spain*. New York: Palgrave, 2002.

———. "The Secularisation of Castilian Episcopal Office Under the Habsburgs, c. 1516–1700." *Journal of Ecclesiastical History* 38, no. 1 (1987): 53–79.

Reinhard, Wolfgang. "Papal Power and Family Strategy in the Sixteenth and Seventeenth Centuries." In *Princes, Patronage, and the Nobility: The Court at the Beginning of the Modern Age, c. 1450–1650*, ed. Ronald G. Asch and Adolf Birke, 329–56. Oxford: Oxford University Press, 1991.

Remensnyder, Amy G. "The Colonization of Sacred Architecture: The Virgin Mary, Mosques, and Temples in Medieval Spain and Early Sixteenth-Century Mexico." In *Monks and Nuns, Saints and Outcasts: Religion in Medieval Society*, ed. Sharon Farmer and Barbara Rosenwein, 189–219. Ithaca: Cornell University Press, 2000.

Reston, James, Jr. *Warriors of God: Richard the Lionheart and Saladin in the Third Crusade*. New York: Doubleday, 2001.

Rey Castelao, Ofelia. *La historiografía del voto de Santiago: Recopilación crítica de una polémica histórica.* Santiago de Compostela: Universidad de Santiago de Compostela, 1985.

————. *Los mitos del Apóstol Santiago.* Vigo: Nigratrea, 2006.

Riches, Samantha J. E. *St. George: Hero, Martyr, and Myth.* Thrupp: Sutton, 2000.

Rietbergen, Peter. *Power and Religion in Baroque Rome: Barberini Cultural Policies.* Leiden: Brill, 2006.

Río Barredo, María José del. *Madrid, urbs regia: La capital ceremonial de la monarquía católica.* Madrid: Marcial Pons, 2000.

Rodríguez, Isaías. *Santa Teresa de Jesús y la espiritualidad española.* Madrid: CSIC, 1972.

Rodríguez, Juan Luis, and Jesús Urrea. *Santa Teresa en Valladolid y Medina del Campo.* Valladolid: Caja de Ahorros Popular de Valladolid, 1982.

Rodríguez Carretero, Miguel. *Epytome historial de los Carmelitas de Andalucía y Murcia.* 1807. Seville: Ediciones de la Provincia Bética, 2000.

Rodríguez-Salgado, M. J. "Christians, Civilized and Spanish: Multiple Identities in Sixteenth-Century Spain." In *Transactions of the Royal Historical Society,* 6th ser., 8 (1998): 233–54.

————. "The Court of Philip II." In *Princes, Patronage, and the Nobility: The Court at the Beginning of the Modern Age, c. 1450–1650,* ed. Ronald G. Asch and Adolf M. Birke, 205–44. Oxford: Oxford University Press, 1991.

Roncero-López, Victoriano. *Historia y política en la obra de Quevedo.* Madrid: Editorial Pliegos, 1991.

Sahlins, Peter. *Boundaries: The Making of France and Spain in the Pyrenees.* Berkeley and Los Angeles: University of California Press, 1989.

Sallmann, Jean-Michel. *Naples et ses saints a l'âge baroque (1540–1750).* Paris: Presses Universitaires de France, 1994.

————. "Il santo patrono cittadino nel '600 nel regno di Napoli e in Sicilia." In *Per la storia sociale e religiosa del mezzogiorno d'Italia,* vol. 2, ed. G. Galasso and C. Russo, 187–208. Naples: Guida, 1982.

Sampson Vera Tudela, Elisa. *Colonial Angels: Narratives of Gender and Spirituality in Mexico, 1580–1750.* Austin: University of Texas Press, 2000.

Samson, Alexander. "Florián de Ocampo, Castilian Chronicler and Habsburg Propagandist: Rhetoric, Myth, and Genealogy in the Historiography of Early Modern Spain." *Forum for Modern Language Studies* 4, no. 4 (2006): 339–54.

Santiago y la monarquía de España (1504–1788). Madrid: Sociedad Estatal de Conmemoraciones Culturales, 2004.

Santos Fernández, Carlos, and Fermín de los Reyes Gómez, eds. *Impresos en torno al patronato de Santiago, siglo XVII.* Santiago de Compostela: Xunta de Galicia, 2004.

Schulz, Andrew. "The Porcelain of the Moors: The Alhambra Vases in Enlightenment Spain." *Hispanic Research Journal* 9 (December 2008): 388–414.

Schwyzer, Philip. *Literature, Nationalism, and Memory in Early Modern England and Wales.* Cambridge: Cambridge University Press, 2004.

Signorotto, Gianvittorio, and Maria Antonietta Visceglia, eds. *Court and Politics in Papal Rome, 1492–1700.* Cambridge: Cambridge University Press, 2002.

Silverio de Santa Teresa. *Historia del Carmen Descalzo en España, Portugal y América.* Burgos: El Monte Carmelo, 1940.

Sluhovsky, Moshe. *Patroness of Paris: Rituals of Devotion in Early Modern France.* Leiden: Brill, 1998.

Smith, Anthony D. *Chosen Peoples.* Oxford: Oxford University Press, 2003.

Smith, Hilary. *Preaching in the Spanish Golden Age: A Study of Some Preachers of the Reign of Philip III.* Oxford: Oxford University Press, 1978.

Spiegel, Gabrielle M. "The Cult of St. Denis and Capetian Kingship." In *Saints and Their Cults: Studies in Religious Sociology, Folklore, and History*, ed. Stephen Wilson, 141–68. Cambridge: Cambridge University Press, 1983.

Stradling, R. A. *Philip IV and the Government of Spain, 1621–1665*. Cambridge: Cambridge University Press, 1988.

Stratton, Suzanne L. *The Immaculate Conception in Spanish Art*. Cambridge: Cambridge University Press, 1994.

Tanner, Marie. *The Last Descendant of Aeneas: The Hapsburgs and the Mythic Image of the Emperor*. New Haven: Yale University Press, 1993.

Thacker, Alan, and Richard Sharpe, eds. *Local Saints and Local Churches in the Early Medieval West*. Oxford: Oxford University Press, 2002.

Thompson, Augustine. *Cities of God: The Religion of the Italian Communes, 1125–1325*. University Park: Pennsylvania State University Press, 2005.

Thompson, I. A. A. "Castile: Absolutism, Constitutionalism, and Liberty." In *Fiscal Crises, Liberty, and Representative Government, 1450–1789*, ed. Philip T. Hoffman and Kathryn Norberg Hoffman, 181–225. Stanford: Stanford University Press, 1994.

———. "Castile, Spain, and the Monarchy: The Political Community from *Patria Natural* to *Patria Nacional*." In *Spain, Europe, and the Atlantic World: Essays in Honor of John H. Elliott*, ed. Richard L. Kagan and Geoffrey Parker, 125–59. Cambridge: Cambridge University Press, 1995.

———. *Crown and Cortes: Government, Institutions, and Representation in Early Modern Castile*. Aldershot, UK: Ashgate Variorum, 1993.

———. "La cuestión de la autoridad en la controversia sobre el patronato de santa Teresa de Jesús." In *De re publica hispaniae: Una vindicación de la cultura política en los reinos ibéricos en la primera modernidad*, ed. Francisco J. Aranda Pérez and José Damião Rodrigues, 293–320. Madrid: Silex, 2008.

Thompson, I. A. A., and Bartolomé Yun Casalilla, eds. *The Castilian Crisis of the Seventeenth Century*. Cambridge: Cambridge University Press, 1993.

Tiffany, Tanya J. "Interpreting Velázquez: Artistic Innovation and Painted Devotion in Seventeenth-Century Seville." PhD diss., Johns Hopkins University, 2003.

Tyerman, Christopher. *God's War: A New History of the Crusades*. Cambridge: Belknap Press of Harvard University Press, 2006.

Van Liere, Katherine Elliot. "The Moorslayer and the Missionary: James the Apostle in Spanish Historiography from Isidore of Seville to Ambrosio de Morales." *Viator: Medieval and Renaissance Studies* 37 (2006): 519–43.

Vélasco Bayón, Balbino. *Historia del Carmelo Español*. Vol. 3. Rome: Instititum Carmelitanum, 1994.

Vilar, Jean. "Introduction." In *Restauración política de España*, by Sancho de Moncada, 5–82. Madrid: Instituto de Estudios Fiscales, Ministerio de Hacienda, 1974.

Villalon, L. J. Andrew. "San Diego de Alcalá and the Politics of Saint-Making in Counter-Reformation Europe." *Catholic Historical Review* 83, no. 4 (1997): 691–715.

Villaseñor Black, Charlene. *Creating the Cult of St. Joseph: Art and Gender in the Spanish Empire*. Princeton: Princeton University Press, 2006.

Visceglia, Maria Antonietta. "Factions in the Sacred College in the Sixteenth and Seventeenth Centuries." In *Court and Politics in Papal Rome, 1492–1700*, ed. Gianvittorio Signorotto and Maria Antonietta Visceglia, 99–131. Cambridge: Cambridge University Press, 2002.

Vollendorf, Lisa, ed. *Recovering Spain's Feminist Tradition*. New York: Modern Language Association of America, 2001.

Walzer, Michael. "On the Role of Symbolism in Political Thought." *Political Science Quarterly* 82, no. 2 (1967): 191–204.

Webb, Diana. *Medieval European Pilgrimage, c. 700–c. 1500.* New York: Palgrave, 2002.

———. *Patrons and Defenders: The Saints in the Italian City-States.* London: St. Martin's Press, 1996.

Weber, Alison. "Saint Teresa's Problematic Patrons." *Journal of Medieval and Early Modern Studies* 29, no. 2 (1999): 357–80.

———. *Teresa of Avila and the Rhetoric of Femininity.* Princeton: Princeton University Press, 1990.

Wilson, Christopher C. "Masculinity Restored: The Visual Shaping of St. John of the Cross." *Archive for Reformation History* 98 (2007): 134–66.

Wilson, Stephen, ed. *Saints and Their Cults: Studies in Religious Sociology, Folklore, and History.* Cambridge: Cambridge University Press, 1983.

Wright, A. D. *The Early Modern Papacy: From the Council of Trent to the French Revolution, 1564–1789.* London: Longman, 2000.

Wright, Elizabeth R. *Pilgrimage to Patronage: Lope de Vega and the Court of Philip III, 1598–1621.* Lewisburg: Bucknell University Press, 2001.

Wunder, Amanda Jaye. "Search for Sanctity in Baroque Seville: The Canonization of San Fernando and the Making of Golden Age Culture, 1624–1799." PhD diss., Princeton University, 2002.

Zen, Stefano. *Baronio storico: Controriforma e crisi del metodo umanistico.* Rome: Vivarium, 1997.

INDEX

Page numbers in *italics* indicate illustrations.